T0163783

Dynamite
The Story of Class Violence in America

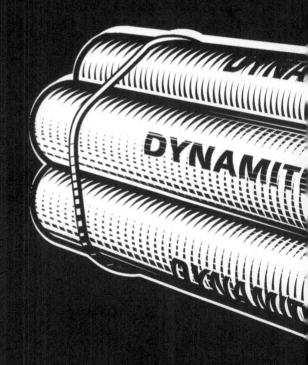

Dynamite
The Story of Class Violence in America

Louis Adamic

Foreword by Jon Bekken

AK
PRESS

Dynamite: The Story of Class Violence in America

by Louis Adamic
Foreword © Jon Bekken 2008
This edition © 2008 AK Press (Edinburgh, Oakland, West Virginia)

ISBN-13 9781904859741

Library of Congress Control Number: 2007939200

AK Press
674-A 23rd Street
Oakland, CA 94612
USA
www.akpress.org
akpress@akpress.org

AK Press
PO Box 12766
Edinburgh, EH8 9YE
Scotland
www.akuk.com
ak@akedin.demon.co.uk

The above addresses would be delighted to provide you with the latest AK Press distribution catalog, which features the several thousand books, pamphlets, zines, audio and video products, and stylish apparel published and/or distributed by AK Press. Alternatively, visit our web site for the complete catalog, latest news, and secure ordering.

Interior illustration by Chris Wright
Cover by Jon Krohn

TABLE OF CONTENTS

PART 5: MASSACRES, FRAME-UPS, AND JUDICIAL MURDERS

PART 6: RECENT TENDENCIES IN THE CLASS WAR (1920–1934)

FOREWORD
BY JON BEKKEN

V ividly written and based on a combination of the author's own
experiences as a working stiff and his wide reading of the available
literature on the history of the labor movement, the book you hold in
your hands is an important document in the historiography of the labor
movement, and, despite showing its age in places, still an enjoyable
read to boot. Published in 1931, *Dynamite* was the first popular general
history of the American labor movement—a distinction it retained for
more than twenty years, despite Adamic's frank admission that he had
not set out to write a comprehensive history, but had rather focused on
the question of the role violence had played in shaping the movement.
This edition reprints the text of the revised 1934 edition (though the
type has been reset, so the pagination differs), later reprinted in 1958
(and in 1984 by Rebel Press, which omitted the material added to the
second edition). This revised edition includes Adamic's appendices
making more explicit his view that labor violence serves as a sort of
spotlight calling attention to social grievances that would otherwise go
unnoticed and discussing the aborted steel strike of 1934, which (soon
after *Dynamite* went to press) laid the foundation for the launch of the
Steel Workers Organizing Committee, while dropping much of his
original conclusion about the role of industrialists, the IWW and other
labor radicals in shaping a more progressive society.

Long out of print, *Dynamite* depicted an American labor movement steeped in violence not of its own making, but which rather had
arisen from the particularly brutal circumstances of American capitalism (a system he was to refer to in his first memoir as "a jungle").
Unions and workers had born the brunt of this violence, he stressed,
but had also learned to use violence not only in self-defense but also to
enforce union jurisdiction and compel recalcitrant employers to come
to terms. The book was generally favorably reviewed, even if reviewers inevitably called attention to various omissions, quarreled with

Adamic's depiction of particular events or issues, and termed the book "a journalistic account."[1]

Searching for Roots in America

Dynamite was Adamic's second book,[2] though in between stints of manual labor he had written extensively for Slovenian and English-language newspapers since emigrating from his native Slovenia (then under Austrian rule) at age fourteen—arriving at Ellis Island on December 30, 1913. Self-taught since being expelled from his third year of Gymnasium because of poor grades,[3] Adamic associated with many leading American literary figures of the 1920s and 1930s, primarily on the left, but also including mainstream writers such as H. L. Mencken, publishing several articles in his *American Mercury* magazine (then one of the leading magazines of the day).[4]

Once in the United States, Adamic worked a series of casual jobs before landing on the staff of a struggling Slovenian-language weekly newspaper, where he translated articles from the English-language press into Slovenian, among other duties. This, in some ways, foreshadowed Adamic's conflicted relationship to America and to his Slovenian roots. Never fully at home in either culture, much of Adamic's literary output was devoted to what one might call a process of interpretation—initially explaining America to Slovenians, and later explaining its immigrant roots to mainstream America. Simultaneously an insider and an outsider to American culture, Adamic once described his journey through America as an "adventure in understanding." Writing in an era of tightening immigration quotas and efforts to "Americanize" the immigrants who made up the lion's share of the country's working class—and were increasingly seen as a threat to national unity—Adamic counterposed to the dominant metaphor of the melting pot his vision of a multi-ethnic America, whose peoples retained their distinct identities and which drew its strength out of the interlocking solidarity of its peoples.[5]

Dynamite in many ways marked a turning point for Adamic, who, after mustering out of the army at the end of the first world war, worked as a merchant seaman, a casual laborer, a journalist, and finally a port pilots clerk in San Pedro, California—sharing the difficulties that plagued many workers as the emerging professional class enjoyed its Roaring Twenties.[6] After the success of *Dynamite* and *The Native's Return*, about a trip he made back to Yugoslavia, which was a Book of the Month Club selection in 1934, Adamic published a series of books between 1938 and 1945 in which he explored the uneasy relationship between immigrant

groups and mainstream American society, including his second memoir, III
My America, From Many Lands, Two-Way Passage, What's Your Name?,
and *A Nation of Nations.*[7] During this period Adamic was eminently
respectable. He received a Guggenheim fellowship, wrote several best-
selling books, was frequently consulted by government agencies, and
in 1942 had dinner in the White House with President Franklin D.
Roosevelt and Prime Minister Winston Churchill—an evening Adamic
later used as a launching point for a scathing critique of U.S. foreign
policy that led Churchill to successfully sue for libel.[8]

Although Adamic writes, in the preface to this edition (p. 4), that
he was never a member of any union or political party, he seems to
have been a member of the Socialist Party until quitting in the mid-
1920s. He explained in a letter to fellow Slovene radical Ivan Molek
"that Socialist propaganda in this country is as futile as spitting into the
ocean with the idea of increasing its volume. It's hopeless. The psychology of the American working stiff is such that he absolutely can't be educated... I'm inclined toward Nietzsche, more than Marx. Democracy,
industrial, political, intellectual, or any other kind, is impossible."[9]
Adamic associated with radicals throughout his time in America, even
if he could not bring himself to identify with any particular current.
He sometimes moved in the orbit of Communist fellow travelers (but
was also criticized by them), though this was the era of the Popular
Front when it could sometimes be hard to distinguish members of the
Communist Party from mainstream Democrats. A lengthy extract from
Josef Stalin on the nationality question in Yugoslavia appeared as an
appendix to *My Native Land* in 1943, but when Marshall Tito broke
with the Soviet Union to pursue his own brand of communism, Adamic
chose Yugoslavia, and brought much of the radical Slovene immigrant
community along with him.

By the end of the 1940s, Adamic was increasingly viewed as a communist, though he never joined the Communist Party. (Indeed, he was
denied a visa when he sought to visit the Soviet Union during his 1948–
1949 visit to Yugoslavia.) In part, this perception rested on Adamic's
association with a variety of Popular Front institutions and his prominent role in Henry Wallace's Progressive Party presidential candidacy in
1948,[10] but the primary cause of his "rapid and personally catastrophic"
fall from grace was Adamic's advocacy for the Tito-led communist regime in Yugoslavia, which alienated cold warriors and Stalinists alike,
and his successful campaign inside the Slovene National Benefit Society
(a mutual aid society aligned with the Socialist Party) to oust its daily

newspaper's longtime editor Ivan Molek and commit the society to supporting the new Yugoslavian regime.[11]

In his final years, Adamic was increasingly prominent in Yugoslav immigrant circles, but marginalized in the broader culture—a reversal of how he lived the bulk of his life in America. Adamic's final book, *The Eagle and the Roots*, counterposed what he saw as a newly freed and vigorous Yugoslavia to the creeping paranoia of the McCarthy era. The book was completed by Adamic's wife and published a year after his mysterious death in the Milford, New Jersey farmhouse he had called home for fourteen years. Adamic's body was found in a second-floor bedroom in the burning farmhouse, a bullet in his head, a rifle across his lap, and a newspaper clipping accusing him of being a Soviet spy on his body. While the coroner ruled this suicide, many were not convinced.[12]

Labor history for workers

When Adamic was writing, there was relatively little scholarly attention to the history of the American labor movement—indeed, *Dynamite*'s bibliography captures most of the then-extant work. That remained the case until the 1960s and 1970s, when there was a veritable explosion of publishing in labor history. However, this work tends to be produced either for members of a particular union, often under the direction of its officers, or written for an audience of graduate students and professional historians. To this day, only a handful of popularly oriented labor histories offer a survey of labor history: *Dynamite*, the United Electrical workers' *Labor's Untold Story*,[13] Thomas Brooks' *Toil and Trouble*,[14] Jeremy Brecher's *Strike*,[15] a coffee table *Pictorial History of American Labor*,[16] and, more recently, *From the Folks Who Brought You the Weekend*.[17] (There are also a number of textbooks written to support college courses in labor history, and multi-volume works including John Commons' four-volume *History of Labor in the United States* and Philip Foner's ten-volume *History of the Labor Movement in the United States*, both of which leave off with the onset of the Great Depression.)

Adamic opens his history in the 1820s, when a nascent labor movement was beginning to emerge, though there had been strikes in the United States at least as early as 1786.[18] This early labor movement was predominantly peaceful despite being considered a "criminal conspiracy" by the courts, publishing labor newspapers, running labor tickets in local elections, and the like. It is true that labor agitators and unions, like the hunger rioters Adamic discusses, were condemned by the press and the ruling class as foreign imports, and also true that the conditions

that led to these upheavals were quite American. But we should also remember, as the larger body of Adamic's work makes quite clear, that the
American working class was predominantly comprised of immigrants,
and thus it is hardly surprising that immigrants figured prominently in
its struggles.[19]

Rather than a systematic exposition of the history of labor strife,
Dynamite is built episodically, around chapters that address particular
disputes or issues that illustrate his broader argument. Thus, following
his short opening chapter, Adamic turns to the American Industrial
Revolution and de-skilling of labor following the Civil War, using the
Molly Maguires as his focal point. While Adamic tells a stirring tale of
secret societies with their origins in old Ireland, kidnapping, murder,
and labor spies, some historians were arguing that the Maguires were
a concoction of the Pinkerton detectives and mine owners even when
Dynamite went to press.[20] The railroad strikes of 1877,[21] which follow,
have drawn strikingly little detailed attention from historians, though
they figure prominently in all historical surveys of the American labor
movement. The Haymarket bombing is one of the most famous incidents in U.S. labor history, and one that reverberated around the world.
Modern historians have been rather kinder to the Knights of Labor than
is Adamic, even if many share his dim view of its leadership. Adamic's
account of the Haymarket demonstration is vivid and compelling, but
today we have a much richer understanding of the movement so often
reduced to the May 4, 1886 explosion as police assaulted a demonstration of workers protesting an earlier police massacre.[22]

The section that follows paints the decline of the labor movement in
very broad strokes, with rather too much emphasis on the sound, busi-
ness-like leadership that emerged. The American Federation of Labor
may have been led by shrewd men, but as Adamic concedes, they were
men of limited vision concerned only with the immediate interests of
the skilled workers they set out to represent. And Adamic may be correct when he says that this business union approach attracted grafters
and racketeers, though many union officials took a firm stance against
such criminal elements. But the hostile legal climate that forced unions
to wage a long struggle for the right to exist, and which allowed police
and private thugs to assault and kill strikers with impunity, surely has
done far more to encourage timidity, on the one hand, and the occasional resort to violence on the other.[23]

The Homestead and Pullman strikes (chapters 9 and 11) demonstrated labor's weakness in the 1890s, and the desperation that drove

activists like Alexander Berkman to turn to individual revenge against the perpetrators of wholesale violence against their fellow workers. Coxey's Army sits somewhat uncomfortably in between, neither violent (except to the extent that hunger and unemployment are properly viewed as violent acts enforced by the coercive power of the state), nor particularly labor-oriented.[24] Nor was there any significant violence in the Pullman strike; troops were turned out less to quell incidents of vandalism than to bring an end to the mass picketing and the refusal of rail workers across the country to handle Pullman cars. However, the strike's suppression did much to persuade a new generation of labor radicals that unionism could not continue down the path of craft unionism and localized struggles without certain disaster. When the Western Federation of Miners—a union steeped in the blood of its members, and which resisted the employers' ceaseless armed assaults upon their strikes and union halls with whatever means were available, from the ballot box to the weapons they often had at hand—reached similar conclusions, the stage was set for a new kind of unionism.[25]

That union, the Industrial Workers of the World, sought to organize all workers on the same job into the same union, all workers in the same industry into the same industrial union, and all workers into One Big Union of the working class—all prepared to act in solidarity to win workers' immediate demands, and to lay the groundwork for a future society in which workers would control the means of production. While the IWW never believed that its objectives could be won through violence, union members did sometimes defend themselves from attack. In the McKees Rocks strike Adamic discusses, workers were able to turn back the thugs through such a policy; more commonly, as in Lawrence and the free speech fights, the Wobblies relied on the power of their numbers and of publicity to confront the violence of the employers and their police. As Adamic notes at the end of Chapter 16, "the Wobblies refrained almost completely from violence. All the violence in I.W.W. strikes and free-speech campaigns between 1910 and 1916...was perpetrated by the police, the militia, and hired gunmen" (p. 126)—a situation that has continued up to the present day. And despite this fact, the popular press and some history books are replete with references to the IWW's violent past—by which the writers apparently mean that the prospect of working-class solidarity is so frightening that the union is responsible for whatever violence is unleashed against it.[26]

Adamic then turns to stories of actual labor violence, beginning with the Ironworkers' effort to defend their union's work against the contractors by dynamiting structures built by scab labor—a campaign he says led to the explosion at the *Los Angeles Times* building that killed several workers. The *Times* explosion, however, does not fit the pattern of these bombings, and to this day many do not believe the McNamara brothers' confession, given in exchange for promises of leniency (many explosions could be proved against them, and in the heated political climate convictions seemed inevitable) and a pledge by some of the city's leading employers to seek peaceful coexistence with the labor movement. Neither promise was honored, and James McNamara died in prison in 1941.[27] This episode receives the most detailed treatment of any in the book, presumably because for Adamic it captures both the desperate straits that, in his view, drive labor to violence and the consequences such incidents have for the movement. Adamic—who evidently believes not only that the brothers were guilty, but that their guilt was known throughout the labor bureaucracy (though why AF of L officials would then have invested themselves so heavily in the defense is not satisfactorily explained)—argues that the craft unions determined less to avoid such incidents in the future than to contract out their dirty work to professionals. In the meantime, the AF of L entered into headlong retreat, leaving the difficult work of organizing in a, now, much more hostile environment to the IWW and other left-wing unions.

Adamic is uncharacteristically cautious in his chapter on the Ludlow Massacre, saying that the "camp took fire" (p. 186) when the historical consensus is that company gunmen and militia set fire to the tents, shooting those who tried to escape the inferno.[28] While Ludlow was an extreme case, miners in particular continued to commonly suffer armed assaults on strikers through the 1930s and beyond. Adamic tells the story of the great steel strike vividly, though his focus on the violent repression does obscure how labor activists in this strike (like the organizing drive in the Chicago stockyards a few years before that collapsed with the 1919 race riot) were trying to maneuver around the limits of AFL-style craft unionism, and were ultimately defeated as much by the Federation's structure and narrowness of vision as by the bullets and clubs of the employers' thugs.[29]

While still controversial in the early 1930s, the Mooney-Billings and Sacco-Vanzetti cases (Chapters 26 and 29) are now almost universally acknowledged to have been frame-ups.[30] Like Mooney and Billings, the last of the Centralia defendants (Chapter 28) was still in prison when *Dynamite* went to press, released only in 1939 (he could have gotten out earlier, but refused to apply for a pardon—insisting

VIII upon full exoneration).[31] Adamic is on target when he notes that the judicial murder of Sacco and Vanzetti was aimed less at the executed than as a warning to other agitators, and as such too strong a prosecution case might even have been counterproductive. "Most of the violence in the class struggle in the United States was perpetrated by organized capitalist interests, acting largely through their agents in the government," (p. 230) he concludes. (This may underplay the role of employer-organized vigilantes and gun thugs, but the basic point is sound.) But, "these massacres, frame-ups, judicial murders are not going unavenged... The underdog in America is getting his vengeance." This is the unfortunate lead-in to chapters on racketeering (which has nothing to do with the spontaneous revenge of the dispossessed) and sabotage, which Adamic largely abstracts from its social context. There can be no doubt that the individual and group malingering Adamic discusses is common, but it has little to do with the sort of sabotage the IWW once endorsed, and which workers of all ideological stripes have had recourse to in the course of their industrial struggles.[32]

Adamic opens his concluding chapter by admitting that he has told "a rather dreadful story... the story of American industry...from the standpoint of labor, the underdog." Despite its battles, the working class is (at the time he wrote, in the midst of the Great Depression) in desperate condition; "perhaps, in a worse plight than it was ever in before." (p. 283) Adamic attributes this to massive unemployment caused by increased productivity and mechanization, and to the industrialists' indifference to the human and social costs of their business decisions. Even such enthusiasts for unbridled capitalism as *Forbes* magazine could see that this policy is, in the long, run suicidal (today, that lesson has been lost), but since each employer makes decisions individually, nobody considers the broader consequences. What is needed, he says, is for capitalism "to civilize itself" (p. 289) by increasing wages (and hence workers' consumption) proportionately to increased productivity.[33] However, business has evolved into bureaucratic institutions "incapable of developing a social conscience and of consistently functioning for the benefit of society." (p. 291) Society must compel business to respond to its needs, Adamic concluded, "not only for the social good but for the good of business itself. Business would have ruined itself and the country long ago, were it not for occasional spurts of social action to curb it." (p. 296) Adamic offers a stark contrast between the dire misery suffered by millions of people—some working themselves to death, others starving for lack of work—and the equally desperate efforts of the rich to spend their enormous wealth. Since then, of course, a massive governmental apparatus has been built up to ameliorate the consequences of capitalism's unbridled greed, and, as I write, hundreds of billions of dollars' worth of the wealth created by my fellow workers is being handed to the banks and other capitalists in order to encourage them to release their death grip on the economy. One suspects this is not quite what Adamic had in mind when he wrote of the need for enlightened industrialists and government to prevent the ordinary workings of the market from destroying us all.

History from the bottom up?

Curiously, although Adamic's literary reputation fundamentally rested on his efforts to reconnect America to its immigrant roots, and to use the immigrant experience as a prism to understand both America and its place in the world, race and ethnicity are subordinated in his history of the labor movement. To be sure, the Molly Maguires are placed squarely in the romanticized tradition of Irish rebellion, but while *Dynamite* mentions the immigrant origins of particular figures or groups of workers, Adamic pays little attention to the implications of the predominantly immigrant character of the American working class, or to the important role immigrants' organizational networks played in sustaining a vibrant labor movement against overwhelming odds. African-Americans appear only fleetingly, despite a long history of race riots and employers' often-successful efforts to pit black and white workers against each other,[34] though Adamic's later books recognize the importance of race to an understanding of the American experience. Race and ethnicity were largely invisible in the modest body of historical scholarship on labor when Adamic undertook his task, but it is hard to imagine anyone better positioned to confront this absence.

However, these issues were left for a later generation to take up. *Labor's Untold Story*, issued two decades after *Dynamite*, offers a somewhat more comprehensive overview. Recognizing that the story they tell goes against the historical narrative taught in school textbooks and reinforced by the media, the authors packed their account with specific details and source notes. Boyer and Morais' lively narrative is, they note, as much a social history of the United States told from a working-class perspective as a history of unions *per se*—and one constructed with an eye to inspiring workers to embrace labor's progressive legacy.[35] While the book briefly looks back to the formation of the first U.S. trade unions in the 1790s, the narrative really begins with the Civil War, which com-

X   pletely reshaped the country economically and politically. Writing from the perspective of the Congress of Industrial Organizations' left wing, they give substantial attention throughout the volume to issues of race and ethnicity, pointing out many unions' failure to see the need for an inclusive labor movement. While violence plays an important role in their narrative, it is the violence of the police, militia, and private guards—supplemented by the daily brutality of child labor, twelve-hour days, and brutal working conditions. Less episodic than Adamic's history, *Labor's Untold Story* tells what is, at root, a heroic tale of workers gradually discovering their power, organizing on a more inclusive basis, and putting the country on a progressive path. This glorious, labor-led Popular Front culminates in the organization of the CIO, until it succumbs to the employers' anti-Communist hysteria, ending in the expulsion of the federation's most militant and democratic unions, including the UE which sponsored the book. But the book ends on a hopeful note, with the anti-communist crusade discredited, the AFL and CIO reunited, and "every reason for confidence that the time will come when war and poverty and persecution for opinion's sake are only memories of a cruel past... The path [of labor] since the day of Sylvis has been long but in the end, despite all difficulties and all reverses, it has always led forward."[36]

Murolo and Chitty's *From the Folks Who Brought You the Weekend* in many ways follows a parallel path, beginning somewhat earlier with colonization and relying upon a prolific array of historic events rather than personalities to drive the narrative. They incorporate women and minorities at every level, offer a more comprehensive survey of the field than any other labor history, and bring the story up to the 1999 Battle of Seattle, where unions marched with anti-globalization forces. This comprehensiveness is also one of the book's weaknesses; cramming so much history into a few pages means that analysis and contradictions often receive short shrift.[37]

Jeremy Brecher takes a very different approach in *Strike!*, focusing on the role of ordinary workers (which he sees as more central than their unions or leaders) in mass strikes and other labor insurgencies over the years. Writing in an era of social upheavals almost totally disconnected from the official labor movement, Brecher saw union leaders often functioning as brakes upon workers' struggles—but (unlike Adamic) as obstacles that workers could circumvent, and wage effective struggles on their own initiative. Most labor history, Brecher concludes, suffers from too limited a sense of what is practical—accepting capitalist control of industry as inevitable, and workers' attempts to exercise control over their workplaces and working lives as hopelessly utopian.

A vision of emancipated labor

While he seems to recognize the limitations of what sociologist C. Wright Mills termed "crackpot realism,"[38] Adamic has trouble articulating an alternative. Elsewhere Adamic wrote that workers made a fundamental mistake in measuring their lives against the myth of unbounded social mobility—a mobility whose limits he documented over his literary career.[39] This American dream was not only isolating—celebrating the individual at the expense not just of the broader society but of his own sense of place and identity—it created a culture of ungratified (and ungratifiable) desires and insatiable consumption. While Adamic ultimately supported the emerging Congress of Industrial Organizations, much of whose membership came from the "new American" groups Adamic championed, he did not believe unions could resolve the underlying social cleavage. As Shiffman summarizes his views, "stronger unions would have limited impact on the lives of workers...unless workers, owners, and labor leaders transformed the jobs they held, provided or protected into endeavors that brought people into open contact with one another and linked them to a nation that was developing, both materially and spiritually."[40] Unfortunately, Adamic combined this realization of the need for fundamental social transformation with a deep cynicism about the capacities of American workers to organize, united by bonds of solidarity and inspired by a vision of a new society.

Rather than trusting to workers, Adamic urged industrialists and union leaders to create a just society. Adamic recognized that capitalism was predatory, and class conflict not only endemic but also necessary to call attention to the need for social reform, but he stood aloof from such struggles. "The function of the new radical labor movement," he wrote in *My America*, "will be to *scare*—terrorize the capitalists and the leaders of the leading political parties... The effect of the new radical movement will be similar to that of the radical movement during hard times a couple of decades ago, when the stirrings of the working people and considerable body of the public at large became finally crystallized into the emergence of such progressive politicians as Theodore Roosevelt and Woodrow Wilson."[41] Enlightened capitalists, Adamic believed, would eventually come to recognize that general prosperity requires well-paid workers with steady jobs organized such that work becomes a source of fulfillment rather than something to be merely endured.

Adamic's work is simultaneously inspiring in its story of often heroic resistance, and bleakly pessimistic about the possibilities for American workers to successfully organize to build a new society. That pessimism led him to leave the Socialist Party in the 1920s, and is a recurring theme in his first memoir, *Laughing in the Jungle*, published between the first and second editions of *Dynamite*. Not believing in workers' capacity to overcome the conditions of their lives and the country's deeply ingrained individualism, Adamic instead looked to individuals: whether lone dynamiters who could terrorize particularly oppressive employers, union officials who could lead (or, more often, stymie) particular groups of workers in efforts to improve their own conditions, or visionary capitalists who might recognize the societal advantages of a less brutal economic system. His postscript, "Tragedy in Steel," is a good example. This is a story of a steel workers' insurgency told from the top down; Adamic offers a vivid portrait of the doddering head of the Amalgamated Association, of inexperienced but well-meaning local officials who are easily bamboozled, and of backroom deals and parliamentary trickery against which honest workers are defenseless. (Reading this demoralizing account, one would hardly suspect that within a few years the CIO would gain union recognition from the country's largest steel makers.)

Adamic repeatedly derides the IWW and other labor radicals as "ultra-emotional," as in the opening paragraphs of Chapter 27. But how are workers who organize to defend themselves against wage cuts, speed-ups, and lay-offs, rather than meekly accepting their fate, being "emotional?" Meanwhile, he accepts at face value the capitalists' claimed inability to distinguish between Bolshevik revolutionists and AFL head Sam Gompers and the conservative business unionists (who had just delivered the members into the maw of a capitalist slaughterfest). This attempt at even-handedness is ill-considered; better to just lay out the facts of the employers' brutal campaign of vigilantism and let readers draw their own conclusions.[42]

A real labor movement—one whose leadership had intelligence, patriotism, social vision and character—would have seized on the opportunity offered by the onset of the Great Depression (and the hard times for workers that preceded it) "to become the greatest power in the United States, a power for the good of labor and the whole country." (p. 302) The American Federation of Labor, of course, was incapable of playing such a role, and while Adamic saw useful activity on the part of some local unions, the overall situation seemed to him bleak indeed. But I would argue that Adamic was blinded by his focus on union leaders and AF of L headquarters. While workers were unquestionably in desperate straits, organized labor was hardly monolithic. The Amalgamated Clothing Workers, for example, sought to harmonize conditions in its industry and advocated a form of social unionism quite close to what Adamic seemingly envisions.[43] The currents that led to the formation of the Congress of Industrial Organizations were well underway. More inspiring, from my perspective, were the forms of alternative unionism that emerged in agriculture, coal mining, meatpacking, rubber, textile, and other industries in the 1930s, until the mounting industrial unrest led to efforts to channel workers' discontent into the confines of the new National Labor Relations Board. Adamic offers the Auto-Lite strike as an example of what could be accomplished through a fighting union policy, but the thrust of his argument seems to be that labor's ineffectual leadership is so deeply entrenched that the prospects for revival are slim.[44] When he ends his final chapter with a call for the organization of unions along industrial lines and the "formation of a new movement, a real American labor movement, fresh, radical, and revolutionary, along industrial and political lines" (p. 321) this reads more like a distant hope than a future he imagines is within grasp, particularly appearing in a chapter titled "What next—More dynamite?"

Adamic follows that conclusion (extensively revised from the first edition) with three postscripts discussing the role of violence in the labor movement and his immediate impressions of the emerging labor militancy which led to the formation of the Congress of Industrial Organizations shortly after this edition of *Dynamite* was first published. It is an awkward place to halt the story (though it is where things stood in 1934, and also where Foner and Commons stop their multi-volume histories, even though they wrote much later), since the labor movement was on the eve of a resurgence that left it institutionally much stronger, but ultimately entrenched a business union vision that left organized labor further isolated from the broader working class than it ever was in the period Adamic writes about.[45]

Violence or Power?

Does violence protect unions? While Adamic argues that it is often the chief factor in propping up unions with weak power on the job, the most mob-ridden unions in the United States have, in fact, had substantial industrial power. Criminals are not known for their philanthropic impulses to protect the poor and powerless; rather, they gravitate to unions with real industrial power, where there are substantial resources to be pillaged.

Nor is it necessarily true, as Adamic suggests in his note on violence as publicity, that violence is the key factor in drawing press attention. It is certainly true that police responded to the unemployed demonstrations with clubs, and that this bloodshed drew the attention of the press. But peaceful demonstrations, where police allowed them, and the growth of direct actions where activists prevented evictions, also drew press attention.[46] Similarly, while journalists did largely ignore the atrocious labor conditions in the Southern textile industry until workers went on strike, those strikes were violent only in the sense that they struck at the employers' very heart—their profit and loss statements—and so the employers brought out their gunmen to put the strikes down. The sit-down strikes in the auto industry drew widespread coverage even though there was no violence until police tried to evict the strikers. Certainly, conflict is often necessary to draw journalists' attention; newsrooms are organized to routinely cover the doings of the rich and powerful, but there is no "beat" dedicated to the homeless or poor. Breaking through the institutional norms and practices that marginalize the lives of the vast majority of the population is by no means easy, but violence is just one of the methods available to radicals seeking journalistic attention, and by no means the most effective. While it is true that incidents of violence will generally attract attention, labor often needs public sympathy to win, and sympathy cannot be built with dynamite.[47] Indeed, Adamic recognizes that workers rarely initiate violence; certainly, as he quotes perennial Socialist Party presidential nominee Norman Thomas writing, workers cannot renounce violence without some other method at hand not only to advance their cause but also to preserve their very lives. When IWW strikers at McKees Rocks faced the bloodthirsty state Cossacks, they did not turn the other cheek—they took steps to defend themselves against attack. More recently, the Civil Rights Movement relied primarily upon nonviolent civil disobedience, but not a few activists prepared to defend themselves when the Klansters started blowing up churches and homes.[48] And the IWW explicitly offered direct action and the general strike as a means for workers to wield their power on the job—where they were the most powerful—rather than engaging in some sort of romantic but ultimately futile armed combat with an employing class that has at its disposal weaponry capable of destroying all life on this planet, and which the available evidence suggests may well be deranged enough to use it.[49]

The book's final words, that "the American working class will be violent until the workers become revolutionary in their minds and motives and organize their revolutionary spirit into force—into unions with revolutionary aims to power," offer sounder counsel. An organized working class, one that has decided what it wants and is determined to use the power already in its hands to gain it, has little need of violence. And if labor is well enough organized, the violence that has been visited against the labor movement for the past two centuries will be of little avail against it. As Joe Hill wrote, many years ago, "If we workers take a notion, We can stop all speeding trains; Every ship upon the ocean, We can tie with mighty chains; Every wheel in the creation, Every mine and every mill, Fleets and armies of all nations, Will at our command Stand Still."[50]

Jon Bekken
October 2008

Endnotes

1 See, for example, reviews of the first edition by Edwin Witte (*Journal of Political Economy* 39, 1931, pp. 826–828), Robert Lovett (*International Journal of Ethics* 41, 1931, pp. 513–516), Ben Reitman (*American Journal of Sociology* 37, 1931, pp. 314–316), Benjamin Stolberg (*Annals of the American Academy of Political and Social Science* 155, 1931, pp. 248–249), and Sterling Spero (*Political Science Quarterly* 47, 1931, pp. 305–307). For an academic to describe something as journalistic is an insult, by the way.

2 His first was a short biography (almost a pamphlet) of the poet Robinson Jeffers, published by the University of Washington in 1929. Adamic had also translated fellow Slovenian Ivan Cankar's *Yerney's Justice* (Vanguard Press, 1926), and published a number of articles and stories in *The American Mercury*.

3 In his memoir, *Laughing in the Jungle: The autobiography of an Immigrant in America* (Harper & Brothers, 1932), Adamic wrote that as a student he had become active in the Yugoslav nationalist movement, and was expelled from Gymnasium after being arrested during a demonstration against Austrian rule in Lublyana. Although this account is accepted as true by many scholars, Adamic conceded to the long-time editor of the Slovenian labor daily *Prosveta* that the story was based on the police killing of another Adamic. (Ivan Molek, *Slovene Immigrant History 1900–1950: Autobiographical Sketches*, Mary Molek translator and publisher, 1979, p. 224.) For an example of a scholar who

accepts Adamic's arrest account, see Dale Peterson, "The American Adamic: Immigrant Bard of Diversity," *Massachusetts Review* 44, 2003, pp. 233–250. Dan Shiffman (*Rooting Multiculturalism: The Work of Louis Adamic*, Fairleigh Dickinson University Press, 2003, pp. 27–29) notes that it is difficult to know the truthfulness of Adamic's descriptions of his early life and impressions. In some accounts Adamic admits that he failed out of school, in others he tells the story of his expulsion for nationalist activity; Shiffman opens his discussion by unequivocally stating that Adamic failed his third year of studies. A Slovenian scholar concludes that Adamic "altered, modified and invented" facts and persons in *Laughing in the Jungle*, even if the main outlines of his life are true. (Ivo Vidan, "An Adventure in Understanding (Louis Adamic's America)," in J. Stanonik, ed., *Louis Adami – Simpozij – Symposium: Ljubljana, 16–18 September 1981*, Univerzitetna tiskarna, 1981, pp. 145–53.) See also Mirko Jurak's "The Relationship Between Fictional and Non-Fictional Elements in Adamic's Autobiographical Novels" in the same volume (pp. 125–136). Not having this volume at hand, I take this reference from Henry Cooper Jr., "Are Louis Adamic's Novels Slovene Novels?" *Obdobja* 21, pp. 617–626.

4 For a bibliography of Adamic's published writings, see Henry Christian, *Louis Adamic: A Checklist*, Kent State University Press, 1971.

5 In addition to Shiffman's *Rooting Multiculturalism*, see Peterson, "The American Adamic."

6 Adamic discusses this phase of his life in some detail in his first memoir, *Laughing in the Jungle* (Harper, 1932), which was reissued by Arno Press in 1969 as part of their American Immigration Collection. For economic conditions in the 1920s see, e.g., Irving Bernstein, *The Lean Years: A History of the American Worker, 1920–1933*, Houghton-Mifflin, 1960.

7 For an overview of this literature, see Henry Christian, "'From Many Lands': Ethnic Literature Then… And Now?" *Modern Language Studies* 8, 1977, pp. 48–56. While these books were well received by popular audiences, professional historians took up arms against the interloper. See, e.g., reviews of *Nation of Nations* by George Stephenson (*Mississippi Valley Historical Review* 32, 1946, pp. 598–599) and Harvey Carter (*American Historical Review* 51, 1946, pp. 505–506), the first of which calls upon Adamic and other immigrants to emerge from their inferiority complex and recognize that in entering America "they were poured into the Anglo-Saxon mold."

8 Adamic had suggested, in *Dinner at the White House* (Harper & Brothers, 1946), a book criticizing the West's failure to play the progressive role he felt was urgently needed in the aftermath of World War II, that Churchill's policy on Greece was influenced by his debt to a bank with investments there.

9 Cited by Matjaz Klemencic, "American Slovenes and the Leftist movements in the United States in the first half of the twentieth century," *Journal of American Ethnic History*, 1996. The March 9, 1925; letter is in the Molek Archives at the Chicago Historical Society. Klemencic notes that Adamic expressed similar ideas in a letter to Upton Sinclair on August 10, 1926. In his memoir (p. 224), Molek recounts a conversation where Adamic insisted that he was wasting his time: "The majority of workers, Slovene and others, were incapable of learning anything." While Molek initially promoted Adamic's

career in *Prosveta*, Adamic's embrace of Tito's regime led to a sharp break in which Adamic joined forces with pro-communist elements in the Slovene National Benefit Society to remove Molek from his position as editor. Molek devotes several pages of his memoir to these events.

10 Klemencic, "American Slovenes and the Leftist movements..." Adamic served on the five-person committee that wrote the Party's platform, and as president of the United Committee of South Slavic Americans, he worked to mobilize immigrant voters behind the Wallace ticket. Shiffman notes the visa denial on page 61.

11 Peterson, "The American Adamic," p. 233. The struggle within the Society is described from Molek's perspective in his *Slovene Immigrant History*. The Moleks had been close to Adamic in the 1930s. See Irena Milane , "Louis Adamic as Viewed by Slovene-American Writer Mary Jugg Molek," *Slovene Studies* 19 (1997), pp. 101–19.

12 Shiffman, *Rooting Multiculturalism*, p. 64.

13 Richard Boyer and Herbert Morais, *Labor's Untold Story*, Cameron, 1955. A second edition was released in 1965, and a third edition issued by UE in 1970. The union has kept the book in print to this day, and it is beyond doubt the most widely read popular history of the labor movement. The three editions appear to be essentially identical.

14 Thomas Brooks, *Toil and Trouble: A History of American Labor*, Delacorte, 1964. A second edition was released in 1971 by Dell. *Toil and Trouble* is solidly ensconced in mainstream liberalism, portraying unions as having played an essential role in social progress, but now needing to be regulated (along with business) to ensure that they do not become too powerful.

15 Jeremy Brecher, *Strike!*, Straight Arrow Books, 1972. A second edition was issued by South End Press in 1997.

16 William Cahn, *A Pictorial History of American Labor*, Crown Publishers, 1972. While Cahn's book is primarily devoted to its hundreds of images, his chapters offer substantive overviews of the evolution of the labor movement from the Colonial era through the 1960s as a narrative of steady progress to the point that many fear unions may have become too powerful and may need government regulation to protect the public.

17 Priscilla Murolo and A.B. Chitty, *From the Folks Who Brought You the Weekend: A Short Illustrated History of Labor in the United States*, The New Press, 2001. Perhaps I should also mention Daniel Guerin's *100 Years of Labor in the USA* (Ink Links, 1979), although this was originally written for a French audience and is less a history of the movement than an analysis of its revolutionary potential.

18 Henry Rosemont, *American Labor's First Strike: Articles on Benjamin Franklin, The 1786 Philadelphia Journeymen's Strike, Early Printers' Unions in the U.S., & Their Legacy*, Charles H. Kerr, 2007.

19 I address this question in "A Collective Biography of Editors of U.S. Workers' Papers: 1913 and 1925," *American Journalism* 15, 1998, pp. 19–39. For glimpses of the early labor press (and by extension the movement that produced these newspapers) see C. K. McFarland, and Robert L. Thistlewaite, "Labor press Demands Equal Education in the Age of Jackson," *Journalism Quarterly*

65, 1988; and Rodger Streitmatter, "Origins of the American Labor Press," *Journalism History* 25, 1999. There is a large and growing historiography on the role of immigrants in U.S. working-class movements. A good starting point is Dirk Hoerder, ed., *Struggle a Hard Battle: Essays on Working-Class Immigrants*, Northern Illinois University Press, 1986. The leading biography of Frances Wright, who opens chapter 1, is Celia Eckhardt's *Fanny Wright: Rebel in America*, Harvard University Press, 1984.

20 Anthony Bimba, *The Molly Maguires: The True Story of Labor's Martyred Pioneers in the Coalfields*, International, 1932. There is an extensive historiography on the Molly Maguires; probably the leading work is Kevin Kenny, *Making Sense of the Molly Maguires*, Oxford University Press, 1998. For the sordid history of labor spies, see Stephen Norwood, *Strikebreaking and Intimidation: Mercenaries and Masculinity in Twentieth-Century America*, University of North Carolina Press, 2002.

21 Philip Foner, *The Great Labor Uprising of 1877*, Pathfinder, 1977; Marilynn Johnson, *Street Justice: A History of Political Violence in New York City*, Beacon Press, 2003.

22 Leon Fink, *Workingmen's Democracy: The Knights of Labor and American Politics*, University of Illinois Press, 1983. Peter Rachleff's *Black Labor in the South: Richmond, Virginia, 1865–1890* (Temple University Press, 1984) discusses how black and white workers came together in the heart of the old Confederacy through the Knights of Labor, building substantial working-class support to directly challenge racial segregation before the movement was crushed.

David Roediger and Philip Foner offer an overview of the struggle for shorter hours in *Our Own Time: A History of American Labor and the Working Day* (Verso, 1989). The most recent work on the Haymarket events (and one told in a stirring style that should appeal to readers who appreciate Adamic's lively narrative) is James Green's *Death in the Haymarket* (Pantheon, 2006). Bruce Nelson gives a rich social history of the grassroots Chicago movement in *Beyond the Martyrs* (Rutgers University Press, 1988), particularly valuable for his work with the movement's foreign-language press. Paul Avrich's *The Haymarket Tragedy* (Princeton University Press, 1984) still offers the best recent treatment of the movement's ideas. *The Haymarket Scrapbook*, edited by David Roediger and Franklin Rosemont (Charles H. Kerr, 1986) offers an eclectic but invaluable collection of documents pointing to the global impact of the Haymarket events.

23 William Forbath, *Law and the Shaping of the American Labor Movement*, Harvard University Press, 1991; Daniel Fusfeld, *The Rise and Repression of Radical Labor, 1877–1918*, Charles H. Kerr, 1992. My research examines one such example: Chicago newsboys' efforts to unionize, which the publishers responded to by hiring gangsters. The newsboys union ended in the control of gangsters after the labor movement proved unable to protect them. "Crumbs from the Publishers' Golden Tables: the plight of the Chicago newsboy." *Media History* 6, 2000, pp. 45–57.

24 Paul Krause, *The Battle for Homestead, 1890–1892: Politics, Culture, and Steel*, University of Pittsburgh Press, 1992; Carlos Schwantes, *Coxey's Army: An*

American Odyssey, University of Nebraska Press, 1985; Richard Schneirov, Shelton Stromquist and Nick Salvatore, editors, *The Pullman Strike and the Crisis of the 1890s*, University of Illinois Press, 1984.

25 The major histories of the WFM include Vernon Jensen's *Heritage of Conflict* (Cornell University Press, 1950); David Brundage, *The Making of Western Labor Radicalism*, University of Illinois Press, 1994; Jerry Calvert, *The Gibraltar: Socialism and Labor in Butte, Montana*, Montana Historical Society Press, 1988; and George Suggs' *Colorado's War on Militant Unionism*, Wayne State University Press, 1972. Some of the violence charged to the WFM did not even occur, as Maryjoy Martin documents in her history (*The Corpse on Boomerang Road: Telluride's War on Labor*, Western Reflections, 1998) of the framing of WFM/IWW organizer Vincent St. John for the murder of a man the authorities knew was not dead. The most comprehensive book on the Steunenberg murder, though it is flawed by the author's determination to solve the "mystery" of WFM involvement through idle speculation in the final chapter, is J. Anthony Lukas' *Big Trouble* (Simon & Schuster, 1998).

26 The most comprehensive overview of the IWW is the union's official history, *The Industrial Workers of the World: Its First 100 Years*, compiled by Fred Thompson and Jon Bekken (IWW, 2006), which includes extensive bibliographic notes for those seeking more information on specific incidents. The most complete account of the McKees Rocks strike is John Ingham's article in the *Pennsylvania Magazine of History* (1966, pp. 353–377); the Lawrence strike is the subject of Bruce Watson's *Bread & Roses* (Viking, 2005); Everett Massacre survivor Jack Miller recounts his experiences in Bud and Ruth Schultz's *It Did Happen Here: Recollections of Political Repression in America* (University of California Press, 1989, pp. 236–248); Gibbs Smith's *Joe Hill* (University of Utah Press, 1970) remains the best biography of the union's best-known martyr, though several other books have been published. For a highly readable overview of the union and its history featuring articles, songs and other items from the IWW's own press, see Joyce Kornbluh, editor, *Rebel Voices: An IWW Anthology* (expanded edition, Charles H. Kerr, 1988).

27 Herbert Shapiro, "Lincoln Steffens and the McNamara Case: A Progressive Response to Class Conflict," *American Journal of Economics and Sociology* 39, 1980, pp. 397–412. Fred Thompson notes that the Times building "evidently went up from a defective boiler" (*The IWW: Its First 100 Years*, p. 81), while an online history of the Ironworkers Union (www.geocities.com/ironworkers373/iwhistory) concedes that the McNamaras did blow up some buildings, but argues that unlike the employers they were careful not to endanger lives. The story of the San Francisco building trades and their effort to establish union conditions up and down the coast is told in Michael Kazin, *Barons of Labor: The San Francisco Building Trades and Union Power in the Progressive Era*, University of Illinois Press, 1987

28 H. Gitelman, *Legacy of the Ludlow Massacre*, University of Pennsylvania Press, 1988; Scott Martelle, *Blood Passion: The Ludlow Massacre and Class War in the American West*, Rutgers University Press, 2007; George McGovern and Leonard Guttridge, *The Great Coalfield War*, Houghton Mifflin Company, 1972.

29 David Brody, *Steelworkers in America: The Nonunion Era*, Harper Torchbooks, 1969; James Barrett, *William Z. Foster and the Tragedy of American Radicalism*, University of Illinois Press, 1999.

30 See, e.g., Curt Gentry, *Frame-Up: The Incredible Case of Tom Mooney and Warren Billings*, Norton, 1967; Paul Avrich, *Sacco and Vanzetti: The Anarchist Background*, Princeton University Press, 1991; Herbert Ehrmann, *The Case That Will Not Die: Commonwealth vs. Sacco and Vanzetti*, Little Brown, 1969.

31 Tom Copeland, *The Centralia Tragedy of 1919: Elmer Smith and the Wobblies*, University of Washington Press, 1993).

32 The IWW referred to sabotage as "the conscious withdrawal of efficiency," arguing that workers could more effectively win their demands by striking on the job. See Salvatore Salerno, editor, *Direct Action & Sabotage: Three Classic IWW pamphlets from the 1910s*, Charles H. Kerr, 1997; Kornbluh's *Rebel Voices* and Thompson and Bekken's *The IWW: Its First 100 Years* each devote a chapter to the sabotage agitation. Contemporary instances of the malingering Adamic focuses upon are discussed in Martin Sprouse, editor, *Sabotage in the American Workplace: Anecdotes of Dissatisfaction, Mischief and Revenge*, Pressure Drop Press, 1992. This sort of sabotage is quite common, and there is an army of consultants working to root out "time theft" and other forms of slacking. Such behavior can be quite rational, by the way. During a stretch when I was temping, I did a few short stints in a large office. The first time I was there I noticed a fellow temp taking hours (quite literally) to copy a few dozen pages. Working as slowly as I could, I worked myself out of the job in a couple of days, but when I was called back a few weeks later he was still there, drawing a steady paycheck and getting as much work out in a week as I did in a couple of hours working as slowly as I could. Under the circumstances, it seems clear he was the more skilled worker.

Adamic's claim that the IWW was advocating sabotage in the 1920s, by the way, is untrue. As Thompson notes, a number of articles and pamphlets on sabotage were issued by the union between 1912 and 1915, at which point the IWW shut down the semi-autonomous publishing bureau that had issued them. Eldridge Dowell found, in his *History of Criminal Syndicalism Legislation in the United States* (Johns Hopkins University, 1939, p. 36) that there was "no case [on record] of an IWW saboteur caught practicing sabotage or convicted of its practice." IWW organizing of harvest workers in the 1920s is discussed in Greg Hall's *Harvest Wobblies* (Oregon State University Press, 2001) and Nigel Sellars' *Oil, Wheat & Wobblies* (University of Oklahoma Press, 1998).

For racketeering, see Robert Fitch, *Solidarity For Sale: How Corruption Destroyed the Labor Movement and Undermined America's Promise*, Public Affairs, 2007; James Jacobs, *Mobsters, Unions, and Feds: The Mafia and the American Labor Movement*, New York University Press, 2006. Adamic's discussion of racketeering addresses only its use against employers and scabs, or in jurisdictional disputes or battles for control of union offices; he does not touch on its use to control union dissidents.

33 Adamic is not a fan of shorter hours or other more sociable means of redistributing this surplus productivity, despite his concern with alienation. As I have argued elsewhere (*Arguments for the Four-Hour Day*, Boston IWW,

2000), slashing work hours is an immediately practical measure that could XXI
simultaneously address massive systemic unemployment (much of which
is concealed in official government statistics), curb the enormous waste of
human energy and time spent in unproductive labor, and free up people's time
to live their lives and rebuild their communities.

34 A good introduction to the subject is Philip Foner and Ronald Lewis, editors, *Black Workers: A Documentary History from Colonial Times to the Present*, Temple University Press, 1989.

35 Despite this aspiration to social history, the book is still embedded in the great man school of history, in part reflecting the state of the history profession at the time (there was relatively little of what we would now recognize as social history to draw upon) but also the authors' evident belief that a story built around major protagonists would be easier for a popular audience to follow. Thus, we learn of the debate over whether to build an inclusive labor movement that welcomed the newly freed African-Americans into its ranks, or a more narrow craft-based approach through the frame of William Sylvis's role in unsuccessfully advocating for the former course.

36 *Labor's Untold Story*, p. 379. I take this from the third edition, but it is not clear that the book was revised between editions; certainly the later editions do not extend the coverage beyond the mid-1950s.

37 And it seems they had something more to say, hinting at the need for a quite different kind of labor movement than the one they chronicle. Capitalism, they note in their epilogue, has dominated American society to the present day, consigning workers to lives of dependency, subordination and insecurity. They close with this: "Labor really does create all wealth...only working people can also organize to abolish the system altogether. When the final conflict comes—as it will—working people will have to be ready; the world will hang in the balance." While the IWW Preamble puts it more directly, and more poetically, it seems that Murolo and Chitty recognize the need for a labor movement built on its principles.

38 *The Causes of World War Three*, Simon and Schuster, 1958.

39 I lean heavily on Shiffman's *Rooting Multiculturalism* for this discussion.

40 Shiffman, *Rooting Multiculturalism*, p. 20. He draws upon several works for this analysis, frustrated by Adamic's vagueness in his writings on social reform.

41 Louis Adamic, *My America: 1928–1938* (Harper, 1938), pp. 428–429, emphasis in original. Shiffman argues that this was a rhetorical stance, and that Adamic's support for such tepid reformers constituted a way station in a broader project of more fundamental social reform.

42 See, e.g., Michael Cohen, "'The Ku Klux Government': Vigilantism, Lynching, and the Repression of the IWW," *Journal for the Study of Radicalism* 1, 2006, pp. 31–56.

43 Steven Fraser, *Labor Will Rule: Sidney Hillman and the Rise of American Labor*, Cornell University Press, 1993. One should not idealize the Amalgamated, which despite its ostensibly socialist leadership was firmly committed to the maintenance of capitalism and managed by professional union managers who would not brook dissent from the rank and file. Indeed, they turned to

racketeers in the 1920s to help maintain control against a faction associated with the Communists, though by the time *Dynamite* appeared the union was booting the mobsters out of its ranks.

44 Staughton Lynd, editor, *"We Are All Leaders"*. For the Auto-Lite strike, see Philip Korth and Margaret Beegle, editors, *I Remember Like Today: The Auto-Lite Strike of 1934*, Michigan State University Press, 1988; Irving Bernstein, *The Turbulent Years: A History of the American Worker, 1933–1941*, Houghton-Mifflin, 1969.

45 Adamic did say in his Preface that he intended to revisit this book, but the closest he came were the chapters in *My America* that recount many strikes and conversations from the Depression years. The leading account of the CIO is Robert Zieger's *The CIO: 1935–1955*, University of North Carolina Press, 1995. A collection edited by Staughton Lynd, *"We Are All Leaders": The Alternative Unionism of the Early 1930s* (University of Illinois Press, 1996) offers an important corrective, demonstrating that the possibility for rebuilding the labor movement on a very different (and much sounder) footing existed.

46 Franklin Folsom, *Impatient Armies of the Poor: The Story of Collective Action of the Unemployed, 1808–1942*, University Press of Colorado, 1991; T. H. Watkins, *The Hungry Years: A Narrative History of the Great Depression in America*, Macmillan, 2000

47 I discuss this issue in "The Invisible Enemy: Representing Labour in a Corporate Media Order," *Javnost/The Public* 12, 2005, pp. 71–84; and "The Kept Press' War on Workers: Labor & the News Media," *Anarcho-Syndicalist Review* 39, 2004, pp. 15–23. See, also, Christopher Martin, *Framed! Labor and the Corporate Media*, Cornell University Press, 2003; Charlotte Ryan, *Prime Time Activism: Media Strategies for Grassroots Organizing*, South End Press, 1999; Todd Gitlin, *The Whole World Is Watching: Mass Media in the Making and Unmaking of the New Left*, University of California Press, 1980.

48 See, e.g., Lance Hill, *The Deacons for Defense: Armed Resistance and the Civil Rights Movement*, University of North Carolina Press, 2006.

49 Ralph Chaplin, *The General Strike*, Industrial Workers of the World, 1933.

50 Joe Hill, "Workers of the World Awaken," circa 1914; published in 1916 and subsequent editions of the IWW's *Little Red Songbook*.

AUTHOR'S NOTE TO THE REVISED (SECOND) EDITION

THE first edition of this book appeared in the spring of 1931. At that time it was, on the whole, rather favorably received by critics and reviewers throughout the United States and abroad, and three and a half years later friendly references to it still appear in public prints; but, as I now see it, the original volume had several flaws. Some of those flaws I attempt to remove in this revised edition.

Then, too, much has happened on the capital-labor front since 1931; so I have added paragraphs and sections dealing with those events. Much more is bound to happen on that front in this country, as elsewhere, in the very near future—what will that be?

Although I have rewritten comparatively few pages—chiefly those dealing with the depression years 1929–34, which I now see rather differently than as they appeared to me three or four years ago—the book is almost a new book.

The title and the subtitle, I think, clearly indicate what the book is about, but to all seeming that is not enough. Only a few months ago someone complained, in connection with a review of another book, that *Dynamite* was a sadly incomplete study of the American labor movement and radical or revolutionary stirrings in the United States during the last century. Well, *Dynamite* was never meant to be anything more than an attempt at telling the story of the evolution of violence in the class struggle in America, which, of course, is but one phase of the history of our labor and of our radical or revolutionary movements, stirrings, and upheavals.

In two chapters near the end of the book I go a bit into the phenomenon of racketeering as it has developed in the United States in the last several years; and I do this because I believe that, to a very considerable extent, the highly organized criminal terrorism which reached its heights in the days of Al Capone, back in 1922–32, has its roots deep in America's national life, in the class structure of our

capitalist economic system built upon the ideals of liberty and democracy. Racketeering appears to me an inevitable result of the
chaotic, brutalizing conditions in American industry, a phase of the
dynamic, violent drive of economic evolution in the United States.
To understand it, one must know something of the history of the
class struggle in this country during the last hundred years. One must
know something, also, of the American labor movement, its tragic in-
efficacy from its inception to the present day; and particularly of the
American Federation of Labor, which for half a century has dominated—and at the moment still dominates—the field of organized labor
in this country.

In this revised edition I have added some remarks on the A.F. of L.
under the New Deal on violence as publicity for the underdog, on the
impersonal nature and social irresponsibility of capitalism as we have it
in America, and on the probable developments in the class war in the
immediate future; which, I trust, will be helpful to those sincerely trying
to understand the current labor situation in this country.

I am not, and never was, a member of any labor union or political
party or movement in the United States. I wrote this book uninfluenced
by anyone with a special ax to grind. I wrote it as truthfully as I could
determine truth. My aim was not to please anyone. The book undoubt-
edly still has flaws. I hope I shall be able to remove them in the next
revision (perhaps two years hence).

The story that I present here is, as I see it, a criticism of our American
capitalist-democratic civilization, the most severe criticism, it seems to
me, that anyone could write; but during the writing of the book my constant attitude toward America—this vast country with its 125,000,000
people, its immense natural wealth and great beauty, its high genius and
marvelous technical equipment—was, and still is, one of love and of
confidence in its ultimate future.

America is at the crossroads. She can't stay where she is, not for
long. Right or left? Probably right first, then left. But eventually it will
be left: for, in its very nature (which I can't discuss here) it is a left or
revolutionary country.

But whichever way she turns first, America will be, within the next
few years, the scene of thousands of bitter disputes between labor and
capital and between radical or revolutionary and conservative (in many
cases racketeering) labor unions. Many of these disputes will be accompanied by violence of an extreme character. One does not have to be a
prophet to see all this just around the corner.

AUTHOR'S NOTE

One need only know something of our socio-economic situation and the story, thus far, of class violence in this country.

And these impending disputes and outbreaks of violence will be a factor of paramount importance in the decision which America will make as to her future course. Intelligent, patriotic citizens should follow closely these events on the capital-labor front as they develop and try to see and understand them, not as something isolated and of mere local importance, but as something that has a deep root in our history and significance in our current national life, and that will profoundly affect the future of the United States.

Louis Adamic
July 1934

PART I
Mild Beginnings

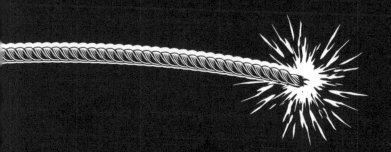

"I can hire one half of the working class
to kill the other half."
—*JAY GOULD*

CHAPTER 1
"IMPUDENT CONDUCT"

The struggle of the have-nots against the haves in the United States was first referred to as "class *war*" in 1826 in New York City by Frances Wright, "that bold blasphemer and voluptuous preacher of licentiousness," as a conservative writer of that day called her; but at that time, and for some while afterward, the war was merely verbal. The fiery Fanny, with other reformers and uplifters then haranguing the young Republic, contented herself with fierce and frequent blasts of eloquence denouncing the social and economic evils of the period.

There were, in the first quarter of the nineteenth century, a few labor strikes for higher wages and for the recognition of workmen's organizations, such as they were. The walkouts usually involved a dozen or a score of men, but they were, without exception, tame, peaceful affairs. So far as any records tell us, not even a fist was lifted in any of them; strikers, it appeared, got even with scabs by calling them "rats" and other bad names. Strikes were considered "conspiracies" or "malicious enterprises," coming under the old common law of England against interference with trade which continued in force in the United States after the Revolution; and more often than not workmen were arrested and fined or jailed as soon as they struck, and replaced by unorganized men.

But that was no serious matter to the strikers. The country was young and vast beyond conception, and one could move on and very likely better oneself. The frontier lured the adventurous man who found himself at odds with the New Industrialism in the East. In the West, land was to be had for the asking, at no expense save that of a journey, a few implements, and a beast or two. There was no sense in fighting for a job. And if one wanted excitement, the wilderness was full of Indians still to be killed.

Toward the end of the eighteen-thirties, however, immigrants—for the most part Germans, Irishmen, and Dutchmen—began coming to

8   the Land of Promise in considerable numbers, and thenceforth incidents of labor violence were frequent.

Conditions in Europe at that time were bad, and rising American
industrialists who found native labor too independent in regard to
wages and working hours sent agents to Ireland and to the Continent
to lure the poor people there to the United States with fantastic tales
of mountains of gold and unbounded freedom and opportunities. *The
Voice of Industry*, a leading labor and reform paper of that day printed
in Massachusetts, editorialized indignantly against the "importation of
strikebreakers" and charged the employers with providing themselves
"against walkouts by creating a numerous poor and dependent popu-
lace... whose abject condition in their own countries made them willing
to work fourteen and sixteen hours a day for what capital sees fit to give
them."

This indignation was justified. The majority of the immigrants then,
as later, were unskilled laborers and lowly peasants. American employers, with the development of machinery and ever greater specialization
of tasks in the shops, could use them advantageously, paying them low
wages and working them from before sunrise till after dark, to no small
detriment of the native mechanics. American workmen naturally resented the presence of these low Europeans—"dung," they called them.
Some of the trade unions, which were then coming into existence in
Pennsylvania, New York, and the New England States, eyed them with
deeper dislike than the employers who were directly responsible for this
class of immigration.

Foreign laborers were employed in large numbers in construction
gangs upon canals in New Jersey, New York, Maryland, and Pennsylvania
at from $5 to $12 a month "and found." They worked, too, at slightly
higher wages, on railroads under construction. Often, when some over-
seer absconded with their money, they lost even these meager earnings,
and in such cases they had no legal redress. The canals and railroads
passed through marshy regions, and laborers were dying of malaria and
other diseases. But contractors found no difficulty in replacing the sick
and the dead, for nearly every ship that arrived from Europe brought
in more "dung."

During the second quarter of the nineteenth century frequent "riots"
occurred, as the press called the disturbances, most of which, no doubt,
were spontaneous, unorganized, leaderless strikes for higher wages and
better working conditions of these wretched foreign laborers driven to

desperation. The militia was often called out to quell the outbursts; men were killed and property was destroyed or damaged.

In most of the riots the Irish predominated. The Germans, the Dutch, and other immigrants were comparatively patient sufferers.

II

In 1836, a gang of Irish harbor workers in New York City "rioted for higher wages" and for their "impudent conduct," as a local newspaper put it, the police distributed among them "some severe and probably dangerous wounds."

Irishmen also took part in the riot at Allegheny City in the summer of 1848. The Pennsylvania reformers had just succeeded in inducing the legislators of the State to pass an act limiting the workday to ten hours and forbidding the employment of children under twelve years of age in cotton, woolen, silk, paper, and flax mills. This had displeased the up-and-coming manufacturers of Allegheny City very much. They immediately laid off 2,000 operatives, who, living from hand to mouth as they did, could not afford to be jobless. Within two weeks most of them starved, or were on the verge of starvation.

One day, in their desperation, several hundred men, women, and children tried to return to work on the old twelve-hour basis, or upon any terms whatever. Such was their eagerness to get back to their machines and benches that they attempted virtually to break into the mills. The armed guards repulsed them; but before they returned home, a riot occurred at one of the factories in which several people were injured and some property was damaged. About twenty arrests were made; thirteen of the rioters—five of them Irish—were convicted and fined, but the majority, unable to pay the fines, went to prison. A few days after the riot a settlement was made on the new ten-hour basis with a 16 percent reduction in wages.

The high-toned New York *Journal of Commerce* referred to the riots as "an exotic phenomenon in this country which has been imported with the dregs and scum of the Old World that we so much covet," and the supercilious *Pennsylvanian* called the rioters "foolish and hot headed foreigners."

III

Such were the extremely mild beginnings of violence in the class struggle in the United States—mild as compared with the violence that flared up

10 with great frequency in the later decades of the nineteenth century and early in the twentieth.

Ignorant immigrants were "dung" and "dregs and scum," and were treated accordingly. They spoke a variety of tongues; there were other important racial differences among them; and even if native labor leaders and reformers had had any sympathy with their lot, which they lacked completely, organization among them would have been impossible.

In consequence, hunger and general wretchedness drove them to sporadic "impudent conduct," which the hundred per cent Americans of that day were perhaps justified in characterizing as a "foreign phenomenon" in the sense that only—or largely—immigrants were guilty of it; but the conditions which provoked them to riots were quite American. It was the American industrialists who imported these foreigners and then treat them inhumanly.

CHAPTER 2
THE MOLLY MAGUIRES

During the two decades immediately preceding and the two directly following the Civil War, the American labor movement was in a constant state of confusion. The Industrial Revolution was rather overwhelming in its effect upon labor.

Before this, the worker with a pair of able hands and a set of good tools had stood on fairly even terms with the master; he had produced directly for purposes of consumption and, indeed, had consumed much of his own actual product. Now, however, the factory system was becoming general. Tools yielded to machinery. Immense factories appeared employing thousands of men, women, and children. Suddenly, machines were of greater importance than hands. Labor depended upon conditions created by machinery. Skilled mechanics, once proud of their crafts, were now reduced to common laborers, mere appendages, servants, to the machines. Labor became a commodity on the market, no different from raw materials or coal. Its object was no longer directly to produce, but to keep the machines going for the enrichment of their owners. All human considerations in industry became secondary to the accumulation of great fortunes by those who owned the machines and the raw materials.

And immigrants—more "dung"—came in hordes. Child and female labor increased because it was cheaper than male; besides, women and children were easier to handle than men, who, if they disliked the work, were more likely to bundle up and head West.

There were fine-fibered, tender-minded men in the Republic to whom these swift changes in the industrial field were a source of deep perturbation. Philosophers and reformers put their heads together and there were much pondering and lamenting, vague Socialistic or "humanistic" idealism and speculation. In the forties, Emerson wrote to Carlyle: "We are all a little wild here with numberless projects of social reform; not a reading man but has the draft of a new community in his waistcoat pocket." There was the Brook Farm group of idealistic thinkers and dreamers who, in their optimistic moods, entertained charming visions of the future—not so distant—when, among other social improvements and embellishments, disease-breeding factories would be replaced by "grand palaces devoted to Labor and Love" and the whole world, at all events the United States, would be, instead of a chaos of misery and exploitation, a wilderness of sweets. But capitalism, growing stronger by day and by night, took no heed of the learned Brook-Farmers, who, to quote Samuel P. Orth, are now remembered mainly "as an example of the futility of trying to leaven a world of realism by means of an atom of transcendental idealism." All intellectual movements against the New Industrialism were defeated before they started.

Trade-unionism was tame and timorous. Most of the strikes ended disastrously for the labor organizations concerned. There were labor unions whose membership pledged itself to "avoid exciting topics." Labor leaders, so called, were for the most part men who neither labored nor led: aspiring third-rate politicians and windy orators who had little capacity for understanding the new industrial forces as they affected the worker; or reformers and lopsided idealists, full of lovely vagaries and longings, who had drawn their original inspiration and their terminology from the writings of the utopian Socialists and the Brook-Farmers. They met in labor conventions to pronounce solemnly upon the nobility of toil and recite verses about the golden sweatdrops upon the laborer's honest brow, which "shine brighter than diamonds in a coronet." They used rhetoric to hide their confusion in the face of reality. With the exception of Horace Greeley, who, however, devoted himself mainly to the printers, the labor movement of the time produced no leader of any ability. Opportunities to enrich themselves lured competent men into commercial enterprises and into politics on the side of big money.

The worker was told by his leaders that he was "Nature's nobleman," while as a matter of fact he was the cheapest commodity on the industrial market and was lucky if his immediate circumstances permitted him to throw up his job in the mill or the mine and find himself a tract of land in the wilderness.

II

In sharp contrast with the ineffective regular labor organizations of that time, we have the Molly Maguires, a secret miners' society in the anthracite region of Pennsylvania in the late-sixties and early-seventies, whose principal method of achieving its ends was terrorism—murder.

The background of the American Molly Maguires reaches back into feudalistic Ireland of the fourth decade of the nineteenth century. There lived then an energetic dame, the widow Molly Maguire, who did not believe in the rent system that was in effect in her country and became the leading spirit of a loosely organized resistance to it.

She was a barbaric and picturesque character. She blackened her face and under her petticoat carried a pistol strapped to each of her stout thighs. Her special aversions were landlords, their agents, bailiffs, and process-servers, and her expression of hatred was limited to beating them up or murdering them. This she did with her own hands or through her "boys," who called themselves Molly Maguires, or Mollies for short. She was down on the government, which aided the tyrannical landlords in collecting the rent. She was the head of the so-called Free Soil Party, whose banner was her red petticoat. If a landlord or his agent evicted a peasant who was not meeting his payments, that landlord or agent was usually as good as dead. The Mollies, if not Mrs. Maguire herself, were sure to hear of it; eventually the man's corpse would be found in some ditch or even upon the floor of his own house.

Molly's systematic assassinations were so effectual that for a time parts of Ireland—notably Tipperary, West Meath, King's and Queen's Counties—became uninhabitable except for Mollies. Finally, the authorities, at the behest of desperate landowners, began to persecute Molly and her "boys," until, in the fifties, hordes of them, including, it appears, Molly herself, emigrated to America.

Many of them sought work in the Pennsylvania coal mines.

The Molly Maguires, as a secret order, already existed in the United States in the mid-fifties. To become a member one had to be Irish or of Irish descent, a good Roman Catholic, and also "of good moral character." More or less officially (for the organization acquired a charter in Pennsylvania under the name of "The Ancient Order of Hibernians") their purpose was to "promote friendship, unity, and true Christian charity among the members; and, generally, to do all and singular matters and things which shall be lawful to the well-being and good management of the affairs of the association." Officially, they meant to attain these ends "by raising or supporting a stock or fund of money for maintaining the aged, sick, blind, and infirm members." Their constitution further declared "that the Supreme Being has implanted in our natures tender sympathies and most humane feelings toward our fellow-creatures in distress; and all the happiness that human nature is capable of enjoying must flow and terminate in the love of God and our fellows."

But while such was the pious basis for the order's official existence, actually the Molly Maguires became fiercer in the United States than they had been in the Old Country—and, perhaps, with good reason. When the Mollies were at the height of their power—early in the seventies—outrage followed outrage until the coal regions of Pennsylvania became a byword for terror. Wives trembled when their husbands spoke of visiting the mining districts. People feared to stir out after dark, and never budged in broad daylight without a pistol—which, however, availed them little, for the assassins seemed invariably to get in the first shot.

A contemporary writer, in the *American Law Review* for January 1877, described the anthracite regions of that day as "one vast Alsatia."

...From their dark and mysterious recesses there came forth to the outside world an appalling series of tales of murder, of arson, and violent crime of every description. It seemed that no respectable man could be safe there, for it was from the respectable classes that the victims were by preference selected; nor could anyone tell from day to day whether he might not be marked for sure and sudden destruction. Only the members of one calling could feel any certainty as to their fate. These were the superintendents and "bosses" in the collieries; they could all rest assured that their days would not be long in the land. Everywhere and at all times attacked, beaten, and shot down, on the public highways and in their own homes, in solitary places and in the neighborhood of crowds, these doomed men continued to fall in frightful succession beneath the hands of assassins.

III

There can be no doubt, however, that the treatment accorded the workers by the responsible mine operators was such as to justify the feelings of resentment and revenge that could prompt these Irish miners to such drastic deeds. The wages were low. Miners were paid by the cubic yard, by the car, or by the ton, and, in the driving of entries, by the lineal yard; there was much cheating in weighing and measuring on the part of the bosses. Little, if any, attention was paid by the owners, of their own accord, to the safety of the miners. Cave-ins were frequent, entombing hundreds of men every year. When and wherever possible, the employers took advantage of the men.

There were all sorts of petty difficulties at the mines. There were, for instance, "soft jobs" and "hard jobs." A miner naturally preferred a soft job. Irishmen considered themselves superior to the other foreigners, who were also beginning to come to the mines, and hence demanded the soft jobs for themselves. If refused, a Molly was naturally displeased, and his displeasure could immediately get the boss thrashed within an inch of his life, if not eventually murdered. On the other hand, if the boss should hire a Molly, there was always the possibility that the two would get into a row over the measuring of the quantity or the estimation of the quality of the miner's coal. And to disagree with a Molly was almost certain death. For a time many bosses refused to employ Irishmen altogether, but they all died by violence. If a superintendent dared to come forward in support of his mining boss against the Molly, he, too, became a marked man and eventually was beaten up or assassinated.

But the bosses were not the Mollies' only enemies. The Mollies also had a thoroughly Irish contempt for the faint-hearted, ineffectual methods of the regular labor unions. Several labor leaders and Socialistic orators were murdered in Pennsylvania during this period—in all probability by the Mollies.

Some of the foremost Mollies were also leaders of non-secret miners' organizations. A group of them, for example, controlled the Miners' and Laborers' Benevolent Association, and were responsible for the unfortunate "long strike" for higher wages in 1874–1875, during which, after suffering had become acute among the strikers, the Mollies kept them from returning to work by threats of murder.

IV

The killings were performed in a cool, deliberate, almost impersonal manner.

The Molly who wanted a boss assassinated reported his grievance in the prescribed manner to the proper local committee. If the latter approved of the wronged Molly's request, as it ordinarily did, two or more Mollies not personally or directly interested in the case were selected from a different locality, usually from another county, to do the "job," so that, being unknown, they could not be easily identified. If a Molly to whom the killing had been assigned refused to carry it out, he himself was likely to die.

16   The grievance committees were wont to meet in the backrooms of saloons run by fellow Mollies and, after the completion of the act, celebrate the "clean job" with the killers in good Irish fashion. Most Mollies were true sons of their spiritual mother, the widow Maguire: strong, dynamic robust fellows, carousers, drinkers, fighters, brawlers, but good and faithful husbands and fathers. They led a "pure family life." Most of them were deeply religious. Meetings at which murders were planned often began with prayers. They went regularly to confession. Molly Maguire killings were not considered personal sins by the killers, but incidents in a "war," so they did not confess them, although the Roman Catholic Church in America had, of course, officially condemned the organization and its terroristic doings.

James Ford Rhodes, in a paper which he read in 1909, before the American Academy of Arts and Letters in Washington, ventured to explain the Molly Maguire psychology as follows:

> Subject to tyranny at home, the Irishman, when he came to America, too often translated liberty into license, and so ingrained was his habit of looking upon government as an enemy [due to the seven centuries of misgovernment of Ireland by England] that, when he became the ruler of cities and stole the public funds, he was, from his point of view, only despoiling the old adversary. With this traditional hostility to government, it was easy for him to become a Molly Maguire, while the English, Scotch, and Welsh immigrant shrank from such a society with horror.

V

In the decade beginning with 1865, Molly Maguire killings were frequent, with few arrests, fewer trials, and never a conviction for murder in the first degree. The killers were always strangers in the locality, usually young men, quick on their legs, who had already made their escape before anybody began to pursue them. If one was caught, there always were a dozen Mollies ready to swear by the Lord God and the Holy Virgin that the accused had been with them every minute in the evening of the murder. They packed juries and selected judges.

Using the same drastic tactics, Molly Maguire leaders invaded the political field and, setting themselves up as "bosses," installed mayors and judges who were members of the order (just as nowadays "racketeers" put their men into public office in New York, Chicago, and Philadelphia). Early in the seventies they developed considerable political power in Pennsylvania, especially in Schuylkill County, where five or six hundred Mollies ruled communities of tens of thousands.

Molly Maguire-ism was at its height in 1873 and 1874. Mining bosses and other men displeasing to the Mollies were falling dead week after week. Coal trains were wrecked. However, many killings and outrages attributed to the Mollies unquestionably were committed by other persons.

There were then several thousand Molly Maguire lodges in Pennsylvania, with a central executive body. The organization was about to gain a foothold in West Virginia when, on the initiative of a young mine-operator whose bosses were being killed with great regularity, the part of organized society in Pennsylvania not controlled by the Mollies began a determined secret action against the terrorists. Detectives of Irish descent went to work in the mines and, after joining the order, became the "biggest Mollies of Mollies," or killers of the first water, and as such were in position to spot the leaders.

In 1875, after a number of especially gruesome murders, several leaders and members of the order were arrested and tried. Pinkerton detectives—notably one James McParland, who subsequently figured in other labor cases—were practically the only witnesses against them. Whether any of the accused were directly guilty of the murders with which they were charged is extremely questionable, but in the course of the next few years ten Mollies were executed and fourteen imprisoned for long terms.

Thereafter the Molly Maguires as a terrorist organization rapidly disintegrated. The Ancient Order of Hibernians, however, exists to this day.

VI

However shocking it may seem to a person who has led a sheltered life, the appearance of organized terrorism at that time and place was quite natural; indeed, it is a wonder that it was not more widespread.

Some of the explanations for the Mollies—namely, the utter ineffectiveness of the regular labor unions in the face of brutal industrial conditions, the criminal disregard for the miners' safety on the part of the employers, and the intense Irish temperament produced by centuries of misrule and injustice in the Old Country—I have already offered. Coal and more coal, was the important thing; the countless new machines in the factories and the new railroad locomotives had to have their motive power; and the men who mined the coal scarcely mattered. Immigrants

18   hungry for work, any kind of work, were coming to the United States by the thousands every week. Hence, if a dozen miners lost their lives in a disaster, it was a matter of scant importance to the employer, and he was little inclined to do anything to prevent accidents in the future—unless he happened to fear the Mollies. By killing mine-owners and bosses by the dozen, by beating up hundreds of others, the Mollies unquestionably improved the working conditions not only for themselves but for all the miners in the anthracite regions of Pennsylvania, and saved many workers' lives. There is no doubt, however, that many Molly Maguire killings were motivated by petty, personal grudges.

On the occasion of the thirtieth anniversary of the Molly Maguire executions by the State of Pennsylvania, Eugene V. Debs, then at the height of his career as a radical leader in America, wrote in the *Appeal to Reason*:

> They all protested their innocence and all died game. Not one of them betrayed the slightest evidence of fear or weakening. Not one of them was a murderer at heart. All were ignorant, rough and un-couth, born of poverty and buffeted by the merciless tides of fate and chance... To resist the wrongs of which they and their fellow-workers were victims and to protect themselves against the brutality of their bosses, according to their own crude notions, was the prime object of the organization of the Molly Maguires... It is true that their methods were drastic, but it must be remembered that their lot was hard and *brutalizing*; that they were the neglected children of poverty, the product of a wretched environment... The men who perished upon the scaffold as felons were labor leaders, the first martyrs to the class struggle in the United States.

In the Molly Maguires we have the first beginnings of "racketeering" in America, especially labor racketeering—to use a term that has come into use since 1920. The Mollies whom the State of Pennsylvania hanged in the seventies are considered heroes today by not a few leaders and members of some of the "conservative" labor unions. The Molly Maguire organization disintegrated in the seventies, but the Molly Maguire spirit, constantly stimulated by the brutal and brutal-izing working conditions in industry, went marching on through the eighties and the nineties into the current century, and—as we shall see toward the end of this book—it marches on today with a firmer step than ever before.

CHAPTER 3
THE GREAT RIOTS OF 1877

B y the end of the sixties the "Gilded Age," as Mark Twain called it, had begun, and the United States was absorbed in the exploitation and organization—mainly exploitation—of its vast material resources, to the neglect of practically every other consideration. The nation launched upon a crusade of material success. Success at all costs! The Devil take the hindmost and the public be damned!...

An intense feeling about wealth motivated and inspired life in America almost entirely. It produced a philosophy with a healthy enough basic principle: the necessity and desirability of the survival of the strongest and the best; but when that doctrine appeared in practice, it was bare, unrelieved selfishness—fierce, cruel, anti-social. No doubt there was much in industry, and generally in the life of the country, that was admirable, but most of that was dimmed by the sordid individual motives and acts of the financial and industrial giants, untempered by any social feeling or intelligence. The keenest and highest-minded social and political observers of the time were remarking upon "the decline of public morality"..."the evil combinations of capital"..."the new slavery."

There were bitter wars among capitalists commanding resources, the vastness of which was unknown even to themselves. The competitive spirit grew fiercer every year. It was the beginning of relentless business methods: of secret rates and rebates, graft, subterranean intrigue, murder, special legislation passed by bought lawmakers for the benefit of some capitalist or small group of capitalists. Financial and industrial magnates were struggling tooth and claw to determine who should survive and dominate. When two of them saw that a fight between them would be mutually destructive, they combined to fight a third. The trusts were started... Theodore Dreiser has captured the spirit of Big Business of that period in his novels, *The Financier* and *The Titan*... It was industrial and financial anarchy, exuberant, hard, irresistible.

20 The Constitution of the United States passed for a joke, and so did the Presidency and the Supreme Court. An honest politician was one who stayed sold to one group of interests. The Federal Government became centralized beyond Alexander Hamilton's fondest hopes; it was virtually the Central Office of Big Business.

The capitalists as a class were thoroughly agreed upon one thing only—their opposition to the proletariat's strivings to improve its status. In this, the police club was the symbol of their power. On one occasion Jay Gould boasted, cynically: "I can hire one half of the working class to kill the other half."

In the labor market every worker competed with every other. Class solidarity was impossible, for, by the natural power of example of the man on top, and by other means of influence, the very rich imparted to the entire population a large measure of their own feelings and ideas in regard to the aims of life in America. The millionaire's estimate of the value of wealth was almost universally accepted. Essentially, the rich and the poor were dominated by the same ideas, and fired by the same feverish urges and desires. And the universal feeling about wealth naturally and necessarily developed the intense and unlimited competition which made life a bitter struggle, not with Nature to obtain shelter and subsistence, which would seem to be the normal life for man, but of man against man and class against class, in which an ever-increasing number must inevitably fail and be crushed. The rich were getting richer, and the poor poorer.

II

Certain labor leaders and reformers were casting about for some scheme whereby labor might be emancipated from the dominion of employers, but the conditions in general were so chaotic, changing so rapidly and unexpectedly, that one scarcely had time to realize a situation when it suddenly presented a problem different from what it had originally suggested. The labor movement was, therefore, a fitful movement; its impulses were uncertain and confused, stimulated mainly from without, hardly at all from within. The eight-hour day victory of Australian labor in the late sixties, for instance, prompted the American trade unions to start an agitation for the eight-hour system in the United States. Resolutions were endlessly passed; leagues and committees were organized in the larger industrial centers; and politicians in Washington were induced to present bills to establish the eight-hour workday. Several strikes were started on the eight-hour issue, but with the ignorant, unorganizable immigrants arriving in great numbers, ready to take any sort of job at almost any pay, and work twelve and fourteen hours a day, the employers had no difficulty in crushing such walkouts.

Labor at this time scored but one notable victory—in the great strike of 1872 in New York City, in which nearly 100,000 men participated, for the introduction of the eight-hour system in the building and mechanical trades. The fight lasted several months, whereupon the employers yielded.

A great victory, but only a momentary one. It did the workers little good in the long run, for within a few months the dire panic of 1873, the after-effects of which lasted six years, swept the country, and labor everywhere in the United States started on a most critical period in its history.

III

The country was in deep economic distress.

There had been a too rapid building of railroads, wharves, plants, and other projects requiring tremendous sums of capital but offering small immediate returns. A contemporary historian wrote: "Men had no longer any vision for realities, but built upon illusions and impossibilities as if they were the solid facts and laws of nature... The sheer wastefulness of that period, if it could be adequately portrayed, would appear incredible to all who did not witness it." Finally, with the failure of an important bank, the economic machine jumped out of gear; the "mad gallop" of American capitalism ended abruptly in a great crisis.

The working class, of course, received at once the full impact of the panic. Hundreds of thousands were suddenly thrown out of work. Wages were reduced. These reductions caused prolonged and desperate strikes. Every one of them failed. Some of the strikes were followed by lockouts, so that vast numbers of people could not get work on any terms. Labor leaders were blacklisted. Between 1873 and 1880 real and nominal wages were cut to almost one-half of the former standards. Labor organizations went out of existence. There were no leaders to lead them and no workmen to pay the dues. In New York City alone the trade-union membership dropped from 45,000 to under 5,000.

At a mass meeting in Cooper Union, New York City, in December of 1873, there was a display of placards which told a terrible tale:

10,000 HOMELESS MEN AND WOMEN IN OUR STREETS
7,500 LODGED IN OVERCROWDED CHARNEL STATION
HOUSES PER WEEK
20,250 IDLE MEN FROM II TRADE UNIONS; ONLY
5,950 EMPLOYED
182,000 SKILLED UNION WORKMEN IDLE IN NEW
YORK STATE
110,000 IDLE OF ALL CLASSES IN NEW YORK CITY

But in other large cities the working people were hit no less cruelly. That winter thousands starved and lacked proper clothing and medical attention.

Meetings of the unemployed were held, but frequently, on the announcement of such gatherings, the conscience-pricked communities took alarm, fearing that a great mob of hitherto patient sufferers, suddenly brought together, might imperil lives and property. Early in January 1874, for instance, the leaders of the poverty-stricken in New York City gained permission from the Police Department to parade the streets on the thirteenth, and then assemble in Tompkins Square, but on the twelfth the department suddenly revoked the permit. It was impossible for the leaders to inform the scattered pauper army of the changed order. When the mob—men, women, and children—poured into the square, the police came and there followed a scene which *The World* the next day confessed was indescribable. "People rushed from the gates"—so runs a contemporary account—"and through the streets, followed by mounted officers at full speed, charging upon them without provocation. Screams of women and children rent the air, and the blood of many stained the streets."

A week after this occurrence, *The World* printed a survey of the conditions, showing that thousands "lived on from 70¢ to $14 a week"; that hundreds subsisted on the refuse of the city—"veritable scavengers."

Early in 1877, the *Inter-Ocean*, an organ of the Administration at Washington, admitted that there

> never was a time in the history of the United States when a greater amount of misery, poverty, and wretchedness existed than at the present time. New York is full of want... Workingmen are parading the streets, publicly setting forth their suffering and calling for relief... Nor is this pressing state of affairs confined to the East. In Chicago, today, there are hundreds of well-born, well-bred, and well-informed men walking the streets without a cent, and without a knowledge of where to get a dinner or a bed.

For four years the fuel had been piled up for the conflagration which suddenly burst forth in connection with the so-called strikes on the Baltimore & Ohio Railroad in the summer of 1877—less than a month after the Molly Maguire leaders had been hanged.

The railroad companies, in common with other industries under the stress of panic, or else using the panic as an excuse, had been cutting their employees' wages since the start of the crisis, and, openly hostile to trade unions, were unceremoniously discharging the men who dared to serve on grievance committees.

Early in July, the B. & O. announced another ten per cent cut of its firemen's and brakemen's wages, effective on the sixteenth of the month. The news brought panic to the employees, who already were scarcely able to support their families on what they received. Desperate, they held protest meetings and sent committees to the manager of the road. He declined to see them. With the other officials of the company, he believed that the hard times would prevent the men from walking out. Besides, if they did, so much the worse for them; for there were hordes of jobless men all along the B. & O. lines to choose from.

On the morning of July 16, the trains were manned as usual. There had been strike talk, but, to all seeming, no action had been decided upon. In the middle of the afternoon, a gang of firemen and brakemen quit at a junction in Maryland. It appeared to be a local movement. The company had no difficulty in replacing them. Hungry men were begging for work everywhere.

But as the afternoon wore on, the company officials received word of difficulties all along the road. Nothing definite as yet; merely "trouble"…"discontent"…"insubordination." And the trouble seemed most intense at Martinsburg, West Virginia, where, toward evening, the men sidetracked their trains and quit.

Elsewhere the situation became equally acute and dramatic. News came that the canal-boatmen were quitting. By midnight the entire system dominated by the B. & O. was paralyzed.

It was a spontaneous movement, with practically no organization behind it.

Abashed, the company officials appealed to Governor Matthews of West Virginia for armed protection of their property. The Governor responded at once, and on the morning of July 17 the first shots were exchanged in Martinsburg between strikers and militiamen. A locomotive fireman was shot. The situation became tense. Mobs of townspeople and farmers from the surrounding country joined the strikers, and finally two companies of Martinsburg militia, officers and men, went over to the workers' side.

Hearing of this, the Governor, as commander-in-chief of the armed forces of the State, decided to lead a detachment to Martinsburg in person, but meanwhile the strike spread to Wheeling, the capital. Alarmed, he wired President Hayes in Washington for Federal troops.

The President acted at once. Regulars were ordered out and within three days the B. & O.'s difficulties in West Virginia were considerably lessened. Trains began to move again.

Meantime the trouble spread swiftly—alarmingly—to other B. & O. points. Federal troops and the militia appeared at once wherever the railroad company asked for them; in several places their arrival incited open warfare.

At Baltimore, for instance, soldiers armed to the teeth marched about in platoons and companies. In some sections the streets were choked with proletarian mobs—strikers, sympathizers, hoodlums, the unemployed. Someone yelled an insulting remark at the soldiers. A few paving-stones and bricks flew through the air, injuring a militiaman. Immediately, without order from the commanding officer, several soldiers fired into the crowd, killing or wounding a number of people. The terrified mob retreated before the soldiers' guns; then more paving-stones and bricks, and the militiamen fired again, strewing the streets with more dead and wounded rioters.

For three days the riots continued in Baltimore. The strikers, who were practically leaderless, were joined by thousands of laborers and mechanics out of work as well as by the entire criminal class of the city, eager for an opportunity to plunder. A large number of men in various other occupations, who had recently suffered reductions in wages, were in a sullen mood. They welcomed what they thought was an attempt on the part of the railroad men to right a common wrong. They aided the rioters and stimulated the movement by reckless and inflammatory talk, until it became a loose, haphazard mob action.

In Cumberland, Maryland, the militia killed ten workmen and wounded twice that number.

V

Within a few days of the B. & O. outbreak, the strike epidemic spread to the Pennsylvania Central. Here, too, the action was spontaneous.

Two days previous the idea had scarcely occurred to the men. Their
grievances were similar to those of the workers on the B. & O. road. The
company, holding the upper hand in the situation because of general
unemployment, refused to bargain with them.

In Pittsburgh, which became the center of trouble in Pennsylvania,
the strikers took all the locomotives to the roundhouses and went home.
But as the news of their walkout spread through the city, the streets filled
with mobs not unlike those in Baltimore. The public was sympathetic.
The militiamen, who were Pittsburgh boys, fraternized with workmen,
whereupon the railroad company called for a regiment of militia from
Philadelphia, and later for Federal troops.

The jobless and the hungry formed mobs in various sections of the
city. Soldiers attempted to disperse them. Within a few days over twenty workmen were shot dead and more than fifty wounded.

One night several hundred box-cars in the Pittsburgh yards were
soaked with oil and set on fire. The conflagration quickly spread to the
shops and the roundhouses, and before morning over $5,000,000 worth
of equipment was destroyed. The strikers, of course, were charged with
having started the fire, but labor and radical writers insist that most of
the cars were old and useless and that the company had hired firebugs
to touch off the equipment, so that it might collect damages from the
State for losses suffered during the strike. In her *Autobiography*, Mother
Jones advances the theory that the business men of Pittsburgh, who had
felt for a long time that the railroad was discriminating against their city
in the matter of rates, were behind the arson.

Mobs, rendered furious by the deadly fire of the military, surged
about the city, sacking stores for arms and food. For a time it seemed
that the rioters, albeit leaderless, would gain the upper hand over the
authorities. As was the case in Baltimore, the striking railroadmen who
engaged in the riots were few as compared with the hungry and desperate men who had not worked for months, or even years.

Riots occurred elsewhere in Pennsylvania. At Reading, thirteen
were killed and over twenty wounded in a single day.

VI

In Chicago, too, with widespread unemployment and starvation, the
situation was extremely tense. Radical orators harangued the wretched
proletariat about "the Revolution," which they proclaimed was imminent. Albert Parsons, not yet an avowed anarchist, was already in the

city. Several strikes—all hopeless—were in progress and a number of big factories had recently locked out their employees.

The Daily News issued extra after extra about the riots at Baltimore, Cumberland, Pittsburgh, Reading, and elsewhere. Its circulation of over twenty thousand doubled in a day and more than trebled in another.

On the night of July 23, the switchmen of the Michigan Central struck against the threat of another cut in their wages, which had very recently been reduced from $65 to $55 a month. Three days previously the men had had no thought of striking. Now they formed eager audiences for such extremists as Albert Parsons.

The strike spread and within twenty-four hours the entire Mid-Western transportation system, "the pride of Chicago," was paralyzed.

On the night of July 24 the police dispersed three crowds of workers who had gathered to be addressed by Parsons and other leaders of the Socialist Labor Party. Parsons issued circulars appealing to the strikers and sympathizers to avoid violence at all costs and thereby solidify the public sentiment behind the eight-hour day movement, which was then being sponsored by his party. "The grand principles of Humanity and Popular Sovereignty," he said, "need no violence to sustain them."

But it was too late to preach non-violence. The next day a battle occurred between the police and the strikers near the McCormick Reaper Works. Men were killed and wounded. Lloyd Lewis and Henry Justin Smith, in their *Chicago—A History of Its Reputation*, say:

> Twenty thousand men, police and citizens, were under arms. Squads of house-holders shouldered rifles and patrolled the residence districts. [At one time] fifty different mobs were clashing with militiamen and volunteer "specials." Saloons were closed... Citizens brought rifles and horses to City Hall... At the Chicago, Burlington & Quincy roundhouses on West Sixteenth Street, locomotives were destroyed and volleys fired. A pitched battle was fought at the viaduct between Halsted and Archer Avenues. Terror had the business men by the throat, and...they demanded 5,000 militiamen to put down "the ragged Commune wretches."... Scores among the "upper classes" left town.

Then a battalion of the United States regulars, commanded by Lieutenant-Colonel Frederick D. Grant, son of Ulysses, arrived in Chicago, and that was the end of strife. The strike was broken.

On July 26 *The Daily News* said editorially:

For years the railroads of this country have been wholly run out-side the United States Constitution... They have charged what they pleased for fare and freights. They corrupted the State and city legislatures. They have corrupted Congress, employing for that purpose a lobby that dispensed bribes to the amount of millions and millions... Their managers have been plundering the roads and speculating on their securities to their own enrichment. Finally, having found nothing more to get out of the stockholders...they have commenced raiding not only upon the general public but their own employees.

VII

The warfare spread all the way to the Pacific Coast. In San Francisco the workers dashed with the police and Vigilantes. Throughout the country the number of casualties ran into hundreds; the exact number has never been determined. The number of troops on actual riot duty approached twenty thousand.

By the end of July the rioters were entirely subdued—beaten. Thereupon, the conservative press and the pulpit began to urge, implore, and demand from the Federal Government and the separate States that they reorganize and strengthen their military forces, so that in the future they might be in position to deal more effectively with such outbreaks— for behind the riots they discerned "a dreadful force"..."the awful presence of Socialism, which has more than once made Europe tremble on account of its energy, its despotism, its fearful atrocities."

The riots had been spontaneous movements, produced by hunger, desperation—and this, upon reflection, impressed the authorities and the respectable element as worse than if it had come about as a deliberately planned, concerted action. Had the riots shown any sign of organization, the failure of the movement would have been a better promise of the underdog's submission in the future. But in this unorganized upheaval they perceived an elemental spontaneity which showed the existence of deep and widespread discontent among the lowly; indeed, of a powerful disposition on the part of the proletariat to subvert the existing social order. What would happen should this discontent become organized under a strong leader—say, a Danton, a Bakunin?

The underdog had given capitalism in America its first big scare. The memory of the Paris Commune of six years before was still fresh.

Frightened, capitalism decided that it must tighten up the screws that held down the working class. The erection of great armories in the

28   large industrial cities dates from 1877. The War Department published a manual of tactics in riot duty. And it was but a few years later that General E. L. Molineux read before the Military Service Institute of the United States a paper upon "Riots in Cities and Their Suppression" and Stephen H. Olin published a pamphlet, "for private circulation," entitled *Suggestions Upon the Strategy of Street Fighting.*

VIII

Those of the strikers who could do so returned sullenly to their jobs at reduced wages. Some of them were required to sign pledges that they would not join any more unions, nor support the eight-hour movement.

Many trade unions, as I have said, went out of existence during the panic, and most capitalists, while still thinking with alarm about the riots, already exulted over "the end of labor unionism."

The panic lasted for two years after the riots.

The Socialist agitators, who had become numerous during the hard times, rejoiced in the "revolutionary spirit" that the mobs had evinced during the two bloody weeks. Now they knew that they had something to work on.

Also, following Bismarck's anti-Socialist decree of 1878, there emigrated to the United States hundreds of educated German Socialists, many of them extremists. They joined the loosely organized radical movement in the various cities, notably in New York and Chicago.

For several years it was extremely unwise for workers to join the unions or support radical political movements. The inevitable result was that after the riots many commenced to gather in secret revolutionary meetings. The underdog movement was thus driven underground. Groups of workers even began to provide themselves with arms and to drill in the woods in preparation for the forthcoming final battles with capitalism—"the Revolution"—in which they meant to meet the police and the soldiers with guns and bombs.

The explosion of the Haymarket Bomb was but a few years in the future.

PART TWO
"DYNAMITE...THAT'S THE STUFF!"

"Extirpate the miserable brood!"
—*JOHANN MOST*

CHAPTER 4
AN APOSTLE OF TERRORISM
COMES TO AMERICA

Such European anarchists as Bakunin, Kropotkin, and Guillaume, living in London and the Jura, had been keeping their eyes on the United States for years, as a possible fertile field for anarchist propaganda and action. Indeed, Bakunin, upon hearing of hunger parades in New York and elsewhere, was thinking of going to America as early as 1874, but affairs in Europe and his ill health, which presently resulted in his death, kept him from making the trip. Now, in the summer of 1877, receiving reports of the battles in several States, they were all filled, as Guillaume put it, "with a lively emotion." In the *Bulletin* of the Jura Anarchist Federation, Kropotkin immediately published a lengthy review of the riots. He was enthusiastic in his praise of the "revolutionary qualities" which the American proletariat had exhibited. "Its spontaneity, its simultaneousness at so many distant points, the aid given by the workers of different trades, the resolute character of the uprising from the beginning, call forth our sympathies, excite our admiration, and awaken our hopes."

Then, in 1882, Johann Most, a German anarchist, arrived in the United States and became the chief exponent of the ideas of Bakunin, Nechayeff and other European "propagandists of the deed."

But first it is necessary to know something of the radical movement in the United States prior to the riots of 1877.

II

Modern American radicalism dates from the late forties, when the country began to receive numerous political refugees from Europe, especially from Germany, following the upheavals there in 1848. They represented the Socialism that was then being crystallized in the mighty literary efforts of Marx and Engels. They were not of the underdog element, but rather the *élite*, the intelligentsia of immigration. The movement was intellectual, refined, tame, romantic. It was, for about two decades, a vague expression of a multiplicity of ideas aiming at the introduction of drastic social reforms, the basic one of which was a reconstruction of the economic scheme so that the entire product of labor should accrue to the laborer. They did not mean to abolish capital, but to do away with a distinct capitalist class, though, of course, no one had a plausible notion how that might be accomplished in the United States. The movement was a babel of voices in which the most strident note was the wail of discontent.

In the fifties, numerous German-American "revolutionary societies" and "educational clubs" were formed in New York City, Baltimore, Philadelphia, Chicago, and other large centers, aiming to start "a revolution in the minds of the people." Barricades and violence played no part in the thought of the overwhelming majority of the Socialists of that day. They were opposed to "lawbreaking," holding with Marx and Engels that such tactics were injurious to the cause.

After the Civil War, and even during that conflict, Marxism had begun to appeal—vaguely—to some of the more thoughtful native Americans whose energies were not entirely absorbed by the exploitation of the country and their fellow citizens. Abraham Lincoln himself became—not too publicly, of course—a sort of Socialist. Serious-minded people were disturbed by the rise of influences affecting the vitality of the government and of the individual social conscience as guardians of public order and morality.

There was little interest in politics and government from the broader viewpoint of social welfare or civic patriotism. Under the sway of the passion for material success which had taken hold of the country, honor and social intelligence vanished from public life. Men of honor fled or were driven from official positions. The influence upon the government of one unconscionable millionaire outweighed the votes of a million common people. Except on the frontier, sportsmanship and fair play had ceased to be vital qualities of American public life.

All this outraged the sensibilities of many people. Beneath the roar and bustle of industrial America there was an undercurrent of ideas, hopes, and fitful strivings to restore the government to social interests and to extend its power for public welfare so as to include the lowest worker.

Throughout the sixties Socialism remained tamely idealistic, polite, refined, intellectual, almost respectable. Its appeals were not addressed to the underdog element as such, but to all classes. There were a few hot-headed, wild-eyed radicals here and there, but while industrial conditions were yet bearable to the majority of workers and the frontier was still open, they received little attention.

Then, with the panic of 1873 bursting upon the country, there followed the conditions described in the preceding chapter and, almost overnight, the Socialist movement lost its genial, intellectual temper. The hunger parades in the terrible winter of 1873–1874 were organized by Socialist leaders, both native and foreign-born, and thenceforth Socialism was largely—almost exclusively—an underdog, belly-hunger movement.

As such, it naturally became emotional and *violent*. It was seized by the desperation of the hungry mob.

III

The most radical city in the United States in the seventies and eighties was Chicago. The Socialist Labor Party of Chicago, whose early career was linked with the bloody events that occurred during the panic, acted under the energetic leadership of such men as Philip Van Patten, Albert Parsons, and G. A. Schilling, strike tacticians and agitators of exceptional ability.

Almost from its inception, the Socialist Labor Party contained an extremist element. From time to time, some of its leaders despaired of accomplishing anything for the working class through politics. They were acquainted with the Marxist ideas, but they also read Hegel, Kropotkin, Bakunin, Alexander Herzen, and Spencer. In addition to the S. L. P., they were organized in the so-called "Revolutionary Clubs," meeting in secret halls and beginning to despair of starting "a revolution in the minds of the people." Similar clubs appeared in other cities during the panic.

In 1881, a national convention of the Revolutionary Clubs was held in Chicago and the "Revolutionary Socialist Party" came into existence, competing with the S. L. P. For a year and a half the character of this movement was very vague. There was loose talk of violence, dynamite, and assassination, but the party as a whole dangled self-consciously between Marxism and Nihilism, between theory and action.

Then Johann Most came. He was a man in his late thirties, an intense, striking personality, somewhat of a Bakunin even in looks; possessing a fiery intelligence and violent temperament; largely self-educated, dynamic, irrepressible; with a picturesque prison record as a result of his revolutionary doings in Vienna, Berlin, and London. In London,

34   on the occasion of the assassination of Tsar Alexander II by the Russian
Nihilists in 1881, he had published, in his paper *Freiheit*, an article ex-
tolling the act and urging others to do likewise with rulers elsewhere.
For this he had been sentenced to eighteen months of imprisonment.
After serving the term he departed for the United States.

In America he was hailed as a hero by the comrades of the
Revolutionary Clubs and became at once the leader of the extremists.
His cry was: "Extirpate the miserable brood!"—meaning all politicians
and exploiters of the masses. He was an avowed, thoroughgoing
revolutionary. His principle of action was the Bakunin principle: "Let
us rely upon the unquenchable spirit of destruction and annihilation
which is the perpetual spring of new life. The joy of destruction is a
creative joy!" Most believed in dynamite and street-fighting and, in
his contentions with the non-violent American Socialists, made no
secret of his belief.

He was a frequent visitor in Chicago, where violent revolutionary
doctrines and tactics gained a considerable following among workmen and their leaders. Under Most's influence, *Die Arbeiter Zeitung*,
a Socialist paper, turned out-and-out anarchist. He resumed the pub-
lication of his own *Freiheit*; a group of Czech anarchists began a sheet
in Bohemian; and for the English-speaking anarchists, Albert Parsons,
who, along with many other Chicago agitators, had accepted Most's
ideas and leadership, edited *Alarm*.

IV

Soon after his arrival in the United States, Most published in New
York a booklet entitled *Science of Revolutionary Warfare—A Manual of
Instruction in the Use and Preparation of Nitroglycerine, Dynamite, Gun-
Cotton, Fulminating Mercury, Bombs, Fuses, Poisons, Etc., Etc.* In 1885
and 1886 chapters of the book were reprinted in anarchist sheets in
Chicago and Cleveland, which, in addition, carried inflammatory edi-
torials, appeals, and manifestos.

I quote from *Die Arbeiter Zeitung*:

> [*April 8, 1885*] Here is something worth hearing. A num-
> ber of strikers in Quincy, yesterday, fired upon their bosses, and
> not upon the scabs. This is recommended most emphatically, for
> imitation.
>
> [*May 5, 1885*] Workmen ought to take aim at every member
> of the militia, and do with him as one would do with some one of

whom it is known that he is after taking one's life. It might then sooner be difficult to obtain murdering tools... Workmen, arm yourselves!

[*March 18, 1886*] If we do not soon bestir ourselves for a bloody revolution, we cannot leave anything to our children but poverty and slavery. Therefore, prepare yourselves! In all quietness, prepare yourselves for the Revolution!

And the following appeared in Parsons' *Alarm* on February 21, 1885:

Dynamite! Of all the good stuff, that is the stuff! Stuff several pounds of this sublime stuff into an inch pipe (gas or water pipe), plug up both ends, insert a cap with a fuse attached, place this in the immediate vicinity of a lot of rich loafers who live by the sweat of other people's brows, and light the fuse. A most cheerful and gratifying result will follow. In giving dynamite to the downtrodden millions of the globe science has done its best work. The dear stuff can be carried in the pocket without danger, while it is a formidable weapon against any force of militia, police, or detectives that may want to stifle the cry for justice that goes forth from the plundered slaves. It is something not very ornamental, but exceedingly useful. It can be used against persons and things. It is better to use it against the former than against bricks and masonry. It is a genuine boon for the disinherited, while it brings terror and fear to the robbers. A pound of this good stuff beats a bushel of ballots all hollow—and don't you forget it! Our lawmakers might as well try to sit down on the crater of a volcano or on the point of a bayonet as to endeavor to stop the manufacture and use of dynamite. It takes more justice and right than is contained in laws to quiet the spirit of unrest.

The story of dynamite—the actual "stuff"—in the United States, as a weapon of the have-nots in their warfare against the haves, dates from Most's arrival in the country.

CHAPTER 5
THE STAGE IS SET FOR THE
HAYMARKET TRAGEDY

M any of the factors that finally led to the explosion of the Haymarket bomb in Chicago had been in operation long before Johann Most's arrival.

The intense public reaction to the Molly Maguire outrages and the riots of 1877, as already suggested, had an unhealthy immediate effect upon labor organizations. The few strikes that occurred between 1878 and 1880 were promptly and brutally put down by the police, the militia, and hired gunmen. But the labor movement was much too elemental and primal, too powerfully motivated by the belly-hunger of a great mass of people, by the desires of individuals to get on, by the prevalent spirit of America, to be kept down for long by the self-righteous condemnation of the pulpit, the conservative press, the respectable mob at large, or even the police clubs and the fire of the soldiers and the gunmen. The workers' living conditions became worse. Immigrants continued to pour into the country by the hundreds of thousands every year, expanding the slums, working for less than the native workmen were willing to take. "In the cities," says Mother Jones, in her *Autobiography*, "there was hunger, and rags, and despair."

Within a year or two—at any rate by 1880—it began to appear that the riots and the subsequent reaction, which included the hasty building of new armories and general tightening up of capitalist lines against labor, had given the wage-earners of the country a new and powerful impulse to organization. The fact that whole regiments had been called out to subdue them stirred in the laborers a resentment which began soon to assume vague political aspects and prompted labor leaders to think of organizing the unskilled workers whose part in the riots had been so startling and important.

II

Many of the old unions were reorganized and numerous local amalgamations were effected. But the most important labor bodies at that time were certain secret societies whose initiation rites were absurd, fantastic ceremonials conducted by magniloquent officers with high-sounding titles, and whose members recognized one another by elaborate signs and secret passwords.

Of these, the most significant was the Noble Order of the Knights of Labor, founded in 1869 by a Philadelphia garment-cutter, Uriah S. Stephens, and six of his fellow craftsmen. Stephens has been described as "a man of great force and character…with love of books…and feeling withal a strong affection for secret organizations, having been for many years connected with the Masonic order." He had associated with radicals, some of them German refugees of 1848, and from them had acquired a few vaguely Socialistic ideas that fitted into his natural but even vaguer humanistic idealism.

The principles of the K. of L. were set down by Stephens in the secret ritual. "Open and public association having failed after a struggle of centuries to protect and advance the interest of labor, we have lawfully constituted this Assembly," and, "in using this power of organized effort and co-operation, we but imitate the example of capital heretofore set in numerous instances"; for, "in all the multifarious branches of trade, capital has its combinations, and, whether intended or not, it crushes the manly hopes of labor and tramples poor humanity into the dust." The K. of L., however, meant—timidly, carefully—"no conflict with legitimate enterprise," whatever that was, and "no antagonism to necessary capital." It meant, rather, "to create a healthy public opinion on the subject of labor…and the justice of its receiving a full, just share of the values…it has created."

For three years the Order was a garment-cutters' club, its membership remaining less than one hundred. In 1872, several ship-carpenters, plumbers, and other workmen were allowed to join, and thereafter it expanded rapidly into a national organization. The secrecy and ceremonials appealed to the men, and within the lodges were numerous official positions with magnificent titles and uniforms.

Grand Master Workman Stephens—for such was his title—declaimed sonorously about "justice," "the nobility and dignity of labor," "the great brotherhood of toil," and hinted at the evil doings of the capitalists. But his successor, Terence V. Powderly, a machinist by trade, who was elected Grand Master Workman in 1878, cut a still more absurd figure in the national labor movement. He excelled even Stephens in vague social idealism, love of abstract words, and bombastic oratory. A windbag, a figure of lath and plaster, vain and jealous, loving power, never knowing his own mind, he was blown hither and thither by the force of events. He had an expansive manner and held that "labor was noble and holy," was opposed to "wage slavery," as he boldly called it, but looked with deep disfavor upon the strike as a method to fight it. His ignorance of the forces inherent in modern industrialism was abysmal. He spoke grandiosely on all sorts of subjects, night and day. The man was full of strivings and gropings, a valorous idealist on the platform, but timorous when action was suggested.

The K. of L. was essentially an assembly of windbags, full of half-hearted revolutionary impulses and crude chicane, affording men, like Stephens and Powderly, who loved to hear themselves talk, an opportunity to orate and receive the applause of simple workmen, in whose capacity to help themselves as a class they had no intelligent faith. Nearly everything that the K. of L. achieved in the course of its dramatic career was achieved in spite of its leaders.

During Stephens's regime the order was entirely secret; not even its name was known to outsiders. Its meeting-halls and gathering places in the forests, and its official announcements in the press were indicated, romantically, by five stars (*****). People would see the mark appear on the door of some auditorium and then hordes of workmen would come flocking there. What were they up to? How strong was this mysterious Order of the Five Stars? The conservative, respectable mob, to say nothing of the capitalists, made uneasy by the upheavals of the proletariat in Paris and their famous Commune of 1871, by the Molly Maguire disclosures, and by the riots of 1877, feared that the organization might be dangerous. Suddenly some fateful day a bloody terror might burst upon the country! Fear…fear.

Finally, the press and the pulpit began to demand that the ***** come out in the open and announce their aims. Powderly was a politician, a self-seeking, self-conscious public character, sensitive to public opinion. So, in 1878, under his leadership, the order complied with the demand, and the public was informed that the K. of L. were eager to "enjoy the blessings of life" and that their battle-cry was "Moral worth, not wealth, is the true standard of individual and national greatness." Powderly spoke pretentiously of "uplift"…"ideals"…"principles."

III

Notwithstanding Powderly's and his cronies' opposition to strikes as a means of gaining for labor a greater share of industrial profits, numerous walkouts, big and small, occurred the country over, commencing in 1880, when conditions began slowly to improve after the dire effects of the panic. The K. of L. leaders, so-called, were forced to make concessions to strong elements within the order which insisted upon action.

Most of the K. of L. strikes, however, as well as others at that period, were unsuccessful because dishonestly or incompetently led. A typical K. of L. strike in the early years of Powderly's regime was that of the telegraphers, in 1883. They had organized nationally and become affiliated with the K. of L. the year before. The impulse for the movement came from below, strong enough to overcome the objections of the timorous general officers, conscious of their inadequacy. The walkout occurred on June 19 against all commercial telegraph companies, of which Jay Gould's Western Union, employing some 4,000 operators, was the greatest. The men demanded one day off in seven, an eight-hour day shift and seven-hour night shift, and a raise in wages.

The strike was a national affair, a topic on the floor of the United States Senate. Jay Gould was just then in deep disfavor with the public for his over-contemptuous attitude toward it, and a large portion of the press gave its support to the strikers, not with any real feeling for the justice of their cause, but rather to cater to a public prejudice. The country was once more reminded of the existence of the labor problem.

But the blacklist was already a well developed method of the capitalists to subdue the workers. In this instance, the Western Union and other companies employed the mere threat of it successfully. Frightened, one by one, the strikers returned to work on the old terms, and by the end of July the strike was a dead failure. There had been no leadership, no discipline, no adequate strike fund.

In the early and middle eighties there were numerous minor disturbances all over the country, for the most part spontaneous outbursts of badly organized, practically leaderless workers. Yet, in the midst of all the failures, there appeared occasional signs that by and by organized labor might become effective.

Of the few successful strikes, the most notable were the K. of L. railroad strikes in 1885. On February 16 of that year, Jay Gould's Wabash road announced a ten percent cut in the wages of its shopmen. Other Gould companies had preceded the Wabash with similar announcements. Within two weeks, close to 5,000 shopmen struck on three Gould lines. The engineers, brakemen, firemen, and conductors declared themselves in sympathy with the walkout and seemed ready to translate their sympathy into action.

The wage cut did not go into effect; the men won the strike.

The following summer, however, the Wabash discharged a large force of K. of L. shopmen, which amounted practically to a lockout, in direct violation of the agreement that had ended the strike in the spring. The K. of L. then ordered a boycott of the Wabash rolling stock, which, had it been put into effect, would have disorganized over 20,000 miles of railways. The boycott was by this time an effective weapon in the hands of labor to which even the K. of L. uplifters did not object very strenuously.

Jay Gould took alarm; the terrible riots of 1877 were still fresh in his mind. Before matters had gone much further, he hastily invited the K. of L. railwaymen's leaders to a conference with the managers of his roads, at which he lent his influence in favor of yielding to the unions. The unions recalled the boycott order, and in the final settlement the Wabash made several concessions to them.

The concessions were meager, but the victory was nonetheless tremendous, in view of the fact that in the dispute the labor leaders were for the first time accepted on equal terms by one of the outstanding plutocrats in the country who had been, and inwardly no doubt continued to be, a leading union-hater. To all seeming, the mighty Jay had been *compelled* to recognize organized labor as a power equal, if not superior, to himself. Soon after the settlement a Chicago divine and lecturer on social problems was saying:

> It is not long since William H. Vanderbilt dismissed a reference to the will of the people with a profane sneer which showed his utter contempt of the people's rights. Now one whose power in the railroad world is only second to that of Vanderbilt finds that today the demands of his laborers cannot be dismissed that way.

There was something intensely dramatic and spectacular in this first important labor victory. Immediately after it, there began a veritable stampede of the loose laboring masses to join the K. of L. unions. The membership of the order increased so rapidly that the general officers, fearful lest the organization should become so huge as to be utterly unmanageable, began to refuse charters to new locals. Among the new members were tens of thousands of unskilled and foreign-born laborers.

The press of the country, both labor and conservative, helped blindly to exaggerate the significance of the victory, little dreaming that within a year it would lead to troubles almost as great as, and more significant than, those of 1877.

IV

Meantime, radical ideas were spreading in America. The most widely read book in the eighties was Henry George's *Progress and Poverty*. In three years it went through more than a hundred editions and George's analysis of the economic and social conditions was discussed before labor groups, in colleges, from pulpits.

There was a reason. The industrial conditions were horrible. I quote a few statements that appear in the official surveys of the National Bureau of Labor Statistics in Washington for 1885 and 1886 which contain a hint of the working people's plight at that period.

Said a clergyman of Fall River, Massachusetts:

Perhaps...the evils which exist arise from...the increasing tendency to regard the operative simply as a wheel, or a pin to a machine. He is, in the eyes of the employers, very much what a mule or a spindle is, and no more... The employers care not who or what the operative is, or where he lives, or what his character, except as any of these things bear on production... We are preparing for new Liverpools and new Lancashires on American soil, with ignorance, vice, and stupidity as the characteristics of the working population.

A physician in the same city:

Every mill in town is making money...but the operatives travel in the same old path—sickness, suffering, small pay.

The Labor Commissioner of New Jersey said officially:

The struggle for existence is daily becoming keener, and the average wage-laborer must practice the strictest economy, or he will find himself behind at the end of the season... The men's remuneration because of female and child labor competition has been reduced to such an extent that only with the aid received from other members of the family are they able to keep the wolf from the door... Children are occupying the places of adult labor here.

And the Labor Commissioner of the State of New York:

Grinding poverty is a very general cause of prostitution. The prominent fact is that a large number of female operatives and domestics
earn such small wages that a temporary cessation of business, or
being a short time out of situation, is sufficient to reduce them to
absolute distress, and it becomes a literal battle for life.

I could quote endlessly from the same source. On the other hand
there were many people who were inclined to agree with the New York
World when it said:

The American laborer must make up his mind, henceforth, not to be
so much better off than the European laborer. Men must be content
to work for low wages. In this way the workingman will be nearer to
that station in life to which it has pleased God to call him.

V

The labor movement—the K. of L., the independent trade unions, and
the railway brotherhoods—looked formidable numerically. Actually,
with such leaders as Powderly, it was anything but effectual. Its ideas
were crude, undeveloped. It was, like every other movement in America
at that time, chaotic, utterly lacking in statesmanship. This lack is apparent throughout the history of the K. of L.. When unemployment
was general, for instance, the K. of L. leaders, in an effort to decrease it,
officially urged the workers to break beer and milk bottles after empty-
ing them and thus increase employment in the glass industry. This, incidentally, was one of the first cases of sabotage propaganda in America.

Thousands of workers, many of whom were members of the K.
of L. or of regular trade unions, gathered in secret meetings, at which
extremists inflamed their minds and emotions, and attended shooting
practice in the woods, preparing themselves for the "big war." In the
open labor market their necessity impelled them to struggle ceaselessly
against members of their own class, but at these underground meetings
the idea was impressed upon them that they could obtain redress for
their wrongs only as they compelled it by violence. Capitalists used force
in keeping down the proletariat; therefore the proletariat was obliged to
resort to force.

Behind this extremist attitude were the abnormal, desperate impulses born of starvation and abuse.

VI

In the mid-eighties, as I have suggested, Chicago was the center of extreme radical propaganda in the United States—and with good reason. Nowhere in America was the capitalists' contempt for the public interest stronger than in Chicago—for folk who had failed to make big money in general, and for the working class in particular. In no American city was class demarcation sharper, nor, it may be added, did the press anywhere else more vehemently uphold to such extremities the sacred rights of property. The Chicago rich were notorious for their debauchery. After the great fire in 1871, which destroyed the city, the more sanctimonious citizens of Boston and Philadelphia declared that the flames had been sent as a judgment from On High upon a modern City of the Plain. Preachers likened it also to Babylon, Tyre, and Pompeii. In the rebuilt, booming city the manners of the rich were unchanged.

In the late seventies and early eighties, the militant radicals of Chicago still clung to political action as a possible means of improving the conditions of the underdog. In municipal campaigns they managed, now and then, to send one or two men to the city council, though of course their presence there was ineffectual. Then, in the election of 1885, the Socialist Labor Party was badly defeated, losing all representation in the city's political life, with the result that the extremists in the movement became even more rabid and violent.

Thenceforth anarchism was definitely a growing movement in Chicago. The active membership of the anarchist clubs perhaps never exceeded three thousand, surely a small number in a community of 850,000, but among the leaders were picturesque, intense men—-Parsons, August Spies, and Michael Schwab, of *Die Arbeiter Zeitung*; Samuel Fielden, an ex-Methodist minister; Oscar Neebe, organizer of the Beer-Wagon Drivers; Adolph Fischer, a printer; George Engel, a toy-maker; and, to mention but one more, Louis Lingg, organizer of the Carpenters' Union. They talked much of "the Revolution," dynamite, human rights, justice, firearms, liberty, arson, and received much sensational publicity in the big conservative newspapers, which referred to their agitation as "the Menace." To some of these men dynamite was little more than a word, a vague symbol of people's uprising; to the others—Lingg, for one—it was the "real stuff."

Reading *The Tribune*, *The Times*, and *The Daily News*, the general public was, of course, alarmed. The community developed a state of mind not unlike the Bolshevik scare that gripped the United States after the World War. Soon every radical, no matter how mild his views actually were, was considered an anarchist, just as forty years later every one who held notions not endorsed by the Ku Klux Klan, the American Legion, and the Daughters of the American Revolution, was branded a "Bolshevik."

With the industrial depression in 1884–1886, the situation was intensified. Tens of thousands were unemployed. There were hopeless strikes, wage cuts, lockouts…*misery*. And agitators were busy. "The workers," writes Mother Jones, "asked only for bread and a shortening of the long hours. The agitators gave them visions. The police gave them clubs." The feelings on both sides ran high. *The Tribune*, according to Mother Jones, "suggested that the farmers of Illinois treat the tramps— unemployed workers that poured out of the great industrial centers—as they did other pests, by putting strychnine in their food."

VII

After the K. of L. victory over the formidable Jay Gould, there was, as I have said, a veritable rush on the part of unorganized labor to join the unions affiliated with the order. The conservative press, as I have also mentioned, helped to bring this stampede about by exaggerating the significance of Gould's defeat.

On the streets of Chicago, in saloons, and wherever else workers gathered, one could hear, early in 1886, such songs as—

Toiling millions now are waking—
See them marching on;
All the tyrants now are shaking,
Ere their power's gone.
Chorus: Storm the fort, ye Knights of Labor,
Battle for your cause;
Equal rights for every neighbor—
Down with tyrant laws!

The situation had slipped entirely out of the hands of Powderly and other big labor officials.

Some trade unions not affiliated with the K. of L. had decided, in 1884, to start an intensive campaign for the eight-hour workday. Subsequently, May 1, 1886, was fixed as the day on which it should be put into effect. As the day—*der Tag*—approached, the movement gained in volume and determination, especially after the railwaymen's momentous tiff with Jay Gould. This was true not only in Chicago, but all over the country. Eight-Hour Leagues were formed in the cities and

46   huge labor rallies conducted through the fall and winter of 1885 and the
early spring of 1886.

In Chicago the agitation was most intense. Late in 1885, George A.
Schilling, a Socialist, organized the Eight-Hour Association, to which
the principal labor bodies in the city, including K. of L. unions, gave
immediate support.

The anarchists at first viewed the eight-hour movement with
scorn, insisting that it was useless to demand anything from the capitalists; the thing to do was to arm the working class and "take over the
whole damn system and change it." But as the movement became the
all-absorbing topic of the proletariat, they—Parsons, Spies, Schwab,
Fielden, and other ultra-radical orators and publicists—joined and,
with their talents, soon became the outstanding, if not the most popular, agitators of the cause.

The conservative press, of course, now immediately branded the
whole eight-hour agitation as "foreign," "un-American," "anarchistic."
Individuals who participated in it, whether they were trade-unionists,
K. of L., or whatnot, were not only dirty, low-down foreign scum, but
enemies of the United States and everything that was decent and holy.
"The city was divided into two camps," quoting again from Mother
Jones's *Autobiography*. "The working people on one side—hungry, cold,
jobless, fighting gunmen and police clubs with bare hands. On the other
side the employers, supported by the newspapers, by the police, by all
the power of the great state itself."

The employers and the authorities were being warned by liberal,
discerning speakers and publicists that the existing state of affairs was
leading to upheavals worse than those of 1877. A few months before
the Haymarket explosion a prominent Illinois clergyman was saying in
Chicago:

> And, my friends,...the laboring classes constitute the bulk of
> our population, and it will be an unhappy day for this country when
> any great numbers of them become "fire and blood" Socialists [*i.e.*,
> anarchists]. But many things in these days are driving and draw-
> ing them that way... The country at large would be horrified to
> see, in plain English, the utterances which are daily circulated by
> Socialistic journals among the laborers in our great cities... And
> there are other tokens than the noisy threats and appeals of the
> Socialists. The laboring men have awakened to the power of orga-
> nization. They have begun to assert themselves where recently they
> only complained, or were silent... A power which suddenly dares to
> measure swords with a railway millionaire like Jay Gould has sprung
> up. It is growing. It declares its purpose to continue to grow.

CHAPTER 6
THE FIRST BOMB

The eight-hour agitation continued all winter throughout the country.

In Chicago, the anarchists ran the whole show. They held meetings on the lakefront, their crowds consisting mostly of jobless, hungry men, many of whom had no place to sleep. The red flag was displayed at these rallies, the speakers explaining that it was "a symbol of the people's revolutionary spirit." Then the black flag appeared, "symbolical of poverty and hunger of desperation." Parsons and Fielden were the most popular speakers. They denounced the Chicago Board of Trade ("the Board of Thieves") which had recently dedicated its new $2,000,000 building ("the temple of usury") while two and a half million men were jobless in the United States.

"How long will you be content with fifteen-cent meals," asked Fielden, "when those fellows are sitting down to banquets at twenty dollars a plate?"

More than a thousand members of the so-called *Lehrund-Wehr Vereine* drilled with rifles in secret halls and practiced shooting in the woods.

At the same time the employers were meeting in George M. Pullman's residence, or in the office of Wirt Dexter, Chicago's foremost corporation attorney, to discuss the sinister eight-hour movement, "the damned anarchists," and what they could do about it all.

The public at large was torn between a vague, distant sympathy for the hard-pressed proletariat and the fear that within the mobs of these sullen-eyed, rough-looking men, jobless and homeless, most of them foreign-born, there lurked something awful and gigantic; and the people shuddered in their homes, their offices, their pews. Fear...fear.

Carter H. Harrison was Mayor of Chicago, serving his fourth consecutive term in office. He was rich and fat, wore silk underwear, hobnobbed with the town's wealthiest men, but at the same time consistent-

47

ly stood up, in all sincerity and in the face of great opposition, for the rights of the underdog. He loved "the plain people" and enjoyed their affection. He was in sympathy with union labor and insisted on having a wide-open town because it was "good for business." He believed in freedom and, as a gesture in that direction, appointed radicals to minor offices. He loved Chicago; the city was his "bride," who, he said, "laves her beautiful limbs daily in Lake Michigan and comes out clean and pure every morning."

The Mayor tried his best to lessen the tension that had gripped the city during the eight-hour movement. He declared that he would not allow troops to be brought in to slaughter workers, insisting that they, too, were citizens of Chicago. But he was practically the only sane man of any influence in town; everybody else had gone mad. The business leaders in the city were too panicky to listen to reason; they believed that the agitation had already proceeded too far. It must be stopped. *The Tribune* printed articles and letters from its subscribers urging the authorities to break up the workers' meetings with gunfire—and, if necessary, with dynamite!

Everything seemed to conspire to bring the crisis to a head. The winter was a severe one, causing fearful suffering among the poor. The Mayor and charitable institutions opened soup kitchens, but this was a mere drop in the bucket. Gaunt, ragged men and women paraded the streets carrying red and black flags, and the police often dispersed them, kicking and clubbing them, contrary to Mayor Harrison's orders. The police, obviously, received their orders from other sources.

On Christmas Day, the anarchists organized a march, on fashionable Prairie Avenue, of several hundred starved and wretched-looking men and women. One old woman carried a red flag, another a black flag. They stopped before the residences of the wealthy, uttering groans and cat-calls, ringing doorbells. The parade, says Mother Jones, "had no educational value. It only served to increase the employers' fear, to make the police more savage, and the public less sympathetic to the real distress of the workers."

The anarchist papers printed violent editorials. *Die Arbeiter Zeitung* said on April 21, 1886:

> He who submits to the present order of things has no right to complain about capitalistic extortion, for order means sustaining that; and he who revolts...is a rebel, and has no right to complain if he is met by soldiers. Every class defends itself as well as it can. A rebel

who puts himself opposite the mouth of the cannons of his enemies, with empty fists, is a fool.

The same paper, a week later:

The police and soldiers...must be met by armed armies of workers... Arms are more necessary in our time than anything else. Whoever has no money, should sell his watch, if he has one, and buy firearms. Stones and sticks will not avail against the hired assassins of the extortionists. It is time to arm yourselves!

II

Winter passed and the Big Day—*der Tag*, the first of May—drew near.

The employers determined that they would yield no more concessions to labor. The eight-hour idea must be fought. Jay Gould had been a damned fool to recognize the unions! They would crush the unions and run their factories on the "open shop" basis.

Accordingly, in February the McCormick Reaper Works locked out hundreds of its men who were union members and hired scabs and 300 Pinkerton "detectives"—gunmen—to protect the scabs. This was one of the most important immediate factors in rousing proletarian bitterness, and the agitators, naturally enough, stressed the situation for all it was worth.

One of the organizations involved in the McCormick lockout was the International Carpenters' Union, of which Louis Lingg, an outspoken anarchist, was the most energetic leader. He believed in dynamite, "the real stuff," and advocated its use. Shortly after the lockout he addressed a circular to his men:

...I say we must resist these monsters [i. e., the capitalists and their hired gunmen]. We must fight them with as good weapons, even better than they possess, and, therefore, I call you to arms!... The first of May is coming near. You must kill the pirates. You must kill the bloodsuckers... Our work is short; we do not want a Thirty Years' War. Be determined!

Parsons, Fielden, and Schwab held meetings near the McCormick Reaper Works. Minor riots occurred every few days.

The situation was extremely tense. On one side, hunger and desperation; on the other, greed and fear.

On May 1st, *Die Arbeiter Zeitung* shouted:

> Bravely forward! The conflict has begun… Workers, let your watchword be: No compromise! Cowards to the rear! Men to the front! The die is cast! The first of May is here… Clean your guns, complete your ammunition. The hired murderers of the capitalists, the police and militia, are ready to murder. No worker should leave his house in these days with empty pockets.

The thronged streets were full of rumors.

Almost at the last moment the executive body of the Knights of Labor in Chicago had withdrawn its endorsement of the general strike on May 1st for the eight-hour day. Such men as Powderly had become frightened by their own power; besides, everybody was saying that the movement was "anarchistic" and "foreign," and they certainly were no anarchists, nor foreigners.

The public was in suspense. Some of the men in the streets looked desperate. There was some talk that the anarchists intended to bomb the police stations and exterminate the whole force.

But nothing terrible or decisive happened on the first or the second of May.

On May 3, *Die Arbeiter Zeitung* said: "A hot conflict!… Courage! courage! is our cry."

On that day the locked-out McCormick employees held a mass meeting near the Works. The men had been out of work for three months. They were desperate. August Spies was speaking to the mob about the eight-hour movement when the factory whistle blew and out came the scabs, done with the day's work.

A pitched battle followed with stones, bricks, fists, and sticks. A few shots were fired. Then the police arrived on the scene and, opening fire on the crowd, killed several men in a few minutes and wounded many more.

Spies, enraged, rushed to the office of *Die Arbeiter Zeitung* and printed his famous "Revenge!" circular, reproduced here. A few hours after the shooting the streets were flooded with leaflets. "Revenge!"

REVENGE!

Workingmen, to Arms!!!

Your masters sent out their bloodhounds — the police — ; they killed six of your brothers at McCormicks this afternoon. They killed the poor wretches, because they, like you, had the courage to disobey the supreme will of your bosses. They killed them, because they dared ask for the shortenin of the hours of toil. They killed them to show you, ' Free American Citizens" that you must be satisfied and contended with whatever your bosses condescend to allow you, or you will get killed!

You have for years endured the most abject humiliations; you have for years suffered unmeasurable iniquities; you have worked yourself to death; you have endured the pangs of want and hunger; your Children you have sacrificed to the factory-lords — in short: You have been miserable and obedient slave all these years: Why? To satisfy the insatiable greed, to fill the coffers of your lazy thieving master? When you ask them now to lessen your burden, he sends his bloodhounds out to shoot you, kill you!

If you ar men, if you are the sons of your grand sires, who have shed their blood to free you, then you will rise i your might, Hercules, and destroy the hideous monster that seeks to destroy you. To arms we call you, to arms!

Your Brothers,

Rache! Rache!

Arbeiter, zu den Waffen!

Arbeitendes Volk, heute Nachmittag mordeten die Bluthunde Eurer Ausbeuter 6 Eurer Brüder draußen bei McCormid's. Warum mordeten sie dieselben? Weil sie den Muth hatten, mit dem Loos unzufrieden zu sein, welches Eure Ausbeuts Ihnen beschieden haben. Sie forderten Brod, man antwortete ihnen mit Blei, eingedenk der Thatsache, daß man damit das Volk am willfamsten zum Schweigen bringen kann! Viele, viele Jahre habt Ihr alle Demüthigungen ohne Widerspruch ertragen, habt Euch vom frühen Morgen bis zum späten Abend geschunden, habt Entbehrungen jeder Art ertragen, habt Eure Kinder selbst geopfert — Alles, um die Schatzkammern Euer Herren, zu füllen, Alles für sie! Und jetzt, wo Ihr vor sie hintretet, und sie ersucht, Eure Bürde, etwas zu erleichtern, da hetzen sie zum Dank für Eure Opfer ihre Bluthunde, die Polizei, auf Euch, um Euch mit Bleikugeln von der Unzufriedenheit zu kuriren Sklaven, wir fragen und beschwören Euch bei Allem, was Euch heilig und werth ist, rächt diesen scheußlichen Mord, den man heute an Euren Brüdern beging, und vielleicht morgen schon an Euch begehen wird. Arbeitendes Volk, Herkules, Du bist am Scheidewege angelangt. Wofür entscheidest Du Dich? Für Essklaverei und Hunger, oder für Freiheit und Brod? Entscheidest Du Dich für das Letztere, dann säume keinen Augenblick; dann, Volk, zu den Waffen! Vernichtung den menschlichen Bestien, die sich Deine Herrscher nennen! Rücksichtslose Vernichtung ihnen — das muß Deine Losung sein! Denke der Helden, deren Blut den Weg zum Fortschritt, zur Freiheit und zur Menschlichkeit gebahnt — und strebe, ihrer würdig zu werden!

Eure Brüder.

THE FAMOUS "REVENGE" CIRCULAR.
Engraved from the Original by direct Photographic Process.

III

Next morning *Die Arbeiter Zeitung* screamed on the front page:

BLOOD! Lead and Powder as a Cure for Dissatisfied Workers.—This is Law and Order! ... In palaces they fill their goblets with costly wines and pledge the health of the bloody banditti of Law and Order. Dry your tears, you poor and suffering. Take heart! Rise in your might and level the existing robber rule in the dust!

On the streets appeared more leaflets calling the workers to a protest mass meeting in Haymarket Square that evening. "Workingmen, Arm Yourselves and Appear in Full Force!"

In the evening some three thousand men, women, and children gathered in the square.

Mayor Harrison, much disturbed, was there. His "bride," it seemed, was having a fit. He waddled nervously between the square and the nearby police station, where a small army of officers waited in readiness. He mingled with the ragged, sullen-eyed proletarians, striking match after match without lighting his fat cigar. He explained to a friend: "I want the people to know that their Mayor is here." Some of the men wore dark looks, but to the Mayor the meeting seemed "tame." The speeches were not violent. Parsons discussed economics.

Drops of rain fell. Overhead were dark, threatening clouds; a sharp wind blew from the lake. People were beginning to go home, lest they be caught in the storm.

At ten o'clock Mayor Harrison, chewing his unlit cigar, waddled back to the station house and there remarked to the Inspector-in-Charge: "Nothing is likely to occur to require interference," and went home.

But less than fifteen minutes later, the Inspector ordered one of his subordinates to turn out the entire force—176 officers—and march to the square and order the meeting to disband. Palpably, the Inspector had orders from some one more powerful in the Police Department than the Mayor; from someone, no doubt, who wanted a riot.

It rained. The crowd had dwindled down to about five hundred people, mostly men. The meeting was anything but a success.

Fielden, the last man to speak, was saying: "I shall be through in a few minutes and then we'll all go home."

His beard dripping, he spoke briefly. "In conclusion—"

Then he saw the army of policemen marching to the square.

Coming within a few feet of the crowd, the captain in command called "Halt!"—and, with drawn sword, advanced toward the speaker.

"I command you," he said at the top of his voice, "in the name of the people to immediately and peaceably disperse!"

A moment of intense silence; only the sharp wind from the lake swished through the crowd and the police ranks, driving the rain in their faces.

"Why, Captain," said Fielden at last, "we *are* peaceable." (It is certain that he did not say: "Here are the bloodhounds! Men, do your duty and I'll do mine," as he was quoted, later, by the police.)

Another spell of silence. Few in the crowd knew what was going on.

Then—suddenly—a blinding flash, a cloud of gray smoke—a terrific detonation, a sickening smell... Some one—possibly an anarchist, probably a hired "racketeer"—had hurled a bomb from the alley a few feet from the speakers' stand, just off the right flank of the police detachment.

Confusion. Firing started. Policemen were shooting at the crowd and at one another. They could not see for the smoke. The workers returned fire and the square was immediately strewn with bodies.

Then the police reformed and made a charge on the workers. The latter yelled and groaned, trying to escape the volley of the enraged officers. Some were dragging their dead and wounded friends and relatives with them.

All this happened in two or three minutes.

On the side of "law and order," 67 policemen were wounded. Seven of them died.

The workers' casualties were perhaps twice, possibly three times, that many; the number has never been determined. Several seriously wounded workmen were taken to the station house along with the dead and injured policemen, but the majority of them were cared for and carried off by relatives and friends.

IV

The following day it was evident that Chicago had neglected to "lave her beautiful limbs in Lake Michigan." She was stunned, horrified, crazed. The front pages of *The Tribune*, *The Times*, *The Daily News* shrieked and howled.

For the first time dynamite had been used in the United States for the destruction of human life... The Haymarket Bomb is the Adam of the "pineapples" that go off nowadays in Chicago, New York, Philadelphia, Detroit, and elsewhere in the cause of all sorts of "rackets," as well as the cause of organized labor.

The papers reported that the city was being "combed" for anarchists, which included practically everybody who had any active sympathy for labor. Several hundred arrests were made. The police raided radical newspaper offices and hangouts. The authorities, it seemed, were "determined to make an example of the leaders of Black Terror." The editorial writers said that the city was "determined to stamp out, once and forever, Socialism, Anarchism, Communism—different labels for the same vile monstrosity."

People stood on street corners, in the middle of sidewalks, along the bars in saloons, excited and feverish, talking about the awful event of the night before. The anarchists did it—of course! No one paused to think, to question.

"Hang 'em and try 'em afterward," was the prevailing sentiment, not only of the well-to-do and the respectable, but of workmen as well. Preachers pounded the pulpits. Each class vied with the other in demanding drastic measures to suppress "the Black International." The Chicago K. of L. issued an official statement:

> Let it be understood by all the world that the Knights of Labor have no affiliation, association, sympathy, or respect for the band of cowardly murderers, cutthroats, and robbers, known as anarchists, who sneak through the country like midnight assassins, stirring up the passions of ignorant foreigners, unfurling the red flag of Anarchy, and causing riot and bloodshed… We hope the whole gang of outlaws will be blotted from the face of the earth.

The police "discovered" bombs; not only single bombs, but secret dynamite factories, whole arsenals of infernal machines. Newspapers the country over printed wild, exaggerated tales of terrible dynamite conspiracies. Editorially, the press of the country called for the blood of the anarchist agitators.

A grand jury composed of prosperous business men indicted Fielden, Parsons, Spies, Schwab, Fischer, Engel, Lingg, Neebe, William Seliger (Lingg's landlord), and Rudolph Schnaubelt. Schnaubelt escaped to Europe; the case against Seliger was dismissed.

No criminal lawyer in the city would take their cases. The venomous press suggested that the attorney who would defend the anarchists was no better than an anarchist himself and ought to be hanged with them. Finally, three men engaged in civil practice dared to go against the hostile public sentiment of the entire country. One was William P. Black, popularly known in Chicago as Captain Black, a pugnacious fellow, impressive-looking, with a mop of gray hair; a serious student of public matters, sympathetic to the cause of labor. Another was William A. Foster, also an able man. The third was a young man by the name of Sigmund Zeisler, a foreigner recently admitted to the bar.

A defense committee was formed, but contributions to the fund came in slowly, in sums from one to five dollars.

Judge Joseph A. Gary, at one time a carpenter, now a reactionary politician, presided at the trial which began on June 21. The State's attorney was the intellectual-looking Julius S. Grinnel, who also had high political aspirations.

The public demanded that the accused be tried, if tried they must be, and strung up as swiftly as possible. Newspapers teemed with stories of wholesale dynamite plots. An unprejudiced jury was impossible. At least four of the twelve men finally selected admitted in the examination that they hated all anarchists, Socialists, and Communists.

The charge was murder. Not that any of the eight men were accused of having thrown the bomb, but merely that their inflammatory speeches and editorials had prompted the bomb-thrower—whoever he was—to the crime. The public was satisfied that none of the defendants, with the possible exception of Louis Lingg, had personally hurled the bomb, but no one questioned that it was thrown by someone inspired by these men. The prosecution exhibited a collection of apparatus which, it insisted, Lingg had used in manufacturing bombs.

On August 19, the jury found the men guilty and Judge Gary sentenced Parsons, Spies, Lingg, Fielden, Schwab, Fischer, and Engel to death. Neebe, who merely owned a financial interest in *Die Arbeiter Zeitung*, was given fifteen years in prison.

When the mob outside the courthouse learned of the verdict it broke into cheers.

V

The condemned men and Neebe were allowed to address the court. Their speeches have since been printed and reprinted in pamphlets all over the world.

Fielden spoke for three hours through his heavy beard. He said:

Today, the beautiful autumn sun kisses with balmy breeze the cheek of every free man; I stand here never to bathe my face in its rays again. I have loved my fellow man as I have loved myself. I have hated trickery, dishonesty, and injustice. If it will do any good, I freely give myself up.

And Spies:

If you think that by hanging us you can stamp out the labor movement, then call your hangman... You cannot understand it.

And Neebe:

Well, these are the crimes I have committed: I organized trade unions. I was for reduction of the hours of labor, and the education of the laboring man, and the reestablishment of *Die Arbeiter Zeitung*, the workingmen's paper. There is no evidence to show that I was connected with the bomb-throwing, or that I was near it, or anything of that kind.

And Fischer:

The more the believers in just causes are persecuted, the quicker will their ideas be realized.

And Parsons:

I am one of those, although myself a wage-slave, who hold that it is wrong to myself, wrong to my neighbor...for me...to make my escape from wage-slavery by becoming a master and an owner of slaves myself... This is my only crime, before high heaven.

And Engel:

I am too much a man of feeling not to battle against the conditions of today. Every thoughtful person must combat a system which makes it possible for the individual to rake and hoard millions in a few years, while on the other side thousands become tramps and beggars.

Schwab chose to define Anarchy as:

a state of society in which the only government is reason; a state of society in which all human beings do right for the simple reason that it is right and hate wrong because it is wrong.

And finally, Lingg—contemptuous, defiant, as he had been throughout the trial:

> I repeat that I am an enemy of the "order" of today, and I repeat that, with all my powers, so long as breath remains in me, I shall combat it. I declare frankly and openly that I am in favor of using force. I have told Captain Schaack [who had arrested him] and I stand by it: "If you fire upon us, we shall dynamite you!" Ah, you laugh! Perhaps you think, "You'll throw no more bombs"; but let me assure you that I die happy on the gallows, so confident am I that the hundreds and thousands to whom I have spoken will remember my words; and when you shall have hanged us, then, mark my words, *they* will do the bomb-throwing! In this hope I say to you: I despise you! I despise your "order," your laws, your force-propped authority. Hang me for it!

VI

Frantic attempts were made by the defense, by radical organizations and individuals to save the men. Europe became interested in the case. George Bernard Shaw went about London with a petition for the reprieve of the anarchists, getting signatures of English literary men. Among those who signed it was Oscar Wilde. William Morris wrote to Robert Browning, four days before the executions:

> I venture to write and ask you to sign the enclosed appeal for mercy and so to do what you can to save the lives of seven men who have been condemned to death for a deed of which they were not guilty after a mere mockery of a trial... I do not know if you have taken note of the events...nor can I give you a full account of my view of the matter. But I will ask you to believe me as an honest man when I say that these men have been made to pay [because of their opinions] for the whole body of the workers in Chicago who were engaged in a contest with the capitalists last year. You know how much more violent and brutal such contests are in America than in England, and of how little account human life is held there if it happens to thwart the progress of the dollar; and I hope that you will agree that the victors in the struggle need not put to death the

prisoners of war they took, after having kept them more than a year in prison.

William Dean Howells took the side of the prisoners. On the other hand, such American radicals or liberals as Robert Ingersoll and Henry George refused to appeal to Governor Oglesby for mercy. Ingersoll explained that, in the Civil War, Oglesby had saved his life and now he did not wish to embarrass him!

On November 10, 1887, Governor Oglesby commuted the sentences of Fielden and Schwab to life imprisonment. On the same day, Lingg blew off his head by exploding a tiny percussion cap in his mouth. His sweetheart had smuggled it into his cell. Parsons declined to apply for a commutation of his sentence to life term, quoting Patrick Henry: "Give me liberty or give me death."

Next morning, before being hanged, Fischer, Engel, Spies, and Parsons spoke from the gallows:

Fischer: This is the happiest moment in my life.

Engel: Hurrah for anarchy!

Spies: There will come a time when our silence will be more powerful than the voices you strangle today.

Parsons: Let me speak, O men of America! Will you let me speak, Sheriff Matson? Let the voice of the people be heard. *Oh*—

CHAPTER 7
THE LABOR MOVEMENT BECOMES
A "RACKET"

A huge procession of radicals, estimated at from 15,000 to 25,000, followed the executed men to the Waldheim Cemetery on the outskirts of Chicago, singing the *Marseillaise*, while 250,000 spectators lined the route. In the year and a half that passed from the day of the explosion to the day of the executions a great many people had changed their minds about the anarchists. According to the New York *World*:

> In the procession were representatives of various trade unions. There was a delegation of the Knights of Labor, composed entirely of women. There were men of education and men of dense ignorance marching side by side. And throughout all the strange procession, silent and sullen and obviously repressed, except when they sang, there ran a feeling that the dead men had in some sense died for them—that they were martyrs in the cause of the poor against the rich, the weak against the powerful.

The *World* added that "the heroism of these men—the heroism of fanaticism—is something wonderful to contemplate."

The people generally began to feel that the whole affair was deplorable, to say the least. A prominent preacher in Newark, New Jersey, reversed himself on his previously expressed opinion, declaring that the four "murdered" men were of "far nobler instincts than many who have denounced them." Pamphlets discussing the unfairness, the utter illegality, of the trial appeared by the dozen. The executions were dubbed "judicial murder," not only by the radicals, but by respectable, safe-and-sane men and women. Clarence Darrow, a successful corporation lawyer and not yet famous as "the big minority man" and "champion of the underdog," deplored and condemned the whole proceeding. A great part of Chicago's population began to feel deeply ashamed of the entire incident; for a time it did Chicago no good to bathe her limbs in the lake; she felt unclean all over.

Not a few intelligent persons began to see that there was no use killing and abusing the radicals. They were but the natural result of our industrial conditions, of the System. And so were the Goulds and the Vanderbilts. If they had never lived, their present positions—those of the millionaires and of the anarchists—would have been filled by other men. While anarchism no doubt had foreign roots, it was an American growth in America, nurtured in American soil. If a member of the working class had hurled the Haymarket Bomb, after all the impulse behind his act had been a not unnatural reaction. Had not the police and professional gunmen, under orders of the capitalists, been shooting down and clubbing laborers? The whole thing was an appalling mess.

The capitalists themselves, of course, could not indulge in any such broad philosophizing; certainly not publicly. They declared loudly that the executions were the best thing that could have happened to Chicago and the rest of the country. Seven years later, when Governor John Altgeld pardoned Fielden, Neebe, and Schwab on the ground that the trial had been illegal, business men denounced him savagely as a traitor to society, an anarchist, and killed him politically. An office building which Altgeld owned in Chicago was rendered worthless by a boycott of Chicago business.

From the narrow, selfish viewpoint of the employers, the Haymarket Bomb was an excellent thing. It stopped the eight-hour movement; not permanently, of course, but all that the up-and-coming industrialists cared about was the immediate situation and results. The bomb had created chaos in the labor movement. It put an end to the rush of the unorganized mob to join the unions. The working stiffs were fighting and abusing one another. Excellent!

In 1909, in commenting upon the twenty-second anniversary of the executions, a Socialist journal said:

> No more powerful blow was ever struck for capitalism than when that bomb was thrown on Haymarket Square. It set the labor movement of America back a generation, and its effects have not yet disappeared.

Whether or not it set the labor movement back depends upon one's viewpoint. There can be no question, however, that it caused labor to come definitely under the control of its most conservative element. Out of the confusion that followed the Haymarket explosion, there sprang into power the American Federation of Labor, an unidealistic, hard-

headed outfit—in whose career also, as will be shown in the last half of
this book, dynamite became an important factor.

II

Immediately after the Haymarket riot, the employers' associations all over the United States reorganized for the purpose of devising and putting into practice more efficient methods of keeping down industrial unrest. They had allowed the eight-hour nonsense to go too far. Now was the time to put the laborer in his place, for the bomb had inflamed the righteous public against the efforts of the underdog to lift himself to a higher level.

Thomas Scott, president of the Pennsylvania Railroad, said: "Give the workingmen and strikers gun-bullet food for a few days, and you will observe how they will take this sort of bread."

Lockouts became general. The few employers who, in 1885 and early in 1886, had yielded to the unions' demands for an eight-hour day, now announced, either on their own initiative or under the compulsion of employers' associations, that the ten- or twelve-hour system would immediately be reestablished in their factories. If the laborers objected too strenuously or threatened strikes, the employers simply characterized their attitude as "anarchistic" and shut down the plants before a walkout could be organized, which naturally had a devastating effect upon the workers' morale.

The employers put spies into the unions, and the most active labor leaders were reported and blacklisted. Many of the best unionists were thus starved out of the movement. In several cases entire unions, some of them affiliated with the Knights of Labor, were locked out and blacklisted.

This caused many organizations to decline, or even to pass out entirely. The Knights of Labor, whose number had gone over the million mark in May 1886, lost more than 200,000 members in a few months after the Haymarket riot. Lockouts and blacklists made a worker who had to have a job think twice before he took out or renewed his union card.

There were other causes for the decline of the American labor movement in the late eighties and the first years of the next decade. The lack of spine and intelligence in the K. of L. leadership, which I have already discussed, was one of them. Powderly and his cronies could not get used to the idea that the strike was an effective means to gain social and economic benefits for labor. They complained bitterly that some unions under their banner were waging war against certain capitalists contrary to their wishes and orders. They had become afraid of the eight-hour movement when it reached its height. The fact that they had at first endorsed an action in which anarchists participated made them feel that they must square themselves with a public whose indignation at the bomb outrage bordered upon hysteria.

Powderly swung to every strong influence within and outside the organization. First he spoke of injustice and the need of more equitable distribution of wealth as though he meant it; then he sermonized upon harmony, good will toward men, and the necessity of every person aiming for the higher things in life. And next he hit upon the idea of inducing the laborer to stop drinking and become a gentleman.

All strikes conducted by the K. of L. after the Haymarket riot failed.

But the basic weakness of the order, perhaps, was that it contained too many elements—skilled and unskilled labor, male and female, native and foreign-born, professional people and even farmers—whose economic interests, in the narrow, immediate sense, were too divergent. Powderly tried in vain to solidify them upon a program of uplift, but the organization was permeated with acrimony, selfishness, and political scheming. Its leaders, national and local, were for the most part professional organizers and promoters who were in the order for the "boodle" and other advantages that they could get out of it. The organization was described by one of its members as

> an asylum for deadbeats and paupers, and a scheming school of politicians. Every man who belongs to it now, and does not make money out of it, is a worse slave to intriguers than he ever was to capital, and is his own worst enemy. He is a tool and a dupe.

III

That the K. of L. were ineffective in most industrial disputes became obvious to some of the keener labor leaders and would-be leaders, in and outside the order, as early as the beginning of the eighties.

In August 1881 several of them met in Terre Haute, Indiana, to discuss the sad state of affairs and the splendid opportunities that the situation offered to bright fellows like themselves who understood conditions and knew what to do about them. They discussed the British trade-union movement, with its intensive local organization, trades autonomy, comprehensive teamwork, and impressive annual congresses, as something worthy of imitation and improvement in America. They decided to issue a call for a convention two months later in Pittsburgh, to which about 150 representatives of international, national, and local unions and K. of L. assemblies responded. Then and there they formed the "Federation of Organized Trades and Labor Unions of the United States and Canada."

The program included political demands, such as compulsory educational laws, abolition of legal restraints on trade unions, and anti-contract-immigration legislation. But the main idea, as it developed, although not clearly expressed in the platform, was "trade-unionism, pure and simple"—its purpose to increase the wages and generally to improve the working conditions of its members *without any concern for the working class as a whole; indeed, if necessary, to achieve those aims at the expense of the rest of the laboring class.*

For several years the organization got nowhere in particular. It had no funds and there was, generally, a depression in the industrial field, At its third convention held in New York in 1883, Samuel Gompers, leader of the Cigar-makers, who were affiliated with the K. of L., was elected chairman.

Gompers was, perhaps, the most energetic opponent within the K. of L. to Powderly's nebulous program. In 1886, following the serious reverses that the order suffered on account of the general reaction to the Haymarket riot, Gompers—clever fellow that he was—saw his big chance and, losing no time, made a successful attempt to combine with his organization numerous other bodies under the name of "The American Federation of Labor." He was elected president of the new Federation, a post which he held, except for one year, up to his death.

The initial membership of the Federation was about 100,000. It included ironworkers, carpenters, boiler-makers, tailors, cigar-makers, coal-miners, printers, and other trades. It grew steadily. It had its basis, like that of Gompers's original amalgamation, in the interests of particular organized trades rather than of labor in general. During the nineties, it developed considerable potency and, in the ensuing decade, grew to be one of the most important factors in the life of the country. It continued as such until the terrible McNamara debacle in 1911 and the "dynamite conspiracy" trials in 1912 deprived it, as will be shown, of its militant spirit. By 1894 the A.F. of L. triumphed completely over the K. of L., which thenceforth was of no consequence in the class struggle.

Gompers was a man of compact energy. He was short and thickset. He had a large head, scantily covered with curly hair; a large, shaven Jewish face, with coarse skin; a high, wide forehead; short, thick nose and wide-spaced eyes; a large mouth with thick lips, drawn down at the corners; prominent jaws and an emphatic chin. The spectacles gave his eyes a false luminousness. His entire personality had a formidable aspect. Aggressiveness was perhaps his chief characteristic. Precise, deliberate in his manner, his oratorical delivery had a ponderous solemnity that was not ineffective. He could say commonplace things impressively. A cigar-maker by trade, he had been associated with labor unionism from his early youth. Before attaining to leadership in trade unionism, he had believed, "with most advanced thinkers," as he put it, "in the abolition of the wage system." He had learned German especially to study Marx in the original. As head of the A.F. of L., however, he became a venomous enemy of Socialism. He was a politician, a victim of his own power, a compromiser, an opportunist. Not a selfish man in a material sense, he died comparatively poor; but he was hungry for power and exceedingly susceptible to flattery, especially if it came from big capitalists or a politician like Roosevelt. Bill Haywood described him as "vain, conceited, petulant, vindictive." He engaged in some unscrupulous transactions; never, perhaps, to increase his bank account, only to stay in office as President of the A.F. of L. and, according to his own lights, serve the men in the Federation.

IV

The attitude of the A.F. of L. toward society at large was, in most vital respects, not unlike that of the capitalists. The trade-union leaders were bent upon getting for themselves and their members everything that could be had under the circumstances, whenever possible, by almost any means—dynamite included—that involved no great risks to themselves or the future of their organization. It did not concern them whether those benefits were attained at the expense of the capitalist class, the unorganized proletariat, the organized labor outside the A.F. of L., or the country as a whole. Politically, they "played the game" as it was played by the capitalists, that is, to gain immediate economic advantages or benefits. They were not antagonistic to the wage system, which Horace Greeley had called "endurable only when contrasted with absolute bondage." After all, it was the wage system that produced their organization. They accepted the capitalist system and proposed to make the best of it. Ideologically, the movement was on a low level; the class

struggle, as a prominent if somewhat indelicate Chicago trade-union
leader and dynamiter candidly expressed himself to me in an interview
during the writing of this book, became "the ass (arse) struggle."

But there is no doubt that the new line-up under Gompers had
more intelligence and a sounder instinct of self-preservation than any
national labor amalgamation before it or since. While the growth of the
A.F. of L. during the nineties was not great, the organization weathered
one of the most critical periods in American industrial life. It was a cautious, hard-headed, conservative, opportunist movement. It had stability. It proposed to profit by the blunders of the K. of L. It let emotional
ultra-radical organizations fight most of the important battles in the
open field and then derived advantage from both their victories and
their defeats. Debs's Railway Union, the Western Federation of Miners,
and the Industrial Workers of the World, with their great uprisings in
the nineties and the first decade of the current century served to fright-
en the capitalists. (During the battles these organizations had in the
A.F. of L. almost as bitter an antagonist as in the employers. Indeed, the
A.F. of L. is known to have furnished strikebreakers in I.W.W. strikes.)
But after the real fight was over and the industrialists were a bit more
inclined "to come across," it was the Federation leaders who profited.
They entered into new wage agreements with the bosses and put over
labor legislation, some of which, it is true, in the long run benefited the
American working class as a whole.

Not a few of the unions in the A.F. of L. became well off financially.
The capitalists did not succeed in luring into the service of wealth all
the competent labor leaders, for now the latter could advance themselves economically and socially by sticking to labor. The unions were
put on a business basis. Officials drew regular salaries. Special organizers were employed. Soon there were marvelous opportunities for graft,
"legitimate" and otherwise; though it was not until the twentieth century that corruption in the American labor movement developed into a
regular science. It was not long before A.F. of L. union officials began to
die rich men, of overeating. Alive, some of them sported diamonds and
silk shirts and drove automobiles. Their wives, to quote Mother Jones,
"strutted about like peacocks." Leaders rode in Pullmans and made trips
abroad. One of them, when accused by naïve members of his union of
having "peddled" the movement, declared cynically: "Sure I'm a grafter.
Whenever you hear that Frank Feeney goes after somethin' you make
up your mind he's gettin' his price. I'm for Frank Feeney." Of course,
there *were* honest leaders in the unions, as honest, that is, as they could

be and stay in; and even the crooked ones occasionally pulled honest moves in the struggle, thereby keeping the "stiffs" satisfied and impressing the capitalists with their power.

The type of leader that Gompers's "pure and simple" movement called for was the man of small abilities, narrow-minded, without social vision. His mental world consisted of a combination of wage and hour issues, and of the different methods by which labor groups might be influenced. He devoted himself diligently to the study of such individuals as might threaten his own job. He steered clear of anything in the nature of a general program. He was not ignorant of his own limitations and, therefore, resisted any step that might unduly extend the field of labor activities, for this would have involved the rise of a higher type of leader, of more intelligence and, perhaps, more character. He opposed independent political action by labor, for the simple reason that it implied other leaders, men with greater ambitions for themselves and society. To him only immediate gains and advantages mattered—and violence was sometimes a quick and simple way of getting results.

Many of the laborites were Irish, with the Molly Maguire blood and tradition in their make-up; and to this tradition were added the anarchistic teachings of Johann Most. The trade unions, especially in Chicago, were full of anarchists to whom Louis Lingg, one-time organizer of the Carpenters, was a hero.

Sam Gompers, as president of the A.F. of L., denounced the anarchists with great vehemence and sermonized against violence on weekdays and Sundays. But it was not long after the Haymarket incident that, under the stimulus of the savage attitude of capitalism toward labor and the public, dynamite—"the real stuff"—became a definite part of the policy and tactics of the American labor movement, including—indeed, especially—the A.F. of L. Only the A.F. of L. dynamite was "pure and simple," devoid of any such wide social idealism and aims as had motivated the original Chicago terrorists.

The labor movement under Gompers became to a great extent a "racket"—to use the word in the sense in vogue many years later—set up in opposition to the capitalist "racket." Gompers spoke idealistically, with uplifted eyes, of the "deep spiritual significance" and the "wide social interest" of his organization, while as a matter of fact there was as little spirituality and social interest in the movement as there was in Carnegie's steel company or in the tariff lobby at Washington. While Gompers orated, the leaders of separate unions "racketeered," employing dynamite and every other means they could think of—and

Gompers, I am satisfied, knew what they were doing. To them only immediate results mattered, just as, on the other side of the fence, the capitalists were concerned only for their profits at the moment. "Get all you can; can all you get."

CHAPTER 8
CRIMINALS ARE DRAWN INTO THE CLASS WAR

In the riots of 1877 the criminal element played an important role. This was natural enough. Here, suddenly, was an opportunity to loot and burn and vent the hatred for the established order which is part of the psychology of every criminal or person criminally inclined.

Marx and Engels, plotting their Revolution, were aware of the part that crime would play in any uprising of the underdog. "The 'dangerous class,'" they said in their Manifesto, "the social scum, that passively rotting mass thrown off by the lowest layers of old society, may, here and there, be swept into the movement by a proletarian revolution; its conditions of life, however, prepare it far more for the part of a bribed tool of reactionary intrigue." The soundness of their view cannot be questioned.

There is no doubt that in industrial warfare the police and other agents of the established order frequently employ criminals to perform deeds of violence which are then blamed upon those who oppose that order, thereby discrediting them as tainted by inhuman acts. European government agents have for many decades been using criminals and terrorists to discredit revolutionary movements. An old trick of the police in Tsarist Russia was to foment and stimulate and finally suppress minor uprisings. At one time the police authorities of Paris subsidized anarchist sheets in that city. Kropotkin tells, in his *Memoirs*, of two occasions on which police agents came to him with money to help start anarchist papers that would advocate violence.

While there may be little doubt that the Haymarket Bomb was manufactured and thrown by some idealistic anarchist of the Louis Lingg type, the idea that the deed was perpetrated by a criminal, hired by agents of the Chicago employers who were interested in destroying the eight-hour movement then in progress, is not unreasonable or far-fetched. Nor—to come to a more recent incident—am I willing to dismiss entirely the belief popular among radicals that the Preparedness

70 Day explosion in San Francisco in 1916, for which Mooney and Billings have spent fourteen years in prison although plainly innocent of that outrage, was perpetrated not by any laborite or radical fanatic, but by some one hired by the representatives of powerful interests in San Francisco eager to wreck the aggressive labor unions in that city.

II

In most civilized countries, at least within the last century or so, all the powers of repression, coercion, and aggression have been in the hands exclusively of the state, with its armies, navies, and local police.

This was true of the United States until the struggle between the have-nots and the haves became a veritable war, shortly after the Civil War. The state has, of course, always been on the side of the great economic interests, but all its resources have sometimes proved to be inadequate. The militia was poorly organized, the police could not always be relied upon when it came to suppressing strikes, and sometimes, too, when the militia was called out, the soldiers' sympathies were with the strikers.

So, already in the sixties, numerous American industrialists, on becoming rich and powerful, began to hire their own forces of armed men. By the end of that decade, Robert A. Pinkerton, a private detective with a talent for business, became wealthy supplying "guards" to employers with labor troubles. Then other individuals, envious of Pinkerton's prosperity, started rival "detective bureaus." Many of these were professional criminals and were in the business of selling the service of other criminals and low characters to the owners of large industries. They sent thieves and murderers to scenes of labor disputes, where the employers appointed them "guards," with duties to protect company property and the scabs, to shoot down and slug strike pickets, provoke riots, commit, and incite strikers to commit, outrages which later were blamed entirely on the workers.

Still others of this type were engaged by the employers' agents to join labor unions and act as spies, create dissension in the organization, and *encourage members to violence and crime.*

Thus criminality was organized in the United States to "racketeer" for the employers in their opposition to the underdog's strivings to lift himself to a higher social and economic level.

And the labor movement—dominated as it was by the American Federation of Labor, whose basic psychology, as I have emphasized, was not unlike that of the capitalists—soon adopted the same methods. The unions began to hire sluggers to slug scabs, gunmen to shoot down superintendents and company assassins, dynamiters to blow up the employers' property, or they developed strong-arm talent within their organizations. Indeed, in the course of a few decades several unions, finding themselves pitted against brutal, unconscionable employers, developed into Mafia-like outfits, with terrorism as the core of their policy.

PART THREE
THE WAR BEGINS IN EARNEST

"…the brutal force which money can exert in America in the workshop, the corrupt force it can exert on the bench and in the capital of every State, make it the most natural thing imaginable for labor to contemplate a resort to such force as it can command—dynamite, sabotage, bad work, the revolutionary strike."
—*J. RAMSAY MACDONALD, IN THE LONDON DAILY CHRONICLE, IN 1912*

CHAPTER 9
THE HOMESTEAD STRIKE

With the rise of the American Federation of Labor, the capitalists were confronted with a hard-boiled organization—and this only a few years after they had rejoiced over the disastrous effect of the Anarchist Trial upon the workers' movement. They began to see that on occasions when labor leaders were unpurchasable labor would have to be dealt with by methods at once more subtle and more brutal than had been employed to subdue the upheavals in the seventies and eighties. They added a new weapon to their war equipment—the injunction. This was an improvement upon the old "conspiracy law," which had made it illegal for workers, in some instances, to strike and picket and generally to advocate their cause.

The first labor injunction case occurred in 1888, in Massachusetts, when a court enjoined the strikers of a spinning mill from "displaying banners with devices as a means of threats and intimidation to prevent persons from entering or continuing in the employment of the plaintiffs." The effect was to deprive the workers—most of them citizens of the United States—of their constitutional rights of freedom of speech, press, and assembly, and of the right even to appear in the street near the employers' property.

Thereafter the injunction was used by the capitalists in many big industrial battles, often very effectively, along with the lockout, the blacklist, bullets, police clubs, spying, and propaganda. The courts were almost without qualification on the side of big money and against labor.

Of course, from the capitalist point of view, the injunction was not unjustified. A strike was after all an insurrection against the existing system, and under the circumstances it was not illogical for the chief beneficiaries thereof to abrogate the civil law. During the interval of armistice in the struggle between the classes civil law might pretend to referee in class and individual relationships, but a strike was war— referred to as *war* by both sides—and an injunction was an act of war.

On the other hand, the injunction—which meant that labor leaders were arrested and held as "prisoners of war" as soon as they began a strong movement against the employers—stirred in the working class more and more bitterness. Labor began to lose its illusions about the justice of the country's legal system. Labor's impulse to violence—to dynamite, arson, and assassination—became stronger after each injunction, after the failure of each peaceable effort to better its conditions.

II

The eight-hour agitation was resumed soon after the appearance of the A.F. of L. Gompers and his colleagues were not enthusiastic about it. The idea was too radical for them, and the anarchist affair was still fresh in the public mind. But as soon as industrial conditions improved slightly, in the late eighties, there came a grumbling demand from the rank and file of the unions for a shorter workday.

At the convention in 1888, the A.F. of L. officially decided to declare a general strike on May 1, 1890, demanding the eight-hour system for all industries represented in the organization. The decision was greeted eagerly by the mass of workers; but at the next convention the leaders became terrified by the idea. They felt that the consequences of the probable failure of the strike would be much too disastrous to risk such an action and so they decided instead to have just one union—the Carpenters—strike on the appointed day. The Carpenters were well organized; theirs was a highly skilled trade and they had a large fund in the treasury. The strike was called, and within a few weeks they won the eight-hour demand in over one hundred cities and towns.

Encouraged by the Carpenters' success, the Mine Workers announced their intention to walk out on May I, 1891, but on the eve of the strike the leaders suddenly realized that the union was in no position to do so, and ordered the men to stay on the job. The leaders' fear of failure was justified, for in the mines there was a multitude of unorganized immigrant labor available for scabbing, while the Miners' strike fund was too meager to fight a long battle. The intention to strike had been a mistake; the calling-off of the strike demoralized the entire eight-hour agitation, and it was years before the movement regained any vigor.

For a time Gompers breathed easily. He had been compelled to endorse the eight-hour agitation of the rank and file of the unions, but in his heart and mind he opposed it.

The idea was too radical; it endangered his conservative policies, to say nothing of his position as president of the A.F. of L. He was not a

militant man, nor an impulsive fighter, but a plotter, a politician, a compromiser. He fought openly only when there was nothing else to do.

III

But there was no real peace; indeed, the war was just beginning in earnest.

In 1892 there burst out the fury of the so-called Homestead Strike, which really was a lockout, involving on the one hand the Iron and Steel Workers, who, with a membership of nearly 25,000, were one of the strongest unions in the country, and on the other the Carnegie Steel Company. Three years previously the union had been recognized by the company; indeed, had entered with it into a three-year contract, at the expiration of which Carnegie wanted the men to take a reduction of wages. The union declined these terms and on July 1, before they could declare a strike, the workers were suddenly locked out.

Before that occurred, however, Andrew Carnegie, already famous as a major prophet of American "democracy," anticipating violence, had hurriedly turned the command over to the company's superintendent, Henry C. Frick, a frank and brutal union-hater, and departed for Europe.

Frick immediately indicated by his action that he meant war to the bitter end. He erected a wire fence three miles long and fifteen feet high around the works and called upon the Pinkerton Detective Agency to send him three hundred gunmen.

The locked-out men heard that the Pinkertons were coming, and they watched for their arrival. They knew that the gunmen would be armed and prepared themselves to meet them on their own terms.

On the night of July 5, a boatload of "Pinkertons" attempted to land in Homestead. A battle followed, in which ten men were killed and three times that number wounded. At the end the workers got the better of the gunmen, captured the entire three hundred, minus the few who were killed, held them "prisoners of war" for twenty-four hours, and finally ran them, disarmed, out of town.

Incensed, Frick then called upon the Governor of the State of Pennsylvania for the militia and within a few days the little mill town of 12,000 was an armed camp.

The soldiers stayed till the end of November, when the strike officially ended in the utter defeat of the workers. The union's treasury was empty; winter was coming on, and the men's families were cold and hungry. In desperation, they returned to work as non-unionists.

IV

But Frick did not win the battle unscathed. There was then in the United States a young anarchist, Alexander Berkman, an admirer of the late Louis Lingg and lover of Emma Goldman, who, on hearing of the gunfight between the steel men and the Pinkertons, hastened to Homestead and there burst into Frick's office. (I take the details from Berkman's *Memoirs*.)

"Mistah Frick is engaged," said the negro porter to whom Berkman had handed his card. "He can't see you now, suh."

Berkman sauntered out of the reception-room; then, quickly retracing his steps, passed through a gate separating the clerks from the callers, brushed aside the appalled porter, and stepped into a room where a moment before he had glimpsed a black-bearded, well-knit man sitting by a long table.

There were two other men at the table, obviously holding a conference with Frick.

"Frick—" began Berkman; then the look of terror in Frick's face struck him speechless. "He understands," Berkman thought to himself. "Perhaps he wears armor," he reflected and, pulling out his revolver, aimed at his head.

Frick clutched with both hands the arm of his chair and averted his terror-stricken face. Berkman fired. Frick dropped to his knees, his head against the arm of the chair. "Is he dead?" wondered Berkman. Then some one leaped upon him from behind and crushed him to the floor. Others piled up on him and held him down. Then they picked him up, and he saw that Frick was not dead. Blood oozed from a wound in his neck. His black beard was streaked with red.

For an instant the young and as yet inexperienced terrorist had a "strange feeling, as of shame"; then he was annoyed with himself for entertaining an emotion "so unworthy of a revolutionist."

The police came and hustled him to prison.

"I've lost my glasses," Berkman complained to the officers.

"You'll be damned lucky if you don't lose your head," snapped a policeman.

Berkman was sentenced to twenty-two years in prison. He served fifteen. His act was considered a crime, but behind it—as behind most of the other violent incidents in the class war—was a motive of social revenge, a blind attempt on the part of a social idealist to help the desperate workers on strike by removing the powerful tyrant who opposed them.

CHAPTER 10
COXEY'S ARMY

The year 1893 was the beginning of another panic, and in the industrial centers the "battalions of hunger" paraded once more. The forces that brought about this crisis in finance and industry were many, too many to be discussed here; but fundamentally they had their origin in the ever-narrowing concentration of wealth in the hands of a few stupid, selfish, willful men who dominated the nation's life. Chauncey M. Depew, himself a tycoon, said early in the nineties:

> Fifty men in the United States have it in their power, by reason of the wealth which they control, to come together within twenty-four hours and arrive at an understanding by which every wheel of trade and commerce may be stopped from revolving, every avenue of trade blocked, and every electric key struck dumb.

William Windom, a former Secretary of Treasury, disagreed with Depew, in that the power to create a panic was limited to four men,

> who may at any time, and for reasons satisfactory to themselves, by a stroke of the pen, reduce the value of property in the United States by hundreds of millions. They may, at their own will and pleasure, embarrass business, depress one city or locality and build up another, enrich one individual and ruin his competitors, and when complaint is made, coolly reply, "Well, what are you going to do about it?"

In trying to do something about it, the people were forming new political parties. There was the Populist movement. Out of Populism grew Bryanism, which in the last analysis was another desperate attempt on the part of the masses—who, in the maelstrom of money-getting, had failed to get anywhere near the top—to pull down, and square accounts with, the few who had succeeded at their expense. On the surface of these movements, of course, there was much moral indignation, social idealism, and marvelous rhetoric.

Motivated as it was by the interests of the plutocrats, the political life of the United States was rotten to the core. In the social and official circles of Washington, men and women talked freely of how much this or that senator or congressman had received for his services to such and such a trust or corporation.

At intervals men prominent in public life stood up and viewed the trend of things with undisguised alarm. Shortly before the panic began Senator John J. Ingalls, for instance, spoke in the United States Senate:

> We cannot disguise the truth that we are on the verge of a revolution... Labor, starving and sullen in the cities, aims to overthrow a system under which the rich are growing richer and the poor are growing poorer, a system which gives to a Vanderbilt and a Gould wealth beyond the dreams of avarice and condemns the poor to poverty from which there is no escape or refuge but the grave... The laborers of the country asking for employment are treated like impudent mendicants begging for bread.

Desperation again stalked the country.

On the other hand there was a growing class of idle rich who had difficulty in finding new thrills in life. Charles and Mary Beard, in their admirable *Rise of American Civilization*, tell us of the social life among the rich of that time.

> At a dinner eaten on horseback, the favorite steed was fed flowers and champagne; to a small black-and-tan dog wearing a diamond collar worth $15,000 a lavish banquet was tendered; at one function, the cigarettes were wrapped in hundred dollar bills; at another, fine black pearls were given to the diners in their oysters; at a third, an elaborate feast was served to boon companions in a mine from which came the fortune of the host. Then weary of such limited diversions, the plutocracy contrived more freakish occasions—with monkeys seated between guests, human gold fish swimming about in pools, or chorus girls hopping out of pies.
>
> In lavish expenditures as well as in exotic performances, pleasures were hungrily sought by the fretful rich delivered from the bondage of labor and responsibility. Diamonds were set in teeth; a private carriage and personal valet were provided for a pet monkey; dogs were tied with ribbons to the back seats of Victorias and driven

out in the park for airings; a necklace costing $600,000 was pur-
chased for a daughter of a Croesus; $65,000 was spent for a dress-
ing table, $75,000 for a pair of opera glasses. An entire theatrical
company was taken from New York to Chicago to entertain the
friends of a magnate and a complete orchestra engaged to serenade
a new-born child.

II

To the proletariat the panic meant wage cuts or no work at all, lockouts and hopeless strikes, breadlines, cold and hunger. Immigrants
continued to come. Between 1893 and 1897 the number of unemployed who wanted and needed work was always from three to four
million. There were strikes involving hundreds of thousands of desperate men; bitter struggles, one-sided and unfair from start to finish,
were accompanied by violence and bloodshed. Some of the smaller,
independent unions went out of existence. The Knights of Labor were
nearing their end. But the American Federation of Labor, as already
mentioned, with its dependable instinct of self-preservation, lived
through the crisis without any great decline in its vitality.

During the panic, one of the most interesting of the underdog
movements was the unique march of the so-called Coxey's armies to
Washington.

The movement started in the fall of 1893 at Massillon, Ohio, in
the head of one Jacob Selcher Coxey, a Theosophist in religion and a
Populist in politics, a horse-breeder and owner of a stone quarry. He
had no special prominence before this time. As a Populist he believed
that it was the function of Congress, and of the entire Government, to
relieve social distress. The country was full of misery; thousands starved.
Coxey, therefore, issued a proclamation announcing his intention to
force, if necessary, those in power to act for the poor, by organizing the
unemployed into "peaceable armies" and marching them, without supplies, begging their way for hundreds of miles, to the capital.

The idea became a newspaper sensation. It was treated for the most
part as low comedy. Coxey, obviously, was a harmless idiot. The editorial
writers waxed satirical.

But Coxey's message, as a contemporary historian put it, "came
as rain upon thirsty ground." In California, Colorado, Massachusetts,
Illinois, Oklahoma, the State of Washington, New Jersey, Indiana,
Wisconsin, and Maryland men appeared who, either convinced of

the righteousness of Coxey's purpose or thirsty for notoriety, or both, joined in the cause. "On to Washington!" Local leaders issued separate manifestos. Frye, of Los Angeles, for instance, condemned

> the evils of murderous competition, the supplanting of manual labor by machinery...alien landlordism, exploitation by rent, profit, and interest of the products of toil [which] have centralized the wealth of the Nation into the hands of the few and placed the masses in a state of hopeless destitution.

Early in the spring of 1894 some 20,000 "Coxeyites" were Washington-bound by a dozen different routes. An extraordinary movement. But the country at large, led by the newspapers, was still inclined to consider it a joke. Great hordes of tramps came through towns, laughing, singing *Marching Through Georgia*, carrying banners and Old Glory. They camped on the outskirts of communities, bummed food from farmers, and to get on the right side of the religious folk sang *Jesus, Lover of My Soul* and *Nearer My God to Thee*.

In San Francisco one Charlie Kelly "raised" an army of 1,500 overnight. The city, uneasy at having the tramps in its midst, did everything in its power to help get Kelly started across the bay into Oakland. In Oakland the authorities also alarmed by the organized mob of ragged men, many of whom looked like criminals, helped them with transportation out of Oakland; and so on.

Now and then an "army" would "steal" a whole train and proceed in style, but there was comparatively little plundering. The farmers generally were sympathetic, generous, amused. It was a good-natured movement.

III

Soon, editorial writers commenced to take Coxey seriously. What was the prime motive behind the movement? Some insisted that it was the leaders' craving for publicity, others that it was a popular, spontaneous social uprising, a revolution—"and let us be thankful," remarked one newspaper, "that it is so tame."

Preachers sermonized about it. One interpreter of the teachings of Jesus Christ, from his pulpit in Hoboken, New Jersey, declared furiously: "All we owe a tramp is a funeral," thus agreeing with the New York *Herald*'s idea that "the best meal for a regular tramp is one of lead, and enough of that to satisfy the most craving appetite."

In Washington the movement was discussed by uneasy, bewildered politicians. Ex-President Harrison said to reporters: "We are witnessing now a spectacle that our country has never witnessed before."

But as the "armies" approached Washington, the movement began suddenly to dribble out. The people in the West and the Mid-West were friendly because the Coxeyites were going east, thereby solving in part their local unemployment and hobo problems. The people in the East, of course, felt differently; the oncoming hordes aggravated their unemployment and hobo situation. Coxeyites began to have trouble with the police; the folks along the way generally were unfriendly, and so the men commenced to desert their armies and hike back home by themselves.

Less than a thousand Coxeyites finally reached Washington.

In accordance with his plan, on May 1, "General" Coxey led about 600 of his followers through the streets of Washington to the Capitol grounds, where a solid wall of mounted police barred their way. Leaving the army, Coxey and two of his "adjutants" ran through the shrubbery toward the Capitol steps, intending to make speeches. They were arrested. The "General" was not allowed to address his army.

They were tried for violation of the statute which forbade parading, or assembling, or carrying or displaying any banner designed "to bring into notice any party or organization or movement on the Capitol grounds," and for having trampled on the grass. They were found guilty and sentenced to short terms in jail.

This practically ended the Coxey movement. The Cleveland *Plain Dealer* said:

> What does it all amount to? The enterprise was meaningless when it started and is meaningless in its conclusion, except as an evidence of the unrest that is prevalent.

CHAPTER 11
"THE DEBS REBELLION"

Of the many minor strikes in the early nineties, the most significant was that of the railroad switchmen in Buffalo, in 1892, for shorter hours and more pay. Like most strikes at that time, it failed. It involved, directly, only 300 men, but its consequences were far-reaching. The railway brotherhoods, whose character and policy were similar to those of the A.F. of L., refused to support the strike, which was the main reason for its failure, and which incensed a man by the name of Eugene V. Debs, then Grand Secretary-Treasurer of the Locomotive Firemen. He had tried to induce his organization to declare a sympathetic strike and, failing, now resigned from his office.

At that time Debs was not a professed Socialist, but he had little use for the trade-union movement as an effective instrument. He wanted all railroad men in "one big organization."

Accordingly, in 1893, he started the American Railway Union, which, within a year, grew to a membership of 150,000 and for a time threatened the future of the railroad brotherhoods.

Debs was then in his late thirties, a tall, gaunt man, French-Alsatian by descent; a gentle-voiced zealot of great persuasive power; a messiah aflame with feelings for the lowly and downtrodden; a brave and forthright man; an emotionalist, sentimentalist, with a singular fineness of character, and a manner which endeared him to all who came to know him. At the age of fourteen he had worked in the locomotive shops at Terre Haute, Indiana, and later became a fireman on engines. In the eighties he had been elected secretary-treasurer of the Firemen's Brotherhood at $4,000 a year. His pay as president of the new American Railway Union was anywhere from nothing to $75 a month.

II

The American Railway Union was a year old when a minor sort of trouble commenced to brew in Pullman, Illinois, a "model town for

85

working people," from which, to quote a contemporary description of its charms, "all that is ugly, discordant, and demoralizing is eliminated." Its founder and owner was George M. Pullman, the sleeping-car king, who, on the score of benevolence to his employees, out-Forded Henry Ford of twenty years later. But his critics called the "Pullman idea" feudalistic. Certainly it was anything but pure altruism. The workers paid rent to the Pullman Company, traded in company stores, sent their children to a company school, strolled when they were not working in Mr. Pullman's park, and attended his church and his theater. Everything was Pullman. Even the sewage from the workers' homes went into a tank and was thence pumped to Mr. Pullman's stock farm as fertilizer.

He was a workingman's friend who knew—and there was no room for argument—what was good for the workingman. Liquor, for instance, was bad for him; therefore, Pullman was a dry town. Unions were bad for him; therefore, unions were taboo in Pullman. For the same highminded reason, Mr. Pullman was against the eight-hour workday idea; it encouraged idleness.

But, alas! in spite of all precaution, the agitators of the American Railway Union had sneaked into the lovely town and organized the sleeping-car workers.

In the spring of 1894 business was poor; therefore, Mr. Pullman reduced the wages of his people from 30 to 40 per cent and the number of employees by one-third, neglecting, however, to lower at the same time the rent of his houses and the prices in his stores. The ungrateful Pullman workers did not like the cut, and so in May they quit their jobs.

The strike in itself was a comparatively small affair, but it led to the greatest labor uprising in the history of the United States.

When the A. R. U. met in convention in Chicago on June 12, the Pullman strike was a month old. Business being bad, the Pullman Company did not care how long the men stayed out. Perhaps the only thing that worried the great altruist was the fact that the strikers owed him $70,000 for back rent.

Pullman suspended the strikers' credit in his stores, and by the end of May most of the workers' families were starving. The Rev. William Cardwardine, a Pullman preacher who, however, sympathized with the strikers, went before the A. R. U. convention and said: "In the name of God and humanity, act quickly!"

The convention voted $2,000 for relief, and the delegates began to talk boycott.

Debs tried to arbitrate. He sent representatives to T. H. Wickes,
vice-president of the Pullman Company, but the great man told them
to tell Debs to go to hell; there was "nothing to arbitrate." He added
that the strikers meant no more to him than "men on the sidewalk."

III

Then the trouble began. The A. R. U. felt rather confident of itself.
Two months before Debs had sprung a surprise strike, unimportant in
itself, on the Great Northern Railroad and won it. Now the delegates
to the convention thought that by springing a bigger surprise upon the
railroads they might easily win a bigger victory. They gave the Pullman
Company four days in which to begin negotiating with the strike committee. The company refused even to notice the ultimatum.

On June 26, Debs, authorized by the convention, ordered a boycott
against Pullman cars on all Western railroads, the cars to be cut out
from trains and side-tracked. Within two days all operations between
Chicago and San Francisco were suspended, for the roads were bound
by contract to handle Pullman cars, which *ipso facto* resulted in strikes.

The newspapers let out a howl. Who was this man Debs? How *could*
he do such a thing? His boycott was "interference with the business of
the railroads"; it was a "conspiracy" and, worse, it was "anarchy."

But the movement, as it developed, doubtless was as much a surprise
and shock to Debs as it was to the rest of the country. It had gone farther
than he anticipated. He had lost control of it almost immediately after
the boycott order went into effect. Railroads discharged the boycotters,
whereupon every union affiliated with the A. R. U. struck.

The good, gentle Debs implored the men to commit no violence,
but he might as well have kept silent. In Chicago violence was almost
inevitable. Lewis and Smith, in *Chicago—A History of Its Reputation*,
say:

All the bitterness, the hoodlumism, the despair, stored up at the
bottom of Chicago's soul during the awful winter, boiled over into
the railroad yards. The causes were almost lost to sight...[The railroad magnates] were doughty fighters. They determined to run
trains. Portly officials who had not handled a throttle in twenty
years climbed into cabs; others handled switches. But they found
themselves defeated by howling, hooting, brick-throwing throngs.
Here and there engines were crippled, capsized on tracks; whole
trains of standing freight cars were overturned, towermen were
dragged from switch-towers... Meanwhile, at the stockyards, sup-

plies of livestock were dwindling... A meat famine threatened the Middle West.

Obviously, the thing had to be put down. Troops were needed. John Altgeld was still Governor of Illinois. He was notoriously pro-labor, radical. The year before he had pardoned three anarchists who were serving time for the Haymarket riot. He could not be depended upon in a serious matter such as this. So the Chicago capitalists decided to ignore him and, going over his head, appealed to the Federal Government in Washington.

President Cleveland at once ordered the regular troops into service in Chicago and elsewhere. By July 4, Chicago was an armed camp, with over 10,000 soldiers, infantry, cavalry, and even field artillery. Mobs of workers hooted at them, calling them "scabs."

Soldiers guarded trains and terminals, but the destruction of property continued in spite of them. Debs insisted that the A. R. U. men had no hand in the violence; that property was destroyed by hoodlums hired by the companies which wanted to be compensated for "strike losses" by the State, and by irresponsible sympathizers.

Incensed, Governor Altgeld telegraphed to President Cleveland:

> I am advised that you have ordered Federal troops to go into service in the State of Illinois... Waiving all questions of courtesy, I will say that the State of Illinois is not only able to take care of itself, but it stands ready today to furnish the Federal Government any assistance it may need elsewhere... As Governor of the State of Illinois I protest against this, and ask the immediate withdrawal of Federal troops from active duty in the State.

Never before or since has the Governor of a State addressed so cutting a communication to a President of the United States.

Cleveland replied, lamely, that the Federal troops were in Chicago in strict accordance with the Constitution and laws of the United States, to protect and help to move the mails.

The country, of course, got behind the President. The preachers and editorial writers pronounced "this most gigantic strike in all history" to be "an outrage." Debs was a demon, no less; his unionists and sympathizers were hoodlums, incendiaries, anarchists. And Altgeld was no better. The United States Senate passed a resolution endorsing the Presidential measure.

In a manner typical of the conservative press throughout the country, the Chicago *Herald* editorialized:

> The necessity is on the railroads to defeat the strike. If they yield one point it will show fatal weakness. If the strike should be successful the owners of the railroad property...would have to surrender its future control to the class of labor agitators and strike conspirators who have formed the Debs Railway Union.

Lawlessness continued. Some two thousand railroad cars were wrecked and burned. The losses of property and business to the country were variously estimated between fifty and a hundred million.

IV

On July 7, Debs and several other leaders of the A. R. U. were indicted for "conspiracy," arrested, and held under bail. The court issued an injunction enjoining them from doing anything toward the prolongation of the strike.

On July 12, in defiance of the injunction, Debs held a conference with twenty-odd leaders of unions affiliated with the American Federation of Labor, at which he urged the immediate declaration of a General Strike by *all* labor organizations in the United States. The A.F. of L., of course, rejected the appeal on the grounds that "it would be unwise and disastrous to the interests of labor to extend the strike any further than it had already gone," and advised Debs to call his strike off.

There was no solidarity. The conservative, cautious A.F. of L. leaders, naturally, refused to play into the hands of the revolutionary Debs, who already had become too much of a hero to the great mass of workers. Debs was an extraordinary fool, all too liable to carry out his "one big union" dream if at all given a chance. If that happened, then what would become of their "pure and simple" trade unionism and their comfortable positions? And so they let Debs stew in his own juice. Gompers, one of the twenty-odd A.F. of L. leaders, has been quoted as saying, when he left Indianapolis for Chicago to meet with Debs: "I'm going to the funeral of the A. R. U."

In desperation, on July 13, Debs offered the General Managers' Association, in charge of the capitalist side in the dispute, to end the strike, provided the men should be reemployed without bias. The Association would have nothing to do with him.

The strike was practically broken. The town swarmed with soldiers, guarding the railway property, dispersing mobs of workers.

The same day it was decided to break the strike completely by putting the injunction into operation. The day before Debs had urged a General Strike, which, if declared, would have amounted to civil war; and so he was charged with contempt of court for disobeying the injunction issued on July 7.

That was the end. The strike leaders were gagged and tied hand and foot. Those of the strikers who could returned to work. The rest starved.

The A. R. U. was disrupted soon thereafter.

In the legal proceedings that occupied the next few months and resulted in jail terms for Debs and his fellow leaders of the A. R. U., Clarence Darrow became nationally known as a defender of labor.

General Nelson Miles, commander of the regular troops on strike duty in Illinois—"a vulture stuffed with carrion," Debs described him—pompously declared at a banquet given in appreciation of his services: "I have broken the backbone of this strike."

A few months later the regular army was raised to 50,000 men and more armories were being started in Chicago, New York, and elsewhere, to keep down any possible labor uprising in the future. Military journals printed articles on riot-duty tactics.

CHAPTER 12
VIOLENCE IN THE WEST

Almost simultaneously with the uprisings in the East and Middle West, there were violent labor upheavals in the West.

The Homestead strike of 1892 was not yet over when the miners in the Coeur d'Alene region in Idaho struck against repeated wage cuts. But the strike was as good as lost when it started. The men were badly organized, lacking effective leadership and adequate strike funds,

The mine operators hired scabs. There were battles. Men were killed by the militia. Some one blew up a quartz-mill, and the strikers drove the scabs out of the district. The companies, deeming the state militia inadequate to deal with the situation, had the Governor of Idaho appeal to the President of the United States. Presently Coeur d'Alene was under martial law, with regular troops guarding the property, while the employers brought in more strike-breakers.

The failure of the strike had immediate tragic results for the workers, but it led, eventually, to the organization of the Western Federation of Miners, which in the next decade developed into the most aggressive, violent, and revolutionary labor body in the United States and became, years later, the backbone of the I.W.W. or wobbly movement.

II

In the second half of the nineties an intense situation developed in the mining regions of Idaho, Colorado, and Montana.

By 1896 the Western Federation of Miners was already a powerful outfit. Its leaders were real miners, radicals, fighters, with more "guts" than was good for them, among them Bill Haywood, a product of the West, one of the most interesting characters that has sprung up in the American labor movement. They believed in violence—an eye for an eye!—and made little secret of it. The leaders themselves engaged in fist and gun fights with the scabs and the militia. They carried guns and on a number of occasions shot it out with the enemy. They did time in jails and military "bullpens," along with thousands—literally thousands—of their fellow union members.

For years after the disturbance at Coeur d'Alene, Idaho was the scene of endless outbreaks. Regular soldiers patrolled the mining districts. The State government, it appears, was too weak to deal with the situation. Almost every month some mine or mill was dynamited. Men were shot dead at night and in the day time. Pitched battles occurred between members of the W.F. of M. and non-union men, resulting in hundreds of casualties.

By May 1897 the feeling had become so intense that President Boyce of the W.F. of M. urged every local union in Idaho and Colorado to organize a rifle corps, "so that in two years we can hear the inspiring music of the martial tread of 25,000 armed men in the ranks of labor."

One strike was scarcely over when another began.

The war reached a sort of climax in the spring of 1899, when the $250,000 mill of the Bunker Hill Company was destroyed by the miners with dynamite. Frank Steunenberg was then Governor of Idaho. He had been elected on the Populist ticket, with the support of labor, and had been up to that time in hearty sympathy with labor organizations, having himself been a member of the printers' union. Called upon by the mine owners for redress, he now promptly responded by asking President McKinley for Federal troops and declaring Shoshone County in a state of "insurrection and rebellion."

The President ordered several companies of negro soldiers from Brownsville, Texas. Striking miners were rounded up by the thousands and put into specially erected bullpens. There were white troops available hundreds of miles closer than Brownsville, Texas, and Bill Haywood is justified in writing as he does in his autobiography:

> We always believed that the government officials thought it would further incite the miners if black soldiers were placed as guards over white prisoners. It did raise a storm of indignation, not so much against the colored soldiers as against those responsible for bringing any soldiers into the mining region.
>
> One of the officers, a dirty white scoundrel, sent letters to the wives and sisters of the men in the bull-pen, asking them to entertain the soldiers, saying that they would "receive consideration." The hell-hound was not concerned about the men under him, his action was intended to add insult to the other injuries already in-

flicted upon the helpless prisoners. It was an insult in any case to ask the miners' families to have anything to do with soldiers, and it was a deliberate attempt to add race prejudice to the situation.

III

The miners blamed Steunenberg for nearly everything that happened in the mining country in the late nineties. After leaving office a prosperous man, which he was not before election, he became a sheep-rancher on a large scale and for six years devoted himself also to other business interests.

Then, on December 30, 1905, he opened the gate of his home at Caldwell. It was his last act. To the gate was tied a piece of fish-line, one end of which was attached to a bomb, which instantly tore him limb from limb.

An eye for an eye! "Dynamite…that's the stuff!"

CHAPTER 13
THE REDDENING DAWN OF THE
TWENTIETH CENTURY

By the end of the nineteenth century industrialism was definitely uppermost in the life of the United States. The frontier was gone. The pioneer era was over. Instead of going west, people turned cityward in search of work in factories. In the first decade of the twentieth century there was a sudden decline in the rural population. The mills and the mines were sucking in the young from the farms. Cities expanded at a terrific rate. Child labor increased. Immigrants continued to come.

All vital phases of life were subordinated to industrial expansion, to the accumulation of wealth, to the exercise by the rich of the power that was being crystallized in enormous corporations and trusts. The Populist and Bryan-Democracy uprisings in the nineties, on the part of the petty-middle and small-capitalist classes, trying to capture the powers of government, were defeated, along with the efforts of the industrial proletariat to better its conditions.

President Garfield had said: "Whoever controls the volume of money in any country is master of all its legislation and commerce." A handful of capitalists were in control of the national, state, and municipal governments; of their executive, legislative, and particularly their judicial departments. The celebrated "consent of the governed" doctrine, associated so closely with the Declaration of Independence, and but a few decades before stressed again by Abraham Lincoln, was openly repudiated by political leaders, and treated by them as an outworn piece of eighteenth-century philosophy. To Senator Lodge of Massachusetts it was a mere "aphorism," a "fair phrase that runs trippingly on the tongue." Senator Platt of Connecticut announced that "governments derive their power from the consent of some of the governed." *The Outlook*, then a reactionary weekly, threw the doctrine over entirely: "We do not believe that governments rest upon the consent of the governed."

America was becoming a factor in the worldwide competition for commercial domination, and now, in addition to being a plaything of forces within their own boundaries, the American people became a plaything of forces completely outside even their nominal control. American goods were competing with goods of other nations, produced by cheap labor, and American capitalists now had a new and compelling reason for keeping down the wages of their workers.

The contrasts of social and economic conditions were becoming ever sharper. On the one hand there was, as A. M. Simons put it, "the dollarocracy of beef, pills, soap, oil, and railroads"; and on the other, to quote from John Mitchell's book, published in 1903: "The average wage earner has made up his mind that he must remain a wage earner. He has given up the hope of a kingdom come, where he himself will be a capitalist, and he asks that the reward for his work be given him as a working man."

II

Naturally, the discontent of the underdog, thus caught in the web of the terrible forces of modern industrialism, realizing his own inability to become an upperdog, was deep and widespread. Socialism, nebulous and confused as the movement was, began to have a wide appeal. For a time early in the century it seemed as if Mark Hanna's prophecy, "The next great issue this country will have to meet will be Socialism," would soon come true.

'Gene Debs became the leader of American Socialists. He was but a recent convert to Socialism; as late as 1896 he had looked hopefully upon the antics of William Jennings Bryan. Soon afterward, however, Victor Berger, a German Socialist of Milwaukee, won him over to Socialism, and in 1900 the newly formed Socialist Party of America nominated him for President. He polled a little less than 100,000 votes. Four years later the Socialists piled up a vote of over 500,000.

Conservative magazines began to print articles on the "menace" of Socialism. On sailing for England early in 1905, H. Rider Haggard commented on "the growing Socialistic tendency among the American masses."

Prominent Republicans and Democrats, made uneasy by the spreading of Socialism, urged their parties to become mildly Socialistic and thus stop the militant movement. After the 1904 election, for instance, William Allen White of Kansas declared that "the problems facing Theodore Roosevelt are problems concerning the distribution of wealth."

But the regular parties would not dive deep into radicalism, and so the Socialist movement developed into a vigorous factor in the political life of the country. The Debs meetings in the 1904 campaign were extraordinary. The largest halls were hired, admission was charged, and yet the auditoriums were packed.

By the middle of the decade there were in the United States half a dozen Socialist newspapers, having what might be called a national scope, and a hundred smaller sheets. In 1904 the circulation of the *Appeal to Reason*, a four-page propaganda sheet, was over 500,000. In December 1905 the *Appeal* issued the so-called anti-trust broadside, for which the paid advance orders exceeded 3,000,000, the largest edition of any paper printed to that time.

A young author, Upton Sinclair, published a powerful Socialistic novel, *The Jungle*, and became famous overnight. It was not long afterward that he ventured to prophesy the downfall of capitalism and the coming of the new Socialist order within ten years, or possibly fifteen. He saw the mechanics of this upheaval very clearly. The social evils of that day were the consequences of industrial competition nearing its collapse and end. The economic struggle had resulted in the survival of the Rockefellers and the Armours. There was no longer any competition in prices; there was competition only in labor; and the result of this condition was that the surplus product of industry went to the big capitalist. This the capitalist invested in new industries, and to sell his surplus he sought foreign markets. When new markets were no longer to be had, there was overproduction, which, in turn, produced the insoluble problem of unemployment. The effect of this condition was cumulative, for the unemployed competed and caused reduction in wages, and this meant a diminution of the purchasing power of the community and the cause of a still further shrinkage in markets. These causes operated universally, and the issue of them could only be a world-wide industrial revolution.

Another author, Jack London, was president of the Intercollegiate Socialist Society, formed for the purpose of interesting college students in the movement. Jack was signing his letters "Yours for the Revolution!"

Morris Hillquit already felt justified in writing a full-length *History of Socialism in the United States*. Robert Hunter produced a volume on *Poverty*, and Henry George, Jr., a book on *The Menace of Privilege*, which he subtitled "A Study of the Dangers to the Republic from the Existence of a Favored Class."

Other figures prominently identified with the Socialist movement were John Spargo, J. A. Wayland, editor of the *Appeal to Reason*, Max S. Hayes, A. M. Simons, Charles Edward Russell, W. E. Walling, Bill Haywood, and W. E. Trautmann. There were hordes of wild-eyed soap-boxers shouting on street corners, "Proletarians, unite! You have nothing to lose but your chains, and a world to gain." It was primarily an under-dog, belly-hunger movement, emotional and violent.

Muckraking in the magazines was in full swing. David Graham Phillips, Lincoln Steffens, Ida Tarbell, Upton Sinclair, and Ray Stannard Baker printed exposé upon exposé in the *Cosmopolitan*, *McClure's*, *Munsey's*, and *Everybody's*, which were building up enormous circulations mainly on the strength of their radicalism. The reading public obviously appreciated nasty articles about the capitalists and their political agents in Washington, their habits of life, amusements, dissipations, marital discords, and aristocratic tendencies. Then, too, the people seemed to have the idea that something was fundamentally rotten in the country, that the growing industrial and economic power, which was greater than any individual who exercised it, was crushing the masses into poverty, depriving them of their liberty.

CHAPTER 14
"TO HELL WITH THE
CONSTITUTION"

Meanwhile—early in the twentieth century—bitter battles of capital and labor continued in industry, especially in the mining sections of Pennsylvania and Colorado.

In Pennsylvania the dominant labor organization was the United Mine Workers, under the conservative leadership of John Mitchell, a bright young Gompersite, one of the vice-presidents of the American Federation of Labor and considered Gompers's "crown prince." He was a consistent "trade unionist, pure and simple," and sought to attain naught but the safely attainable. His union accepted the existing industrial system and regarded the employer as its partner; not a very agreeable partner, it is true, but one whom it was possible under favorable circumstances to coax or coerce into certain agreements in regard to its share of the proceeds. Like Gompers, young Mitchell was opposed to strikes when they could be avoided, for reasons already stated. Safety first! He was a calm, calculating, politic, indirect, high-toned fellow. He talked of "common interests of capital and labor." Roosevelt called him a gentleman. He enjoyed social contacts with great capitalists and politicians: Carnegie, Hanna, Belmont, and others. When he died, still a young man, he left a fortune of a quarter of a million dollars in packing-house and railroad stocks and bonds, notes, bank deposits, and real estate.

In Colorado, the Western Federation of Miners was the most powerful labor organization. It was Western in spirit and practically everything that the United Mine Workers' union was not. It had its tone from adventurous American frontiersmen who suddenly found themselves in the degrading position of workingmen—thousands of feet under the earth. Unlike the U.M.W., it was a business enterprise only incidentally. First of all it was a fighting organization. Its philosophy was against the existing industrial system, against the boss. It wanted higher wages, of course, but that was a side issue. Its primary aim was to eliminate the employer from industry. It was revolutionary, Socialistic.

One of its leaders, as already mentioned, was William Dudley Haywood, and Bill Haywood was a he-man, a man of elemental force, with the physical strength of an ox, a big head and a tremendous jaw; hard, direct, immensely resistant, impatient of obstacles, careless, violent, ready and fit to deal blow for blow; a boozer; a son of the Rockies, risen, as he put it himself, "from the bowels of the earth," to grope his way through years of misery and economic injustice to Socialism, to be touched by its idealism, and become a zealot in its cause. He was not only a Socialist, but wanted Socialism put into effect right away. Ramsay MacDonald, in his little book, *Syndicalism*, published in 1912, says of him:

> He is the embodiment of the Sorel philosophy [of violence]; roughened by the American industrial and civic climate, a bundle of primitive instincts, a master of direct statement. He is useless on committee; he is a torch amongst a crowd of uncritical, credulous workmen. I saw him at Copenhagen, amidst the leaders of the working-class movements drawn from the whole world, and there he was dumb and unnoticed; I saw him addressing a crowd in England, and there his crude appeals moved his listeners to wild applause. He made them see things, and their hearts bounded to be up and doing.

He was the toughest fighter the American labor movement has yet produced, and died, one-eyed, in exile, or rather a fugitive from American law, in Russia, where he is buried in the Kremlin.

The U. M. W and the W.F. of M. were typical of the right and left wings, respectively, of the American labor movement early in the twentieth century. It is interesting to see them in action.

II

In the fall of 1900, the Pennsylvania anthracite miners struck for an increase in wages. The union had little over 10,000 members, but before the strike was a week old nearly 100,000 men left the mines. The strike gave evidence of a great solidarity.

But the year was a political year, and Mark Hanna, McKinley's crafty campaign manager, fearful that the strike might become an unpleasant issue in the campaign, effected a compromise. John Mitchell accepted a ten per cent raise and the men were ordered to return to the mines.

At the expiration of the agreement in the spring of 1902, the union demanded a shortening of hours—from ten to nine—and the recognition of the union, which the owners refused, with the result that in May of that year another strike began, involving 150,000 miners. The union had $2,000,000 in the strike fund.

The strike dragged, peacefully, into the autumn. The public sympathized with the strikers until the winter approached. Factories and railroads were short of fuel. Thus far the strikers had the best of the fight.

McKinley had been assassinated and now Roosevelt was President. Characteristically, T. R. summoned the mine owners and John Mitchell to Washington. They agreed to submit the dispute to a commission which the President would appoint. The miners were granted a slight increase in wages, a slight decrease in time, but were refused the recognition of their union.

The militant Mother Jones, who was active in the strike, blamed Mitchell for the non-recognition of the union. She tells in her *Autobiography* that she had implored him to "tell Roosevelt to go to hell," that the miners would "fight to the finish," but that Mitchell replied: "It would not do to tell the President that."

"Mitchell was not dishonest," Mother Jones goes on to say, "but he had a weak point, and that was his love of flattery," which Roosevelt and the interests cleverly used in furthering their designs. The operators won a victory in that they did not have to deal with the union but with the President's commission. Mitchell doubtless was guilty of forfeiting a moral victory in the cause of unionism, which to Mother Jones was "more important than the material gains which the miners received... Labor walked into the House of Victory through the back door."

III

Now let us see Haywood's outfit in action.

On May 1, 1901, a strike was called in the gold and silver mines at Telluride, in Colorado. The local union, affiliated with the W.F. of M., demanded a uniform work-day with a minimum wage instead of the contract or piece-work system.

For a month the mines were idle. Then Arthur L. Collins, superintendent of Smuggler-Union mines, opened a mine with scabs, most of whom were armed and sworn in as deputies.

The strikers were incensed. Vincent St. John, a local union official, took a piece of union stationery and wrote out an order for 250 rifles and 50,000 rounds of ammunition and sent it to a firm in Denver, enclosing a check in payment, also signed by himself.

On the morning of July 3, as the scabs of the night shift were leaving the mine, the strikers attacked them from ambush. Several men dropped; others returned fire. A brother-in-law of Superintendent Collins was seriously wounded. A few strikers were killed.

The battle lasted several hours. Finally, the scabs at the mine, outnumbered and outclassed in arms, put up a white flag, whereupon a parley was arranged between St. John and the agents of the employers, just as in real war. In the negotiations, the union secured the possession of the mines on the condition that the scabs should be allowed to depart in peace with their wounded.

But before the scabs finally left, there was another battle, in which a few more were wounded; whereupon "the rest of the gang," as Haywood put it, "was escorted over the mountains."

The Governor of Colorado sent a commission to Telluride, which reported, correctly enough, that "everything is quiet in Telluride; the miners are in peaceful possession of the mines."

The report created a sensation.

One day Haywood was at the bank in Denver with which the W.F. of M. did business, when the vice-president of the institution approached him. "Is this report true, Bill," he asked, "that comes from Telluride, about the miners being in possession of the mines?"

Bill answered that it was.

"If that's the case, what becomes of the men who have invested their money in these properties?" said the indignant banker.

"If we follow your question to its logical conclusion," replied Bill, "you'd have to tell me where the owners got the money to invest in the mines. Who has a better right to be 'in possession' of the mines than the miners?"

A year later, after the trouble was apparently over, Superintendent Collins of the Smuggler-Union mines was shot dead by an unknown assassin while sitting at a lighted window one evening in his home. The union, of course, disclaimed any knowledge of the killing. In his book, Bill Haywood records the fact, simply: "Some one fired a load of buckshot into him."

IV

There was no end of trouble in Colorado. In 1903 the miners struck in the Cripple Creek district for the eight-hour workday. The governor of

Colorado then was James Peabody, a banker closely associated with
the conservative business of the State. He was determined to end
this radical union movement and, therefore, proclaimed that in the
Cripple Creek district there existed a "condition of anarchy in which
civil government had become abortive and life and property unsafe,"
and declared the place "in a state of insurrection and rebellion," the
only cure for which was martial law. Later he extended his measure
to include the Telluride district as well.

Certain newspapers criticized the State government for such an
action, declaring it unconstitutional, and to this criticism the Judge
Advocate of the State replied: "To hell with the Constitution; we are not
following the Constitution."

More mining bosses were assassinated and mines and mills were
dynamited. Law and order broke down completely. The militia paid
even less attention to legal provisions or moral rights of others than the
unions or corporations. The militia commander at Victor seized a privately owned building for his headquarters and then, marching his army
to the City Hall, informed the mayor and the chief of police that unless
they obeyed his orders, he would occupy the City Hall as well. "To hell
with the Constitution!" He strutted into the office of *The Record* and
established military censorship.

It was military despotism. Miners, most of them native Americans,
were picked up in the streets, dragged from their homes, locked up in
hastily constructed bull-pens, and there held *incommunicado* for weeks.
When their friends instituted *habeas corpus* proceedings in civil court
and the district judge ordered the bull-pen prisoners brought before
him for an orderly inquiry as to whether innocent men were deprived
of their liberty, the military surrounded the courthouse, posted riflemen
on the roofs roundabout and a Gatling gun in the street outside. When
the judge appeared, a trooper aimed a bayonet at his chest. "To hell with
the Constitution!"

The Record was printed with black-bordered blank columns. One
night General Chase, the ranking military officer in the State, appeared
with a troop of cavalry before the newspaper office, arrested the editor
for an alleged criticism of the martial-law administration, and took him
to the bull-pen, along with all the employees he found in the building.

Small boys and women were put into bull-pens for sticking
tongues out at the soldiers or speaking disparagingly of them. Private
homes were entered and searched without warrants. An ex-Congress-
man was attacked in his law office by a squad of soldiers and shot in

the arm. Shopkeepers were forbidden to sell merchandise to strikers, and the unions, lest the families starve, were compelled to establish their own commissaries. Then, quoting Mother Jones—

> the militia raided these stores, looted them, broke open the safes, destroyed the scales, ripped sacks of flour and sugar, and poured kerosene oil over everything... The miners were without redress, for the militia were immune.

Finally, scores of men, most of them union officials, were forcibly deported from the Telluride district, that is, taken to the county boundary line, and later even into Kansas, and told not to return. Some of these men owned homes and had their families in Telluride.

The Smuggler-Union mines were restored to the owners.

Bill Haywood was in the thick of the fight. The following conversation between him and President Moyer of the W.F. of M., recorded by Haywood in his book as having occurred when they were on the point of leaving for Cripple Creek, is indicative of the mood he was in:

"I don't propose to spend any time in the bull-pen," said Bill.

"Well," said Moyer, who was not quite of the same caliber as Bill, "what are you going to do if they arrest us?"

"Let's shoot it out with 'em."

They put a couple of extra revolvers in a handbag. "If we don't need these," said Bill, "we can leave them with the boys."

It was war, frank and open on both sides. Violence against violence.

Ultimately, of course, the strike was broken. The A.F. of L. miners' unions, under John Mitchell, helped the employers and the militia to break it.

CHAPTER 15
THE MURDER TRIAL IN IDAHO

Unquestionably the most significant incident in the war between the have-nots and the haves in the first decade of the twentieth century was the Haywood-Moyer-Pettibone case at Boise City, Idaho, in 1906–1907. Debs called it "the greatest legal battle in American history." Fifty special correspondents from all parts of the country and from England covered the trial. It involved the leaders of the most notorious, the most revolutionary, labor organization in the country, and started William Borah and Clarence Darrow on their different routes to fame. It drew in the President of the United States and, before it was over, threatened to cause a most formidable uprising of the underdog element in America.

As mentioned at the end of Chapter 12, Frank Steunenberg, ex-Governor of Idaho, was blown to pieces by a bomb planted at the entrance to his home, on December 30, 1905.

The next day Governor Gooding of Idaho offered $10,000 reward for the arrest and conviction of the perpetrators of the crime. The Steunenberg family offered $5,000 more. The large sum aroused the interest of the Pinkerton Detective Agency, and one of its managers, James McParland, came from New York to take charge of the work. McParland was in his late sixties, looked like "an innocuous country-man," and had a record that might have made Sherlock Holmes turn green with envy. It was he who, some thirty years earlier, had been largely instrumental in the breaking up of the Molly Maguires.

McParland arrested a man going by the name of Harry Orchard and placed him in solitary confinement. Orchard was known to be somewhat of an underhand-man and occasional companion of Charles Moyer, president of the Western Federation of Miners, and of Bill Haywood. The man was a frequent visitor at the W.F. of M. headquarters in Denver and occasionally acted as Moyer's bodyguard.

Under McParland's examination, Orchard broke down, whereupon it took the detective three days to take down his story, in which he confessed to 26 murders, all of them, he said, planned by an inner circle of the W.F. of M. McParland further obtained a confession from an alleged accomplice of Orchard.

The "inner circle" implicated by Orchard's confession consisted of Haywood, Moyer, and George A. Pettibone, the latter an unofficial factotum in the affairs of the Federation. According to Orchard, the three men had been hiring him to murder mining bosses in Colorado, Idaho and other states over a period of several years. They—especially Haywood—were the brains, he only the hand of the crimes. All three were living in Denver.

The confession was not made public.

Idaho officials proceeded to Denver and presented to the Governor of Colorado their evidence against Moyer, Haywood, and Pettibone, and a request from Governor Gooding for their extradition. But there were legal difficulties in extraditing them; so the resourceful Idaho men-of-the-law decided to kidnap the two labor leaders and Pettibone.

On the night of February 17, 1906, they were arrested; Moyer at the station just as he was leaving for Kansas on some "organization business"; Pettibone at his home; and Haywood in a rooming-house near the W.F. of M. headquarters. In the morning they were put in a special car, Idaho-bound.

At Boise they were lodged in the penitentiary, and later transferred to the county jail at Caldwell. They stayed in prison for eighteen months while the preparation for the historical trial went on.

II

Now Debs raised a cry: "Arouse, ye Slaves! Their only crime is loyalty to the working class!" He wanted to organize an army in the manner of John Brown (whom he admired above all other characters in American history) and march to Idaho and free Haywood, Moyer, and Pettibone by force. But fortunately Debs had a level-headed wife who kept him from embarking upon many a wild venture. Instead of going to Idaho, he wrote melodramatic editorials in the *Appeal to Reason*.

Other Socialist papers the country over raised the cry of "Frameup!" The kidnapping of Haywood, Moyer, and Pettibone was an effort on the part of the capitalists to ruin the W.F. of M. They charged that the Steunenberg murder was part of a plot to discredit labor before

the great American public. In this theory, Orchard, the instrument of 107
the crime, was an agent of the capitalists, and the confession and evidence obtained from him were all pre-arranged between the detectives and Orchard himself. Daniel De Leon's paper, *The People*, reminded its readers that in the railway strike in 1894 it was the capitalists who set the cars afire at Chicago in order to furnish an excuse for sending Federal troops to suppress the strike; that in 1903 in Colorado it was the Mine-Owners' Association that hired thugs to derail trains, blow up mines, and railroad stations. The greedy capitalists were capable of doing anything to advance their interests, to crush labor.

Another suggestion made by the Socialists was that Steunenberg had been mixed up in land frauds and was killed by some enemy he had made in that quarter. Much was made of the fact that Borah, attorney for the prosecution, had recently had some connection with such deals, and had been Steunenberg's friend and personal counsel. As a matter of fact, the president of the lumber company of which Borah was the attorney was in the same jail with Haywood, Moyer, and Pettibone for fraudulently locating certain timber claims.

The case was front-page news throughout the United States, in England, on the Continent. Magazines printed endless articles. *McClure's* ran Orchard's autobiography, written in prison; an amazing yarn which could not have been made up by anyone whose imaginative powers did not measure up to those of a Defoe. One of the editors of the magazine, who had interviewed the man, insisted, in an introductory note to the story, that Orchard's mind was "absolutely devoid of imagination...sane to the point of bleakness...direct, practical, concrete." The *Independent* referred to Haywood and his fellow prisoners as the "Molly Maguires of the West."

Radical labor organizations began to raise defense funds, which by the time the trial began approached $250,000. The best legal talent in the country was engaged to defend the three men. E. F. Richardson of Denver, perhaps the ablest criminal lawyer in Colorado and a partner of United States Senator Thomas M. Patterson, became the chief counsel of the defense, with Clarence Darrow—just turned fifty—as second in command, but, with his dramatic ability, easily the most picturesque figure on the staff.

III

There was a great hullabaloo over the fact that the men had not been legally extradited. An application was made to the United States Supreme

Court for a writ of *habeas corpus*, which was denied eight to one, Justice McKenna dissenting. In his minority report he declared the kidnaping was a crime, pure and simple, perpetrated by the States of Idaho and Colorado.

Debs wrote about the Supreme Court decision:

> Kidnaping, then, being a legitimate practice, we all have a perfect right to engage in it. Let us take advantage of the opening. For every workingman kidnaped a capitalist must be seized and held for ransom... The kidnaping of the first capitalist will convulse the nation and reverse the Supreme Court.

Feeling throughout the country ran high, pro and con. When Maxim Gorky visited the United States, he wired the men in the Caldwell jail "greetings from the workers of Russia," to which Haywood replied that their being in jail was an incident in "the class struggle which is the same in America as in Russia and in all other countries." Immediately after this a howl went up against Gorky in regard to his wife, who had come from Russia with him. American moralists, among them Mark Twain, objected to the fact that Gorky had never been legally married to the woman, although they had lived together many years. Prior to his exchange of telegrams with Haywood there had been no objection to his common-law marriage. Now he was thrown out of hotels, viciously attacked in the press, and finally forced to leave the country.

President Roosevelt addressed a letter to another politician in which he grouped together Moyer, Haywood, Debs, and E. H. Harriman, the bribe-paying capitalist, as types of "undesirable citizens." Haywood replied from jail calling T. R.'s attention to the fact that, according to law, one was considered innocent until proved guilty, adding that a man in Roosevelt's position should be the last to judge until the case was decided in court. Many people, not otherwise sympathetic to Haywood, agreed with him. Roosevelt then elaborated:

> Messrs. Moyer, Haywood, and Debs stand as representatives of those men who have done as much to discredit the labor movement as the most speculative financiers or most unscrupulous employers of labor and debauchers of legislatures have done to discredit honest capitalists and fair-dealing business men. They stand as representatives of those men who... habitually stand as guilty of incitement to or apology for bloodshed and violence. If that does not constitute

undesirable citizenship, then there can never be any undesirable citizen.

Debs, in the *Appeal to Reason*, returned the attack with his usual fury:

He [Roosevelt] uttered a lie as black and damnable, a calumny as foul and atrocious, as ever issued from a human throat. The men he thus traduced and vilified, sitting in their prison cells for having dutifully served their fellow workers and having spurned the bribes of their masters, transcend immeasurably the man in the White House, who with the cruel malevolence of a barbarian has pronounced their doom.

Tens of thousands of men, women, and college boys began to wear buttons inscribed: I AM AN UNDESIRABLE CITIZEN.

IV

The trial of Haywood was set for May 9, 1907. The prosecutors in Idaho had given out the information that the evidence against him and his two fellow prisoners was ample to convict and hang them; that, indeed, should they be returned to Colorado, they could be convicted of, and hanged for, at least a dozen other atrocious murders there. Men prominent in the labor circles in Denver and elsewhere privately shook their heads and said that "things looked bad for Bill" while publicly, of course, they denounced the "frame-up."

Then—in the first days of May—tremendous proletarian demonstrations occurred in the larger cities all over the United States. On May 4, Fifth Avenue in New York was wholly blocked with a procession from sundown till late in the night. The marchers carried Chinese lanterns, banners, flags, transparencies, all swaying to the strains of the *Marseillaise*. On the banners were inscriptions—

ROOSEVELT CAN SHOW HIS TEETH—WE ARE NOT AFRAID. WE STAND BY OUR BROTHERS IN IDAHO

At the same time another procession was in progress on Lexington Avenue, two blocks away, just as orderly and colorful as the one on Fifth Avenue—banners, Roman candles, Greek fire, red flags, bands playing the *Marseillaise*. In both processions from 80,000 to 100,000 people participated.

On the same day Debs wrote in the *Appeal to Reason*:

Let every workingman who has a heart in his breast make a mighty oath that not a wheel shall turn in this country from ocean to ocean until the verdict is set aside and every one of the accused is set free. Let our factories be closed; let our mills stop grinding flour and our bakeries stop baking bread. Let our coal mines close, and let us die of hunger and cold if necessary to make our protest heeded. Let us show the world that the workingmen of America are not so lost to shame, not so devoid of the red blood of courage, that they will allow one of their comrades to suffer death at the hands of their enemies. Hurrah for the Great National General Strike!

V

Now, suddenly, the conviction of Haywood became unlikely.

The trial that followed was more than fair to the defense. The defense had a huge fund. Orchard's story was left uncorroborated. Not, however, that the trial was uninteresting; on the contrary it was full of brilliant clashes between the prosecution and the defense, and startling testimony.

Ed Boyce, a former president of the Western Federation of Miners, for instance, admitted on the witness stand that in 1896 he had "earnestly hoped to hear the martial tread of 25,000 armed miners before the next convention." To which, years later, Bill Haywood remarked in his book: "It gave me a thrill of the old days to hear Ed testify."

The picturesque Darrow called Orchard "the most monumental liar that ever existed," although Prof. Hugo Münsterberg, the eminent Harvard psychologist, who went to Boise for the purpose of making a study of Orchard, announced his belief that the man's confession was "true throughout." But the defense admitted that, when Orchard was arrested, Haywood had wired immediately to the W.F. of M. lawyers to look after his case, and never denied that Orchard had murdered Steunenberg.

William Borah made a long speech, brilliant in spots, but ineffective as a whole. He obviously was not doing his best. He said:

If Orchard had not turned State's evidence, he would now be on trial, and the eminent counsel from Chicago would be defending him with all the eloquence he possesses instead of denouncing him as the most despicable monster on earth.

Richardson spoke nine hours for the defense. Then Darrow for eleven hours. "He stood big and broad-shouldered," as Haywood describes him, "dressed in a slouchy gray suit, a wisp of hair down across his forehead, his glasses in his hand, clasped by the nosepiece." He sketched the history of the W.F. of M., the troubles in Coeur d'Alene in the nineties, then he came to the present trial, which, he said, was but an attempt to put Haywood out of the way.

> To kill him, gentlemen! [he cried.] I want to speak to you plainly. Mr. Haywood is not my greatest concern. Other men have died before him. Other men have been martyrs to a holy cause since the world began. Wherever men have looked upward and onward, forgotten their selfishness, struggled for humanity, worked for the poor and the weak, they have been sacrificed... They have met their death, and Haywood can meet his if you twelve men say he must.
>
> But gentlemen, you short-sighted men of the prosecution, you men of the Mine Owners' Association, you people who would cure hatred with hate, you who think you can crush out the feelings and the hopes and the aspirations of men by tying a noose around his neck, you who are seeking to kill him, not because he is Haywood, but because he represents a class, oh, don't be so blind, don't be so foolish as to believe that if you make three fresh new graves you will kill the labor movement of the world.
>
> I want to say to you, gentlemen, Bill Haywood can't die unless you kill him. You have got to tie the rope. You twelve men of Idaho, the burden will be on you. If at the behest of this mob, you should kill Bill Haywood, he is mortal, he will die, and I want to say to you that a million men will take up the banner of labor at the open grave where Haywood lays it down, and in spite of prisons or scaffolds or fire, in spite of prosecution or jury, these men of willing hands will carry it on to victory in the end.
>
> The legislature, in 1902, was asked to pass that law which the Constitution commanded them to pass, and what did it do? Mr. Guggenheim and Mr. Moffatt and the Mine Owners' Association and all the good people of Colorado who lived by the sweat and blood of their fellow men—all of those invaded the chambers of the House and the Senate and said: "No, you must not pass an eight-hour law; true, the Constitution requires it; but here is our gold, which is stronger than the Constitution." The legislature met and discussed the matter. Haywood was there; the labor organizations were there pleading then, as they have always pleaded for the poor, the weak, the oppressed...

If you kill him, your act will be applauded by many; if you should decree Haywood's death, in the great railroad offices of our great cities men will sing your praises. If you decree his death, amongst the spiders and vultures of Wall Street will go up paeans of praise for those twelve men who killed Bill Haywood... In almost every bank in the world, where men wish to get rid of agitators and disturbers, where men put in prison one who fights for the poor and against the accursed system upon which they live and grow fat, from all these you will receive blessings and praise that you have killed him.

But if you free him there are still those who will reverently bow their heads and thank you twelve men for the character you have saved. Out on the broad prairies, where men toil with their hands; out on the broad ocean, where men are sailing the ships; through our mills and factories; down deep under the earth, men who suffer, women and children weary with care and toil...will kneel tonight and ask their God to guide your judgments...to save Haywood's life.

Haywood thought it was a great speech.

On July 28, the jury, which consisted mostly of poor farmers, acquitted Haywood in compliance with the instruction from the trial judge.

Darrow said: "The trial has been fair, the judge impartial, and the counsel considerate. We have no complaint to make," although but a few days before the Socialist and labor press had referred to the judge and the prosecution as "corporation vultures and vipers."

Some time later Moyer and Pettibone were freed too. Orchard drew life imprisonment and turned religious.

VI

The radical labor movement was openly triumphant. Debs said that the powerful interests prosecuting Haywood had realized during the trial that a conviction would have a decided bearing on the approaching national election and, accordingly, "brought their influence to bear upon the court in favor of acquittal... This," he added, "in my judgment accounts for the instructions of the court, which amounted to a plea in favor of the defendant for the verdict resulting in his acquittal." The victory was great. In his *History of the American Working Class*, Anthony Bimba says that Haywood, Moyer, and Pettibone "were saved from the gallows by the militant section of the working class."

One of the jurors in Haywood's case was reported to have said: "The
jurors all thought Haywood guilty, but some of them said the State,
under the prosecution, had not made out a case against the prisoner.
Gilman, myself, Burns, and Gess were for conviction in spite of the
judge's instruction. Gess weakened at midnight and went over to the
other side. Burns followed soon after. That left Gilman and me to argue
against ten men. It was hard work, especially in the face of the instruction from the bench and the cutting out of so much testimony. And as
Orchard was not corroborated, Gilman and myself went over to the
majority."

The Chicago *Tribune* said editorially:

> The verdict sets Haywood free, but public opinion has not cleared
> him. Under the Idaho statute the jury could not convict on Orchard's
> testimony, even if they believed it, unless it was supported by cor-
> roborative evidence. Public opinion, however, is not bound by the
> Idaho statute. The public believes that Orchard's story is substan-
> tially true.

During Haywood's imprisonment the membership of the Western
Federation of Miners and the Industrial Workers of the World (with
which I deal in the next chapter) increased over 10,000. Haywood was a
hero to a vast multitude of workers even outside the W.F. of M. When
the news of his acquittal spread through the mining districts there was
great jubilation among the boys.

Says Haywood in his book:

> Perhaps tons of dynamite were exploded in the celebration. In
> Goldfield when I went there later they showed me dents that had
> been made in the mahogany bars in the saloons by the hobnails
> of the boys who had danced to celebrate their joy at my release.
> There is no way of estimating how much whisky was drunk for the
> occasion.

Haywood was regarded with respect and awe by the public at large,
in spite of the Chicago *Tribune*'s editorials. Some of those who publicly
denounced him secretly admired him. Everybody believed him guilty
of complicity in Orchard's deeds; he really never denied anything definitely or emphatically. He believed in violence, openly advocated and
practiced it. There was in him none of the tendency to be one thing
secretly and another publicly, the tendency that four years later—in the

McNamara case—involved the leaders of the American Federation of Labor in a disgusting mess.

Haywood's violence was, to use Sorel's phrase, a "clear and brutal expression of the class war," Bakunin-like, consistent, almost heroic and inspiring, and, from a certain angle, constructive in a social way. It was, in brief, revolutionary, not "racketeering." Although the press and the pulpit denounced him, deep down in its heart the country felt instinctively that he was no mere murderer, not an "undesirable citizen." His violence was a reaction, a response to the brutality of the employers. Behind it was the hunger and desperation of thousands of his fellow workers.

CHAPTER 16
THE WOBBLIES

Already in 1903 there was talk within the Western Federation of Miners about starting a movement to join the entire working class of the United States, indeed of the whole world, into one general *revolutionary* organization—"One Big Union"—formed upon industrial rather than trade lines. It was a typically Western idea—big: the sky was the limit.

Then, at the 1904 convention of the W.F. of M. the leaders were instructed "to start the ball rolling." Accordingly on January 2, 1905, a secret conference was held in Chicago, in a small hall which, twenty years earlier, had often been used by the anarchists. Bill Haywood, a leading spirit of the new movement, was made chairman, and, lacking a gavel, he picked up a loose piece of board that lay on the platform, rapped for order, and bellowed:

> Fellow workers!… The aims and objects of this organization shall be to put the working class in possession of the economic power, the means of life, in control of the machinery of production and distribution, without regard to capitalist masters.

About 100,000 organized workers were represented at the conference by 32 delegates, among whom were also such representatives-at-large of the proletariat as Eugene Debs, Daniel De Leon, Mother Jones, and Lucy Parsons widow of one of the executed Chicago anarchists.

The conference adopted a manifesto outlining plans for the new organization, which was to be on the order of the old Knights of Labor, minus all the hocus-pocus and vague uplift that used to characterize that body, plus abundant "guts" and revolutionary fervor. They decided to hold the first convention of the Industrial Workers of the World the following June, also in Chicago.

In June, 186 delegates representing thirty-four labor organizations, large and small, assembled in Chicago; made a pilgrimage *en masse* to the graves of the Haymarket anarchists; and adopted a constitution, in the preamble to which they declared that the workers and the employers "have nothing in common"...that "there can be no peace so long as hunger and want are found among millions of working people and the few who make up the capitalist class have all the good things of life." They proposed simply to take over the industries. All workers were eligible for membership, irrespective of "race, creed, color, sex, or previous condition of servitude." There were to be no big initiation fees, such as the American Federation of Labor required. Indeed, the I.W.W. purposed eventually to put the A.F. of L. out of business and, incidentally, "smash all labor fakers and traitors from Gompers and Mitchell down."

Several speakers at the convention referred to the recent revolutionary events in Russia as—to quote one of them—"an inspiration to the labor movement all over the world." Lucy Parsons spoke about "the terror felt by the capitalists of Russia at the raising of the red flag in Odessa." A resolution was passed encouraging "our Russian fellow workers on in their struggle."

Haywood was urged to become president of the new organization, but, having just been re-elected secretary-treasurer of the W.F. of M., he declined. Then a man by the name of Charles O. Sherman, a Socialist opportunist, was elected.

But as soon as Bill Haywood adjourned the first convention, bitter antagonisms began to brew among the various elements of the new outfit, which included parliamentary Socialists, opportunists, Marxists, anarchists, industrial-unionists and trade-unionists, and people who were none and all of these things. During the first year of the I.W.W.'s existence, these discordant elements fought fiercely for superiority, and very possibly the organization would have died soon after its first anniversary had it not been for the fact that in 1906 the Haywood-Moyer-Pettibone case came along, causing the leaders of the various factions to pause a while in internal strife and join hands to free "the prisoners from the clutches of capitalist law." The I.W.W. was the first organization to issue a call for defense funds and raised a good part of the amount that went to pay Clarence Darrow and other high-powered legal talent.

At the 1906 convention the struggle for supremacy finally resolved itself into two factions; one was composed of petty Socialist politicians who aimed to use the new organization in furtherance of their own ends, and the other consisted of revolutionary laborites who scorned political action in favor of "direct action," with General Strike as their ultimate means to gain control of the nation's industries. As a result of these squabbles, several organizations, the W.F. of M. included, withdrew from the amalgamation, leaving it to its own devices.

In 1908, however, the "direct action" group secured control of the movement and declared, in a new preamble to the constitution, that the struggle between capital and labor "must go on until the workers of the world organize as a class, take possession of the earth and the machinery of production, and abolish the wage system."

II

Soon after the I.W.W. had thus crystallized itself into a purely industrial-action movement, Bill Haywood began having difficulties with other big officials in the W.F. of M. and was finally removed from office, after which he became an I.W.W. organizer.

Other leaders in those early days were Vincent St. John, Elizabeth Gurley Flynn, William Trautmann, Joe Ettor, and Arturo Giovannitti; all of them people from the ranks of labor who had participated in bitter battles, suffered imprisonment or wounds.

St. John was then in his mid-thirties. He had been a delivery-boy, farm-hand, tinner, printer, upholsterer, miner. At eighteen he had drifted into the W.F. of M. country in Colorado and joined that organization. In 1900 he was elected president of the local union at Telluride and managed a strike in 1901. He was arrested with other agitators and driven out of the region by State authorities. In 1903 we find him in Coeur d'Alene organizing the miners there. He was arrested in connection with the Steunenberg murder, but was released after three months in prison. He attended the 1906 I.W.W. convention as a W.F. of M. delegate. A convinced "direct-actionist," he worked at cross-purposes with the W.F. of M. officials who wanted to mix industrial action with politics, whereupon he resigned from the Federation and soon thereafter became a member of the I.W.W. executive board. In 1907 he was a worker and agitator in the Goldfield, Nevada, mines, and at the third I.W.W. convention was elected general organizer. During a dispute in Goldfield he was assaulted and almost beaten to death. Taken to Chicago for treatment, he recovered and became secretary-treasurer of the I.W.W.

Elizabeth Flynn was called "the Joan of Arc of labor"; a young Irishwoman, native of New Hampshire, whose career as a radical began when she organized a Socialist group of her classmates in a New York high school. When still in her teens, she soapboxed on street corners in New York and elsewhere. In 1909, having joined the I.W.W., she was imprisoned in Spokane, Washington, with 500 other wobblies (as the I.W.W. began to be called), and remained in jail till the taxpayers, wearying of paying for their keep, had them freed. Later she played an important part in the Lawrence strike.

Joe Ettor was born in the slums of Brooklyn, New York. His Italian father had taken him to Chicago as a baby. The old man, a militant radical, was severely wounded when the bomb exploded in Haymarket Square. In 1906, after the earthquake and fire, we find young Joe in San Francisco organizing the debris workers, fighting the Pinkertons, serving a short term in jail. Later he became active as a wobbly organizer in various parts of the country, and was beaten up and shot at on several occasions.

Trautmann's father had died in a mine disaster in New Zealand. Coming to the United States in 1892 as a man of thirty, Trautmann became an organizer of brewery workers. Later, as an I.W.W., he was an effective speaker and pamphleteer.

Giovannitti came from the province of Abruzzi, Italy; a poet, rather well educated. In the United States he was in turn a minter, a clerk, a theological student, a mission preacher, a tramp, editor of a small Italian radical paper in New York.

In addition, every big I.W.W. strike or agitation movement produced local leaders of surprising power and ability.

III

From 1906 to 1916 the I.W.W. engaged in some of the bitterest open fights between capital and labor ever fought in the United States. The organization was frankly revolutionary and, for a time, violent. In its battles it was frequently-opposed not only by the capitalists and the authorities but also by the A.F. of L., which a few times went so far as to furnish strikebreakers in wobbly strikes.

The wobblies first made themselves felt in the West. In 1906 and 1907 they organized workers of all occupations at Goldfield, Nevada, a small frontier town, and won the minimum wage of $4.50 per day for every kind of labor. In Portland, Oregon, they led 3,000 saw-mill workers in a six weeks' strike for a nine-hour day and an increase in wages from $1.75 to $2.50 a day, and won the fight, which increased their prestige enormously among the low-paid laborers in the West.

At the first I.W.W. convention Haywood had said: "We come out of the West to meet the textile workers of the East," and by 1907 the wobblies were already a factor in the Eastern labor movement. In Skowhegan, Maine, they organized 3,000 textile operatives and won a strike despite the A.F. of L. strikebreakers.

In the summer of 1909, at McKees Rocks, in Pennsylvania, the wobblies led 8,000 employees of the Pressed Steel Car Company, representing fourteen nationalities, in a bloody strike, pitted against the State Constabulary—"the Cossacks," as they dubbed them—lately organized on the instigation of the mine and mill owners in the State for the express purpose of putting down labor upheavals.

The Pennsylvania Cossacks were—and still are—the most ruthless and efficient anti-labor police force in the United States, but in this instance the wobblies proved themselves a match for them. One day a striker was shot by a Cossack, and then the war was on. The strike committee immediately informed the Constabulary commander that for every striker killed or injured by his men the life of a Cossack would be exacted in return, and that they were not deeply concerned as to which Cossack paid the penalty: all Cossacks looked alike to them—a life for a life! The strikers kept their word. After eleven weeks of minor hostilities a battle took place near the Pressed Steel Car Company's plant between a mob of workers and the Constabulary in which about a dozen men were killed on both sides and over fifty wounded. The Cossacks were finally driven from the streets and into the factory yard. This ended the bloodshed on both sides for the remainder of the strike, which a few days later resulted in a complete victory for the workers.

Strike! Life for a life!—that was what the wobblies meant by "direct action" in 1909. To hell with the ballot-box and the entire political shebang!...

In the autumn of 1909 the authorities at Spokane jailed all wobbly speakers who tried to address street gatherings. The I.W.W. unions resisted and sent out men and women to hold meetings, until over 500 wobblies jammed the city jail. Among them was Elizabeth Flynn. Two hundred of them went on a hunger strike, which complicated the matters for the police and the entire community. Finally, the authorities and the respectable citizenry had to yield and an ordinance was passed authorizing street speaking.

Something similar occurred in Fresno, the center of the enormously prosperous San Joaquin Valley in California, where the wobblies had taken a notion to organize the orchard workers. The Fresno police, supported by the fruit-growers, jailed over 100 wobblies. Thereupon several thousand of them—"blanket stiffs" or hobo laborers, who hiked from job to job with blanket rolls on their backs began to march from Portland, Seattle, Spokane and even Denver, all of them determined to try to hold meetings and go to jail. It was a free-speech fight. The authorities, of course, had no room for all of them in the city prison, and so, fearing a war, granted the I.W.W. civil rights in the entire region. The I.W.W. organized the workers and in the course of the next year improved their conditions to a notable extent.

IV

The outstanding incident in the early I.W.W. history, however, is the Lawrence strike.

Lawrence, Massachusetts, was a great textile center, outranking any other city in the country in the production of woolen and worsted goods, which were protected by a high tariff. Of the 85,000 population, over 35,000 were mill workers, for the most part mere tenders of machines, without skill, and principally of foreign birth, Italians pre-dominating. They were extremely ill-paid, while the output of a single company in 1911 was valued at $45,000,000. In the American Woolen Company's spinning, winding, and beaming departments and dye-houses the wages were $5.10, $6.05, $6.55, $7.15, and $7.55 a week in 1911. This was a full week only; often, when work was slack, such wages as $2.30 and $2.70 a week were the rule. Some of these workers were men with families, whose wives and children had to work to support themselves. Children were undernourished and the infant death rate was very high; for every 1,000 births there were 172 deaths under one year of age.

But until January 1912, Lawrence was a peaceful city; some of the people who did not work in the mills thought it was also a prosperous city. Then, early that month, a new State law went into effect, reducing the hours of labor for women and children from 56 to 54 a week, and the mill corporations reduced the wages proportionately, without any previous notice, while at the same time they speeded up the machines and so got 56 hours of work at 54 hours' pay.

The workers received their envelopes on January 11. "Short pay! Short pay!" was the cry. In many cases the reduction amounted to less than 30 cents a week, but it was enough to turn Lawrence on its head.

The mill managers did not expect any serious trouble.

The next morning—January 12—most of the operatives came to the mills. They were a sullen lot. Tens of thousands of them.

The looms began to turn at the usual time.

At about 9 o'clock, in one of the departments of the Everett Mill, some one let out a yell: "Goddamn it to hell! Let's strike! Strike!"

A few minutes later a mob of excited people was sweeping through the long rooms lined with machines, shouting: "Strike! Strike!" Some one produced an American flag and stuck it on a short pole. "Strike! All out; come on. All out! Strike! Strike!" Everybody shouted, rushing from room to room, arming themselves with the picker sticks used in the mills. They went from loom to loom, persuading and driving away operatives; stopping the looms, tearing weaves, smashing the machines where repeated attempts were made to run them despite their entreaties, which but seldom failed of instant response. As they swept on, their numbers grew, and with them grew the contagion, the uproar, and the turmoil.

About a thousand workers rushed out of the Everett Mill on the street and, splitting into small groups, went to the other mills, crying: "Strike! Strike! All out." Everywhere the cry was picked up, and, in an hour, tens of thousands of workers were milling the streets, while the bell in the Town Hall tolled the alarm—the first time in nineteen years—calling to duty every police officer in the city.

It was a blind, instinctive, primitive movement, which came as a complete surprise to the city, including the mill workers themselves, and sent a shiver through American industry.

Joe Ettor was in New York when he heard the news. As an I.W.W. organizer, he immediately rushed to Lawrence and in a few hours organized a strike committee. He was in his mid-twenties, with a ready smile, a natural capacity for leadership, unlimited physical vitality, considerable personal magnetism and eloquence. He addressed outdoor meetings attended by tens of thousands.

The militia came. At once small riots broke out.

Ettor had a job on his hands. Several nationalities were represented in the strike, with their different temperaments and racial antagonisms. Ettor said to the strikers: "By all means make this strike as peaceful as possible. In the last analysis, all the blood spilled will be your blood!"

The strikers behaved as well as it was humanly possible for people in their situation. They picketed the mills in masses. Where the operatives would not quit in response to their entreaties, they rushed the bridges, forced the gates and invaded the mills. "Come on, strike! Strike!" Those who did not storm the bridges ran to the freight yards and helped themselves to scantlings and coal with which they demolished the mill windows. Pistol shots were fired.

Over thirty strikers were arrested in three days. They were given no opportunity to consult counsel. They were kept in jail several weeks.

On January 19 dynamite was discovered in Lawrence in three different places: a cemetery lot, a tailor shop and a shoe shop next to a print shop where Ettor received his mail. The strikers were blamed; several more were arrested. Ettor declared the episode a "plant," which is exactly what it was. It was proved later beyond doubt that the bombs were planted by agents of the mill owners, eager to create a public opinion hostile to the strikers.

Ettor staged great mass demonstrations. He spoke a dozen times daily, urging the people to refrain from violence and beware of *agents provocateurs*.

On January 20 Arturo Giovannitti came from New York in the interest of *Il Proletario*, an Italian Socialist paper which he edited. He threw himself immediately into the strike. A powerful, incisive speaker, he became a great factor in keeping up the spirit of his countrymen. "Capitalism is the same here as in the Old Country," he said to great audiences. "Nobody cares for you. You are considered mere machine—less than machines. If any effort is made to improve your lot and to raise you to the dignity of manhood and womanhood, that effort must come from yourselves alone."

Giovannitti was a friend of Ettor. Ettor put him in charge of the relief work. It was winter; strikers and their families were cold and hungry. Giovannitti sent out appeals for food and clothing.

Then, on January 29, a girl striker, Annie LoPizzo, was shot dead on a street corner in a riot which resulted from police and militia interfering with picketing.

It was never determined who fired the shot that killed the girl, but Ettor and Giovannitti were arrested, charged with "inciting and procuring the commission of the crime in pursuit of an unlawful conspiracy." They were held as "accessories before the act."

The arrests were an attempt to deprive the strike of leadership and break it. Bail for Ettor and Giovannitti was refused.

But then Bill Haywood came and took charge of the strike committee. With him came also Trautmann and Elizabeth Flynn.

The strike now practically resolved itself into a question of endurance. Enormous pressure was brought to bear upon the strike committee. All sorts of attempts were made to stampede the workers back into the mills. The American Federation of Labor attempted to discredit the I.W.W. leaders with the strikers. The militia obstructed the relief measures, which continued although Giovannitti was in prison.

One of the most disturbing and heart-breaking features was the plight of the strikers' children. Hundreds of them had no appropriate food. So, under Haywood's leadership, the strikers adopted the French and Italian method of strike relief, that is, of sending children to relatives and friends in other cities. Haywood figured that without the cries of hungry children the strikers would be able to hold out longer.

Thus over 400 children were sent to Boston, Barre, Vermont, and New York City, with the consent of parents and under the care of physicians and nurses. Their departure lightened the strikers' burdens considerably, but incensed the mill owners and authorities of Lawrence; for this child migration received a good deal of publicity, highly unfavorable to Lawrence, branding the city as a starvation-wage industrial center.

So steps were taken to prevent further departures. On February 24, a party of 40 children with their escorts assembled at the station to go to Philadelphia, when the police appeared and began to tear the children from their parents, clubbing the latter, throwing them into patrol wagons. Thirty arrests were made. Among those hurt were pregnant women, miscarriages resulting. The militia, drawn up outside the station, "maintained order," while inside the police attacked women and children.

This brutality made matters worse for Lawrence. It provoked nation-wide indignation. One of the United States Senators hurried to Lawrence for a personal investigation and Congress ordered an official inquiry into the situation. The most conservative papers directed scathing remarks at the Lawrence textile interests.

The mill officials invited the strike committee to come and effect a settlement. On March 12 the strike was over, the workers winning an increase in wages of from 5 to 25 percent.

The Ettor-Giovannitti case, however, dragged well into the fall of 1912. The two labor leaders, no doubt, would have been railroaded to prison or perhaps even executed, were it not for the fact that the interests of Massachusetts feared an I.W.W. general strike movement among the low-paid textile and shoe workers of the State.

On November 23 both Ettor and Giovannitti were cleared of the charge and freed. Among those most active in the agitation that led to their liberation was Nicola Sacco.

V

Almost simultaneously with the Lawrence strike, the wobblies engaged in a violent free-speech fight in San Diego, California; most of the violence being perpetrated by the police and vigilante committees.

In December 1911, immediately after the confession of the McNamara brothers in Los Angeles, the San Diego City Council, in response to the urging of merchants, adopted an ordinance barring street-speaking in the center of the city. Fifty blocks were closed. Socialists, single-taxers, the wobblies, and other groups at once formed the California Free Speech League to fight for their common rights. The day the law took effect, 40 speakers were arrested. They were held without trial under excessive bail. A hundred more were soon added, jamming the jails. Overcrowding, bad food, illness, brutality, marked their confinement.

The I.W.W. sent out a call for men to come to San Diego and overcrowd the prisons still more. When the wobblies began to arrive, the reactionary press called for hanging and shooting without trial. The police threw a mounted guard along the county line to turn them back. The fight lasted eight months, in which period scores were seized, beaten, tarred-and-feathered. One group of wobblies was forced to kiss the flag at the point of guns, another to run a gauntlet of thugs who beat them with clubs and whips. One labor man, not a wobbly, was kidnaped, taken into the desert, and warned to keep on going on pain of death if he returned. In the city, the fire hose was turned on those who attempted to speak and on their audiences, injuring many. Finally, in a clash with the police, a wobbly was killed and two policemen were wounded.

That was the end of the fight. The I.W.W. won it.

Four years later, at Everett, Washington, the wobblies fought an even bloodier free speech fight. It started in a strike of the A.F. of L. shingle-weavers, when the police and gunmen broke up picket lines and meetings. The I.W.W. decided then to try their hand at "opening up the town." They tried to rent halls, but were beaten up and run out of town. Then they charted two tow-boats in Seattle and came sailing into the port of Everett, three hundred strong, singing "Hold the fort, for we are coming." They were met by a fusillade of rifle shots, many of the rifles in the hands of deputies recruited by the lumber interests.

Five wobblies lay dead on the decks; others fell into the sea; thirty-one were wounded. The wobblies were unarmed, but two sheriffs were killed and sixteen wounded—by crossfire, the defense contended in the trials, due to firing on the boats from three sides. All the remaining I.W.W. were arrested. Seventy-four were charged with murder. They were tortured and beaten. Of the men charged with murder, one was brought to trial in Seattle and after several months acquitted. The others were freed earlier. None of the deputies who fired on men merely seeking to land in town to speak on the streets was arrested or prosecuted. The sheriff in charge of them later got a State job.

But the wobblies won the fight. Free speech was established in Everett, and the wobblies were even permitted to hire a hall as well as hold street meetings without molestation.

In 1914 there was the Joe Hill case in Utah, a classical example of the "frame-up" used against labor. A strike against the Utah Construction Company occurred at Bingham Canyon. It was, like most wobbly strikes, a success. The I.W.W. song writer, Joe Hill, was the chief agitator and organizer. He was arrested in Salt Lake City for the murder of a local grocer, of whom, no doubt, Joe had never heard before. He was tried and convicted; he appealed and lost. Then started a period of defense activity not unlike that in the Sacco-Vanzetti case, years after. The Governor's mansion was inundated with letters and telegrams. Foreign ambassadors, and even President Wilson, were induced to appeal for clemency in the case. Protest meetings were held in all parts of the world. But all to no avail. On November 17, 1915, Joe Hill faced a firing squad in the yard of the Utah Penitentiary. His body was sent to Chicago, and his funeral was almost as large, if not so impressive, as that of the Haymarket Anarchists.

VI

One of the original aims of the I.W.W. as I have mentioned, was to put the A.F. of L. out of business and sweep the trade unions into the wobbly movement. In this they failed utterly, for the wobblies, almost from the very beginning of their existence, directed their best energies to improve the lot of the lowest class of industrial workers. These, as foreigners or because they owned no property, had practically no rights, no standing in society, and, although their numbers ran into millions, were of no consequence in the politics of the country. The average trade unionist had no concern for the ignorant, helpless foreigners in textile mills, nor for the American working class as a whole. He would not join the wobblies in their free-speech campaigns and other movements to win rights for the underdog. In the first place, he had but slight concern for the underdog; as a skilled mechanic, he was sometimes called "the aristocrat of labor." In the second place, it was all he could do to look out for himself. He usually had a family, or planned to have one. He had a little property, or hoped to acquire some. He had communal responsibilities and a standing in the social scheme. Most of the active wobblies, on the other hand, were footloose men, unmarried, without property or communal responsibilities. It was comparatively easy for them to go out and fight for the underdog, go to jail for the sake of the American working class and enjoy the pleasures of martyrdom. So he, the trade unionist, let the unattached wobblies do the dirty work and, now and then, to enhance his standing in the community, even joined the respectable mob in the chorus of abuse that it directed at the I.W.W.

When the United States entered the World War, the A.F. of L. joined in the campaign against the wobblies, helping to send them to prisons for long terms by the hundreds.

VII

Following the strike in McKees Rocks, the wobblies refrained almost completely from violence. All the violence in I.W.W. strikes and free-speech campaigns between 1910 and 1916, as we have seen, was perpetrated by the police, the militia, and hired gunmen. After McKees Rocks the I.W.W. used mainly what they called "the force of numbers."

In 1912 or thereabouts, the wobblies discovered another weapon—sabotage. But since it was not employed by them very extensively and effectively until after the World War, I will deal with it in a later chapter.

PART FOUR
THE McNAMARA
AFFAIR

"J.B. McNamara is not a murderer
at heart."
—*CLARENCE DARROW*

CHAPTER 17
GENERAL CAPITAL-LABOR
SITUATION: 1905–1910

The wave of radicalism that had begun to roll over the United States
in the first decade of the twentieth century grew amazingly as the
decade approached its end. The people were beginning to realize more
clearly that they were being caught in a combination of circumstances
distinctly unfavorable to their economic and social advancement. Indeed,
this development of the existing system threatened to crush them into
poverty while steadily enhancing the power of a comparatively small
class of capitalists, whose power already was far too great. Legally and
otherwise, capital continued to concentrate. It was organized against
labor and against the public at large. If, now and then, labor succeeded
in coercing capital to give it an increase of wages, capital immediately
increased the price of products, and thus the public, which included
labor, actually paid for the increase.

The struggle between the have-nots and the haves grew ever fiercer.
The American Federation of Labor, as already suggested, gave the labor movement a stability it had hitherto lacked. But this, together with
such wild-and-woolly doings as the "Debs Rebellion" and the western
miners' strikes, only incited the capitalists to ever more efficient and
organized opposition. The A.F. of L. unions, although called "conservative," appeared to the majority of employers to be as dangerous to their
interests as was Haywood's gang of outlaws. True, the coal operators had
managed to handle John Mitchell rather neatly in 1902, but who could
say with certainty that the movement would not eventually come under
the control of some one less diplomatic, less susceptible to flattery and
public opinion? Many capitalists thought they ought to take no chances.
There was great potency in labor unionism even under such leaders as
Gompers and Mitchell. Hardly any employer escaped annoyance from
them. Most of the unions were "unreasonable," and it seemed that the
stronger they grew, the more "unreasonable" they became in their demands. Some labor leaders could be "handled" in one way or another;

but, then, why pay graft to a lot of petty crooks who used the workers to advance themselves?

Some employers' organizations and individual capitalists, in the first decade of the twentieth century, recognized, with Theodore Roosevelt, the right of labor to organize. They declared their willingness to deal with "reasonable" unions, for, they said, industry after all was business, and labor was an important element in it. Most employers' associations, however, were formed to *fight* the unions. Their philosophy was that industry was *war*, and they proposed to use any weapons at their command. For every weapon that labor could lift they must have a counter-weapon.

The unions demanded "closed shop" (closed to non-union men); the employers were for "open shop," or the "American Plan," as they began to call their anti-union policy. The industrialists were for "Industrial Freedom." America was a free country, and any worker in America ought to be free to work for any wage, at any task, anywhere he chose. And so they fought the unions' boycott with the blacklist, the sympathetic strike with the sympathetic lockout, dynamite with gunfire, and so on. Besides, as already mentioned, they had a tool in the courts that labor could not wrest from their hands.

For a time it was difficult to determine which group—labor or capital—was on the defensive, though, of course, in retrospect it is plain that the struggle was always in favor of the employers.

II

The American Federation of Labor conducted few strikes, using, instead, the "union label" and the boycott to force its will upon the industries. Workers and people sympathetic to labor were urged to buy only goods produced by union labor, marked with the union label. This forced many manufacturers to let the unions come into their shops. Conversely, those manufacturers who were unwilling to have their shops unionized found themselves on the A.F. of L.'s boycott list, and workers and their sympathizers throughout the country were urged not to buy their goods, for they were "unfair" to labor. In this way no end of stubborn "open shop" manufacturers were driven to the wall.

Several years before there had been written into the statute books of the country the so-called Sherman Anti-Trust Law, which declared illegal "*every* contract, combination in the form of trust or otherwise, or conspiracy, in restraint of trade or commerce among the several States or with foreign nations," and the boycotted manufacturers began to se-

cure injunctions against the unions under its provisions. The A.F. of L.
was declared a "trust" which was not incorrect; but at the same time
there were in the United States over 500 capitalistic trusts that daily
violated the law, and for which the Sherman Act did not exist.

Between 1900 and 1910 the A.F. of L. conducted several hundred
boycotts and faced dozens of injunctions.

The most famous boycott injunction case was the Buck Stove and
Range Company of St. Louis *versus* the A.F. of L. and a number of its
officials. The records in the case are voluminous, but the main incidents
are simple and, briefly, as follows:

In August 1906 some metal polishers in the complainant's factory
struck, whereupon the Metal Polishers' Union of St. Louis declared the
company "unfair," published that declaration in a labor paper, issued
circulars to the same effect, and sought otherwise to urge the working
people not to buy its stoves and ranges. In November the St. Louis
Central Labor Council endorsed the boycott. The same month, at its
regular convention, the A.F. of L. sanctioned it, and some time later the
company's name appeared in the "We Don't Patronize" list in its official
organ, *The American Federationist*, and in circulars sent to local unions
all over the country.

Within a few months the sales of the Buck stoves and ranges
dropped from over 1,000,000 a year to almost nothing. Dealers all
over the country informed the company that owing to the pressure and
threats of boycotts on themselves by the local unions, they were compelled to cease handling its products.

Then the company secured, from a judge of the Supreme Court
of the District of Columbia, a sweeping injunction against the A.F. of
L. The case dragged through the courts for years. In March 1909 the
Court of Appeals of the District of Columbia sustained the injunction,
observing that "in our opinion, it is more important to wage-earners
than to employers of labor that we declare this combination unlawful, for if wage-earners may combine to interfere with the lawful business of employers, it follows that employers may combine to coerce
their employees"—as if they had not done so already in innumerable
instances!

The A.F. of L., through its officers—notably President Gompers,
who was also editor of the *Federationist*—took the stand that the injunction prohibited the exercise of the constitutional rights of free speech
and freedom of the press, and hence was unconstitutional and void.
Gompers and Frank Morrison, the secretary, and John Mitchell, a vice-

president of the A.F. of L., publicly violated the injunction and were found guilty of contempt of court, for which Gompers was sentenced to a year in prison, Mitchell to nine months, and Morrison to six. The Court of Appeals upheld the sentence, after which the case was taken to the Supreme Court of the United States.

Gompers, Morrison, and Mitchell never went to jail but the effect of the case, as it dragged through the years, was deep and widespread. The most conservative labor unions perceived that the courts of the country were against labor. All of a sudden, the A.F. of L. became a militant organization. The politic Gompers was beginning to lose his temper. He issued solemn warnings to the capitalists and the Government. For once even the Socialists applauded Gompers. He was a hero. He would go to jail. He stormed up and down the country. Demonstrations were organized in honor of "the martyrs to the cause of liberty." Gompers was asking: "Why isn't the Sherman Act enforced against the capitalistic trusts, whose improper, anti-social doings have provoked its passage? Why is it used against labor, when it was originally intended to curb capitalistic trusts?" He called upon an unheeding Congress to pass an amendment to the Sherman law, making it inapplicable to labor organizations.

The A.F. of L. was seeing red. Gompers, of course, continued anti-Socialist, but unempathetically; while within the trades unions the Socialist and the strong-arm elements gained influence by leaps and bounds.

III

And, as already suggested, there was a definite drift toward radicalism among the petty middle-class. The muckrakers continued to turn out reams of copy for *McClure's, Everybody's,* the *Cosmopolitan;* and, incredible as it may seem today, before the end of the decade even the *Saturday Evening Post,* already with a circulation of over a million, began to publish long political and sociological articles written from a definitely radical standpoint. Lincoln Steffens fumed about The Shame of the Cities. Upton Sinclair's story of the stockyards continued to upset people's stomachs. The *Appeal to Reason* had a regular circulation of over 500,000; the *Jewish Daily Forward* in New York of over 100,000. The child-labor question aroused much feeling.

The Socialist movement grew amazingly. Debs's presidential campaign in 1908 was most effective propaganda work. The candidate, with a staff of campaign workers, traveled from coast to coast in his "Red

Special," and in three months addressed over 500,000 people. Tom
Mooney, who eight years later was to go to San Quentin Prison for a
crime he never committed, was a member of the "Red Special" party,
distributing millions of copies of Socialist pamphlets and leaflets.

Socialism compelled notice in the political and economic life of the
United States. In the spring of 1910 the Socialist Party experienced its
first success at the polls, which was followed by more victories in the fall
and in 1911. Milwaukee and Schenectady elected Socialist mayors. St.
Louis nearly went Socialist. The States of New York, Massachusetts,
Pennsylvania, Minnesota, and Rhode Island had Socialists in the legislatures. Victor Berger went to Congress. By the autumn of 1911 over
500 Socialists were elected to office. In May 1911 the *Atlantic Monthly*
published as its leading article of the month a piece entitled "Prepare
for Socialism."

***

Such, in brief, was the American social scene, viewed from the
angle of the class struggle, when the most dramatic, if not the most
important episode in the history of the American labor movement—
the McNamara affair—occurred and took the militant spirit out of the
American Federation of Labor.

CHAPTER 18
THE A.F. OF L. DYNAMITERS

"**V**IOLENCE," testified Samuel Gompers before the Congressional Committee on the Judiciary in 1900, "is not a recognized part of labor's plan of campaign... Labor needs to be strong in numbers, in effective organization, in the justice of its cause, and in the reasonableness of its methods. It relies on moral suasion." He deplored and condemned with righteous vehemence the ideas and actions of the Chicago Anarchists, the Western Federation of Miners, Debs, and the wobblies. He was "unalterably opposed to violence and sabotage." He referred to the industrial conflict as "warfare," but, to all seeming, so far as it concerned the A.F. of L., it was legalistic, polite warfare.

However, while Gompers orated and editorialized on the subject, there was employed by the unions in the A.F. of L. more—certainly better organized—violence than by the radical outlaw movements which he denounced. In an interview published in the New York *World* (June 7, 1903), Gompers admitted strong-arm tactics in his unions, but went on to remark that that was the concern of the police authorities. The public must not expect the unions to turn over the rioter or terrorist, for that "would be prejudicing his case before it went to the jury... The labor union deals with the economic conditions of work; the Government deals with questions of law and order."

As the head of a great labor amalgamation formed for narrowly selfish ends, one of whose means for attaining those ends was a show of idealism, righteousness, and respectability in imitation of upper-class pretenses, Gompers could hardly be expected to behave with less duplicity than he did. It was inevitable in his position that he should, on the one hand, spout pious hokum and, on the other, indirectly and secretly participate in violence. The average big labor leader must suffer all the vicissitudes of the political leader in a modern democracy. If he strives to lead the less educated and balanced workmen by the light that glows in him, he may soon be an ex-leader, unless that light happens to be as fitful and irrational a flicker as the feelings of his followers. The intrigues that center about a big labor leader's desk are as underhanded and perilous as those which make the life of the average Prime Minister in the Balkans the thrilling experience it is.

Apart from the question of the wisdom of strong-arm tactics in the labor struggle, one must find Bill Haywood's and, later, the I.W.W.'s frank advocacy and practice of violence and sabotage immeasurably more sympathetic than the attitude and practices of the A.F. of L. unions. Haywood and the wobblies honestly and openly recognized violence and sabotage as inherent and necessary phases of the struggle, and openly welcomed them. The A.F. of L. leaders denounced dynamite tactics with holy horror, yet their unions engaged in them and, in so doing, commanded, if not the moral, certainly the material support of the Federation's high leadership. This duplicity operated to the great detriment, I believe, not so much of the unions actually practicing destruction of property, thuggery, and murder, as of the labor movement at large. It turned out—during the McNamara case—to be one of the greatest weaknesses of the American trade-union movement; but a weakness, as I have hinted, that was inherent in the A.F. of L.

II

The building trades took the lead in terrorism within the A.F. of L., and of these the most terroristic were the Iron Workers. The International Association of Bridge and Structural Iron Workers, to give this union its full name, was formed in 1896 at a convention in Pittsburgh at which five local unions, from New York, Buffalo, Boston, Pittsburgh, and Chicago, were represented. Steel-building was then a comparatively new trade. The first skyscraper, or what then passed for one, had been erected in Chicago in the late eighties, followed by others in rapid succession. The men employed were ordinarily engaged in bridge-building. In 1891, as their trade expanded to other structures, they reorganized their Bridge-Carpenters' Union into the Bridge and Construction Men's Union of Chicago, which in 1896 became Local No. 1 of the new Iron Workers Association.

The trade required little skill; almost any husky young man with good nerves could pick up all its tricks in a short time. The iron-workers' wages, when they first organized, were much lower than those of other men with whom they came together on the job. The carpenters, for instance, whose craft called for long apprenticeship, had been organized and had fought for higher wages throughout the nineteenth century.

At first the iron-workers' trade was considered inferior not alone by the employers but by fellow mechanics belonging to other trades.

However, as the buildings rose higher and higher, the tasks grew more and more hazardous, and soon the iron-workers' trade became the most venturesome and romantic of all building trades. Only men of great physical strength and courage became skyscraper men; putting their lives in daily danger as they did, they developed a psychology of recklessness and violence that people in less hazardous occupations may find difficulty in understanding. And there are other factors in the iron-workers' trade that must be considered in connection with their violence. "The game is a killer," says Colonel W. A. Starrett in his *Skyscrapers and the Men Who Build Them,* and continues:

> One passing a large metropolitan building under construction is apt to notice the young, virile men, with nonchalant manner, who so confidently go about their tasks. Few people stop to consider these same men after twenty-five or thirty years of this rigorous life. They are hearty eaters and gulp their food, frequently carried to the job cold; or, if bought at the ubiquitous hot-dog stand, it is generally of the fried variety with little thought of the science of dietetics. Their inordinate use of tobacco and small attention to dental hygiene, nowadays recognized as of such importance to middle-aged good health, leave them susceptible to the occupational ailments which their work sometimes engenders... The admiring spectator sees young men, but little realizes the shadow that an uncertain future is casting. [He does not see] the prematurely aged building mechanic, sometimes a pathetic figure, standing on the sidewalk week after week, in the furtive hope that a job commensurate with his now narrowed abilities is available for him.

Then, too, the bridgeman, who must take jobs removed from any habitation, leads an abnormal life. The trade does not attract the typical "good citizen," who loves to sit by the fireside, help the wife, and play with the kiddies. The iron-worker is of the roving, irresponsible class of men—strong, tough, with ready fists. His social habits are not conducive to "ideal citizenship." This was even truer in 1905 than it is today.

The majority of them were Shanty Irish, Bohunks, Dutchmen, "Squareheads," and native American toughs. It is small wonder then that, under the circumstances of the trade, the union developed such leaders as Sam Parks, who, at the beginning of the century, bossed the building trades of New York. He was a "tough guy" who prided himself on having fought as many as twenty fights a day: ignorant, a bully, a swaggerer, perhaps a criminal in his instincts, inarticulate, with no argument but his proficient and rocky fists.

III

And these men, as a union, had to deal with one of the most determined and brutal open-shop employers' organizations in the United States. The National Erectors' Association, formed in 1906, had its membership restricted to such firms as pledged themselves to the "American Plan" principle. About forty of the largest erecting concerns in the country belonged to the Association, a number of them subsidiary companies of the fanatically anti-union Steel Trust, and they waged, individually and collectively, a relentless war against the Iron Workers, who, as the lowest paid of the building trades, were trying hardest to improve their lot.

There were strikes, and there was violence in strikes. At first the men did their own slugging and dynamiting. But, by and by, as I have suggested in an earlier chapter, the unions began to hire criminals or gangsters to attack the scabs for them. If the capitalists hired gunmen to protect the strikebreakers, why couldn't the unions engage hoodlums to slug them?

Another type that began to assume importance in the class war early in the twentieth century was the spy that the employers' associations put into labor unions. The labor spy was hired on the theory that unions were criminal in character. Of course, if he found that the union in which he had a membership was not criminal, he instigated or encouraged his fellow-members to violent acts, for he kept his job as a spy only as long as he had something to report. In the building trades, spies or "operatives," professionally so called, had no difficulty in finding men who were ready to listen to arguments in favor of violence. But there can be no doubt that most of the violence and sabotage in industrial disputes on the side of labor was committed by *bona fide* unionists on their own initiative.

The men in the building trades had a reputation for strong-arm methods very early in this century. That reputation was based upon such acts as the one perpetrated in July 1906 on a building job in New York. Thirty iron-workers, all union men, were employed, along with a few non-union stairway-makers. The latter worked on the lower floors and the iron-workers were constantly dropping on them, as if by accident, bolts, bars, and heavy tools. The company hired special watchmen to see that the stairway-men were left alone. This enraged the iron-workers.

One day a band of them attacked the watchmen, beat them into insensibility, dropped one of them from the eighth to the fifth floor. He died. None of the men who participated in the assault was identified. Union leaders explained that if the watchmen were attacked it was the company's fault for hiring them!

At the time the destruction of property was a common thing in labor disputes. In telephone and telegraph troubles linemen cut wire cables; glaziers expressed their feelings against the bosses by smashing plate glass; and carpenters, in their effort to rise to a higher level, defaced fancy woodwork. The purpose of such vandalism was to put the employer to additional expense and thereby, perhaps, compel him to hire union instead of unorganized labor.

It was natural for the iron-workers to adopt dynamite as the most effective means of destruction. It had been used extensively in labor disputes throughout the nineties and the first decade of this century. The iron-workers could easily get hold of "the stuff"; there was always some around every big construction job. But the method of destruction is not as important as the philosophy behind it. Destruction was usually resorted to only after the other methods to win their demands had failed.

When the iron-workers did not prevent scabs from being employed on a job by smashing their faces or killing their guards, they sought to destroy the work—and often succeeded. The basic motive was the conviction that the particular job belonged to them as union men, even though they might have refused to go to work except under conditions laid down by the union, which were unacceptable to the employer. In their simple reasoning as union men, they were unable to divorce themselves from their jobs. The reason for this is not far to seek: they had fought for years to raise the wages, shorten the workday, and generally improve the job. They had been paying their union fees and attending meetings. They had been through a dozen strikes and lockouts. They had been blacklisted, clubbed, and shot at. They had suffered hunger and hard-ships to make the job as well paid as it was. *Therefore, the job belonged to them.* There was no room for argument; the scab, who not only had contributed nothing to the improvement of the job, but had been one of their worst enemies while they were improving it, had his face punched, and the builder, who in the face of the union's opposition employed him, had his structure dynamited.

Such was "trade-unionism, pure and simple" in action. But it must not be forgotten that this was also trade-unionism in desperation. I am fully aware of not having done complete justice to the A.F. of L. unions. Left-wing radicals and liberal intellectuals are forever finding fault with the A.F. of L. policy and tactics for its obvious short-comings from the viewpoint of the working class and society as a whole. But the A.F. of L. is, I believe, the only kind of labor-unionism that could have been effective and survived in the extremely chaotic, narrowly pragmatic, blindly violent and dynamic period of the last forty years in the United States. Its emergence in the late eighties and its development in the succeeding four decades were a natural and inevitable product of the times; its policy and tactics are defensible if we consider the brutal greed and power of the forces opposed to it.

The union leaders' personal desire to keep their jobs as presidents and secretaries was never the *principal* reason for the development of strong-arm tactics in the American labor movement. These tactics depend fundamentally on the desperation which seizes the membership when the unions, no matter how rich and well organized, are ineffective or have their very existence threatened by the organized efforts of union-hating employers.

I beg the reader of this book who may not be a working-man himself to consider the life of the industrial worker in the United States. The worker has certain political rights and may quit his job whenever he has the humor to starve, but otherwise his lot is no dazzling improvement upon that of the old chattel slave. In some obvious respects, it is worse. The "free" worker of today is, of course, free to go wheresoever he pleases—if he has the price; but, as a practical matter, his travels can have but one aim: the finding of another job. As his earnings by hard labor seldom exceed his needs, he can become a property owner only by extreme self-denial. When he does acquire a house and lot, it becomes a bond to keep him tied down to one locality, where an industrial panic often deprives him of it.

His political rights he cannot exercise intelligently; after working long hours he has neither the time nor the energy to decide on men and issues in a way to benefit himself. He is, moreover, the object of ceaseless propaganda, good and bad, and he is usually unable to distinguish one from the other.

In self-defense he joins other men in a labor union, to coerce the capitalists into giving him more pay, reducing the number of working hours, and generally improving his condition. He and his fellow workers strike, and sometimes they gain their demands, but very often they lose. During strikes they are slugged or shot at by company guards or gunmen, intimidated and starved back to the job on the old terms. Then, very likely, there comes a business depression—unemployment, wage-cuts, lockouts, *desperation*. The union is their only hope, and they are willing to go to almost any length to preserve it. They elect leaders will-ing to use violence when violence is the only means of preserving it.

IV

Between 1905 and 1910, as was revealed in the McNamara case and later, dynamite became definitely a part of the Iron Workers' tactics in their effort to better their conditions on the job and in society, in the face of aggressively anti-union policies of the National Erectors' Association. And dynamite was effective. The Iron Workers withstood the efforts of the Erectors' Association. Indeed, in those five years their wages increased from $2.50 for ten hours' work to $4.30 for eight hours. To achieve this, the Iron Workers' international union dynamited about 150 buildings and bridges in the United States and Canada—or at least most of those explosions can reasonably be ascribed to the doings of official union terrorists.

I repeat: the Iron Workers resorted to dynamite in extreme des-peration, in a life-and death struggle, to save the men's jobs, to save the union, on which the men depended for their jobs and the improvement of their conditions.

The dynamiting operations were directed from the union's head-quarters at Indianapolis by the organization's secretary-treasurer, John J. McNamara, whose principal "outside-man" was his brother, James B. McNamara. John J. had a monthly appropriation of about $1,000 for "organization purposes." He sat in his office and decided on what "jobs" they would pull, while James B. was "handy with the sticks." They conducted these operations with the full knowledge of the leaders in the union and most of the membership—to say nothing of the rest of the A.F. of L., with which the Iron Workers were affiliated. The union elected John J. as secretary-treasurer largely *because* he believed in dyna-mite, and was willing to use it, *in emergency*.

It is not difficult to explain, or even apologize for, the McNamaras. They were Irish, endowed with the same instincts that had produced the Molly Maguires; perhaps a bit more idealistic, social-minded, than the Mollies. Apart from their dynamiting operations, they were what most people would call "good boys." In private they were model family men, good to their mother. One of them was a devout Catholic, mem-ber of the Knights of Columbus and a lay religious organization. Both,

I believe, were Democrats in politics and friends and admirers of Sam Gompers. In their minds, dynamiting for the union was not a sin that one, as a good Catholic, was supposed to confess any more than it was sin for a soldier to fire his piece in war. They were soldiers in the cause of labor, in the war between the haves and the have-nots; Jesuits in the labor movement, their ends justifying any means.

Each was a kind of hero in the union. (They still are.) They saved the union at one of its darkest periods. Early in the current century every single union in the steel industry had been completely destroyed—except the Iron Workers, thanks to dynamite and the McNamaras.

One of the principal apologists for the McNamaras and their doings was—and still is—Anton Johannsen, once upon a time a leader in the San Francisco trade unions which also employed dynamite, now a labor organizer in Chicago. He was implicated in the McNamara affair in Los Angeles, and is proud of it. In 1913 he said:

> If a man says to me the McNamaras should be condemned, my reply is: All right, we will condemn the McNamaras; but we will also condemn the Carnegies and the Steel Trust. If a man says to me that the Iron Workers' Union should be condemned, I say: All right, but we will also condemn the National Erectors' Association. Before the union began to use dynamite their men lived on starvation wages, some of them on less than $400 a year, with families! If they say, we want light on the activities of union men, I say: All right, but light up the Steel Trust also. Light up both labor and capital. Put on the searchlights, and we are willing that our sins should be compared with the sins of the employers.

V

In 1910, after a series of especially big explosions, wrecking buildings erected by non-union labor, the National Erectors' Association engaged William J. Burns, the detective, to trail down the dynamiters.

CHAPTER 19
THE PLOT TO DYNAMITE THE LOS ANGELES "TIMES"

From the viewpoint of the class struggle, a peculiar situation existed in California early in 1910, or just prior to the dynamiting of the Los Angeles *Times*.

San Francisco was a stronghold of trade unionism. Labor had been well entrenched there even before the earthquake in 1906; after that catastrophe it became the dominant element in the city. The unions, especially those of the building trades, had taken advantage of the chaotic situation following the quake and organized so that in a couple of years they controlled practically every job in San Francisco. In achieving this control, the laborites had used strong-arm methods, including dynamite.

After 1908 builders and contractors could not move without considering the unions. Says David Warren Ryder in a historical sketch of the situation, printed in the *American Mercury* (April 1926) :

> Not a hammer was lifted, or a brick laid, or a pipe fitted, or a wall plastered or painted or papered without the sanction of the unions. Let an employer, large or small, discharge a drunken, insubordinate or incompetent workman without the union's consent, and he found himself the next day facing a strike, and compelled to reinstate the discharged workman and pay him and his fellows for the time they were out. The walking delegate roved the town in state, issuing orders and imposing penalties. The power of the unions was absolute and for years they were able to exact the utmost obedience to their complex and extravagant rules and regulations.

Labor leaders in San Francisco, as elsewhere, were go-getters of the first order, motivated by the same psychology as the directors of great trusts and corporations. They demanded high wages for labor and graft for themselves, and, holding an advantageous position, managed to get both. The membership of the trade unions was limited and corresponded to the body of stockholders in a capitalistic "racket."

Being strong economically, San Francisco's organized labor, naturally, developed political potency. The unions already were the strongest element behind the corrupt administration of Mayor Schmitz during the years immediately after the earthquake. Labor leaders shared in the proceeds from vice and in the bribes that traction magnates were paying the Schmitz gang for franchises.

In 1909, after the Schmitz machine was discredited, the laborites put forth a candidate completely their own—Patrick H. ("Pinhead") McCarthy, president of the San Francisco Building Trades Council, "a blatant bulldozer," as the San Francisco *Argonaut* described him, who conducted "the simplest negotiation with the exhibitions of physical and vocal energy adequate to the management of a twenty-mule team." Behind him was a master-mind in the person of another laborite, O. A. Tveitmoe, a dark Scandinavian of powerful build, a "gorilla," who was secretary of the Building Trades Council, boss of the Labor Party, and Sam Gompers's big friend and trusted henchman on the Coast. And the men around Tveitmoe were such fellows as Anton Johannsen and Tom Mooney, thick-fisted, bull-necked, dynamic men, trained in the rough school of labor leadership; intolerant, tyrannical, loud-mouthed, direct. Some of them were frank believers in dynamite. They loved Roosevelt's phrase about "the big stick." They laughed at naïve Socialists who were conducting classes in economics, educating labor groups. "What we need," they said with great emphasis, "is not classes in economics, but classes in chemistry!" They were barbaric Nietzscheans. The Socialists called them "gorillas." One of the few books read by trade-union officials in Chicago, San Francisco, and elsewhere at that time was Ragnar Redbeard's *Might Is Right*, in which the philosophy of power is discussed in terms of physics. They had small concern for the "laboring stiffs" outside the unions; there were thousands of work-men in San Francisco who could not join unions, and therefore could get no work, because of prohibitive initiation fees. As with the rest of the A.F. of L. "racket," there was nothing sentimental or Socialistic in the San Francisco trade unions.

The unions were a thorn in the side of San Francisco business. Labor costs there were higher than anywhere else on the Coast, and San Francisco industrialists found it difficult to compete with Seattle, Portland, and particularly Los Angeles. The wages were nearly 30 per cent higher in San Francisco, and the workday two to four hours shorter, than elsewhere on the Coast. San Francisco was falling down especially in shipbuilding; even repair work under the system of competitive bidding went elsewhere.

Not only did new capital fear to come to San Francisco, but old capital was drawing out.

II

On the other hand, Los Angeles, 500 miles to the south, was a booming open-shop town, its industrial history closely linked with the career of an energetic personage, General Harrison Gray Otis, a union hater, publisher-editor of the Los Angeles *Times*.

Otis had come to Southern California in the early eighties and, acquiring control of the *Times*, then a struggling sheet in a town of 12,000, developed "a tremendous and abiding faith in the future of Los Angeles," with its climate. He was an aggressive man, bound to be noticed in a small city. An ex-soldier of two campaigns, he was full of the martial spirit; when prosperity came his way, he built himself a mansion and called it "The Bivouac," and when he built the fateful Times Building, he made the architect give it the suggestion of a medieval fortress with battlements and other challenging appurtenances. Just before the McNamara case, while fighting the unions, he mounted a small cannon on the hood of his automobile!

He loved a fight and, when in 1890 the local printers' union declared a strike against the newspapers in the city, demanding closed shop and a higher wage scale, he fought the movement with every means at his command, fair and foul. He won the battle and thus became the generalissimo of the open-shop forces in Los Angeles. He had the anti-union idea in his blood; early in the nineteenth century, his uncle and namesake, Senator Harrison Gray Otis of Massachusetts, was an intense opponent to all organized efforts of labor to improve its lot.

During the nineties Otis had become the most savage and effective enemy of labor unionism in the country, and as a result of his doings Los Angeles was—and is today—the outstanding open-shop town in the United States, "the white spot" on the industrial map of the country. Otis fought the unions tooth and nail. Often he picked fights. In the *Times*, referring to organized workers he used such terms as "sluggers," "union rowdies," "hired trouble breeders," "gas-pipe ruffians," "strong-arm gang"—some of which at certain times, no doubt, were justified.

Otis organized a Merchants' and Manufacturers' Association, which was primarily a union of business men against labor unions; and merchants, manufacturers, and contractors were compelled to join if they wanted to operate in Los Angeles. The greatest sin that a Los Angeles employer could commit was to hire a union worker as such.

About 1909 Otis discovered Nietzsche, or rather he was introduced to Nietzscheism by a young gentleman, Willard Huntington Wright (now S. S. Van Dine, the detective story writer), who became literary editor of the *Times*. Wright had not yet written his summary of old Friedrich's philosophy, *What Nietzsche Taught*, nor his Nietzschean novel, *Man of Promise*, but he was even then a Nietzschean, a believer in aristocracy, in superiority, in the exercise of might. He was a great find for Otis. At any rate, during Wright's literary editorship, the *Times* made frequent references to those phases of Nietzsche that seemed to agree with the policies and temperament of General Otis.

Otis, naturally, acquired numerous enemies. He was personally disliked even by some of his business friends. Labor, of course, hated the ground he walked on. Union leaders referred to him by unprintable titles. Plain folks, reading his vituperative attacks on labor, would say: "It's a wonder somebody doesn't blow him up!" One of his journalistic rivals called him a "surly old swill dispenser." W. C. Brann, the iconoclast, could not find a mean enough word in the English language to call him by. Hiram Johnson, then an up-and-coming liberal politician, called him "depraved, corrupt, crooked, putrescent." Still others considered him vain and pompous, quarrelsome and intolerant, unfair in his tactics, vicious in his attacks. One generous woman, Mrs. Fremont Older of San Francisco, said that he was merely "an honest man who believes in the sacredness of property above all other things."

Due mainly to Otis, the unions were extremely weak in Los Angeles, and wages were low and the working hours long.

III

In San Francisco, when Mayor McCarthy got into office, in January 1910, business and industry were ebbing away; but the capitalists, although seriously harassed by the unions, were, as yet, far from helpless in the community. They were organized. The *Chronicle* and one or two other large papers were strongly anti-labor.

The industrial depression, blamed by the capitalists on the unions, of course, seriously affected the working conditions. Much of the business, as already mentioned, was going to Portland, Seattle, and Los Angeles, where industrialists, unharassed by unions, could work labor as long as they liked for low pay. Thousands of union men were unemployed, and their number increased. They could not pay their union fees.

Early in 1910 the big men of San Francisco business and the big men in the Trades Union Council got together and came to the conclusion that it would be mutually beneficial to employers and union labor if the labor situation between San Francisco and Los Angeles was "equalized"—that is, if the San Francisco labor leaders went to Los Angeles and organized the town, compelling employers there to pay labor as high wages as employers in San Francisco were forced to pay.

But how to organize Los Angeles, with Harrison Gray Otis there?

The San Francisco laborites, as already suggested, were violent men. They decided to dynamite the Los Angeles *Times*—and do it so that Otis would be blamed for it. Otis was an old thorn in the side of A.F. of L. organizers. A few years before, the A.F. of L., assembled in convention, had appropriated a sum of money—the so-called "Los Angeles *war* fund"—to be used in defeating Otis and organizing Los Angeles. The money was spent in a one sided battle, Otis emerging as victor. Now, they thought, they would blow him up and capture the city.

Accordingly, San Francisco laborites invaded Los Angeles in May 1910. Among them were O. A. Tveitmoe, Anton Johannsen, Andrew Gallagher, J. A. Kelley, Eric B. Morton, and John S. Nolen. Occasionally two other men, who were introducing themselves as J. B. Brice and Edward W. Miller, appeared in their company, living in the same hotels with them. J. B. Brice, as it turned out later, was the *nom de guerre* of James B. McNamara, and Edward W. Miller was Schmidt, a local San Francisco dynamiter (now in San Quentin). The San Francisco "gorillas" figured that this Los Angeles "job" was an important "stunt" which had to be pulled right, and so they had asked John J. McNamara to loan them James B., who by now was known among union leaders as the most expert dynamiter in the movement.

Another man who traveled about with San Francisco laborites in Los Angeles in the spring and summer of 1910 was Job Harriman, a nationally prominent Socialist politician and spellbinder, a friend of Morris Hillquit, a leader of the Socialist group in Los Angeles and attorney for the struggling Los Angeles labor unions. Harriman was "in" with the "San Francisco bunch" on the political end of the *Times* dynamiting plot and wrote letters (some of them now in my possession) to his friends out of town, discussing the situation. He was slated to run for Mayor of Los Angeles in 1911 on the Socialist-Labor ticket, with the support of the San Francisco union organizers, in return for which, with his influence as a Socialist leader in California, he would swing the Socialist vote to the McCarthy-Tveitmoe machine at the forthcoming election in San Francisco.

Harriman had nothing to do with the actual dynamiting in Los Angeles; he merely joined the San Francisco laborites in their general program of taking Los Angeles from Otis and his group of open-shop employers, who were even then thinking of making the city a great metropolis. He was an ambitious man, an opportunist; although publicly opposed to strong-arm methods, secretly he allied himself with the dynamiters, who, in turn, used him to help them in their "stunt." Through Harriman, the San Francisco laborites, who were opposed to Socialism, took over the Socialist organization in Los Angeles, to use it for their purposes.

On May 30, Harriman brought a crowd of San Francisco men to a Socialist luncheon in Los Angeles. One of them made a speech, ridiculing "political action" and "the whole Socialist moonshine," announcing himself as a believer in "the big stick," and referring to working people as "cattle" and "stiffs," the only cure for whose lethargy was "the empty stomach" and "the stick on the head." He hinted that they—he and his fellow labor leaders from San Francisco—would pull a "stunt" in Los Angeles that would "stir up and solidify the stiffs."

IV

Throughout the summer of 1910, and into the fall, Los Angeles was full of San Francisco "gorillas." Half a dozen strikes were going on. The employers were panicky, Otis dashed about with the cannon mounted on his machine. There were riots; scabs were slugged by labor bullies; pickets were attacked by the police. There was talk of dynamiting this and that building. The *Times* carried frantic editorials.

> Friends of industrial freedom must stand together and back the employers who are at present being assailed by the henchmen of the corrupt San Francisco labor bosses. All decent people must rally around the flag of industrial liberty in this crisis, when the welfare of the whole city is at stake. If the San Francisco gorillas succeed, then the brilliant future of Los Angeles will end, business will stagnate; Los Angeles will be another San Francisco—dead.

On September 3, after the union sluggers had thrashed some scabs,
the *Times* said:

> It is full time to deal with these labor-union wolves in such prompt
> and drastic fashion as will induce them to transfer their lawless-
> ness to some other locality, for the danger of tolerating them in Los
> Angeles is great and immediate... Their instincts are criminal, and
> they are ready for arson, riot, robbery, and murder.

Throughout September the *Times* had endless trouble with the gas
system in its plant. Employees were getting sick from inhaling gas fumes.
One theory—the soundness of which will become apparent in the next
chapter—is that this was part of the "stunt," that the San Francisco
plotters had their own men working in the *Times* shops, punching holes
in the gas pipes.

CHAPTER 20
THE EXPLOSION—AND AFTER

At one o'clock in the morning of October 1910, the *Times* employees, among them a number of union printers, were putting the paper "to bed." General Otis was in Mexico, where he had gone to talk about a land deal with Diaz. He was on his way back to Los Angeles. Harry Chandler, Otis's son-in-law and general manager of the *Times*, who was wont to work late in his office, had just gone home.

At seven minutes past one there was a deafening detonation, "a dry, snappy sound," in Ink Alley, to the rear of the Times Building. Two minutes later the entire place was filled with gas and flames. There were close to a hundred persons in the building. Only about a score of them escaped uninjured. They were jumping from the windows two and three stories up, breaking their legs and heads. Several of them were buried in the wreckage in the rear of the building.

The total number of the dead was twenty.

The building was totally wrecked, but the *Times* came out in the morning with only a brief delay. Otis had built himself an auxiliary plant only two blocks away. He had expected to be dynamited.

"UNIONIST BOMBS WRECK THE TIMES"
was the headline.

Then Otis returned.

O you anarchic scum, [he wrote] you cowardly murderers, you leeches upon honest labor, you midnight assassins, you whose hands are dripping with the innocent blood of your victims, you against whom the wails of poor widows and the cries of fatherless children are ascending to the Great White Throne, go, mingle with the crowd on the street corners, look upon the crumbled and blackened walls, look at the ruins wherein are buried the calcined remains of those whom you murdered…

151

II

Huge rewards, totaling nearly $300,000, were offered for the apprehension of the "criminals." Otis insisted that the unionists had dynamited his building. Who else would? Who else *could* do such a terrible thing? Anyone who dared to doubt him was *ipso facto* a sympathizer of the "criminal unions," a traitor to the future greatness of Los Angeles, an enemy of "industrial freedom." In San Francisco, on the other hand, anyone who dared to say that he believed Otis in this matter was likely to get his face smashed.

Numerous investigations were made by the police, the grand jury, a Mayor's committee, civic bodies, the city council. Their findings were unanimous that the building had been dynamited and the gas set afire by the explosion.

Job Harriman, as attorney for the Los Angeles labor unions, was in charge of the investigation ordered by the Labor Council. His finding was to the effect that the *Times* had not been dynamited at all; that, instead, all the indications were that there had been a gas explosion. To accuse union labor of perpetrating such an outrage was a crime in itself!

Finally, Otis was accused by the unionists of himself being to blame for the awful tragedy in which twenty workingmen lost their lives. Was it not a well-known fact that there had been something the matter with the *Times*'s gas system? Had not employees been sickened by gas fumes for weeks? And wasn't it strange that only minor employees had been killed, that all the big officials and the editors had been out of the building when the explosion occurred? They hinted that Otis, "the old scoundrel," possibly had had the place blown up himself, intending to put the blame on the unions and collecting insurance on the old plant!

Accusations were hurled back and forth, but the public began to incline to accept the gas-explosion theory and blame it all on Otis. As already suggested, he was widely disliked anyhow, believed to be capable of almost anything.

III

The explosion was front-page news throughout the United States.

To the open-shop employers Otis became a great hero. The National Association of Manufacturers, in convention in New York, wired him sympathies, urging him to keep up the splendid fight for "industrial freedom," condemning "the doctrine of rule and ruin which employs dynamite as the instrument." *American Industries*, an organ of the

Association, lost no time in implicating Gompers and the other officers of the A.F. of L. It printed, *verbatim*, a resolution passed at the Norfolk convention of the A.F. of L. in 1907 which provided "a *war fund* for use in attacking the Los Angeles *Times.*"

Gompers refused to answer the accusation; the mere suggestion of such a thing was absurd!

On the other hand, the Socialists raised a tremendous howl. In the *Appeal to Reason* (Oct. 15, 1910), Debs printed a long article, which in the ensuing five months—while the McNamaras were still at large—he elaborated in every issue. "I want to express my deliberate opinion," he said, "that the *Times* and its crowd of union-haters are the instigators, if not the actual perpetrators, of that crime and the murder of twenty human beings."

IV

The tension between Los Angeles capital and labor continued throughout the fall of 1910 and into the winter. Several strikes were going on, including one of the iron-workers. Picketing was prohibited by law. Otis, the cannon still mounted on the hood of his car, went about "like a roaring lion, seeking whom he may devour."

There was wild talk in labor groups of further terrorizing Los Angeles; rumors that the new aqueduct would be blown up, and so on. The rumors did not materialize. If the dynamiting gang had any such plans, it may be that the awfulness of the *Times* affair made them hesitate. I believe that they really did not intend to kill so many people, if any.

Only one more bomb went off in Los Angeles. On Christmas night, 1910, dynamite wrecked part of the Llewellyn Iron Works, where the men were on strike.

CHAPTER 21
"FRAME-UP!"

Williiam J. Burns, the detective who had been retained by the National Erectors' Association months before to ferret out and arrest the men behind the scores of dynamitings since 1905, was in Los Angeles the day after the *Times* explosion. Mayor Alexander engaged him to get the *Times* dynamiters.

Burns had James B. McNamara spotted months before his "stunt" in Los Angeles. Besides, he had his operatives watching the Iron Workers' headquarters at Indianapolis, especially John J. McNamara. They were following around also a man who went by the name of McGraw, but whose real name, as it turned out, was Ortie McManigal. He was James B.'s assistant in doing the "jobs."

The detective let James B. do a few more dynamitings after the Los Angeles "job." "We were determined," as Burns explained later, "to find out to whom he and McManigal were responsible—from whom they were getting money and orders for their work—and it would have been fatal to let them suspect that they were being watched." Finally, he had enough evidence against them and on April 14, 1911, he arrested James B. McNamara and McManigal in Detroit, where they were "on business." Burns claims that McNamara offered the detectives bribes up to $30,000 for his release, and when this was of no avail he turned defiant and said: "I'd blow up the whole damn country if I thought it would get us rights."

McManigal confessed, giving Burns clues to other evidence. Some of the keys found on him and James B. McNamara opened the locks in farmhouses and other buildings near Indianapolis in which they found dynamite and clocks used for timing bomb explosions.

Then he arrested John J. McNamara as well, at his office in Indianapolis.

There were legal difficulties in extraditing them to California, where John Doe warrants were out for them for the *Times* explosion. The prisoners were too great a prize for Burns to jeopardize on legal technicalities, so he "kidnaped" them—illegally took them to California, much in the manner in which, five years before, Haywood, Moyer, and Pettibone had been taken from Colorado to Idaho.

II

The news of the capture of the three men, as it was released on April 23, was a nationwide sensation.

DYNAMITERS OF THE TIMES BUILDING CAUGHT

CRIME TRACED DIRECTLY TO HIGH UNION OFFICIALS

RED-HANDED UNION CHIEFS IMPLICATED IN CONSPIRACY

—such were the headlines in the Los Angeles *Times*. "These villains," the paper said editorially, "are the Camorrists of the United States, and in running them down Detective Burns has unearthed the most tremendous criminal conspiracy in the history of America."

The McNamaras and Ortie McManigal were put in the Los Angeles County Jail. McManigal was a man of the Orchard type. His confession gained him freedom soon after the conclusion of the McNamara case. (He now lives in Los Angeles under another name.) John J. was a stalwart, well-dressed, clean-shaven young man. His brother Jim was slight, with a thin face enlivened by a bitter, uncertain smile and a fanatical look in his shifty eyes. He was not well—with tubercular tendencies.

Once in jail, the McNamaras became of minor importance as individuals. The important thing now was the McNamara Case—the Case of Capitalism *vs.* Labor. The prisoners became symbols of Labor's Struggle—Martyrs—Victims of Capitalist Greed. The case became a National Issue.

Immediately, throughout the country labor leaders and radicals raised a yell: "Frame-up! Fiendish plot!" Debs telegraphed to the *Appeal to Reason*:

> Sound the alarm to the working class! There is to be a repetition of the Moyer-Haywood-Pettibone outrage upon the labor movement. The secret arrest of John McNamara, by a corporation detec-

tive agency, has all the earmarks of another conspiracy to fasten the crime of murder on the labor union officials to discredit and destroy organized labor in the United States... Arouse, ye hosts of labor, and swear that the villainous plot shall not be consummated! Be not deceived by the capitalist press!

Other radicals and laborites likewise declared that the arrests and the kidnaping were a "frame-up"; among them was O. A. Tveitmoe, of San Francisco, who, as secretary of the California Building Trades Council, offered a $7,000 reward for the apprehension of the person or persons really responsible for the destruction of the Times Building and the killing of twenty men.

Gompers raged:

I have investigated the entire case... Burns has lied... The whole affair smacks of well-laid pre-arrangement. The interests of corporate wealth are always trying to crush the labor movement, and they use the best way to strike at the men having the confidence of the working people... I admit that we can't compete with the capitalists in questions of litigation. But we will meet them this time on their ground and fight them in their own way, but it is the last time we will do it. There may come a time when we can't meet them that way any more, and when they hang a few of us we will show them a new way to meet an issue.

The San Francisco *Argonaut* remarked:

And what does Mr. Gompers mean by a "new way"? Surely he can't mean more dynamite, for that is a lamentably old way. There is no novelty about dynamite... It seems that Mr. Gompers protests too much.

On July 27, 1911, the A.F. of L. issued an official appeal to the working class of America to stand by the McNamaras, innocent victims of capitalist greed.

Funds must be provided to ensure a proper defense, a fair and impartial trial. Eminent counsel have been engaged. In the name of justice and humanity all members of our organization and all friends of justice are urgently requested to contribute.

Money began to pour in. Secretary Morrison of the A.F. of L. was made custodian of the defense fund.

III

Job Harriman, as counsel for the Los Angeles union, was temporarily in charge of the McNamara case immediately after the "boys" were brought to California. "We have witnesses living in Los Angeles today," he declared early in May, "who will be called to the stand and will prove that they left the Times Building early in the evening [before the explosion] utterly unable to stand the odor of gas that flooded it." He was building up the defense on the gas-explosion theory.

Burns, however, said: "We shall have no trouble convicting these men. We have a complete case against them."

It unquestionably was a most critical time for organized labor, and its leaders recognized the fact.

Immediately after the "kidnaping," Gompers went to Indianapolis to confer with President Ryan of the Iron Workers and the union's lawyers. They decided that they must have a huge defense fund and the best of legal talent. They asked Darrow to come to Indianapolis.

Darrow came at once. When he returned to his home in Chicago he said to the reporters: "I hope I shall not be retained. I know what it means, for I have gone through such trials before." He said that the labor leaders in Indianapolis were "panicky."

Finally Darrow took the case. Labor was determined to spare no expense, and, according to Frank Morrison, Darrow was given $50,000 in a lump sum outright as a retainer and the assurance of a very large defense fund. He went to Los Angeles and, while there, as chief of the McNamara defense, received from Morrison, between June and November 1911, $200,000 in sums of from $10,000 to $ 25,000.

CHAPTER 22
THE TRIAL AND THE POLITICAL
CAMPAIGN

In May 1911, barely a month after "the boys" had been brought to Los Angeles, Job Harriman was nominated for Mayor by the Socialist-Labor party of Los Angeles, which by now was completely under the boss rule of San Francisco laborites. His nomination, as already hinted, was part of the trade unions' "war" against Otis and the open-shop forces. The plan was to capture Los Angeles with one grand swoop, not only economically but also politically. John J. McNamara sent word from his cell at the County Jail: "There is but one way for the working class to get justice. Elect its own representatives to office."

Most of the Los Angeles Socialists, of course, were unaware of the fact that Job Harriman, a rather subtle fellow, was allied with the San Francisco "gorillas."

The Los Angeles municipal campaign became of national interest, chiefly because it was so closely tied up with the McNamara case. Whatever its outcome, it was bound to have powerful influence upon the fate of the accused men. The National Headquarters of the Socialist Party sent Alexander Irvine, an experienced politician, to manage Harriman's campaign.

The McNamara case was a great emotional issue in Harriman's campaign; besides, he had no end of excellent economic and civic matters to talk about. There were all sorts of scandals in the political life of the city, which the Socialist-Laborites made the most of.

Already in August it became probable that Harriman would be elected. His leading opponent, as it happened, was Mayor George Alexander, an old retired rancher, a tool in the hands of the local corsairs. He ran for re-election on the ticket of the so-called "Goo-goos," or the Good Government League. He was in sympathy with the policies of the Otis gang.

160   The people of Los Angeles believed that Otis and other capitalists had hired Burns to frame the McNamaras. They believed it was a dirty stunt, and many supported Harriman for that reason alone.

II

Early in July, in Judge Walter Bordwell's court in Los Angeles, the McNamaras pleaded "not guilty" to the charge of having dynamited the Times Building and killed twenty persons.

District Attorney John D. Fredericks asked that the trial be set for an early date, say, August 1, but Clarence Darrow objected on the ground that the defense could not possibly get the case ready before December. The judge set it for October 11.

While in jail at Los Angeles, waiting for trial, John J. McNamara was re-elected secretary-treasurer of the Iron Workers.

Darrow, from his statements to the press after the trial, must have known for some time before the confession the responsibility of "the boys" for the explosion, although he was never prepared to admit that they were "murderers." At all events, the prosecution had a complete case against them; short of some strong external influence, such as public opinion, conviction was certain. The gas-explosion theory could be expected to do little in the courtroom itself; at most it might affect the masses outside, who already believed the men innocent and would continue to believe that even in case of conviction.

But when considered in relation to the whole situation in California and in the United States at large, with the wave of radicalism rolling over the country, there were a few rays of hope. For one thing, the 1912 presidential election was but a year off. A few well-organized mass demonstrations in the meantime, such as had been staged during the Haywood trial in 1907, would scare the politicians of the big parties into bringing pressure to bear upon the interests and authorities in Los Angeles. "The boys" would go free like Haywood.

The McNamara case was a powerful factor in favor of Harriman in the political campaign, but in a lesser degree the same was true the other way around. Should Harriman be elected Mayor, he would have Otis arrested and jailed on the charge of having had a defective gas system in the plant, which had caused the death of twenty workingmen. That would confuse the situation, which already was a fearful mess, and in the long run the confusion was expected to react in favor of the McNamaras. This was freely discussed as a probability in the Socialist-Labor circles during the campaign. There were plans and rumors galore.

Many of them found space in the *Appeal to Reason*, whose circulation in Los Angeles during those months, was almost greater than that of the *Times*.

The common people of Los Angeles were turning red.

III

In mid-September, Gompers came to Los Angeles. He visited "the boys" in jail, was photographed with them, conferred with Clarence Darrow, and spoke before a vast audience of workers and plain people, extolling "the majesty of labor," predicting its "ultimate triumph," endorsing Job Harriman, "candidate of the people," for Mayor of the city of Los Angeles. He also issued a statement to the working people of the United States, assuring them that "the boys" were innocent, urging them to stand by the case and hasten with their contributions to the defense fund.

Money poured in. Practically every town and city had a McNamara Defense League, collecting quarters and dollars from the "toiling masses." Much of this money never reached Frank Morrison, who was in charge of the fund. Local labor grafters found use for huge sums that the people had contributed for the defense.

On Labor Day the great anti-Otis public in Los Angeles joined the proletariat, marshaled by Harriman and the San Francisco laborites, in staging a tremendous demonstration. Some 20,000 marched through the town. Some rode horseback, carrying banners with challenging inscriptions: "Register Your Protest Against the McNamara Frame-Up!" "Harriman for Mayor!" From his cell, John J. McNamara issued a "Labor Day Message to the Toilers of America," in which he bubbled with optimism for the working class; all that the toiling masses needed to do was to stand by their leaders.

On the same day, McNamara demonstrations were held also in San Diego, San Francisco, Portland, Seattle, St. Louis, Chicago, Cleveland, Indianapolis, and in numerous cities and towns in the East.

Discerning political and social observers were fearful of a great class struggle upheaval.

IV

The trial began on the appointed day, October 11.

If Harriman was to win the mayor's chair, the election would have to occur before the conclusion of the trial; for the fact that "the boys," who of course were considered innocent of any crime by the public, were still in jail in Los Angeles, continued to play in Harriman's favor. Fortunately, from this point of view, finding an unprejudiced jury in Los Angeles was like looking for needles in a haystack. Darrow's jury-picking attracted national attention, and provoked a deal of comment on the jury system in general. In the first eighteen court days only two permanent jurors acceptable alike to both sides were obtained.

Election day was December 5. By the middle of November the jury-box was only half filled. And Harriman campaigned furiously. The man's energy was amazing, and he was aided by a big staff of speakers, many of them nationally prominent Socialists.

Otis and his cohort were alarmed. "Protect Los Angeles Homes!" cried the *Times* editorially.

> Don't let Socialist Harriman and his hungry crowd of office seekers fool you, home-owning, working, and other voters of Los Angeles! Socialism in the saddle will mean less civic and private credit, less building, less industry, and thereby less work and less wages...less money with which to comfort your family, and far less protection for your home than you now so happily enjoy.

Other Los Angeles newspapers were equally panicky. Los Angeles then had a population of 290,000 and the go-getters already had visions of a city with millions of people.

In the primary elections on October 30, Harriman was the leading man with 15,000 votes against 13,000 cast for Alexander, the next highest candidate. The third candidate, receiving 6,000 votes, was eliminated in the primary. The final election was a little over a month in the future.

On primary night the Harriman supporters staged another demonstration, thousands of people marching in the streets, singing the *Marseillaise*.

The *Times* and the entire "Goo-Goo crew" were panic-stricken. Should Harriman win, then what would become of the city—*their* city, for they practically owned it—of their valuable subdivisions, of their financial credit in the East? "Can Los Angeles sell $17,000,000 of its bonds in the next year if Harriman is elected mayor?" asked the *Times*, frantically.

> In that question is presented the real issue of the campaign that is to be decided December 5. If Los Angeles fails to sell bonds in

that sum it cannot carry on the great undertakings on the success of which its continued growth and future prosperity alike depend. Failure in those undertakings means municipal disaster.

Eastern bankers, visiting Los Angeles, gave interviews stating that Los Angeles's credit in the East would be suspended should the city go Socialist.

The Los Angeles *Express* cried: "Harriman must not win!"

But how to prevent his election?

V

Early in November, District Attorney Fredericks accused the defense of an attempt to rifle his desk and files. Darrow challenged him to produce proof. Accusations flew back and forth. On November 10, Darrow and Fredericks almost came to blows during the examination of a prospective juror. Judge Bordwell ordered them to behave.

With the final election but three weeks off, the "Goo-Goos" became desperate. Harriman *must not* be elected! But it seemed as if the McNamara trial, which was the biggest thing in his favor, would never start, to say nothing of ending, by election day; and even if it should end in a conviction, most voters would still believe the case was a frame-up. Darrow was still picking jurors.

The "Goo-Goos," of whom the District Attorney was one, seemed to believe that Darrow, in common with most high-powered criminal lawyers, could not be over-ethical.

After the trial the prosecution claimed that, by November 20, they had known that some of the jurors had been tampered with. At any rate, immediately after the primary, the prosecution planted dictographs in Darrow's rooms, and their own agents in his employ. On November 29, the District Attorney's detectives arrested two of Darrow's agents—of whom one, at least, had been planted on him—and charged them with bribing prospective jurors.

The jury-bribing arrests were a sensation. One of the defense attorneys said: "This is a damned frame-up!" Darrow himself declared to the reporters: "What can you expect? We told our friends what would come before we went into this trial. I have no knowledge of any attempt at bribery."

The "Goo-Goos," on the other hand, were jubilant. At last they had Darrow where they wanted him, and, having Darrow, they thought they had Harriman. The election was the important thing. The Socialist ticket was now as good as beaten. Los Angeles was saved! Their Los Angeles, their enormous real-estate properties! The *Express* rejoiced:

> Forces that stand for violence and disorder never can obtain ascendancy in the government of Los Angeles. The Socialists will not be permitted to ruin Los Angeles.

VI

While the above was taking place in Los Angeles, Gompers, at the A.F. of L. convention in Atlanta, issued another statement to the effect that the case in California was a "frame-up." He asked for more defense money, insisting the McNamaras were innocent.

In New York, Chicago, Philadelphia, Pittsburgh, Cleveland—in all American cities—plans were under way for huge demonstrations to be held early in December, the purpose of which would be to protest against "the dastardly frame-up," as Debs called it; to *force* the capitalist class to release John J. and James B. McNamara.

Millions of people throughout the country stood on their toes, tense, indignant, getting more radical every day. They gave their money for the defense. They were as yet unaware that the case was about to end in a fiasco for the American labor movement.

CHAPTER 23
"THE BOYS" CONFESS AND
GOMPERS WEEPS

On December 1, something seemed to be in the air at the Los Angeles courthouse. At ten o'clock, when the court convened, the District Attorney rose nervously and said: "Your Honor, for the first time in this case I must ask a postponement of proceedings. I have certain grave matters to consider between now and the time for convening court this afternoon."

In the afternoon, the courtroom was jammed with reporters.

The defense withdrew the pleas of "not guilty" in the case; James B. McNamara pleaded guilty to the dynamiting of the Times Building and the killing of twenty men; and John J. McNamara to the dynamiting of the Llewellyn Iron Works. "It was my intention to injure the building and scare the owners," said James B. "I did not intend to take the life of anyone. I sincerely regret that these unfortunate men lost their lives."

"Jesus! Ain't it fierce!" exclaimed one of the reporters aloud.

The court adjourned. The judge named December 5 as the day on which he would pronounce sentences in the case.

The reporters surrounded James B. "Well, if I swing," he spoke incoherently, "I'll swing for a principle. Poor Darrow, he's all in. If I swing, it'll be for a principle—a principle." Then the officers led him out, with his brother.

The newspaper men turned to Darrow. He seemed on the verge of losing composure and looked tired to death. "We didn't see any way around it," he said. "They had it on us. The county had a complete case. There was no loophole. No loophole. We have been working on this for a week. There was no hope. I hope I have saved a human life out of the wreckage. With John J. it's only a question of how many years. I guess you newspapermen realize what I mean when I say there was no other way out. Form your own conclusion and be lenient."

LeCompte Davis, one of Darrow's assistants in the defense, was reported by the press as saying: "Under the circumstances we did the very best we could for ourselves and our clients."

Darrow muttered something to the effect that he was through with law forever.

"Mr. Darrow, how about the gas-explosion theory?" asked a Los Angeles *Times* reporter, with understandable malice.

"Why," said Darrow, "maybe it was gas—or something. I'm very tired. I'm worn out and very sorrowful."

The *Times* man persisted with the gas-explosion question.

"I understand that in the explosion of the dynamite," said Darrow, "a pipe was broken and gas escaped—perhaps it was gas." He broke off; then added: "I want to say one thing. I'm perfectly sure that J. B. never meant to kill anyone in that building. Murder was never in his thoughts. He is not a murderer at heart."

Later, in his office, Darrow was asked by newspapermen: "Why was this confession made today? Why not, say, a week from today?" They realized the political significance of the court scene that afternoon.

"Well," said Darrow, "you have to take advantage of clemency when it is extended."

"Did the bribery arrests have anything to do with the confession?"

"Not a thing," snapped Darrow. "We knew before that the evidence the prosecution had was dead open and shut." Still later, in a long statement, Darrow said:

> Doubtless there will be keen disappointment throughout the country among those who have stood by the men. But I am sure that everyone who knows me understands that I would never have consented to their pleading guilty if I had thought there was a chance left... I have known for months that our fight was hopeless... Then Lincoln Steffens came to us a week ago Monday with the statement that prominent men of Los Angeles were anxious that an agreement should be reached that would end the trial and wipe the bitter controversy off the boards.
>
> I felt free then, the suggesting having come from the outside, to say that we were willing to consider whatever concessions they might be able to secure from the prosecution. Following that there was a lot of conferring back and forth, these business men sending someone to District Attorney Fredericks and Steffens coming to me from them.
>
> Early this week there were some conferences direct with Fredericks...and the result of all these was the understanding that if

our clients would plead guilty, James B. on the charge for which he was on trial, and John J. on the charge of dynamiting the Llewellyn Iron Works, as an accessory, of course, [for John was in Indianapolis when the Llewellyn Works was blown up] he, the District Attorney, would recommend them to the mercy of the court.

Davis and I spent nearly all Thanksgiving Day with John and Jim in their cell. We went over the whole thing with them with great care. They knew long before that we did not believe we could save them. We pleaded with them to consent to the only course that would save their lives.

Each was willing to plead guilty to the separate charge, but unwilling that the other should plead guilty. Finally, consent of both was given and after Davis left me at our office at seven o'clock he went out to Captain Fredericks's residence and final understanding was reached...

I was anxious to settle it as soon as possible after the negotiations started and I was worried sick with the fear that news of it would leak out and spoil the last chance to effect an agreement and save the lives of these men....It was intimated to us that we must act promptly, and then there was the danger that rumor of what was being considered would get out and make settlement impossible. So we acted entirely on our own responsibility and accepted the terms offered. Job Harriman knew nothing of our intention. I did not want to worry him with this problem, and he has practically been out of the case since the first week of the trial, on account of the campaign... We were responsible to our clients alone; we did not wait for the consent of any of the labor leaders or others interested in the defense.

However, in spite of Darrow's assumption of sole responsibility in the negotiations for the confession; the officers of A.F. of L., at least, must have had some suspicion of what was going on; for "Big Ed" Nockles, a prominent Chicago labor leader and Gompers's personal representative in Los Angeles in connection with the McNamara trial, was in touch with the case.

District Attorney Fredericks and Judge Bordwell were both emphatic in stating that the chief reason behind the confession at this time was that Darrow's agents had been caught bribing jurors. In short, Darrow's enemies were outspoken in their belief that the McNamaras had been induced to plead guilty in order to save Darrow from prison. Darrow's partisans, on the other hand were equally emphatic in stating that the bargain had been struck only for the sake of saving "the boys" themselves from the otherwise inevitable death penalty.

Later Darrow was tried twice for jury-bribing. In one case the jury was hung; in the other Darrow, after his plea to the jury in which he accused the prosecution of having framed him, was acquitted.

II

The effect of the confession upon Los Angeles was terrific. People would not believe the headlines in the afternoon papers, thinking it all some sort of political trick. A reporter rushing to his office paused on a corner to tell the news to a laborite he recognized; the latter, outraged, called him a liar and knocked him down with his fist.

Harriman denied having had any knowledge of the forthcoming confession. He acted surprised, hurt. There was an enraged mob of Socialists in front of his campaign headquarters; he and Alexander Irvine, his campaign manager, became alarmed, jumped into an automobile and drove off.

In common with all "Goo-Goos," the *Times* was hysterical with joy.

The God that is still in Israel [it said] filled the guilty souls of the dynamiters with a torment that they could not bear... Viewed fundamentally, the stupendous climax of the case was *in essential particulars the most consequential event that has occurred in this country since the close of the Civil War...* The class bitterness which has been engendered by the demagogic and inflammatory appeals and misrepresentations of Debs, Gompers, the "Appeal to *Treason*," Job Harriman, and such leaders was frightful to contemplate. Murder and arson were openly urged by some of these shouters. "Deliver the carcasses of the plutocrats to the furies!" wrote Debs. The tide of feeling rose to a fearful height. Many sober observers detected signs of impending revolution, and trembled for the safety of their families and their country.

But the crisis has passed. The firebugs are quenched. It will be impossible for inciters of crime and violence to longer deceive honest men. Their influence is gone. Their bedevilment is at an end. The country will settle down. Years of peace are assured because Liberty and Law will triumph and prevail.

If the McNamaras had been found guilty by juries and had been sentenced to be hanged, God only knows what the effect on the country would have been. No matter how complete the evidence—no matter how fair the trial—tens of thousands of men would have asserted that the accused were martyrs. Tens of thousands of throats would have shouted that the condemned had been railroaded to the gallows. Probably there would have been riots and bloodshed. Monuments would have been erected to the McNamaras, and memorial exercises would have been held in their honor, so intense has this craftily cultivated class hatred become. Now, no monuments, no memorials, no misapprehensions. It is all an open book. The Times Building WAS *dynamited by agents of the vicious elements of union labor, as the owners believed from the very beginning. With their own lips, in open court, have those dynamiters confessed. Not only is the* Times *vindicated, but the cause of Industrial Freedom and Law Enforcement is assured.*

On the first Sunday after the confession, the preachers—not alone in Los Angeles, but throughout the country—hailed the incident as of supreme importance.

We were standing on the edge of a yawning cliff [said one of them]; the volcano of prejudice and class strife was ready to belch out a lava of turmoil and stagnation, but now the hand of God has visibly taken hold of the ship of State, and the voice of God echoes in the ears of the world in the one word "guilty." This clears the air like an electric storm. Many thousands who honestly believed the McNamaras innocent now will prove their honesty by voting for the cause of Good Government.

For days following the confession, the gutters of downtown Los Angeles were strewn with Socialist-Labor buttons inscribed "Vote for Harriman!"

Not a few radicals and labor sympathizers in Los Angeles as well as elsewhere in the United States, on hearing of the confession, went insane; at least three persons committed suicide because of the McNamara debacle.

In the United States as a whole the reaction was but slightly less intense than in Los Angeles. As I have said, for months millions and millions had believed the McNamaras innocent; Darrow, Gompers, Debs and others had been assuring them to that effect—now this terrible fiasco!

III

Theodore Roosevelt wired William J. Burns: "All good Americans feel that they owe you a great debt of gratitude for your signal service to American citizenship."

Burns became a sort of national hero. Wherever he appeared reporters trailed him. He talked: "The confessions end the case only so far as the McNamaras are concerned." He hinted that others involved in the dynamitings might be arrested any day. Gompers? Burns shrugged his shoulders meaningfully. He intimated, too, that the McNamara confession had served to avert serious upheavals, attended by bloodshed.

IV

Gompers received the news of the confessions while returning from the convention in Atlanta.

"I have been grossly imposed upon!" he exclaimed and began to shed tears. "It won't do the labor movement any good!" he blubbered.

In New York City Gompers stopped at the Hotel Victoria. He was interviewed by the New York *Times*—and during the interview there stood or sat around him O. A. Tveitmoe, of San Francisco, and the latter's lieutenant, Anton Johannsen, and other strong-arm men from the Coast who had also attended the Atlanta convention.

Gompers looked haggard; he had not slept for nights. There is no doubt that he had had word of what was coming from his personal representative, "Big Ed" Nockles, in Los Angeles. (Anton Johannsen, whom I saw during the writing of this book, said to me: "Gompers talked and acted all right. I was there with 'im.")

"Can you explain how it happens that you were kept in ignorance?" the reporter asked Gompers.

Gompers: "Explain? Kept in ignorance? Why, we want to know that ourselves. We, who were willing to give our encouragement, our pennies, our faith, why were we not told the truth from the beginning? We had a right to know."

Tveitmoe and Johannsen solemnly nodded their heads, in support of the A.F. of L. chief's indignation.

"We had a right to know," repeated Gompers.

"Do you blame the men in charge of the case for not setting you straight?" he was asked.

Gompers shook his head. "Am I in any position to blame till I know more of what happened?"

"Well, are you in a position to say what would have been your advice if they had sought it on the question of the McNamaras' pleading guilty?"

Gompers's tear-washed face became self-righteously stern. "I would have told them to plead guilty, sir. If they were guilty, if they did this thing, and if they had told me so, I would have said to them to plead guilty. I believe in truth. I believe in candor. I do not believe in violence. Labor does not need violence."

"What will be the attitude of the American Federation of Labor?" the *Times* asked him.

"There will be no particular attitude taken by the Federation," Gompers replied. "If they are guilty, then that ends the case for us, our connection with it. There is nothing more to say except to repeat that we have been cruelly deceived."

But Burns, not a single one of whose statements in connection with the case, as it happens, has yet been proved untrue or inaccurate, said that Gompers had known right along—"from the beginning"—that the McNamaras were guilty.

Reporters asked Burns what he thought of Gompers.

"Why, boys," said Burns, "what I think of that man is unfit to print. Had Gompers been honest, he would have demonstrated it by apologizing, not to me—but to organized labor and the American people generally for his abuse and vilification of me when I arrested the McNamaras. If Gompers is arrested on his contempt charge [in the Buck Stove and Range Company boycott case] now pending against him in Washington, it will be to the interest of labor—decent labor—to lock him up and throw away the key. Gompers cried that the kidnaping of labor leaders by Burns would have to stop. Did he ever open his mouth about stopping murdering men like rats in a trap? Gompers said that the McNamaras and Darrow deceived him. The truth is that Gompers did the deceiving."

Of course, under the circumstances, no one could reasonably have expected Gompers to act differently.

V

Like their chief, trade-union leaders the country over were "shocked" by the confession. They were "stunned" and "pained," and they denounced the McNamaras and "abhorred their crime." John Mitchell was "astounded" and Frank Morrison was "simply thunderstruck." Separate unions and central labor councils in numerous cities and towns passed resolutions, which they sent to the district attorney and the judge in the case in Los Angeles, urging them to "show no mercy" to the dynamiters, to "give them the limit," "the full penalty of the law."

Burns remarked that some of the leaders denouncing the McNamaras were sincere, others—"most of them"—were not.

Tens of thousands of people throughout the country believed that the men had confessed "to save Darrow from going to prison." Thousands believed—some still do—that they were not guilty at all, but that they had sacrificed themselves for Darrow; which, of course, is absurd on the face of it.

Meantime Burns and the United States Department of Justice agents were working on other dynamite cases. "We're going after the men back of the McNamaras," said Burns. "When Gompers says he was deceived, he is uttering a lot of drivel and buncombe."

The conservative press of the entire United States turned upon Gompers and other leaders of the labor movement, upon Darrow, upon the Socialists. Said the New York *Tribune*:

> Mr. Samuel Gompers wept when he heard of the confession. The precise cause of his grief is left to speculation. Perhaps no injustice will be done in assuming that it was more subjective than objective. He probably wept more for his own distress and that of the close corporation which he arrogantly calls "labor" than for the fate of those two friends of his whom he was only yesterday commiserating as the victims of a hellish conspiracy and whom he was quite prepared tomorrow to mourn as holy martyrs.

The *Wall Street Journal* was delighted with Gompers's predicament:

> Doubtless the trusts bribed the McNamaras to confess in order to discredit labor... Mr. Gompers seems almost too good to be true. He has managed to reach the highest position in labor politics while preserving a pristine innocence of mind beside which the new-born babe seems wallowing in original sin. This good man was moved to tears when he heard [the news]. He never suspected it was coming, although others with inferior sources of information had ample notice... No one short of a congenital idiot could have ascribed [the numerous dynamitings between 1905 and 1910] to anything but the *deliberate* policy of violence pursued by this particular union; and we do not believe for a moment that Mr. Gompers is a fool, whatever else he may be.

Burns said: "I dare Gompers to put his statement that he knew nothing of the dynamite plot into an affidavit. I'm willing to make an affidavit that Gompers went to Indianapolis and sat and talked with men who worked with the McNamaras."

Gompers could do nothing but ignore the challenge.

VI

But few people had kind words for the McNamaras. One of these was John J. Keegan, member of the Indiana State Legislature and State organizer for the Machinists' Union, who said: "I'm just as proud of the friendship of John J. as I was two weeks ago." President Ryan, of the Iron Workers, said he had "no desire to see the brothers repudiated." Bill Haywood, of course, stood by them. "You can't view the class struggle," he said, "through the stained-glass windows of a cathedral, or through the eyes of capitalist-made laws. I'm with the McNamaras and always will be."

Most of the Socialists suddenly turned against the dynamiters. Said Bouck White:

> Every true Socialist should rejoice at the McNamara fiasco. For that hideous exposure laid bare the hiding places of the heart of trade unionism. *Trade unionism stands for violence.* That is the lesson which John J. McNamara sculptured enduringly on the tablets of every intelligent reader of events, for that dynamiter was more than a private in the ranks. Rapid was his promotion, swift was the preferment over his fellows—and by his fellows—to a high post of leadership; he is the kind of man trade unionism delights to honor. After his arrest, their official magazine continued to hint the end of further violence. To be sure, disclaimers are now being uttered sonorously and tearfully. But these vociferations are muffled into muteness by the thunder of fact—fact palpable as the day. I press it upon you: it was trade unionism and not an unofficial set of irresponsibles that decreed and did this wrecking of property and this slaughter… No clear shining idealism illumines trade unionism. Its aims are material aims; therefore its warfarings are material warfarings, with burning and fuel of fire, with confused noise and garments rolled in blood.

André Tridon, who later became well-known as a psychologist and author of books on psychoanalysis, then active in the Socialist movement, wrote to the New York *Tribune*, rejoicing over the McNamara

174   confession, for it was a blow at "trade unionism, pure and simple," whose policy was "akin to the trusts' policy."

Having taken such an active part in the McNamara defense, Socialist leaders were self-conscious; and to get over the uneasy feeling, they turned savagely on every one connected with the case except the Socialists. They began wantonly to accuse Darrow of having manipulated the case so as to get money out of the workers and then sold their cause to the capitalists just in the nick of time to prevent Harriman's election!

The *Appeal to Reason* was breathless for two issues after the confession, unable to utter a word about the case. Then it said: "The McNamaras were Democrats." That was the biggest comfort the Socialists managed to get out of the mess: The McNamaras were not Socialists, they were Democrats. The comrades wanted to forget that John J. McNamara, sitting in his cell in Los Angeles, was Job Harriman's leading campaigner.

Debs said: "Now that the trial in this celebrated case is ended, let us calmly review the principal features of this thrilling chapter in the class war." Only three weeks before Debs had been issuing calls for revolt; now, all of a sudden, he was in favor of calm. "McNamaras were Democrats, not Socialists, and not only this, but they were members of the Catholic Church, whose priests were and are denouncing Socialists as unclean."

VII

On December 5, James B. McNamara was sentenced for life to San Quentin. John J. received a term of fifteen years; he served not quite ten, having been released May 10, 1921. James B. is still in the penitentiary, now an aged man.

On the same day that the McNamaras were sentenced, Job Harriman was beaten in the election for Mayor of Los Angeles.

VIII

General Harrison Gray Otis, on the other hand, became a hero, second, perhaps, only to William J. Burns, among the patriots. The Employers' Association of the State of Washington wired him: "We offer you our congratulations…deep sympathy to you and the strong men of Los Angeles who have stood by you in the long fight for the principles of freedom." Myron T. Herrick of Ohio wrote him: "Sincerely congratu-

late you on the vindication of your position and the triumph of good
government."

Ever since the McNamaras' confession Los Angeles has been safely conservative and open-shop. Wages of labor now are lower in Los Angeles than, perhaps, in any other large city in the United States. In its advertisements, urging big Eastern industrialists to establish branch factories in Southern California, the Los Angeles Chamber of Commerce is stressing the fact that in Los Angeles "cheap non-union labor is plentiful."

In San Francisco, as a result of the general public's righteous reaction to the Los Angeles horror, the labor-union political machine was put out of office at the next election and in subsequent years the power of the unions began to decline also in the economic field, till of late years numerous industries in that city have become open-shop.

In fine, the "stunt," from the viewpoint of the San Francisco labor leaders who had organized it, was a total failure—and worse.

CHAPTER 24
THE A.F. OF L. LOSES ITS
MILITANCY

On October 16, 1911—five days after the opening of the McNamara trial—President Taft, visiting Los Angeles, was told by prominent conservatives in town some of the things that Burns had uncovered in connection with the McNamara arrests; things which amounted, practically, to a disclosure of a nationwide dynamite conspiracy on the part of certain big labor unions against open-shop employers and communities. On his return to Washington, the President ordered the Department of Justice to make a full investigation, and by the time that the McNamaras pleaded guilty scores of Government agents had unearthed incriminating evidence against a number of high union leaders. Burns himself continued investigations.

One motive in the McNamaras' confession, perhaps, was the desire to protect other men, for, if the trial went on, big leaders of the Iron Workers connected with the dynamite operations would be drawn into the affair. But it was in vain. After the McNamara débâcle, the so-called "Dynamite Conspiracy" cases were brought before Federal grand juries at Indianapolis and Los Angeles.

In Los Angeles, O. A. Tveitmoe and Anton Johannsen were indicted for complicity in the Times Building blowing-up party, but at the end nothing came of these indictments. When I saw Johannsen in Chicago, in the summer of 1929, he remarked: "The bastards couldn't stick anything on me!" As a matter of fact, Los Angeles had had enough of dynamite trials. Tveitmoe was later indicted and convicted at Indianapolis as a participator in the "Dynamite Conspiracy."

At Indianapolis, sensation followed sensation. By the summer of 1912, fifty-four officials and members of international unions affiliated with the A.F. of L. were indicted as dynamite conspirators, among them President Ryan of the Iron Workers, along with the rest of the executive committee of that union. They were charged with transporting dynamite on passenger trains for unlawful purposes or conspiring to cause such violations of Federal laws.

The famous "Dynamite Conspiracy" trial, which was a direct outgrowth of the Los Angeles *Times* blow-up, began October 1, 1912. Of the fifty-four accused men eleven were not tried, one was never apprehended, one was ill, several were already in prison, and three were discharged on motion of the Government. The cases were covered by thirty-two indictments, but as all the men were named in several of the indictments one general trial was possible.

Ortie McManigal, the dynamiter and tool of the "higher-ups," was the principal witness against the defendants, and his testimony, involving practically every official of the Iron Workers, was largely corroborated by other witnesses and material evidence. The Government prosecutors offered 620 exhibits, including pieces of exploded bombs, old nitroglycerin cans, cartridges, fuses, magazine guns, some of which were found in the Iron Workers' headquarters. In addition, the Government had letters written by the defendants, and seized in the Iron Workers' offices, in which they discussed their dynamiting operations. The New York *Tribune* remarked during the trial that the dynamitings could be accounted for only in some such way as McManigal described; on the other hand the St. Louis *Labor* was "convinced that while the scoundrel, McManigal, may have had close relations with the McNamaras and may have received money from them, he was at the same time in the employ of the enemies of labor, with duties to discredit the movement."

My belief is that McManigal was not in the employ of the enemies of labor, but that he turned State's evidence to save himself.

II

The trial cost the United States Government upward of a million dollars and was generally characterized as "the most remarkable trial in the history of the country."

Thirty-eight defendants were convicted on all the counts of the indictment, two were acquitted, five found guilty and released on suspended sentences. President Ryan of the Iron Workers was given seven years in prison; John T. Butler, vice-president, Herbert S. Hockin, secretary of the same union, and O. A. Tveitmoe, secretary of the California Building Trades, were sentenced to six years each. The others' sentences ranged from one to four years. Burns remarked that the conviction of Tveitmoe, friend of Gompers and the brains behind the Los Angeles dynamiting, was "more important than all the others."

The Los Angeles *Times*, full of righteousness and self-satisfaction, commented on the wholesale convictions: "Let this be a warning to all dynamiters and assassins in the labor unions. It is well." All other conservative and reactionary papers in the country editorialized to the same effect. The press in England and on the Continent dealt with the trial and the exposure largely in terms of amazement; such things, palpably, could happen only in America!

The respectable pulpit and press demanded: "What is Mr. Gompers going to do about the Iron Workers' union? Is it still eligible for membership in the American Federation of Labor?"

Gompers, of course, took no action against the Iron Workers. At the 1912 convention of the A.F. of L., he talked as a man in his position would: "For high motives, for altruism, for righting the wrongs, for the winning of rights, for human progress, there is no other body in the world, man for man, that will compare with the American Federation of Labor."

The "dynamite conspirators" were lodged in the Leavenworth Penitentiary. When in prison but a few months, President Ryan was re-elected to his office by the Iron Workers—which the self-righteous conservative press immediately characterized as "a direct incitement to dynamiting," "an abominable perversion of the natural instincts of justice and conscience." In chorus with hundreds of other newspapers, large and small, the New York *Tribune* asked: "What will Mr. Gompers do about it?"

Gompers did nothing about it. He merely continued to spout pious generalizations about the "principles" of his movement. Had he tried to do anything about Ryan's re-election or the Iron Workers in general, there can be little doubt that at the next A.F. of L. convention the "gorillas," the strong-arm element in the building trades unions, which were the backbone of the Federation, would have de-throned him as president. And to Gompers the presidency of the A.F. of L., to which he was sincerely devoted, was his whole life.

Besides, as the St. Louis *Labor* put it, the trade-union movement could do nothing but "stand by these men and their families in this hour of storm and stress. Whether innocent or guilty, they are the victims of a system of social crime."

Before long three other "dynamite conspirators" doing time in Leavenworth were re-elected to their respective offices by the unions. And, from the unions' point of view, logically enough. They, like John J. McNamara, had originally been chosen to their offices because they believed in dynamite in case of emergency. Behind their "dynamite conspiracy," as I have emphasized, was the desperation of big labor unions finding themselves face to face with brutal anti-union capitalist associations; behind their doings was the desperation of tens of thousands of workers to whom the union was the only hope of a better life.

III

Gompers was right when he remarked, following the McNamara confession: "It won't do the labor movement any good." Indeed, the affair, as it turned out, took the militant spirit out of the American Federation of Labor.

For half a decade prior to the terrible débâcle in Los Angeles, the A.F. of L. was, as we have seen, a fighting organization, trying to meet capitalism on its own ground, in the courts of law. Gompers, Morrison, and Mitchell, "martyrs of capitalist greed," were about to go to prison for contempt of court in the Buck Stove and Range boycott case. During the McNamara case, while the United States Supreme Court decision was still pending in the boycott affair, Gompers, with more fight in him than ever before, threatened the capitalist class and the Government with dire consequences unless "the boys" were freed. At the Atlanta convention in 1911, only two weeks before the confession, he threatened to be done with the Republican and Democratic parties once and for all. The trade unions and the Socialist Party were getting closer and closer together. In California in 1910 they had actually joined hands with the approval of Gompers and the national leaders of the Socialist movement. There were signs of a great upheaval, in which the A.F. of L. would play the most important role. Roosevelt and Wilson, candidates for the Presidency of the United States, were being alarmed by the rising tide of radicalism in all parts of the country. The A.F. of L., feeling that it was unable to measure up as an equal of the trusts and corporations in the capitalist courts, was becoming revolutionary, abandoning its "pure and simple" trade-union principles. The words of Debs were but a trifle more violent than those of Gompers. After the McNamaras' pleas of guilty, the conservative press and representative capitalists openly admitted that they had feared a terrible uprising, bloodshed, perhaps a general strike, if the case had continued. Never before had there been such nationwide class-consciousness on the part of the working class of America as in the last half of 1911. There were practically no right and left wings in the movement.

Then, with the McNamara fiasco, while Gompers blubbered his unconvincing denials and alibis, all the "guts" went out of the A.F. of L. Its militancy had been based upon a false righteousness, idealism, and nobility of purpose, which the McNamara confession, followed by the revelations of the "Dynamite Conspiracy," turned to nothing in the eyes of the righteous and moral public whose support was an essential factor in the attainment of its aims. Now the conservative press began, gleefully, to compare the trade unions to the Molly Maguires and the Mafia.

Poor Sam Gompers! That this terrible thing should happen in his old age! He was no longer invited to orate before liberal civic and patriotic organizations about the ideals and noble hopes of organized labor. When the news of the McNamara confession came out, his name was on the programs of two civic organizations; then, without explanation, it was taken off. He and his organization were in disrepute in the eyes of the moral public.

And now the only way that he could regain some of the outward respectability and prestige for himself and the A.F. of L. was to be good; that is, avoid all radicalism, scorn the Socialists, refrain from strikes and boycotts and further demands for higher wages, fight the evil I.W.W., furnish strikebreakers in wobbly strikes, and, when the war to make the world safe for democracy came on, cheer the flag and denounce such filthy pacifists as Ramsay MacDonald and Eugene Debs.

Soon after the collapse of the McNamara case, the Buck Stove and Range affair was quashed; there was no use prosecuting Gompers, Mitchell, and Morrison any longer. With the shame of the McNamara guilt behind them, they were utterly harmless as leaders of the havenots against the haves.

Immediately after the dynamite cases and following the war, all important industrial battles were fought by the I.W.W. and other leftwing unions, while the A.F. of L., trying to live down the disgrace which Gompers's tears could not wash away, degenerated into deepest respectability and ineffectiveness regarding the wider interests of the American working people. Indeed, its effectiveness regarding even its own members has greatly diminished.

As I write this, in the fall of 1930, the *Nation* prints an article entitled "The Collapse of the A.F. of L."

Today the A.F. of L. is utterly spiritless. Its leaders are pompous, high-toned Babbitts, some of them with stock-exchange tickers in their offices. Its conventions compare with those of the Elks, the Rotarians, and the National Association of Soap Manufacturers. They invite Army generals to address them. William Green, Gompers's worthy successor, goes to West Point to review the cadet corps and receive honors such as are ordinarily rendered only to visiting royalty, while in Massachusetts they let Sacco and Vanzetti go to the chair and in California Tom Mooney, a trade unionist, stays in prison for fourteen years although innocent of the crime for which he was convicted.

IV

The McNamara fiasco *temporarily* suppressed the impulse to dynamite in the A.F. of L. unions.

Gompers had always been against violence. He was a cautious, scheming man, but he lacked the moral and intellectual power to enforce his views within the movement. He had talked against violence, but, in order to stay in office, had shut his eyes and stopped his ears every time an A.F. of L. dynamiter placed a bomb.

Now, however, with the terrific effect of the McNamara guilt apparent to everybody, his anti-dynamite preachments began to be heeded even by the "gorillas" in the building trades unions. The latter were compelled to agree with Gompers that dynamite was dangerous stuff. It, perhaps, did no damage to the unions using it, but it played the devil with the movement as a whole, because the A.F. of L. officially, was opposed to violence and pretended to moral principles. It had done no harm to the Iron Workers, who believed in dynamite and used it to save the organization, but it put the A.F. of L. into a dreadful mess.

So Gompers pleaded with the "gorillas" to refrain from dynamite in the future, and for a few years he was heeded.

The war came on, the wage scale rose, and for a little while labor, organized and otherwise, had little to complain of.

Immediately after the war, however, the unions once more found themselves in a desperate struggle for existence, especially in Chicago, *and dynamite once more was the only means of salvation.* Only now the union leaders were more careful. There must be no more McNamara cases. So they commenced to hire professional criminals exclusively, men who, unlike such fanatics as James B. McNamara, were practically beyond the reach of the law—"racketeers," as they began to be called about 1922.

Desperate labor unions, indeed, as I show in a later chapter, were one of the most important factors in the inception, early in the last decade, of what is now called "racketeering."

PART FIVE
MASSACRES, FRAME-UPS, AND JUDICIAL MURDERS

"Many people witnessed this horrible
murder. The guilty men were named
openly in newspapers and from a hundred
platforms. Yet no one was ever punished
for the crime."
—*WILLIAM Z. FOSTER*

CHAPTER 25
SLAUGHTER EAST AND WEST

The capitalists and industrialists of the United States took advantage of the public's intense reaction to the exposure of the A.F. of L.'s dynamiting operations and once more tightened up their lines against further efforts of labor to improve its conditions. Encouraged by General Otis's shining victory for the open shop in Los Angeles, they took up the battle for the "American Plan" against the "Mafia-like unions," and in not a few instances they were highly successful. On the other hand, excepting the Lawrence strike in 1912, led by the wobblies, there was no great labor victory between the end of the McNamara case and 1917, when the United States entered the World War.

The climax of the employers' war for the open shop was reached in the spring of 1914, in the so-called Ludlow Massacre.

In the coal-fields of southern Colorado several thousand miners had been "out" since September 1913. They were loosely organized, but motivated by bitterness born of ill treatment. The mines in which they worked when they were employed were for the most part controlled by the Rockefeller interests. Their demands included the eight-hour day, pay for "narrow and dead work," a check weighman without interference of company officials, the right to trade in any store they pleased, the abolition of the criminal guard system, ten per cent advance in wages, and recognition of the union. Of these demands five were guaranteed under severe penalty by the laws of the State of Colorado. They were, however, not enforced, for the mining interests, interlocked with other interests in the State, controlled and ran the State Government through the politicians they installed in office. And so the miners were compelled to resort to a strike in order to put into effect a series of laws which it was the obligation of the employers to obey and of the State to enforce! But the demand that the operators opposed most strenuously was that for the recognition of the union. They, with John

D. Rockefeller, Jr., as their leader, were determined to keep down any effort which might endanger the lofty open-shop "principle." John D. spoke eloquently of his devotion to "principles." He said:

> We would rather that the unfortunate conditions should continue, and that we should lose all the millions invested, than that American workmen should be deprived of their right, under the Constitution, to work for whom they please. That is the great principle at stake. It is a national issue.

The strike dragged into the spring of 1914. Mines were being operated by non-union men, most of them foreigners. To protect the properties and the non-union miners, the Rockefellers and other operators engaged hundreds of "guards" or gunmen, while the State called out considerable bodies of militia. Martial law was declared long before there were any riots; then strikers were beaten up and shot at, and disturbances occurred. The striking miners, to protect themselves, began to procure arms and ammunition. They moved off the companies' grounds and camped in tents. They dug trenches around the camps and holes inside the tents, into which women and children might crawl in the event of attack.

On April 20, 1914, either a striker shot a non-union miner or a soldier fired at a striker near the camp outside of Ludlow, whereupon a battle started and soon spread over an area of three miles. About 500 miners were opposed by approximately 200 militia, but the soldiers, many of whom were but recently sworn-in gunmen, were equipped with machine-guns and other superior weapons, which made the strikers' numbers count for nothing.

Machine-gun bullets riddled the tents; then the camp took fire. "In the holes which had been dug for their protection against the rifles' fire," says one contemporary account of the battle, "the women and children died like trapped rats when the flames swept over them."

Thirty-three people were either shot or burned to death. More than half of these were women and children. Over a hundred others were wounded or badly burned.

The Ludlow battle lasted fourteen hours, after which the camp was abandoned and most of the women and children, dead and alive, were taken to Trinidad, while the strikers began to organize into military companies, taking up positions on the hills. Several mine-shafts were attacked and burned. More battles occurred.

The Denver *Express*, which, though not a labor paper, favored the
strike, printed a vivid characterization of the Ludlow slaughter:

> Mothers and babies were crucified on the cross of human liberty.
> Their crucifixion was effected by the operators' paid gunmen who
> have worn militia uniforms less than a week. The dead will go down
> in history as the hero victims of the burned offering laid on the altar
> of Rockefeller's Great God Greed.

President Wilson ordered out Federal troops but, before they arrived in southern Colorado and disarmed both the strikers and the gunmen wearing militia uniforms, about a dozen more miners had been killed.

Ultimately Rockefeller won; he did not recognize the union. His great passion for "principles" was gratified.

II

Gunmen, supplied by private "detective" agencies, were employed by industrialists in numerous strikes that occurred shortly before the United States entered the World War. Usually these thugs were decorated with deputy badges and endowed with local police power, which they often exceeded.

It was war, called "war" by both sides. In March 1913, during a bitter and violent miners' strike, Mother Jones and forty-nine miners were tried in a military court at Paint Creek Junction, West Virginia, which was under martial law, on the charge of "conspiracy to commit murder." In defending them, their attorney asked: "Was the battle of Gettysburg murder?" He claimed that, if the miners killed, it was in a war and should not be characterized as murder. He introduced as evidence three proclamations issued by the Governor of West Virginia calling the great industrial struggle in the Paint Creek district "war." "The miners accept it as war," said the attorney. "If they will resort to violence, their acts will be aimed at a system and not at individuals. And their acts will be acts of war, which society should not judge by ordinary rules of law and morality." But in spite of such occasional utterances, labor in that period was comparatively non-violent. Most of the violence was committed by the other side.

An incident that was typical of, perhaps, dozens of minor labor massacres throughout the country between 1913 and 1917, occurred in New Jersey early in 1915. On January 2, about 900 employees of two fertilizer factories, situated in the swampy region along the New Jersey Central Railway between Elizabeth and Perth Amboy, struck for higher wages and shorter hours. They were peaceful, unarmed, but, hearing that the companies might employ strikebreakers, watched for their arrival. Both factories were guarded by a force of "deputy sheriffs" hired from a Newark "detective agency."

On the morning of January 19, a crowd of strikers gathered at a tiny railroad station near one of the plants, waiting for a train from New York which they heard would bring in several hundred scabs. A member of the police force of the Borough of Roosevelt was on duty at the station, and this is what happened according to his story as he told it to a reporter of the New York *World*:

> I am positive that not a man carried a revolver or any other sort of weapon unless it was a pocket-knife. The men seemed most peaceful, and I knew they were not bent on making trouble. Several of them told me that they simply were going to do picket duty, and were going to try to persuade the strikebreakers to return to their homes or join in the strike. They stood on public property and I had no authority to interfere with them.
>
> [The train arrived and then] the big gates of the Williams & Clark mill swung open, and out rushed the deputies. The shooting began at once. If those deputies say they fired in the air and that the strikers fired at them first, they lie. The strikers did not fire. They had nothing with which to fire. They simply were butchered. It's impossible to describe how those unarmed, defenseless men were shot down. Some ran and escaped injury. Those who were unable to get to high ground made for the swamps, and it was those men that were shot, beaten, and then shot again... I got into the thick of the trouble, but one man in that frantic mob and savage crowd of gunmen was nothing. The deputies shot until their leader gave the signal. At that time men were all about, wounded and screaming for help. The deputies made not the slightest effort to aid the men they had shot down. They simply marched back into the plant and locked themselves in.

Twenty-eight men were wounded; two of them died the same day, four more within a week. Even the most conservative newspapers were outraged by the massacre. The New York *Sun*, which had never been guilty of undue leanings toward the employees' side, called the gunmen's shooting "wanton and outrageous."

Twenty-two deputies were arrested on charges of manslaughter, but that was as far as it went. They were later released.

III

Throughout 1915 and 1916 strikers were killed by hired thugs in Colorado, West Virginia, New Jersey, and other States. In the summer of 1915, for instance, eight men were killed and seventeen severely wounded during a strike against the Standard Oil Company at Bayonne, N.J, which employed "guards."

After every massacre, the conservative press editorialized disapprovingly of private gunmen. Following the Bayonne riots, the New York *World* said:

Hired ostensibly to guard property during the progress of strikes, these men usually operate aggressively against everybody who approaches them... The fact cannot be too often emphasized that industrial disputes take on the character of private warfare chiefly for the reason that the States in most cases have no disciplined force for the preservation of order, like that of Pennsylvania, with its State Constabulary.

On which the New York *Call*, a Socialist paper, commented:

In a word, what the *World* wants is to give the workingmen more variety in the matter of being shot. Murder by deputy sheriffs is getting monotonous. Let us have State Constabulary butchers, who know their business better, and who can always be defended by the press on the ground that they are more regularly "official" than the haphazard killers picked up any old where to "settle labor disturbances."

The *Call* was not unjustified in this comment. We have seen the brutality of the Pennsylvania State Constabulary—"the Cossacks"—in the wobbly strike at McKees Rocks in 1909. In a later chapter we will again witness "Cossackism" in the Great Steel Strike of 1919.

CHAPTER 26
THE MOONEY-BILLINGS FRAME-UP

The reaction to the McNamara blowing-up party in Los Angeles and to the "Dynamite Conspiracy" revelations, which sent "Boss" Tveitmoe of the San Francisco Labor Party to prison, was—naturally—more intense in California than elsewhere in the United States. The San Francisco industrialists proposed to take full and immediate advantage of it and "Los Angeles-ize" San Francisco, namely, make it an open-shop town.

A savage "crush the unions" movement was already afoot in the city of the Golden Gate in 1912. It was headed by the big executives in the utility corporations. Because of the annoyances they had been compelled to suffer at the hands of the unions in the years following the earthquake, the San Francisco capitalists and employers now were an angry lot, giving free vent to their wrath. With the shame of the McNamara case upon the unions, they saw their chance of freeing themselves from labor domination and re-capturing the city economically and politically. They openly declared themselves in favor of the "American Plan" and General Harrison Gray Otis's methods in dealing with labor.

Their movement was very successful.

The unions' power declined rapidly. In 1912 they lost the city politically. Then they began to lose control of the jobs, and by 1915 the labor element, as such, was no longer of great importance in the political life of the city. The so-called "conservative" labor leaders, oppressed as they were by the guilt of the McNamaras and other "dynamite conspirators," were largely ineffectual against the onslaughts of organized capitalists, who now had the full support of the great moral mob in the community. Big industries became open-shop, and the wages dropped and the number of work-hours went up.

This collapse of conservative unionism, however, strengthened the left-wing faction in the labor organizations which believed in "di-

192   rect action" and in "getting tough" with the capitalists. These scorned
Gompers's pleas to the unions that they should steer clear of dynamite. "To hell with the old fogy!" they said. "To hell with Gompers's
polite trade-unionism, pure and simple!" Although members of trade
unions, they called themselves Socialists and attended secret anarchist meetings.

In 1915 or thereabout, the foremost labor radical in San Francisco
was Thomas J. Mooney, a moulder by trade and virtual leader of the
considerable left-wing bloc in the California Federation of Labor. He
was a gifted and energetic organizer and strike leader, sensational in his
words and actions, which yielded him a good deal of publicity. He associated with known anarchists, both of the philosophical and the "deed"
varieties, and was violently against war. He raged against the European
war and the efforts of American patriots and militarists to embroil the
United States in the conflict. He was known to be a believer in dynamite, "the actual stuff," and had once been indicted for attempted
dynamiting of property of a San Francisco utility, but after three trials
was acquitted.

In the spring of 1916, Mooney and his wife were leaders in a bitter
and unsuccessful fight to organize the ill-paid carmen of the United
Railroads of San Francisco. They thereby brought upon themselves
the wrath of the most powerful corporation in the city, whose managers were leaders of the local "crush the unions" campaign.

The United Railroads' money and their personal and moral support were behind the so-called Law and Order Committee of the San
Francisco Chamber of Commerce, one of whose functions, along with
cheering Old Glory and agitating for Preparedness, was to defend private gunmen when, in labor troubles, they slugged and killed union
men. The United Railroads' money and moral support were also behind Charles M. Fickert, a leader in the "crush the unions" drive who,
in 1914, had been elected county district attorney. On coming into
office, Fickert began at once to hound labor leaders and radicals. Tom
Mooney was his particular prey.

II

In 1916, with the European war two years old, the United States was
suddenly afflicted with a high "get ready for war" fever. Ex-President
Roosevelt and his crony, General Leonard Wood, advocated universal
military training, for, to their minds, it was inevitable that the country
eventually would be involved in the world conflict. Preparedness was

an issue in the 1916 presidential campaign. In the larger cities parades were held, while radical soap-boxers fumed against militarism and imperialism and the American jingoes who were trying to drag the country into the frightful mess across the Atlantic. The preparedness movement was headed largely by high-powered Republicans and, in its political significance, was an attempt to rebuke President Wilson for being "too proud to fight" and doing nothing decisive about Germany's attacks upon American commerce.

In San Francisco, as elsewhere, the preparedness leaders, who were also the leading spirits of the Law and Order Committee, had a local reason for wanting to stage a great patriotic military demonstration. They wanted, as one of them was quoted, to "show the sons-of-bitches [that is, labor leaders like Mooney] where to get off." It was, in fact, intended to be a gesture of defiance to labor's efforts to improve its lot, or rather to retain the advantages it already had won, in San Francisco. It was to be a warning to laborites and radicals that, should they "start something," they would be dealt with in a manner no gentler than that of the aggressive employers in Colorado and New Jersey.

Early in July, after Mooney and his wife had already been defeated in their attempt to organize the United Railroads carmen, the city authorities were persuaded to proclaim the twenty-second of the month as Preparedness Day, and all civic, patriotic, military business, and fraternal organizations—except the labor unions—were invited to participate in the parade.

On the twenty-second, between noon and two o'clock, an immense mob of people in military and fraternal uniforms, with flags and bands, with all the symbols of their high standing in the community on display, assembled on the Embarcadero and in the side streets off lower Market Street. At six minutes past two, the head of the column, with the Governor of California and the Mayor of San Francisco prominently in view, swung up Market, while a detachment of Spanish War Veterans came in from Steuart Street to fall into the main line of march.

Then—suddenly, while the band ahead played a martial piece—a dynamite bomb exploded by a saloon wall on Steuart near Market, instantly killing six persons and injuring over forty, of whom four died within the next few days.

III

San Francisco, to say nothing of the rest of California and the United States as a whole, was deeply stirred. It was a terrible crime. Aggressive police activity was started at once and the press was filled with clues and theories for the solution of the tragic mystery. "The radicals did it!" The situation was a mild repetition of the immediate consequences of the Haymarket explosion in Chicago, thirty years before.

Five days after the explosion Tom Mooney and his wife, Rena Mooney, Warren K. Billings, Israel Weinberg, and Edward D. Nolan were arrested.

Billings, twenty-two years old, was a rising young left-winger in the San Francisco labor unions, a friend of Mooney, a believer in "direct action." He had previously been convicted of carrying explosives on a passenger train. Weinberg was a jitney-bus driver who had occasionally driven Tom and Rena Mooney. His son was a pupil of Mrs. Mooney, who was a music teacher. Nolan, too, was a radical laborite and a friend of Tom.

But Mooney, because of his prominence in the labor movement, was from the start the center of the case.

On the prosecution's side next to District Attorney Fickert, the most important character was a private detective named Martin Swanson, a secret operative in the "crush the unions" movement. He had formerly been employed by the Pacific Gas and Electric Company, which in its passion to kill the unions was second only to that of the United Railroads. While in the employ of the Gas and Electric, only a few months before, Swanson had tried to connect Mooney with the dynamiting of some property, but failed, it appears, because Billings and Weinberg refused his offers of "reward" to testify against their friend. Now Swanson was appointed an "investigator" on District Attorney Fickert's staff, with the special duty to build up the case against Mooney and the others, or rather to help Fickert build it up.

Billings was tried first, in the fall of 1916. A jobless waiter, John McDonald, who since has stated that he had perjured himself under instructions from Fickert and Swanson, testified that at 1:50 p.m. on July 22 he had seen Billings place a suitcase against the saloon wall on the corner of Steuart and Market Streets and then confer for a few moments with Tom Mooney in the saloon doorway. Several other witnesses more or less substantiated McDonald's tale. Billings protested his innocence, but in vain; he was convicted on the charge of manslaughter and, because of his youth, let off with a life term in Folsom Prison.

The Mooney trial was delayed until January 1917, but by this time the prosecution's case was considerably weakened. Photographs taken during the parade on the roof of the building where Mrs. Mooney had her music studio—*a mile from the scene of the explosion*—were developed and enlarged, showing by a clock in the picture that Mooney and his wife were on that roof at 1:58, which conflicted with McDonald's testimony that he had seen Mooney at Steuart and Market at 1:50. But then McDonald—obviously instructed anew by Fickert and Swanson—amended his story to the effect that he had seen Mooney and Billings together in the saloon doorway sometime between 1:30 and 1:45, which would have made it possible for Mooney to get to the roof of that building by 1:58.

But Fickert had other "witnesses." Among them, was one Frank C. Oxman, who seemed a "frank and honest" cattleman from Oregon, a typical product of the open spaces of the West. Oxman testified that he had arrived from Portland that morning and that he had stopped on the corner of Steuart and Market at about 1:30 in the afternoon to watch the parade, and there observed even more than McDonald. He described everything in great detail with a matter-of-fact simplicity, which made his story convincing to the jury and the judge. He said that Mooney and Billings had arrived on the corner in a Ford machine that looked like Weinberg's jitney, with three other passengers, including "a lady." With great foresight, Oxman had noted down the license number, which, it turned out, was the number of Weinberg's jitney.

Ever since his arrest Mooney had been called by the newspapers everything from an anarchist to a pro-German, while, in the courtroom, Fickert denounced him as a dynamiter, a dangerous man, a German agent.

The jury brought in a verdict of guilty, and Mooney, the arch-enemy of the "crush the unions" element, was sentenced to be hanged.

Weinberg and Mrs. Mooney, tried later in 1917, were acquitted. Nolan was kept in prison for nearly two years and finally released without trial, for lack of evidence.

IV

Mooney was sent to San Quentin Prison.

But almost immediately after his conviction facts began to transpire which made the justice of both the Billings and the Mooney verdicts very questionable. Oxman's testimony was impeached. It was established beyond the shadow of a doubt that on July 22, instead of being in San Francisco, he was staying with his friends in Woodland, California, a town nearly 200 miles away. Oxman was later tried for perjury, but, with Fickert prosecuting him and the judge who presided over the case frankly stating his opinion that Mooney was "guilty anyhow," got off with a technical acquittal.

Subsequently other witnesses in the Billings and Mooney cases were completely discredited. By the middle of 1917 it was the American labor and liberal opinion that the men had unquestionably been "framed" and railroaded to prison in an atmosphere of patriotic, anti-labor hysteria, stirred up by reactionary newspapers and agents of large corporations, both in and out of public office.

In April 1917 President Wilson suppressed his aversion to fighting and plunged the country into the war "to make the world safe for democracy." The Mooney frame-up was apparently threatening to become a lively national issue that might deprive the government of some of the labor and liberal support in its war policy. Accordingly, in March 1918, the President addressed an open letter to Governor Stephens of California, urging either that Mooney be given a new trial at once or that his death sentence be commuted.

The "crush the unions" group in California resented the President's "interference with the orderly processes of California justice," as they called it, but Wilson's letter was effective none the less—first it postponed Mooney's execution and then, after the end of the war, prompted the Governor to grant him the commutation.

Mooney's life was saved, but as I write this—in the winter of 1930, fourteen years after the arrests—both Mooney and Billings are in prison despite twelve years of sustained and considerable efforts on the part of labor and liberal groups the country over to have them freed.

All the witnesses and members of the prosecution in the two cases have since been completely discredited. Judge Franklin A. Griffin, who presided at the Mooney trial, has appealed to three successive Governors of California for their pardon. Besides, all the living jurors in the Mooney case have appealed for clemency, and several police officials, prominent in the evidence-manufacturing activities of Fickert and Swanson, have declared themselves convinced that neither Mooney nor Billings had placed the bomb.

All this is to no avail. For political reasons, the executive and legal machinery of the State has been so manipulated all these years as to keep Mooney and Billings in prison. Governors William D. Stephens and Friend Richardson refused outright to consider Mooney's application for pardon. The State Supreme Court, basing its action on thin

legalistic grounds, has refused to grant a new trial for Mooney or to
pardon Billings.

In 1926 an obscure politician pretending to certain progressive principles, C. C. Young by name, was elected Governor of California with the support of labor and liberal groups, to whom he had promised, if elected, to give the Mooney pardon application "fair consideration." But when Young got into the governor's chair, he learned, as I think one is justified in assuming, that it would be political suicide on his part to pardon Mooney. Such great organs of open-shop industrialism as the Los Angeles *Times* and the San Francisco *Chronicle* began to hint that if he freed the labor leader his career would end disastrously.

Young was no Altgeld. In the first three years of his governorship he made an elaborate and hollow pretense of "studying" the case, whereupon—early in 1930, shortly before he became a candidate for re-election—he denied Mooney's application. It was his "final decision."

But, unwilling to shoulder the responsibility in the case alone, Governor Young turned the Billings case over to the Supreme Court of the State of California, indicating that, if that court should recommend the pardon of Billings, he would free both prisoners. The Supreme Court consisted for the most part of politicians of the mentality of Young, and on December 1, 1930, six of the Justices sent a letter to the Governor, concurring in his original opinion that Billings's trial had been fair and just. One of the Justices issued a minority opinion, in which he practically stated that, to his mind, Billings was innocent, and accused his colleagues of treating testimony that had been proved false as facts. However, Young's "final decision" stands upheld by the highest court in the State.

Behind this action of a group of servile politicians in office was the will of the big business interests in California. For Mooney and Billings, in San Quentin and Folsom respectively, are living symbols of the open-shop employers' supremacy in the State. Behind the industrialists' determination to keep Mooney and Billings imprisoned is their old fear of labor unions. They fear that the unions, given the slightest chance, might again seize the power in San Francisco that they had in 1910, and might even capture Los Angeles. This would mean the end of the open-shop status of the rising California industries.

California go-getters need Eastern capital to develop their communities. Not a few big real-estate operators and bankers in Los Angeles and San Francisco believe that California's credit in the East would decline should Mooney and Billings be released. Their belief is not unsound, for, in the eyes of Eastern magnates, one of California's chief virtues is its open-shop status in industry.

Between 1920 and 1930 numerous Eastern industrialists started plants in California upon the assurances of civic and business leaders in the State that the open-shop status would be maintained in the future. The "big fellows" in such organizations as the local Chambers of Commerce, the Merchants' and Manufacturers' Associations and the Better America Federation, whose economic and political potency is enormous, not only in the State but nationally, are determined to maintain that status. In sending out circulars to large manufacturers in the East, inviting them to bring their industries to California, they stress the fact that in their communities "labor is unorganized, cheap." And Mooney and Billings in prison are living advertisements of the California boosters' determination to keep California open-shop; a living proof to Eastern manufacturers and capitalists that they control the State utterly, from the Governor's mansion and the Supreme Court down; a living assurance to Eastern industrialists and financiers that they, using politics, the courts, the police, and every other means, fair and foul, intend to keep labor "cheap and unorganized" in California.

The American Federation of Labor, with the McNamara "stunt" as part of its past, is considered as dangerous and "un-American" in California, especially in Los Angeles, as are the I.W.W. and the Communists. Every effort to organize workers is nipped in the bud; the leaders are usually arrested and jailed. As I write this, scores of organizers and agitators, besides Mooney and Billings, are lodged in various California Jails.

The general California public—the great democratic mob that goes to the polls every so often—has but the faintest conception of the Mooney-Billings case, and that conception is largely erroneous. More than half the present population of California consists of recent arrivals there, tired and retired people mostly from the Middle West. Their concern with politics is slight and superficial. The go-getters, the politicians, and the newspapers can do almost as they please.

V

It will perhaps never be established who placed the bomb. No evidence exists that either Mooney or Billings had anything to do with it.

The idea, shared by many radicals in California and elsewhere, that the outrage was perpetrated by someone connected with the employ-

ers' "crush the union" movement, is not far-fetched. If the bomb was
planted by some anarchist or member of the Mooney group, which also
is not unlikely, the open-shop interests, in their savage efforts to keep
down labor, in taking full advantage of the terrible incident and the
public reaction thereto, have committed a worse crime than the bomb
explosion.

VI

In 1930 Governor Young was defeated for re-election despite the
fact that he kept Mooney and Billings in prison; his defeat was due to
other issues. In January 1931, James Rolph, Jr., for twenty years Mayor
of San Francisco, a machine politician masquerading as a "liberal"
and "friend of the people" but actually a faithful servant of powerful
corporations in his state, became Governor of California. His record
pertaining to the Mooney-Billings case was as disgusting as those of
his two predecessors.

Rolph died on June 3, 1934, and was succeeded by Lieutenant-
Governor Frank F. Merriam, an obscure politician, who in all probability will do nothing about Mooney and Billings. As this edition
appears, California will be in the midst of a heated campaign to
elect a Governor to take office in January 1935. In this campaign, the
Mooney-Billings case will again be a principal issue, whether the candidates discuss it or not.

As I write this (June 1934), Mooney and Billings are about to begin
the nineteenth year of their imprisonment for a crime with which—so
far as it can be determined by the records of their case—they had no
connection whatever. Their crime, in the eyes of those who control the
processes of justice in California, is that they were passionate, incor-
ruptible fighters in the cause of labor. For that crime, if the California
business interests will have it their way, Mooney and Billings will die
in San Quentin and Folsom, respectively. But the California business
interests possibly will not always have it their way.

CHAPTER 27
THE GREAT STEEL STRIKE

D uring the great crusade "to make the world safe for democracy,"
organized labor in the United States, with the exception of the
Industrial Workers of the World, supported the Government. Indeed,
Samuel Gompers, eagerly grasping the opportunity to appear once more
respectable and patriotic and regain the prestige he and the A.F. of L.
had lost in consequence of the McNamara episode, became a sort of
super-patriot. He vied with such representative capitalists as Judge Gary
of the Steel Trust in denouncing all who opposed the war, from Senator
LaFollette down. President Wilson, in his turn, spoke beautifully of
the "New Freedom" and "Industrial Democracy" and the "rewards" that
American labor would justly reap after the war for its patriotism.

But a very few months after the Armistice, the workers' "rewards"
began to come in the form of wage cuts and lockouts and police clubs
and bullets. The war had produced over 20,000 new millionaires and
multi-millionaires who now joined the veteran labor-fighters in a determined and savage effort to keep down the proletariat.

The radicals let out a cry of protest: were these wage cuts and lockouts the "rewards" that Wilson had talked about? Was this the "New
Freedom?" Wilson tried to appeal to the capitalist class to treat the
workers decently, but to no avail. He was only the President of the
United States. Throughout the early months of 1919, as wartime production ceased, there were more wage cuts and lockouts. The war profi-
teers were unwilling to share their war-made millions with the workers
after the war.

A wild-and-woolly, ultra-emotional radical movement sprang
up. The I.W.W. became strong in the West and the East, while the
Communists, a new breed of radicals in the United States, rivalled
the Socialists in proclaiming the wonders of the new Soviet regime in
Russia as compared with the brutal powers-that-were in America.

An anti-Red hysteria seized the capitalist class and the respectable people. Many industrialists honestly believed that Bolshevism was just around the corner and that A.F. of L. trade unionism, with its past record in violence, was merely its forerunner. One could not believe Gompers when he spouted patriotism. One had to take a "firm stand" against the "growing menace."

There was a great deal of whispered talk in the executive offices of large corporations about nipping this or that bit of "incipient Communism" in the bud. Much of the hysteria was stirred up by the Soviet Government, with its declarations about the imminent "world revolution"; by the Federal Government in Washington, with its persecution of harmless radicals; by local and State authorities who joined the Federal Government in that persecution; by private detective agencies trying to build up a new line of business; by ex-Intelligence Division sleuths and Department of Justice agents who, on leaving the Government service, became enterprising dealers in industrial espionage. All these and many others added to the alarm concerning the coming proletarian upheaval. Patriotic societies, such as the American Legion, an organization of World War soldiers and sailors, and the Daughters of the American Revolution, cried out against the Reds; new anti-Red and open-shop associations were formed, with staffs of propagandists and *agents provocateurs*.

Big strikes occurred and were accompanied by outbursts of violence—mostly on the part of the employers' agents and gunmen.

For example, there was the murder of Mrs. Fannie Sellins at West Natrona, Pennsylvania, in the summer of 1919. She was an organizer of the United Mine Workers of America, a woman of great energy and courage, operating for the most part in the notoriously anti-union Black Valley district along the Allegheny River. She had had considerable success and so became a thorn in the side of the coal companies.

In August 1919 the miners of the Allegheny Coal and Coke Company struck at West Natrona in protest against a wage cut. The mine was located in the mill-yard of the Allegheny Steel Company and furnished fuel for that mill. One day a group of "deputy peace officers" on strike duty, led by a mine official, suddenly rushed the pickets, opening fire on them. One striker was mortally wounded.

Fannie Sellins happened to be nearby and, on witnessing the above occurrence, proceeded to get some children that were playing there out of danger. Then she ran back to the mill-yard and pleaded with the "peace officers," who were still clubbing the unconscious picket, to let up on him.

One of the "peace officers" hit her on the head with his club. She fell, tried to rise, dragging herself toward the gate, away from the officers.

"Kill that goddamn whore!" shouted one of the men.

Three shots were fired, each taking effect.

"Give 'er more!"

Then, according to an eye-witness who put the story in an affidavit,

one of the deputies, standing over the motionless body, held his gun down and, without averting his face, fired into her once more. [Another deputy] picked up her hat, placed it on his head, danced a step, and said to the crowd: "I'm Fannie Sellins now."

Mrs. Sellins was forty-nine years of age, a grandmother, and mother of a son killed in France while a soldier in the great crusade "to make the world safe for democracy." William Z. Foster, in his *The Great Steel Strike and Its Lessons*, tells us:

Many people witnessed this horrible murder. The guilty men were named openly in newspapers and from a hundred platforms. Yet no one was ever punished for the crime... A couple of deputies were arrested; but they were speedily released on smaller bonds than those often set for strikers arrested for picketing. Eventually they were freed altogether.

II

On the heels of the Sellins murder came the so-called Great Steel Strike, beginning September 22, 1919, when nearly 400,000 men quit in the iron and steel mills and blast furnaces in fifty cities and towns of ten States—one of the most significant industrial battles in the history of the United States.

On one side were the steel manufacturers, who, as William Z. Foster, the chief leader in the strike, put it in his book, from which I quote above,

have always aggressively applied the ordinary, although unacknowledged, American business principles that our industries exist primarily to create huge profits for the fortunate few who own them, and that if they have any other utility it is a matter of secondary importance. The interests of society in the steel business they scoff at. And as for their employees, they have never considered them better than so much necessary human machinery, to be bought in the market at the lowest possible price and otherwise handled in a thoroughly irresponsible manner. They clearly understand that if they are to carry out their policy of raw exploitation, the prime essential is that they keep their employees unorganized.

With this policy, and owning the country's basic industry, the Steel Trust comprised the most powerful group of capitalists in the United States, controlling no end of newspapers, which "spewed forth poison propaganda in their behalf"; churches, which "had long since lost their Christian principles in an ignominious scramble for company favors"; and unscrupulous city, county, state, and Federal job-holders, whose "eagerness to wear the steel collar was equalled only by their forgetfulness of their oaths of office" and who suppressed the freedom of speech and assembly during strikes, and clubbed, shot, and jailed workers who rebelled against low wages, long hours, and the absence of safety devices in the mills. In the twenty-five years between the Homestead strike in 1892 and America's declaration of war upon Germany in 1917 the Steel Trust defeated all efforts to organize the workers on a large scale. The only exception, as indicated earlier in this book, was the Iron Workers, with their effective "dynamite conspiracy." And the endless series of defeats deprived the organizers of all confidence in their ability to withstand the power and militancy of the steel manufacturers.

In 1917, however, the situation changed in favor of the unions. With men being drawn into military service and the great demand for munitions and other war materials, labor became scarce. William Z. Foster, then one of the most aggressive labor organizers in Chicago, perceived the opportunity to organize the steel industry. He had no faith in Wilson's talk about labor's "rewards" after the war, believing that the workers would achieve benefits only by fighting for them. Therefore, on April 7, 1918, he introduced a resolution before the Chicago Federation of Labor asking the executives of the A.F. of L. "to call a general labor conference and to inaugurate thereat a national drive to organize the steel and iron workers." The resolution passed, but the unmilitant A.F. of L. executives, still oppressed by the McNamara guilt and now trying to rehabilitate themselves before the public with a great exhibition of patriotism, were in no hurry. They took their time about it. Foster had sprung upon them a dangerous idea.

Foster had an ambitious and excellent plan, "to make a hurricane drive simultaneously in all the steel centers, that would catch the workers' imagination and sweep them into the unions *en masse* despite all opposition, and thus put the employers into such a predicament that they would have to grant the demands." He figured that the employers would be unwilling and unable to suspend production—first, because the profits of the

United Steel Corporation alone, in 1917, amounted to $253,000,000, and, second, because for the time being President Wilson and the Federal Government were friendly to the efforts of organized labor.

> The essence of the plan was quick, energetic action... Great mass meetings, built up by extensive advertising, would be held everywhere at the same time throughout the steel industry, to arouse hope and enthusiasm among the workers and to bring thousands of them into the unions, regardless of any steps the mill owners might take to prevent it. After two or three meetings in each place, the heavy stream of men pouring into the unions would be turned into a decisive flood by the election of committees to formulate the grievances of the men and present these to the employers. The war was on; the continued operation of the steel industry was imperative; a strike was therefore out of question; the manufacturers would have been compelled to yield, either directly or through the instrumentality of the Government. The trade unions would have been established in the steel industry, and along with them fair dealing and the beginnings of industrial democracy.

But Foster, it appears, was too aggressive a man for the leaders in the A.F. of L.; if too successful, he might endanger their positions in the movement; and so they stalled and wasted time. It required months to get together a sizable campaign fund. Meantime the steel manufacturers, hearing of the plans for organizing the workers, began to give employees small concessions, in an effort to forestall the movement.

Finally, in August 1918 the representatives of the unions interested in Foster's idea met in a conference in Chicago and formed the National Committee for Organizing Iron and Steel Workers, with Foster as its leader. In October of that year the Committee began work in Pittsburgh.

But, according to Foster:

The outlook was most unpromising. Even under the best circumstances the task of getting the enormous army of steel workers to thinking and acting together in terms of unionism would be tremendous. But the mistake of not starting the campaign soon enough and with the proper vigor multiplied the difficulties. Unfavorable winter weather was approaching. This was complicated by the influenza epidemic, which for several weeks suspended all public gatherings. Then came the end of the war...[and] the mills, dependent as they were on war work, began to slacken production. The workers became obsessed with a fear of hard times, a timidity which was intensified by the steel companies' discharging one suspected of union affiliations or sympathies.

The funds at Foster's command were far from adequate.

But worst of all, the steel companies were now on the *qui vive*... The advantage of surprise, vital in all wars, industrial or military, was lost to the unions. Wide awake and alarmed, the Steel Trust was prepared to fight to the last ditch.

Things looked desperate. But there was no other course than to go ahead regardless of obstacles,

which were greater every day. The mayors and burgesses of the Pennsylvania mill-towns, many of whom were company employees, held a meeting and decided to allow no labor assemblages. The trade-unionists were treated as though they were a predatory outlaw band. They were threatened with mob violence, arrested, released, re-arrested, week after week. Their meetings, when they attempted to hold them, were broken up by mounted State Constabulary, the Cossacks. But for Foster—who then was in his late thirties, a New Englander by birth, calm, confident, unemphatic in outward manner—the movement might have been "nipped in the bud" even before the Armistice. He said: "This is not a fight of today nor of tomorrow, it is part of the fight that's been going on since the time of the Cæsars." His chief lieutenants were old-time trade-union organizers from *Chicago*. The significance of this fact will appear later when we come to the development of modern "racketeering."

Despite all the hindrances, the organization work proceeded through the winter of 1918–1919. Foster and his lieutenants started local committees in separate mill towns and organized unions. It was slow, heartbreaking work, for as soon as men were suspected of having anything to do with the unions they were discharged, among them employees of twenty and thirty years' service.

By mid-summer of 1919 their success was considerable. They had a union in every steel-mill town. The National Committee decided to take a strike vote of the men on the following issues: the recognition of the unions, reinstatement of all men discharged for union activities with pay for lost time, the eight-hour day, one day's rest in seven, abolition of the 24-hour shift, increase of wages sufficient to guarantee American standard of living, standard wage scales in all trades and classifications of workers, and double pay for overtime after eight hours' work.

The unions voted in favor of the strike. Judge Gary of the United Steel Corporation would not deal with the representatives of the organizing committee and September 22, 1919, was named the day on which the strike would begin. President Wilson tried to prevent it. Gompers suddenly withdrew his half-hearted support of the movement, urging the Foster committee to try to postpone the strike.

But it was too late. The movement had gone too far. The bitterness of the men in local unions was very great, and their feelings flared up into fierce indignation when they heard of the murder of Fannie Sellins. The National Committee for Organizing Iron and Steel Workers could do nothing but call the strike. If they had not called the big strike, there would have occurred numberless local strikes, outbreaks without leadership, accompanied by mob violence pitted against the brutality of the Cossacks. The Committee wrote a letter to President Wilson, explaining in detail the situation from the viewpoint of the union men. "Mr. President, delay is no longer possible. We have tried to find a way out but cannot... This strike is not at the call of the leaders, but that of the men involved."

III

The brunt of the strike fell on the Pittsburgh district, the heart of the American steel industry.

> In anticipation of the strike, what do we see? [said the New York *World* editorially on September 22] In the Pittsburgh region thousands of deputy sheriffs have been recruited at several of the larger plants. The Pennsylvania State Constabulary has been concentrated at commanding points. At other places the authorities have organized bodies of war veterans as special officers. At McKeesport alone 3000 citizens have been sworn in as special police deputies

subject to instant call. It is as though preparations were made for war.

Along the Monongahela River from Pittsburgh to Clairton, a distance of twenty miles, over 25,000 men were under arms. In some towns there was a deputy sheriff for every striker, and the striker was unarmed. Professional and small-business men were sworn in. Few of them dared to refuse the badge; for western Pennsylvania was—and is—owned body and soul by the Steel Trust, the life of the whole region centering around that industry. The mill superintendents' wishes were commands to mayors and police chiefs and local business men. The steel companies made no appeal for troops. Their own armies, officered by their own officials, were vast enough to suppress the strike.

But, even so, by September 30 nearly 400,000 steel workers were "out" in Pennsylvania, Ohio, Illinois, Colorado, West Virginia, Michigan, Alabama, and the State of New York. In many districts the shut-down was complete.

Freedom of speech and assembly was utterly abolished throughout the heart of America's steel and iron area, with the Cossacks galloping through the streets, beating up men and women, shooting at them, dragging them to jail, trampling them under their horses' hoofs "in the manner," as Foster puts it, "and under the circumstances best calculated to strike terror to their hearts." At Braddock, Pennsylvania, the Constabulary attacked a funeral procession from ambush, clubbed the participants, and scattered them to the four winds. In the same town, a Slovak Catholic congregation, leaving the church, was suddenly attacked by the Constables, clubbed and trampled by the horses, for no reason whatever except that the priest was known to be a passionate strike sympathizer. And the next day the Cossacks plowed into a group of mill-workers' children going home from school. The Constabulary were in the habit of riding on sidewalks, the better to ride down the pedestrians. Often they rode into doorways—and one can easily imagine the terror of some poor Bohunk woman when confronted by a horseman wielding a club inside her own dwelling!

Mounted Cossacks barred people from grocery stores—an effort at starving them out! In Farrell, Pennsylvania, three people were killed by the Cossacks in one day, and eleven wounded, one of them a woman. She was shot in the back while on her way to the butcher shop.

I could cite literally *hundreds* of such cases.

Besides the Cossacks, the companies had hundreds and thousands of gunmen, the so-called "company police," who seldom lost an opportunity to shoot down or slug a striker. Picketing, of course, was out of the question. Strikers foolhardy enough to attempt it were slugged and arrested and often kept in jail without bond. Here and there mobs of gunmen broke into men's homes and forced them at the point of their guns to return to work! Those who would not be forced, were arrested for "disorderly conduct." The jails swarmed with arrested strikers.

Yet the strikers themselves, heeding the orders of their strike committees, refrained from violence almost entirely. They allowed themselves to be clubbed and ridden down, shot and jailed, without fighting back. Indeed, to fight back would have been futile.

IV

Before the strike was two weeks old, groups of business and professional men in every Pennsylvania mill-town began the so-called "Back-to-Work" movements. They held meetings, telling strikers that their leaders were crooks and grafters and worse, that the wisest thing they could do was return to work,

By mid-October huge posters appeared in the streets—"THE STRIKE HAS FAILED"—with a picture of Uncle Sam shouting over the smoke of a steel mill: "*Go Back To Work!—Idite Natrag Na Posao!—Chodte Nazad do Roboty!*"—and so on, in seven different languages.

In November the terrorized strikers commenced to desert the ranks and return to work on the companies' terms.

Then winter came—cold and hunger. The strike committees had meager funds—and the men, in desperation, were forced to go to work again at any wage. They were driven back by the Cossacks, the cold winter, and hunger.

By the end of December less than 100,00 remained on strike. The National Committee had spent over $400,000 only to find itself defeated by the brutal power of the Steel Trust. Courage had oozed from the men and they were drifting, sneaking back to work, driven by want and fear and the doubtful faces of their women.

There was but one thing to do—end the strike. Foster had but little support from the big unions that had been behind the movement in 1918. He had practically no support from the leaders in the A.F. of L. The press of practically the entire country was against the strike, either by printing no news about the brutality of the Constabulary or by characterizing the movement as one inspired by the Bolsheviks, as something un-American, evil, anarchistic. The strike ended "from slow bleeding."

Accordingly, in January the strike was officially called off. In the dark hall outside the National Committee's office, steel workers, old and young, sobbed out aloud when they heard the strike-ending order read to them.

V

Foster and trade-union leaders who had assisted him in the strike went back to Chicago.

Obviously, *non*-violence was a poor method of winning demands from the employers.

"Dynamite!...that's the stuff!" And it wasn't long before bombs were again popping in behalf of trade unions—first in Chicago, later in New York and elsewhere.

CHAPTER 28
THE CENTRALIA OUTRAGE

The battle in the steel industry still raged when, on November 11, 1919, the respectable citizens of the United States were shocked to read the news of the killing of four American Legion men by members of the I.W.W. at Centralia, Washington. The reactionary press announced that these unoffending ex-soldiers, "heroes," while parading in their uniforms to celebrate the first anniversary of the Armistice, were slaughtered by the wobblies in cold blood—murdered from ambush without provocation of any kind. The incident was characterized as an "outrage," no less, and played up for all it was worth by the diverse organs of super-patriotism and anti-Red hysteria.

As a matter of fact, behind the "outrage" was a long series of far greater outrages—perpetrated against labor by the capitalists in the Northwestern lumber industry, the capitalist-controlled authorities, and the patriotic mobs along Puget Sound—than the killing of four Legionnaires.

The Centralia incident was a sort of climax to a long struggle on the part of loggers and sawmill men in the Northwest to coerce the Lumber Trust, whose character and doings were not unlike those of the Steel Trust, into improving their lot. The wages were low and the workday long. The workers had to buy their jobs from "employment sharks" in the cities, and to keep them frequently were compelled to split their meager wages with unconscionable labor bosses. They lived in filthy, overcrowded bunkhouses, inferior to cow-sheds on cattle ranches, usually hundreds of miles from any town.

Twenty years ago and even more recently, before the loggers' unions acquired strength, these conditions prevailed practically throughout the lumber industry, not only in the Northwest, but in the Maine and the Southern woods as well.

The lumberworkers' unions commenced to be effective when the I.W.W. invaded the Northwest. In 1912 several small outfits joined the

"One Big Union" movement, which soon became known as the "timber beast." It was treated accordingly by the lumber interests and by the authorities, which were controlled by the Lumber Trust as the authorities in Western Pennsylvania were controlled by the Steel Trust. The A.F. of L. had tried to organize the woodsmen, but the *bigness* of the wobbly "One Big Union" idea appealed more to these workers than the close and narrow principles of "trade unionism, pure and simple."

Immediately after the wobblies came into the Northwestern lumber country strikes began to occur. In 1912 the I.W.W.'s were jailed and beaten up by the hundreds in Aberdeen, not far from Centralia, but at the end of a short strike, they forced the sawmill owners to pay their workers $2.50 a day. In the next five years the wobblies fought many other successful battles, with scarcely ever a defeat, and the conditions in the lumber camps gradually improved. Men received higher wages and better food, and the bunk-houses were cleaner.

The I.W.W. became a power in the Northwestern woods that the Lumber Trust had to reckon with.

In 1916 they commenced to agitate for the eight-hour workday. They won their right to hold meetings by invading communities *en masse*, but their victories were never easy. In a previous chapter I have mentioned the Everett massacre, but the wobblies had other encounters with the Lumber Trust gunmen in which dozens of them lost their lives.

Toward the middle of 1917, after the United States had gone into the World War, the demand for lumber in various industries became tremendous, and the lumber companies, taking advantage of the situation, began to boost the prices sky-high. Indeed, some increased them from $16 to $116 per thousand feet in a few days, and before the end of 1917 were selling spruce for Government airplanes at $1,200 a thousand. And most of that spruce could not be used for airplanes. These figures and facts must be kept in mind, for at the same time the workers' wages were but slightly increased where the men had struck and coerced the employers into boosting them.

The brazen profiteering of the Lumber Trust, with its patriotic pretensions, fanned the coals of old discontent into a flame, and in the summer of 1917 the greatest strike in the history of the American lumber industry swept through the Northwestern lumber districts. The tie-up was practically complete. The industry was paralyzed. Suddenly the tremendous war-time profits were stopped.

The loggers and other workers were immediately accused of "disloyalty" by the Lumber Trust, the press, the local authorities, and even the Federal Government. They were accused of having designs on "our form of government." The strike was "treason." And so thousands of strikers were clapped into jails, and, when jails were filled up, "bullpens" were erected. Men were slugged in the streets, killed in open daylight; union halls were raided. Thousands were herded into box-cars and "deported"—that is, taken into lonely country, hundreds of miles away from habitation, and then driven out. Scores of men were tarred and feathered. Several were taken to lonely railroad bridges at night and hanged.

Public opinion was easily turned against the strike. The country was war-mad, hysterically patriotic, and the "hundred-percenters" had no trouble in convincing the people that the strike was pro-German in motive, anti-American, a peril to "our institutions" and "our flag," although one of the most powerful lumber magnates in the Northwest, a high priest of labor hatred, was a native of Prussia!

The strike *must* be put down!

And it was. The entire country, war-blinded, turned against the I.W.W. Armed mobs of patriotic business men, some of them wearing uniforms, attacked I.W.W. halls and offices, looted the desks, smashed all windows and furniture, burned books and papers. Union secretaries were kidnaped and made to "run the gauntlet." The thousands of men in prisons and "bull-pens" were not fed for days at a time. The whole story of atrocities in that strike will, perhaps, never be known. To kill a wobbly was a more patriotic deed than to kill a German.

The strike was broken, but thereafter the wages in the woods increased considerably. Hundreds of wobblies remained in prisons through the greater part of America's participation in the war. When released, many were mere skeletons. Several died in the lock-up from starvation and illness.

Throughout 1918 it was unwise for a wobbly to tell the world he was a wobbly. Those who returned to work in the woods hid their union cards and credentials in their heavy shoes. The movement was driven underground. They met secretly and sent their pay to the families of men who had been killed during the strike or were in jail.

Only in some of the bigger towns—Centralia for one—they continued to keep up their halls and union offices.

II

Immediately after the strike, there was little activity in the I.W.W. hall at Centralia, but even so the place was a source of constant annoyance to the wobbly-hating super-patriots of the Lumber Trust.

In April 1918 Centralia staged a Red Cross and Liberty Loan parade. The Governor of Washington and the Mayor and the Chief of Police of Centralia were at the head of the parade. Behind them marched the Elks, the Chamber of Commerce, and other business, civic, and fraternal bodies. At the rear of the line was also a gang of men, who, the I.W.W. claim, were hoodlums hired and directed by one F. B. Hubbard, then president of the Employers' Association of the State of Washington.

The parade passed the wobbly hall. From somewhere in the rear of the procession a man cried out: "Let's raid it!" Another voice shouted: "Up and at 'em, boys!"

A mob rushed out of the line of march and stormed the little wooden building. Windows were smashed and doors were broken. Inside, the hoodlums tore down the partitions, broke up chairs, tables, pictures.

The few wobblies who happened to be in the building were surrounded, beaten, driven into the street, where they were forced to witness furniture, files, books, and a typewriter burned and demolished. A victrola and a desk were carried into the middle of an empty lot and auctioned off on the spot "for the benefit of the Red Cross." (A local business man bought the victrola and patriotically boasted of its possession many years later. Hubbard himself acquired the desk.)

Then the dozen or so wobblies were knocked unconscious, loaded on a truck, taken outside the county and dumped.

This was the first raid on the I.W.W. hall in Centralia, and for a year thereafter the wobblies had no headquarters there.

Then, in the summer of 1919, the I.W.W. opened another hall in Centralia.

A few months after the Armistice the "One Big Union" movement suddenly sprung into great power along Puget Sound. The I.W.W. captured some of the most important unions in Seattle, Spokane, and Tacoma. For a brief time, they tied up the big industries, including the harbor of Seattle, and were the dominant element in those communities.

In the woods, war-time wages were being decreased and the loggers were turning wobbly in open daylight, meeting publicly, with

Centralia as a center of the lumberworkers' movement. The Employers' Association of the State of Washington concentrated its anti-I.W.W. drive on Centralia. F. B. Hubbard and his lieutenant, George F. Russell, made their headquarters in the Centralia Chamber of Commerce.

Another prominent wobbly-hater in Centralia in the summer of 1919 was Warren O. Grimm, a typical "clean-cut young man," of good family, a small-town aristocrat, who had been with the American forces in Siberia and whose chief bid for distinction in town was a loud-mouthed dislike for the new Soviet Government in Russia. He had participated in the 1918 raid on the I.W.W. hall. On returning from Siberia, he became a leader in the local post of the American Legion and an ally of Hubbard and Russell. He made speeches discussing the "nationalization of women in Russia" and calling the I.W.W. "the American Bolsheviks." He advocated "rough treatment" of the wobblies.

Already in the summer months there was talk that the new I.W.W. hall would be raided. At a public meeting, Hubbard shouted to the town's chief of police: "It's a damned outrage that these men should be permitted to remain in Centralia! Law or no law, if I were chief of police, they wouldn't stay here twenty-four hours."

In periodic and widely distributed official bulletins, signed by George F. Russell, secretary-manager of the Employers' Association, the business people were urged to "suppress the agitation...hang the Bolsheviks...put the I.W.W. in jail...get rid of the I. W. W...import Japanese labor...import Chinese labor...use the rope...keep up the public sentiment [against the I.W.W.]."

At a meeting of Centralia "business men and property owners" held in June in the Chamber of Commerce rooms, Russell dwelt on the need of a "special organization to protect property rights from the encroachments of all foes of the Government." He indulged in a long tirade against the I.W.W., which he characterized as the most dangerous organization in America and one most necessary for "good citizens" to crush. At this meeting the "Citizens' Protective League of Centralia" was organized, of which Warren O. Grimm became a leading spirit.

On October 19, the Centralia *Hub* urged all employers in Centralia to attend a meeting to be held the following day—three weeks before the killing of the four Legionnaires—in the Elks Club for the purpose of devising ways and means to "deal with the I.W.W. problem." Commander William Scales of the local Legion post was chairman of the meeting. Hubbard spoke on the "menace of the I.W.W.," which should be driven out of town. They organized a "secret committee" of several Legionnaires. Grimm was a member of the committee, and on November 6 was elected post commander, taking the places of Scales, who had resigned in his favor.

In the last days of October and early days of November there were frequent references to the workings of the "secret committee" in the Centralia *Hub* and *Chronicle*.

On the other side of the fence, throughout the summer and autumn of 1919, the wobblies were, characteristically, non-violent, peaceful, conducting their agitation and organization work strictly within the law. Indeed, only a few weeks prior to the Armistice Day "outrage," the police chief of Centralia tried rather unemphatically to dissuade Hubbard, Russell, and Warren Grimm from "pulling any rough stuff," for, to his notion, "the I.W.W. is violating no laws in Centralia." C. E. Grimm, a brother of Warren, who was not wholly in sympathy with the persecution, remarked: "There is no law by which you can drive them out of town."

The I.W.W., with the 1918 raid still fresh in their minds, began to take the rumors about the "secret committee" seriously. They printed a leaflet and circulated it in Centralia, appealing to the town's citizenry for fair play.

III

On November 6 the Centralia Post of the American Legion met with a committee from the Chamber of Commerce to arrange for a parade on November 11, or Armistice Day—a "patriotic parade" in which the boys were to wear their uniforms.

The new wobbly hall was in an out-of-the-way section of the town, but the committees decided to lead the line of march past it, "in order," as Scales, one of the "secret committeemen," put it, "to show them how strong we are." It was intimated that a command "Eyes, right!" would be given as the Legionnaires and business men passed the union headquarters. Obviously, this was but an excuse of the "secret committee" to get the parade where they wanted it, luring men who had no desire to raid the hall to participate in the "stunt."

On November 11, when the Centralia division of ex-servicemen came to the I.W.W. hall, a Legionnaire in the uniform of an army lieutenant blew his whistle, which, the wobblies insisted subsequently, was the signal for the raid, and almost instantly guns began to pop, doors were smashed, windows crashed, men fell dead and wounded, while the paraders scattered in every direction.

To tell what actually happened and the order of occurrence required nearly 300 witnesses in the trial which followed, and the testimony was so hopelessly in conflict on important points that the differences of opinion will, perhaps, never be removed. The State contended that the parade, in making a turn a short distance before reaching the I.W.W. hall, became somewhat disorganized and that the Centralia ex-servicemen were halted to close up ranks; and that while the men in front were marking time to allow those in the rear to close up, the paraders were fired upon from four places without the slightest provocation. These four places were two hotels located across the street from the I.W.W. hall, Seminary Ridge, an elevation of ground near the hall, and the hall itself.

The defense contended that the parade was stopped in front of the I.W.W. hall as a part of a preconceived plan to drive out the I.W.W.; that, as soon as the parade was halted, a rush was made upon the hall from the ranks in the street; and that no shots were fired from the hotels. It was admitted that shots were fired from Seminary Ridge and the hall, but it was claimed that they were fired in self-defense and in defense of property.

The shooting resulted in the wounding of several and in the killing of four ex-soldiers, among them Warren O. Grimm.

Following the shooting, everyone in the neighborhood suspected of being an I.W.W. was rounded up, and for days armed men searched the surrounding country for fugitives. Eleven men, all wobblies, were finally charged with the murder of Grimm. They were Smith, McInerney, Becker, Sheehan, Faulkner, Morgan, Everset, Bert Bland, O. C. Bland, Roberts, and John Lamb. Morgan turned State's evidence and was not tried, and Everset was taken from the city jail on the night following the shooting and, after being unspeakably tortured, was lynched—hanged under a bridge near Centralia, the headlights of the mob's automobiles turned on his body.

There followed a long, tense, and complicated trial.

From the very beginning of the trial, a large part of the audience was made up of ex-servicemen, sailors and soldiers, in uniform. They were there for "moral effect." Shortly after the defense began its case, a detachment of United States troops was sent from nearby Camp Lewis and pitched their tents near the courthouse. On the other hand, the presence of the ex-servicemen in large numbers, the charges that the interests behind the prosecution were anti-labor, and the intensity of feeling throughout the section led a number of labor organizations—

not I.W.W.—in the State of Washington to send delegates to watch the trial. These were called "the labor jury." They took a very active interest in the trial throughout and formulated a "verdict" or report in which they unanimously concluded that the defendants were not guilty; that the I.W.W. hall was unlawfully raided by a mob of ex-soldiers before a shot was fired; that Grimm was a party to a conspiracy to run out the I.W.W.; and, finally, that the men did not get a fair trial because the court had ruled out material evidence tending to show in detail a conspiracy to raid the hall.

The "labor jury's" report unquestionably was just. Judge Wilson's rulings throughout the trial were palpably anti-I.W.W. He would not allow a mention of the fact that Grimm had taken part in the raid on the old I.W.W. hall in 1918. Witnesses who testified that they had seen Grimm leading the raid on November 11, 1919, were promptly arrested for perjury on leaving the courtroom! Finally, the judge instructed the jury that the law of self-defense did not authorize the placing of armed men in outside positions in defense of personal habitations, or property inside the habitations, and that a killing from such a position was a crime.

Seven of the men were found guilty of murder in the second degree and sentenced to from 25 to 40 years' imprisonment—obviously, not because they were guilty of Grimm's death, for it was not proved by the prosecution that any of them had personally shot him, but mainly because they were the most active and intelligent members in the lumber-workers' union in Centralia. Six of the jurors in the case subsequently stated under oath that they had been terrorized into rendering the verdict of guilty, and that they had become convinced that the trial had been utterly illegal, unfair.

All efforts on the part of the I.W.W. Defense Committee and various liberal organizations and individuals during the last decade to get the men a new trial have been in vain. It appears to be immaterial to the powers in control of the government in the State of Washington how many jurors in the case declare the trial illegal. In their greed and class arrogance, those powers—the Lumber Trust *et al.*—mean to keep the wobblies in prison without a re-trial, as a symbol of their rule. By such methods as the Everett massacre and Centralia trial they have succeeded in weakening the I.W.W. movement in the West to such an extent that it now is no serious threat to their profits—and they intend to take no chances in the future. Innocent or guilty, the I.W.W. convicted at

Centralia must remain in prison as a warning to all "working stiffs" who incline to I.W.W.-ism, or to unionism of any sort.

IV

Not a few wobblies on the Pacific Coast believe that the shooting on Armistice Day in 1919 was started by some one connected with the Hubbard-Russell-Grimm "secret committee" from the hotel windows across the street from the I.W.W. hall. Indeed, they go so far as to theorize that Grimm was a deliberately chosen victim of the Employers' Association, one of whose agents, perhaps, had "picked him off" before any of the wobblies had fired. The theory is that the Employers' Association wanted to be sure to have his death blamed upon the wobblies because he was the most prominent "war hero" in Centralia.

There is no doubt, however, that some wobblies did fire on the paraders, or rather the raiders, from their hall and from Seminary Ridge, though whether or not any of the seven men who were convicted had done any firing is questionable. But whoever were the actual I.W.W. snipers, there is no doubt, either, that their firing on the patriotic mob is justifiable on the grounds of self-defense—self-defense not only in the immediate sense, that of protecting their own lives and the furniture in their hall, but in the sense of defending their union. For the existence and growth of their union were all-important, as they saw it, not only in their personal lives, but in the lives of thousands of men and their families who were not anywhere near the hall.

Behind the "outrage," assuming that the I.W.W. did kill the four Legionnaires, was the blind, dynamic desperation, the will-to-live-a-better-life, of thousands of working men, women, and children. And pitted against them was the greed of the employers in the lumber and other industries who, through their agents, were manipulating patriotic hysteria so as to help them in crushing the wobbly union movement.

CHAPTER 29
SACCO AND VANZETTI—"THOSE ANARCHISTIC BASTARDS"

Throughout 1919 the American press, in common with the press of other capitalistic countries, published almost daily reports about the various "monstrosities" and "atrocities" of the Russian Revolution, along with predictions of the imminent downfall of the Soviet regime. As these prophecies failed to be realized and the Bolshevik experiment became more and more a challenge to capitalism, while its sympathizers multiplied in all capitalistic countries, the anti-Red hysteria and the militant hundred-percentism seized practically every community in the United States. As already mentioned, many ill-informed and stupid industrialists, uneasy of conscience because of their war profiteering, frankly believed that revolution was just around the corner unless strong measures were taken against the radical agitation. This fear was exploited and cultivated—with frightful results—by professional alarmists who went into the patriotic hysteria business to advance themselves politically and otherwise. Newspapers and propagandists hired by employers' associations fomented anti-Red feelings in order to justify before the public the brutalities in the suppression of such upheavals as the Great Steel Strike and such organization movements as that of the lumberworkers in the Northwest. *"Our institutions are in danger! Protect the flag!"*

President Wilson was a sick man; his attorney-general, A. Mitchell Palmer, having developed high political ambitions, proposed to work himself into the graces of great capitalists by hounding and harrying the radicals with utter indifference to legality—and especially radicals of foreign birth, for the latter seemed to predominate in the growing numbers of Bolshevik sympathizers. Under Palmer's direction, hundreds of United States Department of Justice agents were scattered through the country. In their persecution of Reds, they enlisted the cooperation of local police and judicial authorities and such super-patriotic organizations as the American Legion and the Daughters of the American

Revolution. In many cases, the local authorities and patriotic societies were on the job even before the Federal agents started their dirty work. Municipalities passed ordinances against radical agitation and several States formulated so-called Anti-Criminal Syndicalism laws. Radicalism—every shade of red—had to be put down! *"Save our institutions from the Bolsheviks!"* In the eyes of the hundred-percenters every radical, no matter how moderate in his views, or how ignorant or incompetent, was a "menace." He might overthrow the Government! I know people who, in those days, were afraid to read in public such mildly radical journals as *The Nation* and *The New Republic*. There were anti-Red drives, raids of I.W.W. and other radical halls and offices, wholesale arrests, plot-scares, frame-ups, the third degree, and deportations—all in the name of patriotism, to save the country from Bolshevism.

The outstanding development of this insane period was the Sacco-Vanzetti affair.

II

On May 3, 1920, an Italian printer, Andrea Salsedo, who had recently been arrested in Brooklyn on "suspicion of radicalism," crashed to death from an eleventh-story window of the United States Department of Justice office in New York City. Whether he had leapt or whether he had been flung from the window by the Department of Justice men or someone else is still a mystery. A fellow prisoner, Roberto Elia, also an Italian radical-suspect, was hastily deported; but before leaving he had made an affidavit to the effect that he and Salsedo had both been tortured by the Department of Justice men in order to force them to confess themselves guilty of the charges against them, i.e., that they were violent anarchists—the penalty for which was deportation to the Old Country.

A vigorous agitation began for public inquiry into the Salsedo affair, and the Department of Justice agents, frantically trying to hush it up, spared no pains to stop the agitation.

There had already been a demand by the organized Italian workers in Massachusetts and New York for the release of Salsedo and Elia. The leaders of this movement in Massachusetts were Nicola Sacco and Bartolomeo Vanzetti, two Italian immigrants who were supposed to be connected with the so-called Galleani group of anarchists in Boston.

Sacco had come to the Land of Promise at the age of seventeen and in the course of a few years had become an expert shoe-cutter—a highly skilled, well-trusted workman, always in work in spite of his radical activities. His employer considered him "the fastest edge-trimmer of some 3,000 who have passed through my factory doors." He worked in Stoughton, near Boston. His wages were comparatively good; he lived a frugal life and was able to support his wife and child and to send regular remittances to his parents at Toremaggiore, in Italy. In 1918 he was a minor leader in a long shoe workers' strike, which forced wage increases from various shoe manufacturers in the vicinity of Boston. Prior to that he had worked for the defense of Ettor and Giovannitti. He was then twenty-seven years of age.

Vanzetti's early years in the United States had been a long siege of unemployment and "greenhorn hardships" in New York. Then he went to Massachusetts and worked in brickfields, quarries, and finally in rope-mills. He lived in Plymouth, the landing-place of the Puritan Pilgrims, now the cordage production center of the United States. Here the modern pilgrim from Southern Europe tended the spinning machines of the Cordage Trust, transforming the sisal hemp of the Yucatan Peninsula into rope and binder-twine.

When Vanzetti came to Plymouth, in 1914, the Italians and Portuguese working in the cordage plants lived under worse conditions than the workers in Lawrence before the I.W.W. strike of 1912. Husbands and wives worked side by side in the mills or met each other going to and from the day and night shifts. Women were paid six dollars a week and the men a maximum of nine dollars.

Vanzetti, then in his mid-twenties, began an energetic campaign for economic action. He, too, had heard of the Lawrence strike, of Ettor and Giovannitti, and he was a reader of extreme-radical literature.

In January 1916, due mainly to Vanzetti's agitation, some 4,000 rope and twine operatives walked out in Plymouth, stopping all work in the industry. This was the first strike the Cordage Trust had ever faced— and this in the midst of the busy season, when binder-twine orders for next summer's harvest were coming in.

It was a hard fought battle. Police and specially hired gunmen, along with threats that families would be turned out of company-owned hous-es, failed to break the strike, largely because of Vanzetti's leadership. He worked night and day making speeches, collecting strike funds, taking his turn on the picket lines.

The strike was won. The 4,000 workers went back to work at in-creased wages—except Vanzetti, the leader, whose services were "no longer required." Blacklisted, he became a fish-peddler in Plymouth, continuing as leader of the cordage workers. Indeed, in his simple way, he became a power in Plymouth, loved by his countrymen working in the rope-mills.

Sacco and Vanzetti were personal friends and brother-radicals. They both inclined to extremist views and were not entirely opposed to violence. When arrested, they had on their persons revolvers and cartridges, which they explained later were a means of self-protection. It is not beyond imagining that as anarchists they were allied in some way with terrorists and even criminals of the underworld, but there is no doubt that the most powerful motives in their lives were highly idealistic, and their innocence of the crimes charged against them is almost beyond question.

They were of the type of men that the Department of Justice operatives were picking for deportation in the brutal anti-alien drives, which local industrialists and politicians used to serve their anti-labor purposes. Primarily they were agitators, encouraging their fellows to resist wage cuts and open-shop campaigns. They were leaders.

III

On May 5, a week after Salsedo's death, Sacco and Vanzetti were suddenly arrested at Brockton, Massachusetts, after they had made arrangements for a Salsedo protest-meeting to be held the following Sunday. At the local police station they were questioned closely about their beliefs and their movements on the evening of their arrest, which occurred on a street car. They refused to give any definite information, fearing that, if they did so, they would only reveal the names of their fellows in the Salsedo movement, who would then be subjected to the same sort of persecution. Neither they nor anyone else who knew them doubted that they had been taken merely as radical-suspects.

But the following day they were charged with robbery and murder. They were accused of being members of a gang of motor bandits who had carried out a daring daylight raid at South Braintree, near Boston. The paymaster of a big shoe-factory and his bodyguard had been shot dead outside the factory gate and the $15,000 in their care had been carried off. A series of just such crimes had been shocking eastern Massachusetts.

Vanzetti, in addition, was accused of an attempted payroll robbery, at Bridgewater, also near Boston. For this he was hastily tried in the court of the reactionary Judge Webster Thayer. Vanzetti was found guilty and sentenced to fifteen years' imprisonment. The character of the trial may be gauged by the judge's remark in his summing up: "This man, although he may not have actually committed the crime attributed to him, is nevertheless morally culpable, because he is the enemy of our existing institutions."

The news of the astounding charge brought against these two radical labor leaders—anarchists, or whatever one likes to call them— roused the Italian workers of New England, especially those around Boston, to vigorous action for their defense. From the beginning there could be no room for doubt that it was a frame-up. The crime and the alleged criminals simply did not fit. The crime was obviously the work of experienced professional bandits. The alleged criminals were poor, hard-working men of unimpeachable integrity, known for their fanatical, self-sacrificing devotion to their social ideals. Such men might kill or be killed for a cause, but they were as little likely to be guilty of highway robbery as was John D. Rockefeller to be implicated in a Communist conspiracy.

The case began to attract national attention. Scores of radical labor unions in various parts of the country became interested in it and contributed to the defense fund started by Italian workers in Massachusetts.

IV

The Sacco-Vanzetti trial for the Braintree crime began on May 31, 1921. It lasted seven weeks. By a terrible coincidence or design, Judge Thayer presided over this trial, too. He was openly prejudiced against—indeed, hostile to—the prisoners. He was openly anti-radical, anti-alien—an old pillar of old New England traditions which now were threatened by the stirrings of the European immigration. He was not only pro-capitalist and anti-labor, but pro-New England, pro-Nordic, pro-Back Bay, anti-alien, anti-Italian.

The prosecution depended chiefly upon the evidence of witnesses who had either seen the crime or identified one or both of the accused as members of the gang, or who swore to having seen them in Braintree on the day of the murder. The evidence of these witnesses—given fourteen months after the occurrence—was confused and contradictory. One swore that Vanzetti was driving the bandits' car; another that he was sitting next to the driver; still another that he was in the back seat. One swore that Vanzetti arrived in Braintree by train on the morning of the murder; another that he arrived by train the night before. As a frame-up, which it unquestionably was, it was a crude piece of work.

The witnesses who "identified" Sacco were equally confused, equally contradictory, and equally shifty under cross-examination.

On the other hand, nine witnesses from Boston testified to having seen and spoken with Sacco in that city during the afternoon of April 15. (The murder took place at three o'clock.) Among them was the clerk of the Italian Consulate, who swore that a few minutes before three Sacco had come into his office seeking a passport to go to Italy.

The evidence of all these witnesses was entirely unshaken by the prosecution's cross-examination.

So with Vanzetti. Six witnesses swore to having seen and conversed with him on the day of the murder in Plymouth, 35 miles from Braintree, where he was, as usual, hawking fish. And this evidence also stood the test of cross-examination.

But in spite of everything the judge summed up dead against the two proletarians. He referred to them as "conscious of guilt as murderers or as slackers and radicals"—"slackers" because both had refused military service in the war. He played upon the racial prejudices of the jurors. Indeed, from beginning to end, every theatrical device had been used to work the jury into an anti-alien frenzy.

The verdict was guilty; the sentence, death. Judge Thayer, characteristically, did not once look at the prisoners as he condemned them to the chair.

After the sentence had been pronounced upon the two Italians, on April 9, 1927, Vanzetti, in an amazing exaltation of spirit, said:

> If it had not been for [this case], I might have live out my life, talking on street corners to scorning men. I might have die, unmarked, unknown, a failure. Now we are not a failure. This is our career and our triumph. Never in our full life can we do such a work for tolerance, for joostice, for man's onderstanding of man, as now we do by an accident. Our words—our lives—our pains—nothing! The taking of our lives—lives of a good shoemaker and a poor fishpeddler—all! The last moment belongs to us—that agony is our triumph!

Which, in all likelihood, will be the verdict of history.

V

After the trial there were six years of indescribable agony for Sacco and Vanzetti and, in a lesser measure, for those vitally concerned with justice in their case.

The defense asked for a new trial on the grounds that the first trial had been illegal. Judge Thayer refused the motion. That very day he attended a football game at Dartmouth, where he was heard boasting in a loud voice to a professor of his acquaintance: "Did you see what I did to those anarchistic bastards the other day? I guess that will hold them for a while. Let them go to the Supreme Court now and see what they can get out of them."

The case was appealed to higher courts, after which it dragged tortuously through the early nineteen-twenties, while the entire world became interested in what later began to be called the Passion of Sacco and Vanzetti—implying that their ordeal compared with that of Jesus Christ and other martyrs, real and legendary, in human history. All this time Sacco and Vanzetti were in prison and, as the London *Outlook* put it in 1927, they became "a symbol to millions of people throughout the world as victims of the 'capitalist' system of justice, which has one law for the poor and another for the rich."

The appeals to higher courts were in vain, for all the highest judicial positions in the State of Massachusetts were occupied by faithful servants of New England capitalism and Back Bay aristocracy, with its decaying traditions. But, as the case dragged on, working people and liberals of means, native and foreign-born, contributed over $300,000 for the Sacco-Vanzetti defense.

Finally, the Governor of Massachusetts became the only official agency that could save Sacco and Vanzetti, and he—Alvan T. Fuller, by name—was a New England plutocrat who was more directly interested in the suppression of radical agitation among foreign workers than was even Judge Thayer. Appeals for clemency poured into the State House in Boston by cable and telegram from all over the world. There were demonstrations in some of the principal cities in the United States. In foreign countries, Sacco-Vanzetti sympathizers paraded before American embassies and consulates.

Fuller seemed from the start determined to have Sacco and Vanzetti executed. The affair was too raw, however, and he hesitated to assume the final responsibility. He, therefore, appointed an advisory council, consisting of Judge Robert Grant, President A. Lawrence Lowell of Harvard, and President Samuel W. Stratton of the Massachusetts Institute of Technology—all three pillars of New England traditions, all three unfailingly faithful to the existing social and economic system, anti-radical, pro-Nordic, anti-alien.

Time passed—endless months.

At last, on August 10, 1927, the Governor announced the decision: Sacco and Vanzetti must die! Their trial, he averred, had been fair; they were guilty; most of the defense witnesses were liars, and so on, and so on.

The world-wide reaction to the Fuller-Grant-Lowell-Stratton decision was intense. The windows of the American Consulate at Buenos Aires were smashed. Expressions of horror-struck outrage came from one country after another. Prime Minister Ramsay MacDonald of Great Britain exclaimed: "The whole affair is too terrible!" Ex-Prime Minister Herriot of France declared: "I am against this punishment which has lasted seven years. Sacco and Vanzetti ought to be released. They have earned such a measure of clemency." A group of outstanding London jurists was unanimously of the opinion that the men ought to be freed, whether guilty or innocent, since even the crime of murder, of which they were convicted, does not merit the unusual and cruel punishment of being kept in torturing suspense—between life and death—for seven years. The London *Daily News* said that "no one ought to be treated as these men, whatever they have done." And the Paris *Temps*: "We wish to see these men spared, whether they are innocent or guilty, because we think they have suffered enough in these seven years of nightmare."

Governor Fuller granted a respite of twelve days. This served only to prolong the torture. They were twelve days of extreme tenseness all over the world. Bombs timed and placed so as to kill no one, went off in New York subways and elsewhere. In Boston no meetings or demonstrations were allowed.

The defense was making eleventh-hour attempts to postpone the execution. Justices of the United States Supreme Court were appealed to—without result; they had no power to act in the case.

Just after midnight on August 22, the good shoemaker and the poor fish-peddler were executed by the State of Massachusetts. They died with dignity, unafraid, with nothing in the manner of their death to shake the belief of many persons that they were utterly innocent of the crime.

On the night of the execution a terrific tension prevailed, not only in Boston, but in the principal cities of the United States and in the world at large—as if the killing of Sacco and Vanzetti was a most significant event. And it unquestionably was; its significance will grow with years. Sensitive persons who had but the vaguest notion of the issues behind the dreadful affair sought one another's company, in an inarticulate sort of desperation and agony. In Union Square in New York City a great mob gathered. When news came that Vanzetti, who was first to go, was dead, some one in the *Freiheit* office hung out of the window a sign reading,

"VANZETTI MURDERED!"

—whereupon, to quote the New York *World's* moving depiction of the incident:

The crowd responded with a giant sob. Women fainted in fifteen or twenty places. Others, too, overcome, dropped to the curbs and buried their heads in their hands. Men leaned on one another's shoulders and wept. There was a sudden movement in the street to the east of Union Square. Men began to run around aimlessly, tearing at their clothes and ripping their straw hats, and women ripped their dresses in anguish.

But the State of Massachusetts was not yet satisfied. On August 28, when 7,000 peaceable men and women marched the eight miles from Boston to the Forest Hills Cemetery behind the bodies of Sacco and Vanzetti, and over 200,000 people lined the streets along the funeral route, detachments of city police and State Constabulary attacked the procession, injured several, and dispersed the crowd.

VI

The Sacco-Vanzetti case was a barbaric, cowardly act on the part of a great commonwealth, controlled by profit-driven, powerful capitalists and industrialists who were bent upon crushing the efforts of underpaid, abused foreign laborers to improve their lot. The killing of Sacco and Vanzetti, after keeping them in suspense for seven years, was intended not only to put out of business two rather obscure radical agitators, but to be, first of all, a lesson and a warning to all other agitators and would-be agitators. As such, of course, it was an act of war, for Sacco and Vanzetti were soldiers in the open class war on the underdog side. From the viewpoint of justice in its highest sense, however, the Sacco-Vanzetti executions seven years after their arrest constituted a crime far worse than the Braintree murder and robbery of which they were convicted and with which, in all likelihood, they had had no connection whatever.

While Sacco and Vanzetti were still alive, and Governor Fuller could have saved them, there existed evidence that the attempted

230   holdup at Bridgewater, of which Vanzetti was first convicted (which
conviction was one of the most important factors in the subsequent
conviction and death sentence of Sacco and Vanzetti in the trial for
the Braintree crime), had been perpetrated by two Boston underworld characters, Frank Silva and James Mede. Governor Fuller and
his advisory committee, while considering the Sacco-Vanzetti application for pardon in the summer of 1927, were cognizant of that
evidence. They refused to consider it. These four pillars of the social
and economic scheme of New England were bound to decide for the
death of the two Italian labor leaders and anarchists, whose activities
among immigrant laborers threatened the profits of great industries
in the State of Massachusetts and the supremacy of New England cul-
tural and social traditions. Behind the committee's rigidity of mind
was the machinery of the entire government of Massachusetts and
the anti-Red hysteria which, in that State, was kept alive long after it
had begun to wane elsewhere in the Republic. If Sacco and Vanzetti
were not guilty of robbery and murder, they were guilty—in the
eyes of the capitalist-patriotic powers in Massachusetts—of an even
greater crime. They were two "anarchistic bastards," enemies of the
social and economic system of which the government of the State of
Massachusetts was a principal agency.

A year after the executions, *The Outlook* gathered the evidence of
Vanzetti's innocence of the Bridgewater crime and printed it in its issue for October 31, 1928. The editor called the material to Governor
Fuller's attention, but that politician again declined to consider it,
thereby proving once more that Vanzetti's guilt or innocence of the
Bridgewater holdup or any other such crime was of minor importance.
The important fact in the affair was Vanzetti's confessed radicalism, his
avowed opposition to the order of which Fuller was a high beneficiary
and priest, and, therefore, Vanzetti and Sacco had properly been done
away with.

In fine, to conclude this part of my book, from the end of the
McNamara case in 1911, until, say, 1920, most of the violence in the
class struggle in the United States was perpetrated by organized capitalist interests, acting largely through their agents in the government. It
was a period of massacres, frame-ups, Red scares, mass arrests, judicial
murders—dirty doings, far worse than the acts of such characters as
Alexander Berkman, Bill Haywood, the McNamaras, and the Centralia
I.W.W. The latter, at least, were not perpetrated by the powerful against

the weak, were not anti-social, brutal, brutalizing, inhuman in the motives behind them.

But these massacres, frame-ups, judicial murders, are not going unavenged. The class war goes on. The underdog in America is getting his vengeance—and this vengeance, as we shall see in the ensuing chapters, is becoming nearly as anti-social and inhuman as were the terrible acts I have described, and which, directly or indirectly, have provoked it.

PART SIX
RECENT TENDENCIES
IN THE CLASS WAR
(1920–1934)

"Fight or Starve!"
—COMMUNIST AGITATORS

CHAPTER 30
LABOR AND THE BEGINNINGS OF
"RACKETEERING"

With the Republican nomination of Warren G. Harding for the Presidency, which meant his election, the country began to get "back to normalcy." Incidentally, it meant that many of the most important departments of its national government would come completely under the control of some of the most crooked and unconscionable capitalists under the sun. The nomination of Harding, a good-natured, naïve machine politician, was the signal for new anti-labor moves on the part of the industrialists. This time their efforts were directed not only against the I.W.W. and other extreme radicals, efforts which had already received the support of the Wilson Administration, but also against conservative, long-established trade unions.

The employers, with the power of their war-enhanced wealth, taking advantage of unemployment and chaotic post-war social conditions, as well as of the anti-Red hysteria which they helped to foment, began, by the middle of 1920, nationwide drives to "Americanize" the American worker. That is, they sought to break up the trade unions' control of the labor market in certain industries and cities, to discredit the theory and practice of unionism, to institute open shop everywhere, and, when necessary, to organize the workers into harmless company unions controlled from the main office. The workers were to be lured away and kept satisfied with "company welfare," "personnel activities," "group insurance," "employee stock-ownership" and other such inventions.

Throughout the country, industrialists refused to recognize and deal with the unions any longer. Many of them refused to employ union men altogether; and workers, to get jobs, were obliged to sign the so-called "yellow dog" contracts.

Employers resorted to all sorts of methods. They called their idea the "American Plan"—an old phrase implying that anyone not in favor of open shop stood for something un-American. The word "American," as Robert W. Dunn, a radical writer, explains, "had reached its heyday. Even the Europeans still worshiped at the throne... It was the correct psychological moment for the enemies of trade unions to label their crusade 'American.'" Employers spoke of Industrial Freedom—a phrase meaning that they wanted to have a free hand in exploiting labor. Labor, of course, was to be free too—to accept their wages or go without. Some of the fanatical open-shoppers refused to sell their products to, or buy raw materials from, other employers of labor who would not adopt "the American Plan." They lowered wages to almost the pre-war scale, while the cost of living stayed up. Strikes were broken with court injunctions and hired gunmen.

This was part of the "back to normalcy" movement.

II

For several years after the McNamara affair, the strong-arm element in the A.F. of L. had heeded Gompers's preachments against dynamite; but now, the effectiveness or existence of their organizations was threatened anew. The leaders of certain unions, with the desperate unemployed membership behind them, were again driven to dynamiting and slugging. They believed that only strong-arm methods could save their organizations from annihilation. They had to keep up the wage scale which it had taken them so long to establish. They had to keep *their* jobs under the union's control. They saw that under the circumstances the best possible labor strategy sans dynamite was of no avail against the organized forces of capital.

This last conclusion was especially obvious to those labor leaders who, in 1919, had tried to organize the steel industry and had been defeated, as many were inclined to believe, because they were completely non-violent, because they did not meet the Cossacks on their own terms.

Therefore, dynamite! The old cry of the Chicago Anarchists— "Dynamite!...that's the stuff!"—went up once more, especially in Chicago, where trade unions were full of organizers who had suffered defeat in the Great Steel Strike.

Only now the "gorillas" were more cautious, subtler. They agreed with Gompers that there must not—simply *must not*—be any more McNamara and Haywood cases and revelations of dynamite conspiracies. They must operate with care. The actual dynamiters and sluggers and assassins must have no official connection with the union offices, nor any close relations with the leaders.

They began to hire professional criminals of the type that were soon—by 1922—to be called "racketeers," and these criminals "pulled the jobs." Dynamiting operations were put upon a businesslike, unsentimental basis. Unlike the semi-idealistic James B. McNamara, the professional racketeer had no emotional or intellectual interest in organized labor. All he cared for was his fee, in return for which he guaranteed a good job. He was usually hired through several intermediaries, so that sometimes he was unaware in whose behalf he was doing the stunt. And he was, as a rule, a competent thug, practically beyond the reach of the law, and not a fanatic like McNamara. Sometimes, however, in the early days of racketeering, he had had no previous experience in handling dynamite and had to be specially trained to "pull jobs" for the unions. In fact, there are "pineapple men" still living in Chicago and elsewhere who were started on their dynamiting careers by trade-union agents.

By the end of 1920 bombs burst once more, especially in Chicago. Indeed, large-scale labor racketeering in Chicago and some other cities preceded even the sensational wars between bootleggers in the nineteen-twenties.

There were fifty bombings in Chicago in 1920: sixty-odd in 1921; about the same number in 1922; and over fifty in 1923. More than half of them, it is estimated, had some connection with the labor unions; most of them, especially in 1920 and 1921, damaged buildings under construction and homes of builders and contractors unfriendly to organized labor.

There is no record of slugging incidents, but I know personally a "Chicagorilla" who is chief of strong-arm operations of a big building-trades union in which the Molly Maguire and the Louis Lingg traditions are very much alive—not only with the leaders but among the membership as well. In the summer of 1929 he quite freely discussed with me the nature of his job, and stated that slugging had been a part of his union's tactics since 1920 and was even more effective than dynamite bombs.

He is a typical gorilla, past middle age, who has been active in the labor movement for the last thirty years. He was a friend of John J. and James B. McNamara, was implicated in the blowing up of the Los Angeles Times Building in 1910, and is frankly proud of it. He was one of O. A. Tveitmoe's lieutenants in San Francisco at that time, and was present in the Victoria Hotel room in New York on December 2, 1911, when Gompers was being interviewed by the New York *Times* about the McNamaras' confession. He has a great contempt for the "stiffs," as he calls ordinary workers, and admires only "fighters"—men like the McNamaras.

He introduced me to his slugger, an ex-heavyweight pugilist, who is not a member of any labor union but makes a handsome living from organized labor. He charges $50 for putting his fist in some scab's or labor foreman's face.

I asked the slugger to tell me something about his work. "Oh, there ain't nothin' to it," he said. "I gets my fifty, then I goes out and finds the guy they wanna have slugged. I goes up to 'im and I says to 'im, 'My friend, by way of meaning no harm—' and then I gives it to 'im—*biff*! in the mug. Nothin' to it." One blow from him is enough; the sluggee is usually out for a while. When he wakes up, often in a hospital, he ordinarily makes up his mind never again to displease any union. Scabbing is thus discouraged.

The man I met is but one of a dozen or more professional sluggers in Chicago. He does anywhere from five to ten jobs a week; most of them for labor unions. The effectiveness of his fist is famous in Chicago.

Bombings are still frequent in Chicago, but it is estimated that lately very few have occurred in the cause of labor. In 1929 there were, in over a hundred explosions, probably not more than fifteen that had the earmarks of labor terrorism.

Most of the Chicago labor unions are again safe from immediate destruction by the employers. Dynamite and slugging saved them. This is especially true of the building-trades unions.

Nowadays slugging goes a long way in Chicago, with only an occasional bombing or putting some contractor "on the spot" as a warning to those whom a smash in the face does not convince that the unions mean to stay in business.

III

Labor racketeering, like other species of racketeering, is by no means restricted to Chicago. It merely started there back in 1920; since then—especially from 1925 on—labor dynamitings, assassinations, and arson incidents have been occurring with great frequency in New York City, Brooklyn, and other industrial centers where labor unions are meeting with strenuous opposition from the bosses.

Violence and the fear of violence are sometimes the only methods that save some unions from passing out.

The following are a few bombings and other violent incidents in recent years for which no one was arrested and punished, but most of

which were probably perpetrated by racketeers hired by men connected
with labor unions, or by union men themselves:

On May 25, 1925, two company houses owned by the Glendale Gas and Coal Company, at Wheeling, West Virginia, occupied by non-union miners were bombed and wrecked during a miners' strike.

On August 30, 1926, two bombs exploded in the factory of L. B. Levinson Clothing Company, at Lakewood, New Jersey, tearing off a wall, damaging machinery, and smashing all the windows. The concern employed non-union operatives, and the bombing occurred shortly after certain organizers failed to induce the company to hire organized men and women.

On August 19, 1927, more than fifty non-union negro miners were hurled from their beds early in the morning by an explosion which wrecked two buildings in West Elizabeth, Pennsylvania. The miners were employed by the Pittsburgh Coal Co. There had been a strike a while before.

On the same day, in Henderson, North Carolina, the home of M. E. Partin, who had walked out with eight hundred strikers in the Harriet Cotton Mills two weeks before but later returned to work, was dynamited. The blast tore off the back porch and shattered the windows of other homes in the vicinity. That same night small explosions occurred in the yards of two other ex-strikers in that town.

On July 8, 1927, two persons were rendered unconscious and four others had narrow escapes from injury when a dynamite bomb exploded in front of the home of John McMahon, mine foreman of the Clinton Block Coal Company, near Pittsburgh, Pennsylvania. The dwelling was badly damaged by the blast and the entire neighborhood was rocked. The Clinton Block Coal Company operates an open-shop mine.

On June 30, 1928, a heavy charge of dynamite wrecked the Jonesville Mine No. 1, one of the three shafts owned by the La Salle Carbon Coal Company at La Salle, Illinois. It caused a damage of many thousands of dollars. The explosion was ascribed to a dash between two rival miners' unions in which the company was indirectly involved.

On June 23, 1928, a bomb shattered the fronts of four houses on Parkside Avenue in West Philadelphia. Fragments of the bomb were found imbedded in the front wall of the home of D. A. Ingher, where it apparently had been set off. Ingher attributed the explosion to labor troubles. He maintains a leather manufacturing establishment and told the police he had been having strike disputes.

On March 10, 1928, a bomb wrecked the four-story brick plant of the Manhattan Steam and Scouring Company, of Brooklyn, after the company's employees had failed to win a strike.

During the silk mill employees' strike at Garfield, Passaic, and other towns in New Jersey in 1926 and 1927 numerous homes occupied by workers who refused to strike were dynamited and wrecked or damaged.

On September 3, 1929, Joseph Matraza, a Brooklyn barber, found an unexploded bomb in his doorway. He had been having "trouble with a labor organization."

On July 28, 1929, a bomb tore the front from the showroom of the Dachis Brothers, furriers, in New York City. "Dispute in the fur trade," according to the police.

On December 8, 1929, a bomb exploded in the home of Joseph Falzone, a prosperous marble contractor in Brooklyn, killing three of his children and partly wrecking the house. "Labor trouble," according to press reports.

On February 3, 1930, William Healy, a Chicago contractor, was "put on the spot" and shot. According to the police as reported in the press, he named, before dying three days later, a walking delegate of the Marble Setters' Union as one of his assassins. This was one of the few labor-racket killings in Chicago; union racketeering there, as I have said, consists mainly of sluggings and careful bombings (too many to enumerate here) which at worst throw people out of their beds.

On September 29, 1928, the home of Paul C. Hackett at Rocky River, near Cleveland, Ohio, was dynamited, throwing the family out of their beds. Hackett, a real estate man, said that the explosion probably was intended for the house next door, owned by Charles Montgomery, another real estate dealer. Nearly two years before, Montgomery said, one of his houses was bombed when he refused to employ union labor. He added that he had thought his labor troubles had been settled.

On February 15, 1930, a heavy dynamite explosion wrecked the home of R. W. Baldwin, president of the Marion Manufacturing Company at Marion, North Carolina, where a strike had been on for some time. A few days before, another charge of dynamite went off in the plant of the Clinchfield Manufacturing Company, near Marion, causing heavy damage. Union officials in charge of the strike, of course, denied any connection with the bombings.

On August 11, 1930, a series of labor disorders in the Webster   241
County coal fields in Kentucky culminated in the bombing from an
airplane of two mines near the town of Providence. Nine bombs were
dropped from an altitude of 2,000 feet, as miners—non-union men—
were going to work. No damage was done beyond digging huge holes in
the ground; the "stunt" having obviously been intended as a scare. The
pilot later confessed he had been hired by two men who, he thought,
were connected with a miners' union.

On November 25, 1930, a bomb exploded on the porch of the
home of Carl Wildey, personnel manager of a Ford Motor Company
branch in Chicago. The man and his wife narrowly escaped death.
Their baby was injured and their home was wrecked. Wildey explained that he had lately discharged about one hundred workers.

In the spring of 1929, during the long street-railway strike at New
Orleans three dynamite bombs exploded in two months, wrecking car
barns and damaging equipment.

Since 1926 over a dozen theaters have been dynamited in various
parts of the country in connection with labor troubles, the total damages
running into millions of dollars.

In the fall of 1927 the stagehands employed at the theaters in the
Twin Cities were on strike, seeking one day off in seven, and the mo-
tion-picture operators and musicians were out in sympathy with them.
On October 10 a bomb exploded in the Forrest Theater, a movie house
in the residential district of St. Paul, while the show was on, injuring one
woman and throwing over 300 men, women, and children into a panic.
On the same day the Logan Theater in Minneapolis was also bombed.
The strike leaders denied any previous knowledge of the blasts. And the
year before, also during a labor dispute, a bomb was found behind the
screen of the Wonderland Theater, another Minneapolis movie house.

On August 19, 1927, the Wright Theater at Guerdon, Arkansas, was
partly wrecked by dynamite, causing a damage estimated at $20,000.
"Labor trouble."

On November 8, 1927, the State Theater of Hammond, Indiana,
recently completed and valued at $1,700,000, was completely destroyed
by a dynamite explosion. A business agent of the Motion Picture
Operators' Union was arrested and, according to the police, he confessed to having had a hand in the plot. Others arrested and charged
with having been connected with the bombing were the walking delegates of the Hod Carriers' Union and the Finishers' Union.

On November 3, 1929—to give but one more theater incident—at 12:20 a.m. a nitroglycerin bomb exploded in the projection booth of the Lemay Theater, St. Louis, blowing a hole in the roof of the building and damaging motion picture machines and vitaphone apparatus to the extent of $6,000. Thirty minutes later another bomb went off in the projection room of the Mackland Theater in the same city, doing a damage estimated at $5,000. Union musicians had been out on strike for six weeks in a dispute over a contract concerning the number of musicians employed, and the owners of the bombed houses and the police attributed both incidents to the musicians' union.

Owing to the development and great popularity of the talkies, the radio, and other mechanical amusements during the past three years, most of the theatrical workers' unions now find themselves in desperate straits. The musicians' union, for instance, is a tragic organization, with a majority of its members out of work. Other theatrical organizations have been notoriously strong-arm racketeer outfits for years; indeed, violence alone has saved them so far.

IV

Labor racketeering from the point of view of extreme violence is now at its height, not in Chicago, but in New York.

In the summer of 1929 I sat, late one evening, in a friend's home in the Bronx, when suddenly the neighborhood was lighted up by a fierce blaze nearby. It enveloped a sixteen-story apartment house under construction but almost completed, with all the woodwork finished inside. The building had evidently been drenched with coal-oil from top to bottom and "touched off." It was an incident in the "war" between labor racketeers and builders, the third incident of the kind in the Bronx in a few months. Later there were two more—the total damage exceeding three million dollars. No one was ever arrested for this incendiarism. The builders may know who had hired the firebugs, but it would be suicidal for them or any public prosecutor to act against them.

In the winter of 1929 there was a Grand Jury investigation of the Bronx "building-trades racket," but its only results were the indictments of Anthony Montforte, so-called "racketeer tsar" of the building trades, and Michael McClusky, walking delegate of the Lathers' Union, on the charge of extortion. They were tried, convicted, and sent to prison. When the jury was being picked for the McClusky trial, several talesmen begged to be excused because they were "afraid."

Since that trial there have been two assassinations of contractors in 243
New York. One of them occurred in May, 1930. The contractor stepped
out of his home in Harlem and walked to his car at the curb, when three
gunmen, firing at him simultaneously, "plugged" him in the groin.

In the spring of 1930 several contractors' homes in Brooklyn were
bombed at night, throwing people out of their beds. In April a plumb-
er's foreman was shot dead in front of his house when he returned from
work in the evening—another incident in the "labor war."

On August 8, 1930, there died at Kings County Hospital in
Brooklyn, Jack Albert, one of two painters who, after falling out with
their union, were attacked by six men a few days before and beaten
up. His fellow victim, Morris Leiman, was critically injured.

I have mentioned the desperate plight of the musicians' unions.
Their desperation began even before the appearance of the talkies, with
the radio. Out of it there developed in 1924—by a process too long
to describe here—the so-called Musicians' Mutual Protective Union,
a powerful strong-arm faction within the American Federation of
Musicians in New York. The Protective Union engaged one Antonio
Vaccarelli, alias Paul Kelly, a gorilla of great prowess who years before
had won fame in stevedores' strikes. He was made "business manager"
at $20,000 a year, with special duties to terrorize performers outside the
union. For years thereafter, until the M. M. P. U. was finally put out of
business, musicians who would not join the organization were attacked
by sluggers in stage-entrance alleyways and beaten up. Scores of clarinet
players had their front teeth knocked out and violinists and pianists
their fingers broken! Employers of non-M. M. P. U. musicians were attacked and their amusement places were bombed.

Nor was the musicians' violence restricted to New York. On
November 26, 1927, four musicians were beaten about the face and
head with pieces of lead pipe in Englewood, New Jersey. According
to the press, the victims and police believed that the attack had been
sponsored by the musicians' union, and the lieutenant detective in the
prosecutor's office at Hackensack, New Jersey, was "convinced" that
such was the case.

Certain garment-trades unions in New York are notoriously racketeering outfits. In 1927, the year before he was murdered, Arnold
Rothstein, a Manhattan gang chief, was a big factor in the great furriers' and garment workers' strikes, furnishing the unions with strong-
arm talent and "fixing" the police lest they club the strikers. For his
services he received fees running into hundreds of thousands of dol-

lars. Since then about a dozen garment manufacturers have been assassinated. The last assassination in the garment trades, as I write this, occurred during a strike in February 1930. A gunman shot dead the owner of a great factory as he stepped into an automobile in front of his plant. The gunman got away, and at the time the murder was a mystery. Since then, however, a detective, posing as one of Al Capone's gangsters, traced the woman who had put the millionaire manufacturer "on the spot" and the man who had killed him. The woman confessed they had been hired for the "job" by a man connected with a labor organization.

Slugging, of course, is also a well-developed practice in New York, Brooklyn, and the Bronx. Indeed, as in Chicago, extreme violence—assassinations and dynamiting—is usually resorted to only when slugging and fear of attack are ineffectual.

V

Back in 1920, when labor racketeering was in its infancy, the relationship between gangsters and unions was rather distant and simple. The unions hired dynamiters, killers, and sluggers and paid them for their work—that was all. But, by and by, gangsters—these professional criminals having been thus started on their lucrative careers of violence by the unions—began to "muscle" their way into the union offices and affairs, and in not a few cases took over the control of the organizations.

I have shown that dynamite and slugging often save unions from passing out. The gangsters who do the dynamiting and slugging for the unions realize this. They associate with the "gorillas," who admit that their work is *the* thing; and eventually they begin to consider themselves the most important factor in the affairs of the union, which indeed they are in time of emergency. Presently it occurs to them that the fees they get out of the union treasury are too small for such important work, and too irregular. So they propose to give the union "steady protection" at so much per month. If the union officials reject such an offer, the latter very often are thrown out of office—sometimes physically, sometimes through election—and their places are taken by "gorillas" who are friendly to the "protection" idea. But, of course, few labor leaders who once go in for violence reject such an offer outright, knowing full well that it may mean the end of their labor-leading.

But while the process that puts the gangsters in control of unions is simple, there often develop in that connection very complicated situations. For instance, two different gangs may want to dominate the same union, in which event, to avoid warfare in the organization, the officials usually go to a third gang chief, whose outfit may be larger than the other two put together, and ask him to protect them, not only against the employers' anti-union activities and the scabs, but against the other gangsters as well. And, of course, when the gang leader grants their petition, he becomes the big boss of the union and is in a position to exploit it.

The following appeared in the Chicago *Tribune* of April 20, 1930:

Organized labor in Chicago stands in peril of being delivered into the hands of gangsters, according to labor leaders who expressed their fears today. Already several unions, rated as the most powerful and active in the city, have been taken over completely by Alphonse (Scarface Al) Capone and his crew of gangsters, it was pointed out. Other leading unions are being forced to pay monthly tribute to stave off the gangsters.

In the background of the gangsters' aim for union rule lies the equally significant danger to the building-trades industry, pointed out by builders and contractors, who have a mental picture of the tribute they would be forced to pay when their chances of completing a job lie in the hands of Capone's gangsters.

Beyond this rich field of plunder lies Capone's new harvest ground, already revealed, the field of political patronage. For with the unions under his domination the gang boss would become a political power, able to swing many thousands of labor votes to servile candidates and officials...

The gang chief's power has had its effect also on leaders of the Building Trades Council, according to reports, which have it that the labor men feel themselves helpless to stem the inroads being made by the racketeers on their organizations. Some of the union heads, in fact, have gone to Capone seeking his help in meeting the demands of other gangsters.

This is not in the least exaggerating the situation in Chicago; on the contrary, it is putting it mildly. I have been told by Chicago labor leaders themselves that over thirty large unions in their city are partly or completely under the control of gangsters or racketeers. In other cities, big labor organizations are also being dominated by professional criminals; others—not all, of course—are in immediate danger of such domination.

Al Capone is being continually referred to as a powerful factor in the affairs of the Chicago labor unions. He is, but possibly much against his will. Certainly he never sought very hard to control the unions. To understand this, one must know that Capone is not at all the monster his press given nickname "Scarface Al" may suggest. He started out as a beer-runner, intending to make a lot of money in that racket and quit. But then he became involved in politics and his henchmen put the gang into other rackets, until now it is almost impossible for him to quit without wrecking the gang. This he does not wish to do, if for no other reason than because of his loyalty to other members of the gang. He was drawn into the "protection racket" to protect legitimate business establishments against other gangsters because the police were unable to provide that protection. Several business houses took him, or rather his gang, into partnership for that reason. And similarly, the unions went to him for protection against "Bugs" Moran and other gangsters, because the unions know that Al and his men are straight shooters—not only with their guns but in point of honor and business ethics. Indeed, the Capone gang has more prestige in Chicago, even among legitimate business men, than some of the corporations and institutions properly organized under the laws of society.

The Chicago *Tribune* for April 20, 1930, reported an incident which, I think, illustrates this tendency of the unions to seek Capone's aid. It seems that James McLoughlin, business agent of the Marble Setters' Union, which is associated with the Chicago Building Trades Council, was called to the headquarters of George ("Bugs") Moran, head of the North Side gangster faction which at that time had a sort of truce with the Capone gang.

"What's the take in your union?" Moran asked McLoughlin. The "take" is gang argot for income. McLoughlin was forced to discuss his union affairs with "Bugs." Thereupon "Bugs" told him that he wanted so-and-so much on the first of every month for "protection."

McLoughlin took his troubles to Danny Stanton, who was in charge of Capone's labor-union department. Danny, in turn, took the case to the "Big Fellow," as Capone is known to his men, with the result that Al called up "Bugs" and advised him to cease his demands on McLoughlin and his union.

How far the Capone gang's domination of the unions will go, remains to be seen. At the moment it is just beginning. Most of the year 1930 Capone's well-mannered, gentlemanly gunmen attended labor union meetings, keeping away other gunmen. For the time being that is all.

It goes almost without saying the Capone gang will make use of the unions, perhaps in a political way, or perhaps to gain control of the contracting business in Chicago. In return, the Capone gang will probably be able to do something for the unions. In the summer of 1930, a Chicago laborite said to me: "Aw, hell, Capone may mean more to the unions than our high-toned A.F. of L. 'executives' in Washington," who, he hinted, are still chicken-hearted on account of the McNamara debacle, nearly twenty years ago. "Listen here," he said, "I know what I'm talkin' about. I was in all kinds of strikes. I've been in the movement over twenty-five years. I went to Pennsylvania during the steel strike in 1919—and, young man, I *know* that it takes more than organization and agitation and strikes in the open to save the unions, to raise the wages, and so on. It takes chemistry! Dynamite, by God!"

In the September 1930 issue of *Harper's Magazine* I published an article on "Racketeers and Organized Labor," in which I used most of the material in this chapter. To my surprise, I received a number of very friendly letters from officials in the A.F. of L. unions. I quote from one that came to me on the stationery of one of the largest labor unions in Chicago, signed by one of its officials:

> I enjoyed your article. There is no use beating about the bush; we in the movement realize that we couldn't get to first base without *stronger* persuasion than expounding Karl Marx and the theories of class struggle... I think you drove home the point that labor organizations use strong-arm tactics only when they have no other weapon or defense. Capital has the courts, always, to say nothing of its gunmen, police, and soldiery. The economic "game" in the existing system is loaded against us—and we behave as one does believing one has been roped in an unfair game.

VI

I have little doubt that labor racketeering will increase. In February 1930, when anywhere from four to eight million men were out of work in the United States, I had a rather long talk with the secretary-treasurer of a large building-trades union in one of our larger cities in the East.

"More than half of our members," he said to me, "have been out of work since early in the fall and most of them, it seems, will continue out of work till summer or, perhaps, indefinitely. The contractors are organized against us almost a hundred per cent. They're hiring scabs and we're losing control of the jobs that we've fought for twenty years to improve. They're *our* jobs; they belong to our men—good union men who have been paying their dues—but they're now being filled with hungry men who, of course, need work as badly as our men or worse, but who have done less than nothing to improve the working conditions in the trade. They're scabs. They're the means by which the bosses threaten to wreck our union."

He paused.

"Well?" I said.

"Well," he said, "suppose you were a paid and responsible official of an organization of ten thousand men, all of them skilled workmen and willing to work, but nearly seventy per cent of them unable to find jobs in their trade or any other trade. Remember that most of them are family men. They have mortgages on their homes and are paying for things on the installment plan. They're in danger of losing everything unless you, the official, get them their jobs. You're responsible to the membership for keeping under the control of the union a sufficient number of jobs to go around. That's what the union elects you for. You stay in the office only as long as the men are supplied with jobs… What would you do if you thought—in fact, were convinced—that violence was the only means of saving the situation for the union?"

It was not an easy question to answer. He himself is opposed to violence on principle. He is not a "gorilla," but a rather fine-mannered intellectual. However, unless employment increases, he will have to yield to the dynamite faction in the union or get out. Six months after he spoke to me as I quote him above, I heard that the "gorillas" in the union had taken possession of his office and kept him out of it, physically, for two weeks, after which period he was allowed to return only after "coming around" on the point of engaging a slugger. At this writing, a large percentage of the union's members are still out of work. Employment conditions are not improving, and, as my friend says, "the men are getting desperate as hell." They demand work; they are desperate for work and earnings; and they expect the union officials to see that they get work. They, individually and as a body, are becoming violence-minded. And eventually my friend will either have to hire, not only sluggers, but dynamiters, to terrorize the scabs and the scab-employing contractors, or get out of office. There is, of course, a third possibility, that industrial conditions will improve immediately, before this book appears, beyond the fondest expectations of even such great optimists as President Hoover.

Unemployment and employers' greed breed desperation, for a man   249
and his family must live. Desperation breeds violence—racketeering.
Take, for example, the typical though extreme case of labor racketeering that occurred on February 5, 1930, in Chicago. Two men stopped
their automobile near the Lying-In-Hospital, on the Midway, to which
an addition was then under construction. Casually, they inquired of a
worker if Meagher, superintendent for the contractor, was on the job.
He was pointed out. The strangers walked over and fired two bullets
into his back, dashed back to their car and drove off. This was unquestionably a terrible piece of business, and yet behind its horror and all the
terroristic acts of labor driven into a corner, we should at least see also
the horror of desperate men thrown out of work with their families on
the verge of starvation.

VII

As *Harper's Magazine*, with my article on labor racketeering, appeared
on the news stands on August 20, 1930, two labor officials were assassinated in Chicago. It seems that they had objected to professional
sluggers and assassins taking control of their union offices—and so they
were shot.

Thereupon Chicago's organized business began to take a sudden
friendly interest in the unions. "The Chicago press," as one labor official
wrote me,

> struck off in a different key about racketeers and labor. For years
> the *Tribune* and the *News* were openly hostile to labor. A man getting slugged or shot (even not seriously) in a union hall always got
> page one, although a murder not in a union hall received four lines
> among department-store ads. Now they are shedding crocodile
> tears of concern lest the "racketeers capture the unions." Before labor unions were either Communist or a gang of hoodlums; now
> they are workingmen's organizations in danger of being captured
> by Capone.

Chicago builders and contractors are uneasy about the gangsters'
domination of the several unions. But I believe they can do nothing
about it. If they suffer any evil consequences as a result of it, and I don't
doubt that they will, they will in a great measure have themselves to
blame. *They, along with other employers, have driven organized labor to
seek the aid of racketeers.*

The employers' uneasiness on account of labor racketeering is not restricted to Chicago. In July 1930 the New York newspapers reported that racketeers, whose aid had been sought by the unions in their struggle with the employers and who have since then taken control of several organizations, extort from a million to two million dollars yearly from garment manufacturers in that city under the threat of starting labor troubles in their establishments!

What effect this close contact between unions and gangs will have on organized labor in the long run remains to be seen. The chances are that it will do it more harm than good. At the 1930 convention of the A.F. of L., President Green seemed deeply perturbed by the tendency of racketeers to muscle in on the unions. At the same time some one prophesied that in five years labor racketeers would capture the A.F. of L. and elect their own president.

The great majority of trade unions as yet have nothing to do with racketeers and are steering clear of violence, but the gangsters are making such swift inroads that the situation deserves the concerned attention of social-minded people. Perhaps, very little can be done about it. Labor racketeering, as it has begun to develop in the United States, is a natural and even necessary product of powerful and chaotic social and economic forces that have been operating in this country *uncontrolled* since the beginning of the Industrial Revolution in the eighteen-forties.

We need not be surprised when we realize how close the relationship is between organized labor and organized crime. Nor need we be shocked by the thought that organized labor was a vital factor in the early history of modern racketeering, that, indeed, organized labor, perhaps more than any other economic group, started the professional criminals whose names now shriek in the headlines on their amazing careers. One should bear in mind that gangsterism was a vital factor early in the American class struggle, first on the capitalist side and then on the side of labor; and that its history is inextricably bound up with the history of organized labor.

CHAPTER 31
RACKETEERING AS A PHASE OF CLASS CONFLICT

In an early chapter, I have indicated how criminals were drawn into the struggle between the haves and the have-nots; how they were organized on a large scale by detective agencies and hired out, by the hundreds, as gunmen to powerful industrialists, to protect their property and scabs, and to attack strikers; and how, later, labor organizations, taking their cue from capital, began to hire professional strong-arm men to slug scabs, assassinate employers and foremen, and dynamite mills, mines, and uncompleted bridges and buildings.

There were gangs in the larger American cities before the capitalists began to use criminals in keeping down the proletariat, but those early gangs were comparatively small and loosely organized, operating largely as bandits, pick-pockets and neighborhood toughs. At election time, they acted as terrorists in a small way for crooked political bosses. But in the eighteen-sixties, when criminals began to be used in the class struggle, crime received a tremendous impetus toward becoming the billion-dollar "industry," which it is today. Gangs then became more compact, better organized, headed by managers of "detective agencies," which included some of the brainiest and most ruthless crooks in the country.

Moreover, on becoming a factor in the class struggle, criminality learned the use of weapons employed in that struggle. The idealistic Chicago Anarchists had advocated the use of dynamite as a means of bringing about what they conceived to be a just social order. Then large labor unions, in desperation, resorted to dynamite, and used it, as we have seen, sometimes with gratifying results. Finally, professional criminals, some of them occasional dynamiters for the unions, perceived that it would be effective stuff in other fields of endeavor.

The Haymarket Bomb, as I have suggested, was the Adam of the "pineapples" that now go off in such quantities in Chicago, New York, Detroit, Philadelphia and Cleveland, in behalf, not only of organized labor, but of all sorts of rackets. By using dynamite, criminality became, in the nineteen-twenties, one of the most powerful elements in America's national life, defying practically all agencies of law, gaining control of municipal governments and the courts, and fairly threatening what so far has passed for legitimate business.

In the larger cities all sorts of racket wars are going on day and night; wars in which dynamite, gunfire, daggers, arson, blackjacks, and fists, or the fear of such violence, decide economic and other issues. There are now in the United States hundreds—perhaps thousands—of men whose sole or principal occupation is to dynamite and "touch off" buildings, and commit murder and slug people in the interest of others. They charge regular fees for "jobs" according to the importance thereof. They sell their services at any time, anywhere, for almost any purpose, to almost anybody who has the need of a good assassin, dynamiter, firebug, acid-thrower, machine-gunner, window-breaker, or slugger, plus the required fee.

There are tailor shops in New York and Chicago, and perhaps elsewhere, which specialize in making clothes for gunmen, with leather-lined holster-pockets to conceal weapons.

Since the days in 1920, when men connected with labor unions had to instruct gangsters in the use of dynamite, regular "schools" of violence have appeared in Chicago and New York. Edwin Balmer, editor of the *Red Book* magazine, wrote in a syndicated article in the summer of 1930, that there were eight specialists in various forms of violence instructing criminals in Chicago alone. I am reliably informed that two of the eight—both instructors in the use of dynamite—are former trade-union walking-delegates. Crime, says Balmer, has

developed its own technicians, and the demands and easy profits of the "rackets" have created in Chicago a sort of graduate school which teaches technical refinements. Window-breakers in Chicago, for instance, are not crude heavers of bricks through panes of glass. They are experts in a special sort of blow which, I understand, is delivered as a scooping stroke upward, and which, when properly executed, completely "takes out" a window of any size or thickness. Dynamiting is a trade which obviously calls for special training; there is a definite art in stripping an entire front from a flat building or demolishing the side wall of a garage with one properly placed and carefully wired "shot." Arson also is complex. You must sprinkle your gasoline according to principles which have been found by practice to set the building all ablaze before the firemen arrive.

And when you come to bombs—well, there are a dozen divisions of bombing, ranging from the technique of a "pineapple" planted only to terrorize, to the technique of detonating a "big cough" to do deliberate murder. The acid-throwers concern themselves chiefly with the destruction of expensive clothing in the shops which have not made terms with the racketeers.

In the summer and fall of 1930 several racketeers' "arsenals" were discovered by the police in New York. These contained dynamite bombs, machine-guns, revolvers, blackjacks, and other tools of terrorism.

Almost every week some one is found mysteriously dead, riddled with bullets, on an empty lot in some large city or other. Now and then assassinations occur in open daylight, adroit gunmen, who had gone to "school" for the purpose, picking their victims "on the spot" from speeding automobiles.

II

Next to booze-running, gambling, and dope-peddling, the most widespread are the so-called "protection" rackets. The origin of the last named is easily traced to the trade unions' connection with criminality. Unions in Chicago and New York were already "protected" by gangsters, in the manner described in the preceding chapter, in 1922 and 1923, or years before "protection" racketeering became the $500,000 a week industry it now is in each of those two cities.

A modern "protection" racket usually starts with a small band of "wise guys," sometimes headed by a former city or hotel detective or by some ex-United States Department of Justice agent. They determine to dominate a certain section of the city. They are slick fellows, having started out as petty criminals and served short terms in prisons, where they learned all they needed to know about crime. The leader is usually "in the know." In all probability, as a former "dick," he has some "dirt" on the big boys in city politics, and, holding a club over their heads, has no difficulty in keeping the police out of his way. Indeed, he often takes the cops, as well as judges and ward heelers, "in on the racket." He becomes boss of the section. To attain that position he employs dynamite and other forms of violence.

On "taking over" the section, they call, as a rule in pairs, on all the grocers, butchers, barbers, druggists, laundrymen, florists, restaurant and garage owners, tobacconists, candy stores, beauty shops, and other tradespeople in the neighborhood, and say to them: "Good morning,

254 sir. As you know there's a lot of crime going on. Early this week two stores were burglarized within two blocks of you"; (their own job) "no doubt you've heard about it. Well, we've just formed a protective agency—here's our card—and you're invited to join us. The fee is nominal. Fifty [sometimes a hundred] dollars a month, in return for which we—the Night and Day Detective and Protective Association—will protect you from every evil in the world, including hold-ups and competition. You're invited to join right away"—emphatically.

If the butcher or grocer declines to sign up right away, one or two of the gangsters call again the next day. They "proposition" him once more and, as likely as not, stress their eagerness to have him join the Night and Day Detective and Protective Association by pulling out their guns; whereupon, as a rule, "the bozo comes across." If not, the next morning he may find his windows "taken out" or the whole front of his store neatly blown out by dynamite. If he is a laundryman, his delivery wagon may be dynamited or his driver slugged. Then, if he still continues obstinate, which is unlikely, one nice afternoon a husky customer walks into the place and, hauling off, suddenly smashes him in the face. The next day, if he is not a total wreck in hospital, he is quite ready to be "protected" and, with well concealed reluctance, forks over the first month's "protection" fee.

Thus the gang, without the slightest interference on the part of the police, gains economic control of the neighborhood, which may include anywhere from thirty to a hundred blocks. In return for the tribute that legitimate business people pay the gangsters, they actually are given a sort of protection. In the first place, the gang refrains from holding them up and keeps other crooks out of the neighborhood, which is more than the police can do. Then, they prevent new stores from opening in competition with their "protégés."

Of course, the gang takes control of the liquor business in the section. It opens speakeasies, night clubs, gambling joints, dance halls and brothels. It also "gets in on" the dope business. In all of these rackets they have practically a free hand; all they have to watch for is some other gang of "wise guys" who may have their eyes on the "territory."

There is a gang in charge of a section in the Bronx, whose "protection take" runs into nearly $10,000 a month. The business people must pay, or they may get "bumped off." The gangsters usually shoot or dynamite one or two at the start as a hint to others. The victims cannot call the law to their aid; if they attempt to, they are doomed.

These protection gangs usually expand into other fields. They form partnerships with wholesale pretzel, spinach, artichoke, meat, egg, milk, ice, butter, and bread dealers and then force all the retailers in their domain to buy from them. They force their "clients," as they call them, to install slot-machines and chance boards in their stores. They terrorize scab-employing contractors and builders in behalf of desperate labor unions. They hire out dynamiters, assassins, sluggers, window-breakers, acid-throwers, and other strong-arm talent to almost anyone who has some dirty work to be done.

They often force successful business establishments to take them into partnership. I know of a moving picture theater owner in Brooklyn who is paying a percentage of his weekly income to the neighborhood "mob," the members of which used to drop "stink bombs" in his theater during performances. Since he took them into his business, they have ruined—also with stink bombs—his competitor four blocks away, and now he and his racketeer partners have the only movie house within twenty blocks. To open another theater in that district without taking in the racketeers would be futile—if not fatal.

Since 1927 the neighborhood gangs have begun to amalgamate, and now cities like Chicago, New York, and Philadelphia are swiftly coming under the domination of such powerful groups as the Capone gang. I have it from a police official in New York that there are—in 1930—at least 80,000 practicing, gun-toting racketeers in Manhattan, Brooklyn, and the Bronx. These men, but recently plain workingmen or sons of working people, started out a few years ago as petty bootleggers; now their individual "take" from $100 to $5,000 a week. The "take" of the "big fellows" often amounts to $10,000 a week.

Despite the tendency to amalgamate, however, the interests of one gang occasionally come in conflict with the interests of another, and then there is war. Gangsters are killed by other gangsters; now and then one is killed—as though accidentally—by the police. But these killings have no effect upon gangsterism and racketeering as a whole. Indeed, all rackets are definitely "on the up and up."

Booze, gambling, prostitution, and dope, of course, are the big rackets. Of late—in 1930—the racketeers have begun to go into food racketeering, that is, by means of violence and fear, forcing retailers to pay higher prices. For instance, they have muscled in on the milk business. In certain sections of Chicago and New York milk is seventy per cent "organized." To accomplish this, racketeers have slugged no end of milk dealers and milk-truck drivers, bombed large creameries and small dairies, punctured the tires of milk trucks, and overturned milk wagons. A gentler method, but also effective, is to drop chemicals into fresh milk, causing it instantly to curdle.

During an official investigation into food racketeering in New York in the summer of 1930, it was revealed that gangsters were becoming a power in all the food markets in the city. Their rule is: pay up and shut up, or take the consequences. Incredible as it may seem, the drowsy farmer whom the late motorist sees rumbling cityward with his produce often is confronted at the end of his route by emphatic individuals who insist upon controlling the sale of his goods. He sells to whom he is told and at the price set, else his tires are cut, his truck wrecked, or he himself is beaten.

Employing violence, the racketeers have gained control of the smoked fish business in the Jewish sections of Brooklyn. And so on, and so on. It would require the space of another book to describe all the rackets that have sprung up in the last half of the nineteen-twenties.

In the fall of 1929, the New York *World* estimated that about 250 industries in that city were completely or partly under the control of gangsters, whose total proceeds from the rackets exceeded $100,000,000 a year. Courtney Terret, author of *Only Saps Work*, a book on racketeering, estimates that the gangs' "take" in New York is from $200,000,000 to $600,000,000 a year, or from $33 to $83 for every man, woman, and child in the city. In Chicago, according to a committee of the Employers' Association, there were on January 1, 1930, forty-nine different rackets with legitimate business as their prey, costing tradespeople and the public approximately $136,000,000.

A grand jury sitting in Brooklyn in 1930 expressed the opinion that the racketeers in that community were "a power for the time being greater than the government itself." To put it more exactly the racketeers *are* most of the government in such cities as Chicago and New York, for they have their own men in the police departments and on judicial benches. Men like Al Capone and Arnold Rothstein and Bugs Moran are figures of national prominence, "big men" in the same sense that Henry Ford and Charles Schwab are big men. They certainly are men of consequence. Capone's annual income from his various rackets is said to be about $30,000,000. He has a mansion on the coast of Florida and travels in an airplane of his own. When Jack ("Legs") Diamond was shot in October 1930, the hospital authorities in New York issued bulletins as to his condition twice a day.

Sometimes a big racketeer becomes a sort of hero in the community he dominates. Al Capone, for instance, is considered a modern Robin Hood by thousands of people in Cicero, near Chicago, where he used to make his headquarters. It is Al's policy to spend a few hundred thousand dollars every year in charity, supporting widows, paying poor people's doctor bills, enabling them to send their children to school, giving them baskets of groceries on holidays, and so on. They think Al a "great guy" for taking money from the rich and giving it to the poor. There is a little known gang in the Bronx, whose members also are extremely popular among the poor working people. When one of the gangsters is shot, they give him a funeral costing tens of thousands of dollars, burying him in a silver casket... This hardly differs from the social technique of Tammany Hall district control and similar "legitimate" political processes...

In his annual report issued in May 1930, the Police Commissioner of New York City virtually admitted that he and his force were unable to cope with the "sinister figures who stalk through the underworld and who reign through fear, violence, and murder." In June 1930, the appalling crime situation in Chicago caused the chief of police there to leave his office in defeat. He admitted that he was no match for such organizations as the Capone and Moran gangs, most of whose important members were, to quote the Chicago Crime Commission, "beyond the reach of the police power; for they do their dirty work through anonymous henchmen and, moreover, have powerful friends in the city politics."

The police commissioner of New York blamed the growth of gangsterism in the large cities on Prohibition, which gave rise to the bootlegging industry, "with its natural appeal to the criminal element." The police chief of Chicago said the same thing. Indeed, nearly everybody who ventures to speak on racketeering blames it on Prohibition.

But, of course, to put all the blame of it on Prohibition is to be superficial. Prohibition unquestionably is a tremendous factor in the egregious condition, but only one of several factors.

I have shown that the technique of racketeering, its development and its tools, are to be traced to the class struggle.

III

What is most important in this connection is the fact that the class struggle, growing continually fiercer in the last half century, with long spells of unemployment and low wages, has driven or induced numerous workmen, or boys who under better conditions would have become workmen, into the criminal class.

Racketeering, as it exists today in the United States, is an essential manifestation of the dynamic drive for economic betterment so characteristic of the country. It is a phase of the efforts of the American underdog to raise himself. It is inextricably bound up with the chaotic and *brutalizing* conditions in industry and with the great inner urge of the American people, constantly stimulated by social and economic forces, to get on, to get on, *quickly*, at all costs.

Criminals, including America's high-powered racketeers, are recruited largely from those classes which suffer most from poverty, uncertain and unhealthy employment, and other evil conditions of life and labor. The French sociologist, J. R. Brissot de Warville, said many years ago:

A man is not born an enemy of society. It is the circumstances which give him that title, such as poverty or misfortune. He does not disturb the general tranquillity until he has lost his own. He ceases to be a good citizen only when the name becomes meaningless in his case.

Another Frenchman, Edouard Ducpétiaux, held that

criminality is the inseparable companion of poverty... In the midst of destitution, a man gradually loses the notion of justice and injustice, of good and bad; beset by needs that he cannot satisfy, he disregards the laws, and ends by recoiling from no attempt that appears capable of bettering his condition.

The problem of crime is, of course, a colossal and many sided subject. Here I wish to stress the economic aspect of it, which, in America at least, is, I think, one of the most important.

Since the beginning of the great industrial era, life in the United States, as compared with life in other so-called civilized countries, has been marked by its restlessness, adventurousness, brutality, instability. The country is huge and rich, with *thousands* of real and fairly legitimate opportunities, open to all who wish to seek them, and *millions* of individuals eager for success, who are seeking them. The mathematical result is that a great majority of the people, among them some of the most daring and resourceful, are ordained from the start for a life that is far less agreeable and successful in the material sense than they feel it ought to be in a land where things are plentiful beyond imagining and "all men are equal." So, as failures, which they consider themselves, they are unhappy, desperate.

In Europe, the poor and lowly have been taught to accept their plight without much complaint, but Americans are motivated by a different and powerful spirit, the spirit of democracy, formulated in the Declaration of Independence. The American underdog has been taught to believe that, essentially, he is as good as the next man, if not a little better, and as such has the right to refuse to stay an underdog, and to do everything possible to climb upward. Indeed, his philosophy of values being the same as that of the upperdog, he has come to believe that his principal duty in life is to cease to be an underdog and get on—to make money.

Practically every one has in his make-up certain lawless or antisocial urges, which, stimulated by American individualism and the "get on" philosophy, become easily translated into actual lawbreaking. If one does not succeed in getting on within the law, one tries to find the avenue to success outside the law. This is especially true since the average man has begun to break away from religious inhibitions. Add to this the general knowledge of dishonesty and graft in high places. Someone has said that human society is like a fish: it begins to rot first at the head. The bad example of persons in high places is a subtly corrupting force that gradually but inevitably undermines the integrity of individuals in the lower strata of society.

Prohibition may be blamed for the growth of gangsterism in America in that it afforded a road to success outside the law to a multitude of people who otherwise would have remained poor. The causes underlying the development of racketeering and crime in recent years, however, go much deeper and much farther back.

The more intelligent worker in an industry where employment is periodic and uncertain, and wages and working conditions none too good, realizes before long that, if he continues to work as he does only six months out of the year, he will never get anywhere, that when he becomes prematurely old and his health broken down, industry will, as a matter of course, wash its hands of him. He may be intrinsically as honest and law-abiding as anyone, but when he finds himself out of work and without money, he is already predisposed to look up his bootlegger acquaintance and be initiated into the racket. He may perhaps be caught at it, but in jail he will learn much more about crime and racketeering. He will realize that, even with prison staring him in the face, crime or racketeering is better than being geared to the industrial machine, where, in times of depression, and certainly in his old age, he will be thrown out, a wreck, upon the mercies of the Salvation Army.

The less intelligent underdog is likely to arrive more intuitively at the conclusion that, with the economic game loaded against him, he cannot summon the necessary mental energy and initiative to climb the ladder of success, in the true American sense of the word. But he reads of stealing, in high places and low, for which no one seems ever to get punished. Instead he sees the malefactors well-dressed, with cars, cash, and women—and he, too, feels discouraged. He knows that while he wears the overalls at productive labor he will get nowhere, and how to get rich on the labor of others he cannot see unless he moves outside the law. On the basis of the number of crimes committed as compared with the number of convictions, his chances of immunity in crime would be about fifty-fifty. Such odds he would consider comparatively fair. At any rate one day he too crosses the Rubicon. If he "gets away with it," then he is through with overalls forever. If he joins a "mob," becoming a professional gunman, a racketeer, a spoke in some great booze or "protection" ring, his chances of going to jail dwindle to very low proportions.

IV

In the summer of 1930, Stuart Chase published an article in *Harper's* in which he argued that integrity in America is becoming a luxury that but few can afford. And the poorer a man is, the less he can indulge in honesty—especially since the social structure is becoming more and more corrupt, inhuman, and brutalizing, from top to bottom.

In the middle of the last century Henry Thomas Buckle collected data showing that the number of criminals increased in direct proportion to the rise of food prices. In present-day America, aside from the ever-mounting cost of bare living necessities, one's appetites for material goods are being ceaselessly whetted by persuasive advertisements and high-pressure salesmanship. By these means the manufacturers of luxuries transform their products into necessities, without the possession of which one is made to feel poverty-stricken—a failure. The relatively little actual starvation in America, therefore, is not inconsistent with the fact that there is more poverty—that is, more people with ungratified desires—among Americans than in any other nation in the world.

Then there is the factor of the average American's democratic pride—or, if you will, conceit. To beg a man whom he considers no better than himself for a job is humiliating to him. He resents the insults of contemptuous employment managers. My own encounters, as a worker, with the latter make it easy for me to understand why a man would rather be a racketeer and a criminal than an honest industrial laborer. In a racket a man can at least be a piece of a man. As a gunman or boot-legger he has a man-to-man chance with an opponent; he may fight it out if he has the guts. In industry, on the other hand, he is not only subjected to insults and humiliation; he is at the mercy of the moods of a system which he does not understand and which no one seems able or willing to control for the benefit of all.

The millions of men out of work, as this book appears, are going through a dreadful experience. Unemployment causes more distress in America than anywhere else, for here a man may suffer not only from cold and hunger, but from the agonies of shame at not being able to keep up appearances against enormous odds. A good front is so necessary to the American that his poverty is a hidden, under-ground poverty, much worse than poverty expressing itself, as it does in Europe, in open social protest. Hence, poverty in America drives men, not into the radical movement, which might give them social vision and class-conscious hope of a better future, but into the un-derworld, into bootlegging, into "mobs" and rackets—or to suicide. In the early fall of 1930 the newspapers reported seven suicides of jobless workingmen in New York in one week; three of them, before killing themselves, murdered their wives and children.

Since the World War it has become increasingly harder for a man lawfully to achieve economic independence in the United States. Once upon a time one could bundle up and go West, settle in the wilderness, and thus escape the humiliations and uncertainties of being an industri-al worker. Now the open spaces are gone; all the good land is under the control of big money. Small-scale farming is decidedly unremunerative. And all small businesses, such as neighborhood stores, are being frozen out by big business and chain stores.

Thus millions of men in America are left with but one lawful path to follow: they must sell their labor on the overcrowded market, which they know is not a starting-point to economic independence. And so it is quite natural, given an opportunity, for some workmen, if they are characteristically American in their desire to get on, and if, besides, they have the guts and are free from family ties, to become bootleggers, or racketeers. Racketeers are being recruited almost exclusively from among the working class.

V

Since 1929, when I began to work on this study, I have come into personal contact with a number of racketeers and gangsters, big and petty, in and around Chicago and New York. Nearly all whom I know come of immigrant-labor parentage or had themselves been workers in the years immediately after the war. One is the son of a Polish worker who was injured in the Haymarket bomb explosion in 1886. Several others have sprung also from the numerous class of precariously employed and ill-educated people, poverty-stricken and ill cared for. These spent their early lives in big industrial cities, with their contrasting slums and mansions, with their unwholesome conditions and weak communal conscience, and their opportunities for knowing many persons and, at the same time, being lost to the community as a whole. I believe that these men of my acquaintance are typical racketeers.

Among them I find several who unquestionably are "right guys," men with strict codes of honor and ethics. Their behavior in personal relations, so far as I have been able to determine, is the highest; they are men of their word, and would sooner die than betray a fellow racketeer, friend or enemy, to the police. Their contempt for established authority is boundless; they are self-confessed outlaws, but conscious of their superiority to law and police power.

A few racketeers with whom I have come in contact are high-spirited, intelligent men. One whom I know, perhaps, the best of the lot, is a Yugoslav, a countryman of mine. He is a "big fellow" in one of the Chicago gangs, a well-mannered, well-read man, a former radical capable of discussing Karl Marx and Nietzsche no less than of handling a great booze ring and a vast protection racket. Indeed, he is one of the best informed and, in his way, the most honest and realistic man I know anywhere. He told me in the summer of 1930 that he took to bootlegging, which later led to other rackets, to "save my goddam self-respect!" As an "honest worker" earning four or six dollars a day he got nowhere. He had been a Socialist and a trade-unionist and had found petty graft and intrigue everywhere. He began to realize, he said, that most of the leaders of the Socialist movement, local and national, were either rogues or lopsided emotionalists, while outside the movement was a tremendous mass of stupid proletarians whom the message of Socialism could never reach and who, perhaps, deserved nothing better in life than what they were getting. After the war he lost faith in the radical movement altogether. It was, he decided, all so much claptrap and hogwash; Mencken was right. He continued to work at four or six dollars a day. Sometimes he didn't work at all. And he began to feel like a "damn fool." So he became a bootlegger—back in 1921—and, getting in with the right "crowd," rose swiftly to power in the affairs of what since has developed into a big gang. "Now, by God, I feel like a man again." Now he counts for something. He is somebody. His name appears in news columns. He lives in style. Once he had been clubbed by the police in a strike in Joliet, Illinois; now he has it all over the cops. They can't touch him. In fact, not a few of them are under his orders.

With the understanding between us that I would disguise him if I quoted him in print, he spoke quite frankly about himself and his doings.

Yes, we run booze, mostly beer; [he said] that's our main line. What of it? We supply an insistent demand. Tens of thousands of our customers like our beer and liquor. It's good stuff. It finds its way into the homes of judges and other great men, some of whom, after being drunk tonight, will pass judgment upon others in the morning for drinking.

Our business is illegitimate, true, but the law that makes it so is considered a bad law by more than half of the people of the United States. See the *Literary Digest*. And you know what Thoreau said about bad laws. Break 'em! Well, we help to break the Prohibition law.

As to the other "rackets," as you call them—we call them "business"—they're a damn sight more moral than most of the rackets that usually go by the name of corporation. Let us admit that we, the so-called racketeers, do "extort" money from so-called legitimate business establishments—what of it? Doesn't every other gang of business men do the same thing, one way or another? Isn't practically everything that is sold in America sold for more than it is worth—first by the manufacturer, then by the wholesaler, finally by the retailer? Business is a hold-up game from top to bottom. Those on top exploit those beneath them economically. Capital exploits labor—oh, and *how*! Big business screws small business. Of course they have made it legal and moral. They talk of Service with a capital S and join the Rotary, both the exploiters and the exploited, who, in their turn, as I've said, exploit some one below them.

Yes, we use force—what of it? Are we any worse than legitimate business? Don't big capitalists use force in putting down strikes? They stop at nothing. Of course their force sometimes is legalized; sometimes their gunmen wear uniforms with shiny buttons on them. You told me of the "stink bomb" gang in Brooklyn that has muscled in on a theater. Well, I can tell you for a fact that [mentioning the name of a huge motion picture concern] last year, while acquiring a new string of theaters in Chicago didn't deem it beneath their dignity to employ so-called racketeers to stink-bomb privately owned show-houses all over the country, in order to buy them cheaper from desperate owners, whose customers were being driven away by stink-bombs. Or, for that matter, wouldn't you call Henry Ford a racketeer? Didn't he *force* his dealers all over the country, a couple of years ago, to take a certain number of cars, more than they could handle; if they didn't take them and send him the money, they lost their agencies. What do you call *that?*...

You mentioned that labor unions are hiring dynamiters and sluggers to attain their ends. Well, I may be a lowdown criminal pervert, but I don't think there's anything the matter with that. How do the capitalists treat labor? Is it worse to dynamite a building than to turn out of work, in the middle of winter, thousands of men whose families live from hand to mouth? I marvel there isn't more dynamiting. If there were, I'd probably get a little respect again for the working class. Now, to hell with it! The goddamn stiffs, with their docile suffering, make me sick; and if some of the gangs exploit certain labor unions, I don't care.

But none of the big gangs, so far as I know, really exploit labor unions. Labor is too low; it's weak, and there's nothing in it. We don't go in for the weak, except—in our generous moments—to help them out. Unlike the big capitalists who exploit the weakest class, we reverse the process. We exploit for the most part those above—legitimate business men, the strongest element in our society. I'm not bragging, but in our own peculiar way—and, believe me, kid, I know the thing from the inside—in our peculiar way, we're honest and straightforward about it. We're direct-action *business men*, that's what we are. We're outlaws, true, but we have laws of our own. Some of the boys carry guns and other bad instruments. You've heard of bombings and killings. Now and then the boys just can't help knockin' some guy over. Too bad. But is that any worse than to starve workmen and their families, or shoot down defenseless worn-out proletarians when they strike trying to improve their lot? I don't think that what the so-called racketeers do is half so mean. We go for the strong. They have the law on their side. And if we sometimes get the best of them, which happens, that's all to our credit. We don't exploit the weak. Anybody can do that.

Talk about rackets! I've been reading in *The Nation* and *New Republic* about the new tariff bill—well, if *that* isn't a racket I'd like to know what it is. Behind it is the force of the state, but force just the same; and who is the state but the gangsters known as Big Business or the G.O.P.? The only difference between them and the "protection racket" in the Bronx that you mention is that the tariff is a billion-dollar proposition while the racket in the Bronx takes in only ten grand per month. As a matter of fact, the average "protection racket" is only a miniature tariff stunt—only it isn't signed by Herbert Hoover with a gold pen.

I saw him in New York after a championship boxing bout. He had won a large sum on the fight and hinted to me that the defeated prizefighter had had "a gun against his belly" and had not dared to win; that, indeed, racketeers had muscled themselves into the prizering and controlled it.

We were walking on Fifth Avenue and met a man by the name of Sam, a booze-gambling-labor racketeer from across the river in New Jersey, who had known my Yugoslav friend for years. I had met Sam once before. He is a hearty, generous fellow, an Americanized Russian Jew in his early thirties, a sport from head to foot, with a weekly income of from two to five thousand dollars. He is "in" with most of the big politicians, in and out of office, of several cities in New Jersey. He is, incontestably, a "big shot."

This afternoon he had with him a neat little blonde whom he introduced to us as "Dolly, just in from Hollywood." He said that they were going shopping and wouldn't we come along; he and Dolly were out on a spending jag. Dolly giggled cutely.

We went along and within the next hour and a half visited several of the most exclusive shops on the Avenue. Sam spent three or four thousand dollars on Dolly. In one place he bought her twenty pairs of shoes, each pair costing from twenty to twenty-five dollars, and twenty handbags to match the shoes, which cost anywhere from twenty-five to a hundred dollars each. And it was evident that Sam was in the habit of treating his girl friends in this style.

Later I remarked to my Yugoslav friend that I thought Sam was a damned fool to spend so much money on a girl.

"Maybe he is," he said—"what of it! But then is he any worse than your millionaire who's cleaned up in Wall Street or in some manufacturing racket? Your legitimate plutocrat does the same thing with his chorus girls—so why shouldn't Sam with his Hollywood cutie? Sure, there are millions of people out of work, thousands of them starving, but why should Sam worry about them any more than does John Pierpont Morgan, whose private yacht—so appropriately named the *Corsair*—cost him two and a half million to build and now costs him $3,000 a day to operate... Maybe some day Sam, or Sam's son, if he should have one, will build himself a private yacht as fine as Morgan's and call her the *Racketeer*. Why not?"

And he laughed.

CHAPTER 32
SABOTAGE AND "STRIKING ON THE JOB"

In 1920, following my discharge from the Army, I became, under the bread-and-butter compulsion, a young "working stiff" (I was just twenty) with no particular trade. For several months I hung around the employment agencies—the "slave market"—in Chicago. There I met a couple of rather articulate I.W.W., who, seeing that I was a young ex-soldier, palpably "on the bum," and a "scissor bill" with a radical trend of mind, set out to make me into a class-conscious proletarian, a wobbly. They urged me to give up all ideas of ever being anything else than a working stiff, for the chances of my becoming a capitalist or a bourgeois, in however modest a way, were extremely slender, indeed, almost nil. I was a foreigner, and the number of opportunities was decreasing rapidly even for native Americans. I should make up my mind to remain a worker and devote such abilities as I had to the hastening of the decay of the capitalist system, which was doomed to collapse, they said, within a very few years whether I joined the I.W.W. or not.

I learned of the methods by which, it appeared, sooner or later the workers would attain to power and abolish capitalism and "wage slavery." At first I did not understand everything I was told. The wobblies used a word—"sabotage"—which, as I recalled, I had read some time before in Frank Harris's *Pearson's Magazine* without knowing its meaning. At the public library I did not find it in the dictionary.

Then, in a dingy I.W.W. reading-room I came upon a little book entitled *Sabotage*, written originally in French by Emile Pouget and translated into English by Arturo Giovannitti, in 1912, while he was in jail at Lawrence, Massachusetts, on framed-up charges for his part as a wobbly leader in the famous textile-workers' strike. There I found sabotage defined as

> any conscious or willful act on the part of one or more workers intended to reduce the output of production in the industrial field,

or to restrict trade and reduce profits in the commercial field by
the withdrawal of efficiency from work and by putting machinery
out of order and producing as little as possible without getting
dismissed from the job.

The book was a sort of wobbly gospel.

In the same reading-room I found pamphlets in which sabotage was
discussed from the ethical point of view. A wobbly writer described it
as a "war measure" in the conflict between the capitalist class and the
working class, and in war everything was fair and moral. The wobblies
admitted that sabotage on the part of the workers was no goody-goody
method, but defended it on the ground that it certainly was no worse
than the methods to which the capitalists were resorting in the economic warfare. If the workers, in their efforts to gain economic advantages, damaged property and destroyed materials, did not the bosses,
in the interest of profits, destroy property with a ruthless and careless
hand? Have they not laid waste the country's national resources with
utter lack of consideration for their human values—forests, mines, land,
and water-ways? Did they not dump cargoes of coffee and other goods
into the sea, burn fields of cotton, wheat, and corn, throw trainloads of
potatoes to waste—all in the interest of higher incomes? Did not millers
and bakers mix talcum, chalk, and other cheap and harmful ingredients
with flour? Did not candy manufacturers sell glucose and taffy made
with vaseline, and honey made with starch and chestnut meal? Wasn't
vinegar often made of sulphuric acid? Didn't farmers and distributors
adulterate milk and butter? Were not eggs and meat stored away, suffering deterioration all the while, in order to cause prices to rise?

All of this, the wobblies insisted, was sabotage, just as their doings were sabotage; the ethical difference between the worker and the
capitalist with their respective forms of sabotage was that the former
was open and honest about it, and the latter dishonest, practicing destruction secretly, under the guise of business, the while condemning
proletarian *saboteurs* as criminals.

There was another difference. The wobblies preferred that property
should not be destroyed; indeed, they were more jealous of its preservation than the capitalists, for at the basis of their philosophy was the
idea that the property belonged to them. It was their—the workers'—
creation; some day it would be theirs by right of possession; and until
that day it should be preserved for them.

These things were openly discussed by the wobblies in meetings,
newspapers, and conversation. They didn't care who knew that they be-

lieved in and practiced sabotage. Some of them were veritable evangelists of sabotage, for they saw it as almost the only means—but a powerful one—whereby the cause of the underdog could be advanced. One of my wobbly friends said, in effect:

> Now that the bosses have succeeded in dealing an almost fatal blow to the boycott; now that picket duty is practically outlawed in many sections of the country, free speech throttled, free assemblage prohibited, and injunctions against labor are becoming epidemic—now sabotage, this dark, invincible, terrible Damocles' sword that hangs over the head of the master class, will replace all the confiscated weapons and ammunition of the workers in their war for economic justice. And it will win, for it is the most redoubtable of all, except the General Strike. In vain will the bosses get an injunction against strikers' funds, as they did in the great Steel Strike—sabotage, as we practice it, is a more powerful injunction against their machinery. In vain will they invoke old laws and make new ones against it—they will never discover sabotage, never track it to its lair, never run it down, for no laws will ever make a crime of the "clumsiness and lack of skill" of a scab who bungles his work or "puts on the bum" a machine he "does not know how to run," but which has really been "fixed" by a class-conscious worker long before the scab's coming on the job. There can be no injunction against sabotage. No policemen's club. No rifle diet. No prison bars.

It was some time before I realized how effective—and significant—sabotage really was.

II

Through a Chicago employment agency I found pick-and-shovel work on a long-time construction job outside of Joliet. I was one of perhaps a hundred muckers, among whom, as I soon discovered, were also several wobbly sabotage evangelists.

"Take it easy, kid," one of them said to me smilingly the second or third day. "Don't try to build the road in a day. T'hell with it! You're getting the same as me, three fifty ain't you? Well, then, don't work as if you were get thirty-five."

I had been working steadily, and this not because I wanted to see the road finished as soon as possible, but because, not having worked for months, and being plagued by some sort of blues, I thought that a few months of real work would toughen me up physically and otherwise.

But now as the wobbly prophet of sabotage called me down for working too fast, I blushed—without knowing why. I became self-conscious.

For days the man kept close to me, continuing to urge me to slow down. "Put the brakes on, kid," he would say. Or, "Go take a sip of water." Or, "Say, don't you think it's about time you went to the can again?" Or, "Tomorrow's another day, boy."

Then we would have long conversations, while he pretended to be digging or shoveling beside me; he had stalling down to a science. He evidently was a well-read, self-educated bozo; and when I revealed to him that I was a sort of fan of such writers as Upton Sinclair and Frank Harris, and was interested in the Russian Revolution, he told me about the I.W.W. movement, and about "Big Bill" Haywood and William Z. Foster who, in 1912 had attended an international labor congress in Europe and brought back to America the French ideas of sabotage which since then have been considerably improved by the rank and file of the wobblies. He was a self-appointed apostle of sabotage, with a surprising gift of gab, going from job to job, making wobblies of scissor bills, teaching them what he called "the technique of stalling."

He taught me the technique. He said: "Don't take so much on the shovel, kid. Don't break your back. Which reminds me of what a bunch of stiffs did down in Bedford, Indiana, back in 1908, when the boss told 'em their wages were cut. They went to a machine shop and had their shovels shortened, and said to the boss, 'small pay, small shovel.' They had the right dope. That was a kind o' instinctive, spontaneous sabotage; though sabotage, I mean the word, was then unknown in this country. That still holds good—'small pay, small shovel.' You get three fifty; do you think that's all your labor is worth? Don't be a fool. So give 'em a small shovel; when nobody is looking, no shovel at all. T'hell with 'em! Stall—strike on the job. Savvy?"

I found stalling, even after I had more or less mastered the technique, harder than real work, but my instructor derived a deep satisfaction from it. He encouraged me, saying that by and by I should get used to it.

Originally—back in 1912 and 1913—the wobbly idea was to damage the machinery just before going on strike, so that the scabs could not use it; but by 1920 the I.W.W. and the Communist agitators, who then began also to play an important role in the drama of sabotage in American industry, commenced to "fix" machines while the work went on. On the road-building job I worked on near Joliet the foreman had trouble every few days with the concrete-mixers, trucks, and steam-shovels. Suddenly things would break down in the middle of the fore-noon or afternoon, whereupon ten or twenty men stood around idle while the mechanics repaired them.

My friend the wobbly winked at me meaningfully, smiling. In the evening while we walked about he told me about sabotage stunts in which he had participated or of which he had heard.

One day he said: "I guess I'm a short-timer on this job. Did you notice how the old Irish buzzard"—meaning the foreman we worked under—"watches me all the time the last few days? They're getting wise to me; maybe one of the stiffs that I've tried to educate told them what my religion is." He smiled. "I'll be fired in a day or two. But what the hell! I'll be on another job in a week, doing the same thing."

The next day he and three other men, also wobbly sabotage apostles, were paid off and cautioned to stay away in the future; but before they went I learned that the two miles of concrete road we had laid in the past month and a half would be full of wide cracks within three weeks. They had put something in the cement that would cause it to crack, and the contractor would have to do it all over again.

I stayed on the Joliet job another month, long enough to see the concrete crack; then, with mid-summer near, I went on to St. Louis with two young I.W.W. who were confident that there we should have no difficulty getting work as harvest hands in the Missouri and Kansas wheat fields.

In St. Louis the "slave market" also was full of wobblies. They were all a rather jolly, if somewhat lopsided lot, lame with a sort of fanaticism tempered with good humor. I heard the story (which I later verified) of an incident that occurred one winter before the War when the city was full of starving and freezing unemployed men who had come in from the camps and fields. The wobblies decided to force the city to take care of them; and so one day several hundred of them invaded the restaurants, ordered big meals, and then presented their checks to the cashiers, telling them to charge them to the mayor. Arrested, they made speeches in court that broke on the front page. The town got excited over the prospect of thousands of men heading for St. Louis to eat at the mayor's cost—for that was just what they did, out of jail or in. The city council then hastily passed an emergency bill to start municipal lodging houses with free beds and meals. The "stunt" was a form of sabotage on the community, dramatic and humorous, which, frankly, appealed to me.

Indeed, not a few wobblies with whom I came in contact, though intensely serious, were genial, amusing, and intelligent fellows, quite frank about their ideas and doings. They were free-lance missionaries in the cause of the underdog to whom the end justified the means, with the self-imposed duty to harm the propertied class as much as, and wherever, possible: guerrilla soldiers in the class war.

In the Kansas wheat fields, where I worked for several weeks in the summer of 1920, there was much stalling or "striking on the job," and threshers and other harvest equipment would break down in the midst of work, when every hour counted to the farmer.

Some thirty miles away from where I worked, a wheat field nearly a mile square burned up. It created somewhat of a sensation in our camp. The wobblies I knew, most of them fairly level-headed stiffs, seemed opposed to fire and blamed the stunt on the Communists, who were much more drastic. There were rumors among the I.W.W. that the "Communists" in the United States had orders "from Moscow" to sabotage on American industry. These rumors probably were based upon a "confidential circular" said to be "unquestionably authentic"—but in all likelihood wasn't—which the United States Department of Justice "discovered" and published at that time, and in which some "Executive Committee" in Moscow urged its "representatives abroad," among other things to instigate general and particular strikes, injure machinery and boilers in factories, and do everything possible to disorganize capitalist industries.

There can be little question that, early in the last decade, "Communists" in the United States engaged in such doings; only, let me hasten to say, there was and is no connection between them and the several Communist movements now existing in this country. Most American "Communists" at that time were various kinds of dissenters from the I.W.W., none of whom have now any connection with Communism. Among my notes I happen to have press clippings covering violence and sabotage in connection with the railroad and coal strikes in the fall of 1922:

> *Washington, Sept. 1.*—Between 6,000 and 7,000 loaded cars have been tampered with, and will have to be unloaded and re-paired, it was announced by the Department of Justice today. Their contents will have to be reloaded on other cars in order to prevent a shortage in the Northwest, where many of them were consigned.
>
> *Cumberland, Md., Sept. 5.*—A bridge on the Jerome branch of the Baltimore and Ohio Railroad was blown up with dynamite placed under two abutments; both fell into the street immediately after the explosion.

Memphis, Tenn., Sept. 5.—Eight men will face murder charges,
four of them at Memphis, and four at Hubert, Ark.; one will face an
attempted train-wrecking charge and another a Federal court contempt charge, as a result of a confession said to have been obtained
from striking rail-shopmen now under arrest...

Wilkes-Barre, Pa., Sept. 7.—The feed pipe entering the Beaver
Run dam of the Lehigh Valley Railroad, near Packerton, the chief
source of water supply on its lines, was dynamited and blown up
last night.

Oklahoma City, Sept. 7.—With the arrest of four men in connection with the burning of a bridge on the Chicago, Rock Island
and Pacific Railroad south of Reno, Okla., on. August 17, United
States Marshal Alva McDonald announced here tonight that he
had gathered evidence indicating a state-wide plot among certain striking shopmen to destroy bridges and terrorize "Big Four"
Brotherhood men in an attempt to precipitate a general railroad
walk-out.

Regular leaders of conservative labor unions issued warnings to the
strikers to steer clear of ultra-radical agitators. Even so, during the last
decade, sabotage and "striking on the job" have become part of the psychology and behavior of millions of American workers who would re-
sent being called wobblies or Communists.

III

Late in 1921 I found myself in the East again. Unable to get work
ashore, I went to sea and during the next year sailed on five different
American ships, on all of which I encountered sabotage, both among
the sailors, wobbly and non-wobbly, and the officers (though, of course,
the latter would not have called their doings sabotage).

As a messboy I saw wasted or thrown overboard thousands of dollars' worth of food supplies and as a seaman tens of thousands of dollars'
worth of paint and ship's equipment. I met wobblies on every ship and
made friends with some of them.

One of them, I remember, once said to me: "The American underdog is getting wised up, and so is the American underling; I mean
the small-time bosses and overseers, like the officers on a ship. They're
beginning to realize they're underpaid, and they act accordingly. I've
been going to sea now for fifteen years and, if I know anything—and I
consider myself a pretty smart guy—there is, for instance, more graft,
petty graft, on American ships than ever before. As you know, stewards

ruin food and dump it overboard so that when they get in port they can order more provisions and collect a small commission on the purchase from the provision house. The same is true of mates, engineers, and masters. On some ships I've been on the whole gang of them was in cahoots, selling great big coils of expensive Manila rope in foreign ports or rolling them overboard, throwing over whole cans of ship's paint, and so on—so that they could order more rope and paint, and collect cumshaw."

On a ship on which I made a round trip from New York to the Pacific Coast the fo'c's'le* was almost one hundred per cent *saboteur*— and some of the men had scarcely heard of I.W.W.-ism. The wobblies had what at least they deemed a high social motive when they preached and practiced sabotage; the non-I.W.W. *saboteurs*, however, seemed to be just in an ugly mood and derived a mean personal satisfaction when, instead of washing a paint brush, they tossed it over the rail or threw whole bucketfuls of paint into the sea. There was no shipmindedness. "To hell with 'er!" was the motto. "To hell with the owners!" We discussed the graft that the skipper, the chief engineer, the mates, and the steward were pulling down each trip. I was told that on the second previous voyage the captain and the engineer had "fixed up" the engines so that the vessel had to be laid up in a San Pedro, California shipyard for three weeks for twenty-three thousand dollars' worth of repairs, for which they collected a bonus from the shipyard's agent.

I found out that I.W.W. and other *saboteurs* aboard ships often helped the officers do their dirty work, and with great gusto. I recall that once, when one of the mates ordered a group of us sailors to throw over the side a slightly damaged oil hose nearly fifty feet long and worth several hundred dollars, because the skipper did not want to bother making out a report to the home office the way it had been damaged, most of us laughed; it was a joke on the company—"to hell with it!"

An I.W.W. sailor, perhaps the most intelligent worker I ever met, said to me once when we discussed sabotage on the ships:

> You see in the magazines that the United States is having great difficulties in establishing a merchant marine of any consequence because in America ship-building costs exceed those elsewhere; because American investors would expect a larger return on capital invested in shipping than foreign companies make, and because the wages of American crews are higher than those paid by the lines of other countries—with the logical result, so they say, that the American

---

* the upper deck of a ship.

freight and passenger rates must be higher, and consequently shippers find it advantageous to deliver their goods in foreign bottoms. I'm no "high-powered executive," only a fo'c's'le stiff; but I know enough to realize that all these alibis are only superficially true; the last alibi, perhaps, not even superficially. In point of fact, American officers and men do receive higher wages than the ships' crews of other countries except Canada; but in relation to the wages ashore American crews are hardly as well paid as the Japanese. And, to my mind, therein lies one of the primary causes of the sad state of the American merchant marine. The American go-getter in the shipping business, as his brothers in other lines, is stupidly greedy; for those who, caught between the circumstances of their environment and their own innate qualities and shortcomings, are compelled to sell him their brains and brawn, he usually has small consideration and rewards them as meagerly as he can manage to for all the effort he can exact from them—with the result that in the long run his slaves get back at him, some of them through conscious sabotage, such as our I.W.W. sabotage, which nibbles away at the vitals of the capitalist system; others, half-unwittingly, through sabotage which has no social aim and is purely personal revenge, but which blindly attains the same purpose—hastens the decay of the system. It is true that the so-called maintenance of American ships is higher than that of most foreign ships, but that is solely because the crews don't give a damn for the ships or the owners and willfully waste. I don't doubt but that more is wasted on American ships than the shippers manage to get out of the Government in subsidies.

A few months after he had said this to me—it was in 1922—my wobbly sailor friend and I signed on the *Oskawa* at Philadelphia. She was a United States Shipping Board freighter, 6,100 gross tons, built in 1918 at a cost of nearly two million dollars and equipped with an up-to-date refrigeration system. We sailed to Hamburg with a small cargo. The trip there was uneventful. The crew was the usual crew that one then found on American freighters, perhaps a little worse. The half dozen wobblies I found in the fo'c's'le unquestionably were the best men aboard. The skipper was an old man, not in the best of health, somewhat bewildered by his responsibility. The mates, engineers, and the steward were a collection of bleary-eyed "lime-juicers" and overbearing "squareheads," licensed during the war emergency when almost anybody could have obtained a ticket. There was much drunkenness and brawling, along with poor navigation.

In Hamburg we picked up an enormous cargo of champagne and liqueurs for South America. Then, four or five days after leaving Germany, bottles began to pop in the officers' rooms and the mess-rooms; finally even on the bridge and in the chart-room, and cases of the marvelous liquids found their way into the crew's quarters.

The old skipper—feeble and unresourceful character that he was, scared of his own authority, befuddled by endless Shipping Board regulations and the Seamen's Act, afraid of legal trouble which would entail making all sorts of reports at which he was not clever—was beside himself. The second mate was the only other officer who kept sober. The ship was thrown off her course several times; but, finally and miraculously, thanks in part perhaps to the six or seven I.W.W. who stayed sober and helped the skipper to run the boat, she reached Brazil.

The cargo discharged, it was discovered that the *Oskawa* was short over a hundred cases of champagne, *kümmel*, and other such fancy hooch. The old man, of course, knew what had become of the stuff; but, nearly the whole ship being in a sort of loose conspiracy against him, he was unable to locate a single case aboard or prove anything against his officers. He signed for the shortage, to be made good by the ship. He looked around both in Rio de Janeiro and Montevideo, but realized that he could not pick up any better officers and crew in South America, even should he be so fortunate as to rid himself of his present gang.

The *Oskawa*'s cargo on the return trip to Hamburg was about a thousand tons of frozen meat.

A day or so out, champagne bottles that they had hidden away began to pop once more in the officers' rooms and on the bridge. Most of the officers became openly hostile to the captain, who was at his wits' end. He carried a gun and, in his futile way, threatened to arm a few sailors, including myself and three of the I.W.W., whom he considered loyal.

One day some one fed too much oil into the furnaces, and the fire blazed out of the funnel, belching burning oil all over the ship. The fire destroyed or damaged a good part of the upper structure, including most of the lifeboats, the bridge, and the chart-room; indeed, it was sheer luck that the sober part of the crew—mostly I.W.W.—managed to extinguish it. "We'd let 'er burn," said the wobblies, "if it weren't that we'd go to hell with 'er."

But the worst was yet to come. While still several days from Hamburg, the engineer burned out the dynamos, so that for the rest of the voyage the *Oskawa* was without lights and there was no more cold air for the refrigerator pipes. Indeed, to the great menace of all other ships on that course, part of the time she sailed at night without running-lights. We used oil lamps, which, however, were little better than nothing; and one night the first mate, too drunk in his bunk to raise himself and put out the light, kicked the lamp over—and we had to put out another fire.

Then, instead of pumping out the bilges, one of the men pumped out nearly all the fresh water! There was enough left for drinking but none for the boilers; so we were compelled to use salt water for steam, with the result that presently the valves were choked with salt. We had to stop every few hours to clean them out.

We were about a day off Madeira when the *Oskawa*'s engines went out of commission entirely. We drifted a night and a day while the machinery was being sufficiently repaired to enable us to limp into Madeira, in which port, however, there were no facilities for any extensive repairs, and we procured only water and a few more lamps and some oil for the running-lights. The dynamos, it appeared, were totally ruined.

The refrigeration system not working, the frozen meat began to melt and smell; whereupon, to make a good job of it, some one—I suspect one of the I.W.W.—shot steam into the refrigerator pipes, with the result that before it was discovered much of the cargo was cooked or otherwise spoiled.

Anyhow, the wobblies laughed among themselves, figuring how much the United States Government would have to pay for the ruined cargo.

Somewhere off the coast of Holland, the fuel-oil supply suddenly gave out, and we had to be towed into Hamburg, where the investigations that followed nearly drove the master out of his mind. At the end he was exonerated and some of the officers were jailed and deprived of their licenses. The *Oskawa* was sufficiently repaired to be taken back to the United States and there put in the "boneyard," where there already were hundreds of other ships in no better condition!

One of my I.W.W. friends aboard said to me, "They couldn't have done a better piece of sabotage even if everybody from the skipper down had been a wobbly or a Communist. Hallelujah!"

IV

The *Oskawa* incident—which, by the way, is a matter of record in Washington and also received considerable attention in the Hamburg press at the time, as well as some slight mention in the American newspapers—disgusted me utterly with sailoring, and so I began to earn my living ashore again. From 1923 to 1927 I worked on dozens of jobs all the way from Philadelphia to Los Angeles—in steel, furniture, shoe and textile factories, on farms and ranches, in restaurants, in a stone quarry and a print-shop, in a grocery-store and an automobile plant, on construction jobs, on docks unloading ships—and practically everywhere I found some form of sabotage. Nowhere did I find any real zest for work, any pride in labor.

In a furniture shop in Cleveland, where I managed to get a job as a carpenter's helper, I found cliques of workmen organized to help one another in working for themselves on the boss's time, making parts out of the boss's material, then smuggling them out under their clothes in the evening, and finally assembling them at home into chairs and cabinets, either for sale or for their own use.

In a lace mill near Scranton, Pennsylvania, where I worked for a while, I found the operatives, especially the men, in a bad mood. The management was speeding up the machines, forcing the employees to work faster and faster for the same pay, with the result that there was much sabotage on the machinery. Looms were injured; on the large machines leather bands were cut with safety-razor blades. The foremen blamed these things on "those Communist bastards." On several of the cut leather bands one morning "Sacco-Vanzetti" was inscribed in white chalk.

I worked in three or four restaurants in New York and Pittsburgh and encountered sabotage in at least two of them. In one place a Communist dishwasher before quitting poured several cans of kerosene into barrels of sugar and urinated into containers of coffee and tea. I imagined that he went from job to job doing this sort of thing.

In New York I met another Communist, a handsome red-headed young Irishman, whose special "racket" was to work on soda-fountains in the garment-making sections and serve his Communist friends, men and girls, whom he counted by the score, expensive milk drinks and fancy sandwiches for which he handed them nickel and dime checks to pay the cashier. When he was discovered and discharged he found himself another job in the Bronx or Brooklyn near some factory employing great numbers of Communists.

In a print-shop in Kansas City the men, instead of distributing expensive type, dumped it into the so-called "hell box." A printer friend of mine who has worked in big and small shops, union and non-union, all over the country, tells me that the hell box still is a very popular receptacle for type. Few printers nowadays retain any love for fine type or good workmanship.

In a shoe factory in Milwaukee a man was pointed out to me who was known among some of his fellow workers to be a *saboteur*. An eccentric-looking person, he hated the machines and had all sorts of devices to damage them. He was an indefinite sort of radical, and he considered the machines a great curse to humanity. I have encountered this hate for machines elsewhere. Men vent it in various forms of sabotage, which has no connection with I.W.W.-ism or Communism, but is purely a matter of personal resentment and vindictiveness. I have seen men who—sometimes drunk, sometimes sober—cursed the machine and, passing by, shook their fists at the mills, declaring they were not their slaves. Every big industrial town seems to have "nuts" who believe that machines are alive and hold them—the workers—in their power.

Shortly after the war I read—I forget where—about an American soldier—"a nut"—who believed that machines were killing men in revenge for the work that men made them do. "Stop the machines," he would cry, lying wounded in a hospital, "and there'll be no more war. Machines make war—machines kill us!"

V

During the nineteen-twenties big and bitter labor upheavals were comparatively few in the United States, but the struggle of the have-nots against the haves went on unceasingly and relentlessly just the same; only now it was no longer open warfare. Upon the surface things were quiet, but underneath the workers were being infected with the germs of sabotage and "striking on the job."

As a result of the employers' anti-union drives, the anti-Red hysteria, marked by such incidents as the Centralia trial and the Sacco-Vanzetti affair, and the laborites' and radicals' inability to match the industrialists' brains and weapons in open warfare, there was no effective organized radical movement in the last decade. There was, however, a vast *unorganized* radical movement, including millions of workers outside the unions and the Socialist and Communist parties, skilled and unskilled, each left to his own devices to improve his lot in life and revenge himself upon the system which used a man only when his toil might bring profits for the employer, let him starve (unless he turned bootlegger or criminal) when there was a surplus of production, and utterly discarded him when he became old. After the suppression of the organized radical movement in 1922 or thereabouts, there was perhaps as much radicalism among American workmen as ever before, only now it found scarcely any vent in organized open political or industrial action as it had twenty years ago, or even in the few years immediately after the war. The workers' radicalism now found individual, personal expression in doing as little as possible for the wages they received and in wasting as much material as possible. Their radicalism now lacked all social vision and purpose; its motive was mainly personal revenge.

This sort of radicalism continues today. Workmen are cynical. The motto in a factory where I once worked was: "To hell with 'em all but six; save them for pallbearers!" The more intelligent workers have no faith in politics. They sneer at the Socialist Party, especially those who have witnessed at close range the futile tactics of its leaders. They have no faith in trade-unionism; most of those who belong to the unions belong because they must; because, for the time being, the unions still control certain jobs. They know their leaders are crooked. I have heard members call their officials crooks from the floor in meeting and refer to their organizations as "rackets." They have no faith in a better future for themselves as a class, while at the same time they feel that they are "stuck"—that most of them are fated to remain workmen till they get too old to work. They know that "the system" is unjust to them; they have been told so by numberless Red agitators and demagogues, past and present. They realize that most of their class movements, industrial and political, in the past have been largely ineffectual. They know that the cause of low wages is a surplus of labor, and that unemployment, which hits them every once in a while, is due to overproduction. And so, logically enough from their individual points of view, they strike-on-the-job and waste the bosses' time and material, thereby stretching out, as they feel, their spell of employment and diminishing the profits of employers, who, they believe, underpay them.

This goes on, more or less, as I have hinted, throughout industry, even where the I.W.W., who developed striking-on-the-job and sabotage tactics in America, have never been strong (except, of course, in the great plants with the speed-up system, such as the Ford factories, where the motions of every workman are purely mechanical, prescribed by the management, and the foremen see that he executes them with the required result). Early in the summer of 1930, for instance, the organized cafeteria owners in New York City and Brooklyn gave out the information that *saboteurs* among their employees waste or destroy from one to two million dollars' worth of food a year.

The working class has been driven to sabotage by greed on the part of the industrialists. When the I.W.W. took it up, it was about the only effective weapon left to the underdog. Then the wobblies lost control of it, and sabotage lost its social vision and purpose. Now in many places, as I have shown, it borders upon the criminal—a menace not only to industry, but to our national character. The advocates of sabotage have turned loose in the community a force which they cannot check and whose consequences are far beyond their intention.

Some employers, trying to combat sabotage, hire spies whom they pay more than regular workmen, and whose business it is to spot strikers-on-the-job and *saboteurs* and get them eliminated and blacklisted. But this, I think, is combating one evil with another, which produces a third and even greater evil. With spies in the factories, the workers distrust one another, each believing that the other is or may be a spy. This plays the devil with the men's sense of honor. It tends to make "heels" and "sneaks" of them. I know of cases where workmen practiced sabotage upon one another, "framing" their fellows in order to get their jobs or gain other advantages. I know of a case where a man was beaten up by his fellow workers who believed him to be a spy. He happened not to be one.

Also, spies often encourage sabotage; or, rather, detective agencies which specialize in *saboteur* spying frequently slip *saboteur* instructors into the factories as workers. These teach the other employees subtler means of sabotage and soldiering, so that the detective whom the employers hire to watch the men may have something to report. Thus, in some cases, the industrialists are quite helpless in the face of sabotage and "striking on the job."

Sabotage and "striking on the job" are forms of revenge that the working class of America—blindly, unconsciously, desperately—exacts for the employers' relentless, brutal opposition to its strivings in the past—revenge for the Ludlow massacre, for the Mooney-Billings frame-up, for the Centralia injustice, for the Sacco-Vanzetti horror, for the Cossackism in the Steel Strike.

CHAPTER 33*
WHAT NEXT—MORE DYNAMITE?

I realize that, in the preceding thirty-two chapters, I have put together a rather dreadful story. It is the story of American industry, which is the most vital factor in America's national life, from the standpoint of labor, the underdog, and those people who, like myself, are incapable of being indifferent to misery and crime and other tendencies that are undermining the people's character and driving men wholesale to sabotage, striking-on-the-job, and into racketeering.

Despite all the battles that labor has fought and all the agonies that it has endured in the past, as I have barely sketched them in this book, the working class of the United States today—in these years of the great depression, which is part of the world-wide capitalist crisis—finds itself, perhaps, in a worse plight than it was ever in before, and it is not impossible that that plight will be rendered even more deplorable in the near future. There are now in the United States, according to various estimates, between ten and fifteen million jobless people who need and want to work.

This unemployment is due mainly to the increased productivity of American industry per worker. Ernest J. Eberling, professor of economics at the Vanderbilt University, says:

> Careful study shows that from 1899 to 1914 the output per employee had gone up slightly less than one-half of one per cent per year. In 1919 the physical output per worker was actually three per cent less than in 1914. Beginning with 1921, however, it is the consensus of opinion among students that the productivity of labor has increased about fifty per cent, or an average annual increase in output per worker of seven per cent. This has been due primarily to scientific management and the great increase in the machinery.

* Completely rewritten June, 1934.

283

At the same time the number of workers has been increasing at a rate of over 1,500,000 a year. And not only has this annual increase in the number of workers not been taken care of, but the United States Bureau of Labor Statistics reports that between 1925 and 1928—while Coolidge prosperity was at its height—almost 1,900,000 employees in manufacturing industries and railroads were laid off and not replaced.

The technological changes in industry have been enormous. Before the United States Senate Committee on Education and Labor in 1929 experts testified that

> seven men now do the work which formerly required sixty to perform in casting pig iron; two men now do the work which formerly required 128 in loading pig iron; one man replaces 42 in operating open-hearth furnaces. A brick-making machine in Chicago makes 40,000 bricks per hour; it formerly took one man eight hours to make 450. The most up-to-date bottle-making machine makes in one hour what forty-one workers used to make by hand in the manufacture of four-ounce prescription bottles.

A new forging machine recently developed has doubled the production per man. A machine for manufacturing pressed-steel frames, operated by one man, produces six frames per minute, or 3,600 in ten hours. To accomplish this by hand would require 175 men. One man a few years ago could solder two radiators in one hour; today, thanks to improved methods, he can do at least forty per hour. Rear quarter body panels can now be welded together electrically by an unskilled man at the rate of sixty welds per hour; a skilled man previously, using the torch method, did only twelve in the same period. And so on, and so on; I could fill fifty pages with examples of improved production methods in the last decade. On the farm, also, machinery is displacing human labor at a terrific rate.

Some of the workers thus displaced have managed to become salesmen, gasolene-station attendants, watchmen. But millions of them are being left out in the cold, with nothing to do. "A significant number of them after months of enforced idleness," says Professor Eberling, "admitted frankly [to investigators of the Institute of Economics] that they had taken to bootlegging." But since the repeal of the eighteenth amendment, in 1933, the bootlegging industry, of course, has suffered a great setback, and that avenue of opportunity has narrowed greatly for jobless workers.

II

And the industrialists' attitude while improving the machinery and turning out labor has been as follows:

Business is business. The objective of industry is to make money. We are determined to make money. We concentrate solely on that aim. If we are satisfied that a billion-dollar merger will mean greater profits, we go ahead and engineer it.

One of the easiest ways to cut down expenses being to cut down salary and wage rolls, we of course lay men off right and left. If elderly workers have become less nimble because of their long years of service, they are the logical ones to be dropped first. Naturally, the greater resources at the command of the enlarged combinations are unstintedly used to acquire the very latest labor-saving machinery, enabling us to dismiss still more wage-earners.

In our eyes the most valuable executive is the one who can produce the most with the least amount of labor—the smallest number of workers and the smallest payroll. Our up-to-the-minute methods make it feasible for us to dispense with enormous numbers of workers—it is not uncommon for us to install one machine which enables half a dozen men to do what formerly took half a hundred or even a hundred men.

Yes, we know that through our creation of gigantic enterprises—manufacturing, distributing, retailing, and every other kind—and through our vast expenditures on research, on invention, on machinery, we have caused grave dislocation of employment; but instead of being criticized for all this technological unemployment, we should be commended, since it is conclusive proof of our mastery of the science of management. What happens to all the hordes of workers we release is not our concern. Our responsibility begins and ends with running our business with surpassing efficiency, which means with a minimum of human labor.

No, the unemployment thus created does not enter in any way into our calculations. Our bounden duty is to exercise every ounce of ingenuity we possess to do away with jobs, not to create them. Our objective is money, more and more money, not more and more men, but fewer and fewer men.

We are much too engrossed in increasing profits to give a thought to what happens because of our reducing the number of workers. How to take care of unemployment is a problem for others to solve. Let George do that... We haven't the time to bother with it. It isn't our worry.

The above is quoted from an editorial entitled "Are U. S. Business Leaders Morons?" in *Forbes* (April 1930), a businessmen's magazine, which goes on to say: "American industry may disclaim that it *talks* that way, but it cannot disclaim that, collectively, it has *acted* that way." As a matter of fact, as we have seen, it has acted much more brutally, beating down labor's efforts to improve its conditions whenever it possibly could.

Industry [*Forbes* further editorializes] hasn't one organization, representing its best brains, devoting itself seriously, systematically, scientifically, to handling the whole subject of employment and unemployment. There is no co-ordinated machinery for co-operating with the jobless to find work. Industry feels perfectly free to dismiss breadwinners by the hundred and by the thousand without giving a thought as to how these breadwinners may succeed or fail in earning bread for themselves and their families... The disturbing truth is that our improvements of production methods had released an abnormal number of workers even during our period of greatest prosperity. It is a commentary upon how this whole problem has been neglected that neither Government nor industry has taken the pains even to keep track of the extent of unemployment from month to month, from season to season. It has been nobody's business to lie awake cogitating what happens to breadwinners denied opportunity to earn their bread.

The attitude of the capitalist class to the jobless was best expressed two decades ago by the late William Howard Taft, then President of the United States, when some one asked him, "What is a man to do who is starving and cannot find work?" Taft replied: "God knows."

Ever since the Industrial Revolution about a century ago, American industry has been a cruel, chaotic, inhuman scheme—as if it were run by a gang of morons indeed. It has been an aggregation of rackets, big and small, each preying on the other, exploiting labor, extorting from the public, corrupting the government, using any means—including force, including murder—to advance their purposes. Large immediate profits and to hell with everything else! This was the big idea of American capitalism.

Since 1920, the American industrialists have been concentrating all the brain-power they could buy upon the so-called "rationalization" of factory methods. Making production "rational" from the capitalist viewpoint means decreasing its costs, primarily labor costs. For the laborer, required to do, with the aid of machinery, the work of perhaps twenty

men—while the other nineteen went unemployed or became bootleggers—it seemed distinctly irrational, or worse. In huge "rationalized"
factories, with their "speed up and stretch out" systems, workers were
required to work harder and harder. Each man had to keep up with a
faster machine, or he was given more machines to run, or both. It was
by this means that the production per worker increased about fifty per
cent—while the workers' pay increased less than three per cent.

"Speeding up" became general in the automobile industry, with
its conveyor system introduced by Henry Ford, the Messiah of mass
production. One careful investigator, Robert W. Dunn, reports that

> in 1919 in the [Ford] motor assembly plant, on certain conveyor-
> lines the unfinished motors moved by a given point at the rate of
> 40 an hour; by 1925 they were moving at the rate of 60 an hour. On
> other lines in 1919 the rate of speed was 120 an hour; in 1925…it
> had been increased to 180 an hour. *And this with the same machinery.*
> The difference was made up in human energy, for which the work-
> ers received no substantial increase in wages.

Dr. Arthur Feiler, editor of the *Frankfurter Zeitung*, who after visiting the United States wrote a book, *America Seen Through German Eyes*,
says that workers in the automotive factories "are bound to the conveyor the way the galley-slaves were bound to the vessel." And an actual
worker describes the speed-up system as follows:

> Men work like fiends, sweat running down their cheeks, their jaws
> set and eyes on fire. Nothing in the world exists for them except the
> line of chassis bearing down on them relentlessly. Some are under-
> neath on their backs, on little carts, propelling themselves by their
> heels all day long, fixing something underneath the chassis as they
> move along.

There can be no "striking on the job" along the conveyor. The straw-
boss has received word from the shop-boss: "Get out production or get
out yourself!" So all day long he bawls at the heels of his men: "Step on
it! Hop on it! Come on, boys, you're slipping! Get them out!" or more
threateningly: "If you don't speed up, I'll send you down for your time!"

Thus industry, scientifically managed, became a roaring saturnalia
of speeding up and bullying—wholesale, highly organized racketeering
on the part of powerful industrialists against the workers, who could
not help themselves; *forcing* them to produce more and more at meager
wages. In some shops men were not allowed the time to go for a

drink of water or to the toilet—while other men were being turned out of work.

Even before the great collapse of the Coolidge-Hoover prosperity in 1929, on one side of the factory-gate men were working breathlessly at top speed; on the other, thousands were begging, hoping for jobs. To one group the management—"scientific management"—said: "Come on, you must work faster or get out! Faster! Faster!" To the other group it said: "No, nothing doing. You'll have to stay idle. We have nothing for you!"

Throughout 1929 tens of thousands of men were being turned out of jobs by great corporations, some of whose profits were higher in that year than ever before. The net profit of the Ford Motor Company for 1929 on the "Model A" car, for instance, ran over $80,000,000—and when, in the same year, Ford threw thousands of his employees out of work at Detroit without making any provision for the widespread distress that was bound to follow, he is said to have remarked in Pecksniffian manner that it was "not good for character to feel too insecure."

III

Then, in the fall of 1929, the crash came; suddenly, the Coolidge-Hoover prosperity had slipped out of gear. There was a panic—a financial crisis—and by Christmas of that year the unemployed army was augmented by about 2,000,000, while during the ensuing three years the number of jobless almost doubled every year, till in the winter of 1932–33 their number was variously estimated to be between fifteen and twenty million, or about half of the normal working population of the country.

There were several causes behind the crash, but the chief and basic one was "overproduction," which was greater than the overproduction which had preceded any of the previous panics in the United States. It had been brought about by "rationalization" and the inability of the ill-paid and jobless working people, the most numerous class in the country, to buy and consume the increased products of speed-up factories. When the crash came, there was enough money in the United States to buy, probably, some five times as much of finished goods as the industries and the merchants had in their overcrowded warehouses and stockrooms; only most of it was in the hands of the few—the capitalist-racketeers and the investors—who, of course, had no personal use for, could not themselves consume, the surplus of manufactured products. The many who needed or could have consumed the goods—the mass of working people—had but very little money, for, while prices had remained at a high level, wages had increased scarcely at all despite the fifty per cent increase in the workers' productive efficiency. At the same time the industrialists were unable to expand their foreign markets, or find new ones, on which to dump their products.

"Scientific management," all the rage in American industry since 1920, with all its occasional brilliancy, actually was nothing short of stupid in the long run. Utilized solely by greed for higher profits, its first effect was to "save" labor—that is, cause unemployment, and in so doing reduce labor's buying power. The idea was to pay the workers who as yet could not be replaced by machinery a mere subsistence wage, just enough to enable them to live and work.

The fallacy of this is now obvious. J. A. Hobson, the veteran English economist, says in his little book, *Rationalisation and Unemployment*, published in London in 1930:

> The economic wants of man are illimitable. There are would-be consumers for all the wheat, wool, cotton, steel and other goods that cannot under existing circumstances get produced. There is not any lack of purchasing power or money to buy these goods.

There is but one explanation for the overproduction that brought on the crisis in 1929, and that is underconsumption, due to

> a maldistribution of income (purchasing power), which puts a disproportionate amount into the hands of those who desire to invest and are unable to achieve their desire because the final commodities which [their investments] are intended to supply cannot secure a full reliable market owing to the too small share of the total income vested in the would-be consumer.

Mr. Hobson contends that capitalism could still further increase its production efficiency and capacity without running any danger of overproduction *if* it paid the workers higher and higher wages, on a sliding scale with increased productivity. It would thereby increase the purchasing and consuming power of the public. It would thus take the first step to stabilize itself—to civilize itself.

But Mr. Hobson's is a very tremendous IF, indeed.

IV

Soon after the crash, solemn and hysterical voices began to be heard all over the land uttering pleas and words of warning to industrial and financial leaders of the country. People wrote letters to the press that something must be done "at once" about the unemployment situation, which, they insisted, was growing worse daily. "Drastic steps are needed by and within the industry," to quote a letter to the New York *World-Telegram* early in 1931, "and heroic action for the sake of humanity." Lecturers on social topics called upon industrialists to "stabilize" and "humanize" industry, for periodic slumps such as the present one, they cried in tones of alarm, were having vicious social consequences.

An eminent Yale professor wanted industrial managers to make periodic "human audits" of their industries as well as financial audits and inventories, for, in his belief, they "owed consideration to the human element in their businesses." Dean Donham, of the Harvard Graduate School of Business Administration, wrote a book, *Business Adrift*, in which he outlined the "duties" of business to society and to itself, and suggested what business should do to fulfill them and thus, in effect, save itself, its soul, and the country.

Editorial writers, on progressive and conservative newspapers alike, were pointing to the degenerating effects of unemployment and kindred industrial evils on the national character, and emphasizing the desperate need of "enlightened, social-minded leadership in the business community." Writers in such organs of the Christian religion as the *Christian Century* and the *Commonweal* thought it was urgent for financiers, industrialists, and plain business men to develop social-mindedness in a big way and reorganize their enterprises so they would be able to pay their people higher and higher wages for less and less work; and that, to succeed in this high aim, they must become "real Christians."

During 1930–32 one of the favorite topics of preachers who go in for social problems was "Unemployment—Whose Fault?" and they sermonized (I am quoting from an actual sermon) as follows:

> It is un-Christian, this condition, with millions of men desperate for work and tens of thousands of families in dire want because of unemployment... And who is to blame? In my opinion, our big business men. There has been—there is too much greed for quick, immediate profits in our industrial world. To make money, more and more money, and nothing else! Great industries employ and discharge workers without regard for human and social consequenc-

es... But industry shall have to cease dealing with human beings in this cruel, careless, inhuman, haphazard fashion, or else—indeed, I don't know what our country may come to! It is hard to speak with restraint, for it is imperative that the managers of our great industrial enterprises should acquire a humane, a Christian social attitude toward their fellow human beings in the ranks of labor who contribute so greatly to the production of wealth. The employers must acquire and begin to exercise social sense.

Several big men in industry and finance rose in public and uttered harsh words about the economic system of which they were the chief beneficiaries. Owen D. Young, chairman of the board of directors of the General Electric Company, for instance, labeled unemployment "the greatest blot on our capitalistic system." Daniel Willard, president of the Baltimore and Ohio Railroad (on which began the bloody riots of 1877), stated that, to his mind, "those who manage our large industries, whatever be the character of their output, should recognize the importance and necessity of planning their work so as to furnish as steady employment as possible to those in their service," for that was "an obligation connected with our economic system." He added that, in his opinion, industry "can be stabilized" and all that was needed in that direction was "the will to do" on the part of the management.

Most of these people, no doubt, were sincere in what they said, but as they spoke or wrote they displayed a colossal lack of knowledge of the history, organization, character, and basic motives of business—Big Business—as it happens to be conducted in the United States. They were, or appeared to be, wholly unaware that business, although by far the most important factor in the lives of the American people, was largely dehumanized and, despite all the Rotary and Kiwanis oratory, profoundly—*and inevitably*—indifferent to vital human and social questions; that, by its very nature, business could have no spontaneous and direct, no intelligent, "Christian," or benevolent interest in society.

This is implicit in the story I tell in the foregoing chapters; but let me state clearly, and as briefly as I can, in this revised final chapter, why capitalistic business as we have it in the United States is incapable of developing social conscience and of consistently functioning for the benefit of society; why it cannot consistently function even for its own good, for the good of the capitalist class; why it must behave just as it does.

A hundred years ago business was a comparatively simple thing, even in the United States. An industrial or business enterprise was owned by one man, who operated it with the aid of a few employees. The master and the mechanics, as a rule, belonged to the same trade guild, whose principal aim was to promote good workmanship and service to the community. Living in the same village or town, they often were neighbors and intimate friends. If more than one man owned the enterprise, all the partners lived in the community and actively participated in the business. Close personal relationships existed not only between the bosses and the workers, but also between each of these and the customers, and business was thus an integral, intimate part of the communal life. Basically, of course, business was then, as it is now, mainly an expression of man's acquisitive instinct functioning outside of social motives, but in those distant days, unlike today, the wider humanistic interests, acting through the close personal contact between employers, workers, and the public and the various communal agencies, had no difficulty in curbing it and making it actually serve the community.

Then the New Industrialization came and, of a sudden, huge industrial-financial organizations—corporations—were formed, in which personal relationship vanished almost entirely. These corporations were started because individual business men, suddenly excited by the hugeness and the resources of America, and eager to put over gigantic new undertakings, lacked sufficient capital for their purposes and had to take in as investors a great many other persons, living in various parts of the country, to whom they promised rich and quick returns for the use of their money.

On launching their corporations, the managers' most pressing concern was to fulfill their promises to the investors, mainly because, if they failed to produce dividends, they would be unable to secure financial assistance in the future. To the shareholders (most of whom had no close knowledge of the businesses which their cash was helping to create) the corporations were nothing more than magic instruments producing wealth. Their interest was solely or largely in the coupons. Moreover, the manufactured goods were sold through middlemen and, what is still more important, labor became a "commodity." Thus business became impersonal, unsocial. It became what it is today—Big Business.

Corporations grew and combined, and business became more and more intricate and gigantic, more and more impersonal, dehumanized, inhuman, unsocial, powerful, uncontrollable by society. To be successful corporation managers, men had to become dehumanized, almost inhuman, at least in their capacities as business men. Indeed, it can scarcely be said that corporations were managed by men. They were operated almost purely by policy, which soon jelled into tradition, and which had little, if any, consideration for the human elements in business. The central aim of corporation policy was higher and higher profits. Such slogans as "The public be damned!" and "Beat down the labor movement!" were uttered by individuals prompted by the impelling impersonal, unsocial—in many cases distinctly anti-social—character of the corporations which they headed.

And the character of Big Business is essentially the same today as it was in the time of Commodore Vanderbilt, Jay Gould, and Henry C. Frick; not that the Vanderbilts, the Goulds, and the Fricks, either of the 1880's or of today, are directly or personally to blame for this lack of social sense in business. The lack, you must understand, is inherent in the capitalistic corporation system. It is, I repeat, inevitable. In its very nature, as I have hinted, Big Business can by itself have no social philosophy or social intelligence. It can have no statesmanship or long-range foresight. It is essentially opportunistic, anarchic, fatalistic. "If let alone," said Mr. Garet Garrett a few years ago, "it will seek its profit by any means that serve and then view the consequences as acts of Providence"—as it has been viewing the current business slump and the unemployment situation these several years.

Big Business today, to be sure, has certain ethical rules, but they have nothing to do with the wider social morality. There is, for instance, considerable honesty in transactions between various firms, but not because honesty is a social virtue conducive to a higher civilization and nobler life; only because, quite apart from every other consideration, it is essential to business. Business honesty has nothing to do with honor; it is, as Mr. Garrett puts it, merely "formal honesty."

Society, of course, derives many benefits from modern business, but these benefits are incidental to the main and original purpose of our business organization—that of profit-making. Let us take the tendency of putting on the market dependable goods, which has become noticeable in American industry and commerce during the last two decades. The motive behind it is ethical in a purely narrow business sense, and not in any large social way. It is, like the practice of honesty by firms, simply good business policy, for in the long run, as a rule, the buying public supports the manufacturer of reliable articles, enriching him not only by its purchases but by automatically increasing the capital value of his trademark and his credit, which enables him to sell more shares and expand his business.

In fine, to look for social-mindedness and idealism in Big Business is to be naïve. And to call upon Big Business to discipline itself or become "Christian," to fulfill its "social duty" to labor and to the community, is to appear, I believe, worse than naïve.

Big Business being what it is, its attitude toward labor is naturally, as the above-quoted preacher put it, "cruel, merciless, inhuman, haphazard" from the social or human point of view.

Before business became Big Business, the worker with a pair of able hands and a set of good tools stood, as suggested in Chapter 2, on fairly even terms with the employer. He produced directly for purposes of consumption and, indeed, consumed much of his own actual output. Following the Industrial Revolution, however, when the corporations and the factory system came into existence and hand-tools yielded to machinery, production became indirect and suddenly machines were of greater importance than hands. The worker became an appendage to the machine. He was dependent upon conditions created by machinery. He labored not directly to produce, but to keep the machine going and create wealth for corporations, whose shareholders demanded high dividends. Labor, as I have said, became a market commodity, just as were the raw materials that fed the machines or the coal that was needed to generate power to turn the wheels.

Labor is still a commodity, and an increasingly cheaper one; and the corporations' attitude toward it is practically the same as toward the other cheap commodities on the market. It cannot be anything else. I suggest that here you turn back to page 285 and read again the "confession" that B. C. Forbes put into the mouth of Big Business.

Mr. Forbes, as I have mentioned, entitled his article, of which that "confession" is a part, "Are U.S. Business Leaders Morons?" To my mind, American business "leaders," so called, are no more moronic than practically any other group of average men. The fact of the matter is that they, too, are victims of the immense, chaotic, de-humanized, impersonal, unsocial "system" of Big Business that I have sketched above, though, of course, their worst plight is seldom as acute and tragic as that of workers thrown out of employment. Since October 1929, proportionately, perhaps as many capitalists and industrialists have committed suicide on account of the depression as jobless men, and it is possible that, proportionately, more rich men die of melancholia, caused by the uncontrollable chaos in their businesses, than idle workers of starvation.

I don't deny that some business men *are* morons, nor that the "system" of Big Business deprives not a few industrialists and capitalists of

whatever innate social sense they ever possessed; most of those whom
I know, however, appear quite human—alas! all too human. My observation is that the average American business man does not become intrinsically unsocial or anti-social because of his material interest. It is merely that he does not run his business, but that, on the contrary, his business runs him. He acts according to the policy or tradition of his corporation; and essentially, as I have said, most corporations are alike. His social conscience is often uneasy, but—such being human nature—he never suffers severe pangs of remorse, for he neatly and conveniently blames all evils on the corporation. He passes the buck to the great organization, which, with its impersonal character, easily serves as a hide-out for his conscience. As a manager or director of the corporation, he says: "Well, if this were my own business, believe me, I'd deal differently with labor. But, you see, it isn't mine. I'm but an instrument of our corporation's policy. I'm responsible to our ten thousand shareholders, who, regardless of everything, want their dividends." And each of the ten thousand shareholders comes back with: "Well, what can I do? Am I running the business? I'm not. I'm but one of ten thousand people, none of whom has anything to say personally about how things ought to be run."

No one is personally or directly responsible to society. Corporate business as a whole is responsible only in matters that pertain to business. To society it has only a few *legal* responsibilities, which the social will, struggling against the evils and tyrannies of Big Business, now and then manages to impose upon it through such agencies as Congress, the Department of Justice, the Interstate Commerce Commission, the Federal Trade Board, and just now the New Deal legislation. But very frequently, almost invariably, Big Business, with its money power, gains control of these agencies and thwarts the social will, thus even its legal responsibilities. It can easily hire the most adroit and unconscionable lawyers and public relations experts, bribe judges, and thus often turn against labor laws which Congress and state legislatures passed to protect labor or the general public. That happened, as I have mentioned, with the Sherman Anti-Trust Act. That happened, more recently, with the Clayton and Norris-La Guardia Acts. That is beginning to be the case with the somewhat progressive New Deal legislation pertaining to labor. And that, nine chances to one, will happen with most of the other legislation which President Roosevelt's social-minded but unrealistic "brain-trusters" are apt to think up in the next few years. Those who wish to know more about how reformist social legislation fares at the hands of Big Business I refer to John Chamberlain's excellent book, *Farewell to Reform*.

On the whole, then, Big Business is utterly irresponsible, without social conscience, "free from hope of heaven or fear of hell," as Mr. Garrett put it; "in all ethical respects, anonymous." And it must be remembered that, as it is variously estimated, from two-thirds to three-fourths of our national wealth is owned by these anonymous, impersonal instruments of modern business called corporations. They control, it is safe to say, every important process of the country's economic activity and, thereby, directly or indirectly influence every other phase of our national life. Indeed, every now and then they threaten, with their enormous money power, to gain full sway over the Government and overcome the social will.

The humanistic or social interests of the country have been fighting a feud with Big Business these seven or eight decades. Occasionally the social will gets worked up and, acting through political parties and the Government, imposes itself upon business and makes it behave, or tries to make it behave, at least for a little while, until business, with its single-minded purpose, finds a way to rid itself of social control.

Now and then business willingly endures social control, but only after it becomes plain as daylight that social control is conducive to bigger and better business. Take, for instance, the pure-food laws. In 1906 Upton Sinclair published his novel *The Jungle*, which "hit the country in the stomach" and worked up the social will to such an extent that the pure-food idea became a national political issue. Meat-packers and other food interests fought the idea. Later, however, when the idea was put on the statute book and the industrialists were forced to sell only good food, they gradually perceived that high-quality merchandise was more profitable in the long run than low quality, and since then the food branch of Big Business has been vociferous in praise of the pure-food idea.

Society must always *compel* business to function for the social good, and not only for the social good but for the good of business itself. Business would have ruined itself and the country long ago, were it not for occasional spurts of social action to curb it. If space permitted, I could show that even honesty in business, which I mentioned above, like dependability in manufactured goods, was imposed upon business by laws and other social pressure.

Yet, in 1933, along came Franklin D. Roosevelt and his "Brain Trust," with their New Deal program, which was full of seeming concern for the Forgotten Man, the jobless man and woman, and the future of labor as a whole, to say nothing of the United States, but which—if one may judge it by the way it has been administered—is based mainly upon the theory that Big Business is just full of self-discipline, social conscience, and intelligence, or at least intelligent selfishness, and as such is eager to pay labor higher and higher wages for less and less work! No wonder the labor part of the New Deal turned out so colossal a failure. Mr. Roosevelt may as well smile and talk nicely to the crew of a speeding train urging them not to crush the ants on the rails as to the managers of American corporations asking them to be good to labor.

But let us go back a bit.

V

In November 1929, President Hoover, anxious to prevent just such a serious condition as we later found ourselves in, conferred with big business "leaders" of the country and asked them—requested them—pleaded with them—to refrain from wage-cuts and further lay-offs. They promised him that they would and praised him for his "foresighted measure." But most of the corporations in which they were directors and executives continued matter-of-factly to reduce wages and lay off employees. Between December 15, 1929, and February 15, 1930, the big railroads, which were heavily represented at Mr. Hoover's conferences, dropped over 84,000 men. As a rule, the great, impersonal corporations are bigger than the biggest individual in them, and their traditional policy, dating back to their origins, is to lay off men when it is unprofitable to keep them on the payrolls and cut the wages of those they keep when the labor market is full of jobless men, eager to work for low pay.

In December 1929, when 100,000 men were idle in Detroit, one of the wealthiest cities in the United States, Senator James Couzens, formerly a partner of Henry Ford and now, perhaps, one of the most humanely inclined tycoons in the country, delivered a red-hot lecture to several hundred members of the Michigan Manufacturers Association, blaming them in severe terms for the condition of unemployment. He naïvely denounced them for not being awake to "the responsibilities of man to man." "Just think," he cried, "what it means to hire a thousand men today and a few weeks hence to fire them without any more consideration than if they were some animal other than human." The Michigan manufacturers, as individuals, applauded the Senator for his impassioned speech. Most of them, I am told, personally agreed with him. But in the ensuing three months, in Detroit alone, the number of unemployed men increased by at least another 50,000! Mr. Couzens might as well have kept silent.

All over the country unemployment grew by leaps and bounds, and the wages of those retaining their jobs went down like a rock. And I wager that individually most of the employers who were cutting wages believed in high wages—for the other firm.

In 1931, Mr. James A. Farrell, then president of the United States Steel Corporation, delivered his sensationally honest impromptu talk before the American Iron and Steel Institute in New York, in which he referred to wage-cutting within the steel industry as "a pretty cheap sort of business." He was most severe with companies—"the most talked-of companies, the so-called big companies"—which he knew had slashed wages and were "honeycombing and pinching and that sort of thing" by discharging employees wherever they could. And, ironically, less than a week after his talk, according to press reports, the United States Steel Products, a subsidiary of Mr. Farrell's corporation, dropped fifty men in one department and cut wages in others!

During 1930–32 I talked with dozens of corporation officials in Eastern states, a few of whom were personally very much distressed by the unemployment situation, especially during the winter months, and, conscience-stricken, were contributing liberally to the various emergency relief funds, while their organizations continued cutting wages and discharging more employees.

"But," I said to one of them, pretending naïveté, "couldn't you as a big-shot in your company use your influence to change the policy pertaining to labor in your employ?"

He answered, impatiently: "My influence in our company, like the influence of most corporation presidents, is limited. I can't do much. I can suggest, yes, but a suggestion which goes contrary to long-established policy or tradition always encounters strong opposition. We have a board of directors which decides on matters of policy. Most of our directors are elderly men. Such a change in our labor policy as you suggest would immediately strike them as radical, and they are conservative men with set mental processes. And our company, I think, is a typical one. I, as president, and Mr. B—, as general manager, can be progressive only in such matters as installing new machinery and new methods, whereby our overhead is cut down. We can be radical only when all our directors and our shareholders can see *at a glance* that what we propose is sound business, that is, immediately profitable... I know what you mean, but 'stabilizing' our particular industry, I very much fear, would cause a row in our company. I doubt if I or anyone else could convince our directors that guaranteeing all-year employment to our people would be good business."

But the average employer is incapable even of grasping and discussing the idea of industrial stabilization. He is usually a college graduate, but has no developed social ideas. Socio-economically, he *is* a moron. He is solely a business man. He is keenly alert and opportunistic in keeping up-to-date with "progressive business methods" (most of which operate to reduce employment), but ponderously tenacious when business touches on anything outside business. He is a hard worker and good at routine, conceited, eager to have people look up to him and eager to keep on the good side of his economic superiors. He is anxious to convince you of his own importance in the business he happens to be in; he calls himself an "executive" but, so far as I have been able to detect, he hasn't the faintest idea where he and his enterprise are headed.

In the fall of 1930 I spoke with an "executive" who had just laid off six hundred men and reduced the wages of the remaining seven hundred. I reminded him of President Hoover's request to industry in November 1929. "That's all very well," he said to me angrily. "Mr. Hoover can talk. *We have to protect our stockholders*," he emphasized. "Besides, why should we keep up our 1928 payroll, when other industries are reducing theirs right and left, both by discharging men and by wage-cuts."

And, incredible as it may seem, I have met, or I know of, "executives" who deal with immense resources, millions of dollars and thousands of men, and whose only conception of the depression during 1929–32 was that "business is poor... I hardly remember when it was as poor as this." They had no more notion of what it was all about than had the owl that I once saw caught in a traffic jam on Fifth Avenue in New York City. They were blindly grateful to President Hoover, who in one of his messages to Congress, after trying to apologize for the shortcomings of business, declared—with his customary brilliance and optimism—that the depression was "world-wide" and "recurrent," and insisted that business must be left alone to right itself.

VI

Meanwhile—throughout this period—there was among the great masses of people a degree of misery which I doubt will ever be adequately described. Most of it was hidden misery. On top of unemployment came thousands of bank failures. Every newspaper in every big city reported daily from five to ten suicides on the part of jobless men. Men killed their families and themselves. Going about the country, in every town, one was stopped every few blocks by shamefaced men who said they had families, etc. I have seen people rummaging in garbage cans.

Five—eight—ten—twelve—fifteen million unemployed, and the number still grew; while among the employed were several million workers, including hundreds of thousands of child workers, whose regular shifts were still twelve hours and over, and others who worked long hours overtime.

Some people were working themselves to death; others had no work. Breadlines in the big cities lengthened with haggard men in their twenties, thirties, and early forties who wished they knew how to get into some illegal racket, or who were tempted to snatch women's purses; while at the same time there were in the United States over 3,000,000 child workers between twelve and sixteen years of age, working in textile mills and beet fields and sugar factories, making as little as $6 and $7 a week, in some places working as long as ten hours a day, six and even seven days a week, sometimes at night. The flophouses—or "Hoover hotels," as they were called—were overcrowded with strong jobless men, while in the Pennsylvania silk mills women worked twelve hours a day, making as little as $11 a week.

In February 1930 a Philadelphia employer advertised for a workman; the next morning 5,000 men responded. Such scenes became common through 1931–32 all over the United States.

Early in 1930, the Mayor of Evansville, Indiana, a city of somewhat less than 100,000 wrote in a letter to a friend:

> I have listened to more stories of real distress than I thought could possibly exist in America. This demand has been so insistent that I have had little time to give to regular duties in my office... I have callers at my home and my phone even at home rings almost incessantly due to calls from men who need employment, or from their wives who recite their distress and needs. The whole thing is a nightmare, but I am able to absorb scarcely any of this labor and when I do help a man find a job, it is usually at the expense of some other fellow being thrown out of work. I have had applications from college men, accountants, and school teachers who are willing to accept the lowest type of employment to earn bread and clothing for their families... Evansville has quite a diversity in its industries,

but all branches seem to be suffering. The relief is beyond our power
to supply.

The above, perhaps, is typical of the situation in the smaller cities in 1930, which have continued through the ensuing depression years.

In the spring of 1930 a Catholic parish priest in New York City wrote in the *Commonweal*:

> Whatever the statistics of unemployment may say, whether the number of idle workers runs into many millions or not, I do not know, but I do know, and so do most other pastors in New York, that not for many years have there been so many people out of work, and in such keen distress because of unemployment. Through my reception-rooms last week there passed nearly two hundred of my parishioners, each one begging for help to secure a job, or a job for Jimmy or Jane, or Mary or Bob, thrown out of work without fault of their own... Moreover, there is discontent; there is sullen anger, in addition to bewilderment and distress. The poor are asking why they should suffer, when the rich multiply; and not only is it the very poor who ask that difficult question; for hundreds of families that generally would not be classed among the poor—respectable people, usually quite safe and fairly prosperous—are now sinking down among the indigent class.

But everybody was not smitten so hard. On the day that I read the above Mr. J. P. Morgan launched his new $2,500,000 private yacht, the *Corsair*.

Detroit was a tragic city in 1930 (and became worse in 1931–32). While early in the summer of that year one read in the press that John N. Willys, American Ambassador to Poland and former president of the Willys-Overland Company, had bought five rare tapestries and an altar frontal for $30,000, most of the employees of that concern in Detroit were out of work.

In August 1930, the superintendent of the Bowery Mission in New York wrote in the New York *World*:

> Many men are weak from hunger. They are often practically barefooted and in rags. They have slept on a bench or the floor instead of a bed... The suffering on the Bowery today in midsummer is as acute as it often is in midwinter.

At about the same time the social columns of the New York newspapers contained the following information:

Mrs. Virginia Graham Fair Vanderbilt opened the Long Island social season by staging an unexpurgated open-air performance of Earl Carroll's *Vanities* for the delectation of several hundred members of the smart set at her palatial estate at Manhasset during the early hours this morning...The party cost $200,000.

While writing this chapter in the first edition of this book, I chanced to see a four-line item in a newspaper about a jobless young Pennsylvania worker who killed his girl and himself because they were "too hopelessly poor to get married." That reminded me that a few months before I had clipped an article out of the New York *World* containing interesting statistics about weddings in high society. It appears that the nuptials of Nelson Aldrich Rockefeller and Mary Todhunter Clark, early in June 1930, the "beautiful simplicity" of which had been chronicled in great detail by the country's press, cost, according to conservative estimates, over $100,000. The Rodman Wanamaker-Alice Devereaux and James Roosevelt-Betsy Cushing weddings each cost $150,000. And so on; indeed, a fashionable hook-up in these days of depression and working-class despair never cost less than $50,000, which included $5,000 for engraved invitations, $8,000 for liquor, $1,000 each for organist and singer, and $7,500 for flowers.

In brief, on the one hand, extreme want and misery for the millions; on the other, riotous wealth and luxury for the few. A lunatic system.

The Catholic priest writing in the *Commonweal* ended his report: "I believe that if today or tomorrow there appeared a man of magnetic personality, an apostle of radical revolt, fires would soon flame up in many places; possibly to meet in some great conflagration."

But during 1930–34 no leadership appeared which had the suffering of the masses really at heart and knew what to do about it. There were no great riots or upheavals, only misery and bewilderment. There were only misleaders and confusionists whose function was to deepen the people's bewilderment, deepen the social chaos.

VII

A real American labor movement would have had, during these years of chaos in the business world, an immense opportunity to become the greatest power in the United States, a power for the good of labor and the whole country, if its leadership had intelligence, patriotism, social vision, and character; but, alas! there was no real American labor movement, nor the leadership for one, when the depression came, and none developed.

In 1929, the American Federation of Labor was the country's largest body of organized workers; it unquestionably was American in character, as American as anything that came into existence before the great slump; but it was not a movement and could not become a movement in a hurry, if at all. As always, the A.F. of L. was a loose amalgamation of craft unions, like "a vague alliance"—to quote its most brilliant critic, Benjamin Stolberg—"of autonomous Indian tribes," which for a time after their formation, "with tomahawks and arrows and piercing yells attacked the outposts of the trusts," occasionally scoring a slight victory, but which, "after the frontier spirit disappeared in industry, when the trusts became monopolies and the monopolies the mere pawns of finance capital...[had been] assigned to their respective craft reservations, from which they were not allowed to move."

Once upon a time, as we have seen in the earlier chapters, the A.F. of L. had had spine and vitality, even militancy of a sort. Big business men and regular politicians had been frightened by its "tomahawks and arrows and piercing yells." The current depression, however, found it a sick body, flabby, ineffectual, afflicted with the dull pains of moral decline, which had begun after the McNamara fiasco, and physical decline, which had set in after the war and continued through the period of Coolidge prosperity. By 1929 big industrialists and conservative politicians were no longer worried by it. Indeed, when the crisis began and throughout the period of 1930–34, the more intelligent ones saw (and still see) the A.F. of L. as the best obstacle—temporary at least—to the emergence of a real, militant, and formidable labor movement.

This decline continued during 1930–32. Late in 1931, planning to write an article on labor unionism, I wrote to a number of friends and acquaintances who were officials of A.F. of L. unions, asking them to give me their frank opinions of their organization. Here is the reply, in part, of the secretary of a once leading union in a large industrial city:

> I regard you as a friend of the labor movement, so I can see no harm in writing you frankly... During the ten years that I have held office our membership has declined till we have a mere handful left.
>
> Our State branch of the A.F. of L. has been lifeless all this time. The secretary has been sick for years, and little or no work was done. Through sympathy he was elected year after year, although it was known that he was unable to attend to work. His salary was raised and then it was discovered there wasn't enough money in the

treasury to pay him the increase. I mention this so you can see how carelessly and foolishly we do our work.

Our city central labor union has been dead for many years. A man named ____ held office as business agent and secretary, although everyone knew he was unfit for the job either from the viewpoint of intelligence or courage. He was a good politician, however, and lately he became vice president of the ____ National Union at a salary of $ 12,000 a year...

Throughout our State and the neighboring States there is nothing to give heart to a man who wants to believe that the present labor organization in this country will be a force for the betterment of working conditions. The average working stiff is too indifferent and sour, or selfish, and the men in office are about played out and are mostly labor politicians and grafters, anyhow. We have some very fine fellows in the unions, but they lack the power of control.

The ____ Union is the strongest labor organization in this city. Everything is in their favor. They have a closed-shop agreement. And yet, with a membership of 6,000, they are practically bankrupt today. As in a great many other unions, the officials receive enormous salaries, and high-priced committees are called out on conference for every little grievance. Instead of being a power of intelligent influence, they have become merely a job-holding racket. It's discouraging as hell, but I'm telling you the truth.

In my own union we have so-called organizers on the road at a salary of $3,000 a year "and expenses" (and you should see their expense accounts!). Some are good men, but most of them are hopeless. They are either burned out or never had that passion for labor organizing which is necessary to stir and inspire others...

As for the central A.F. of L. organization itself, I see little cause for encouragement. On real issues they flounder and spend too much time on mouthy protests. At the 1930 national convention in Boston, it was discouraging to see so many dumbbells on the platform trying to look wise. There were fine men among the delegates, but their influence was nil. As a trade-unionist, I was mortified throughout the convention and was glad when it was over... There is little life left in the A.F. of L. The high officials seem unable to formulate policies to meet the great problems of today. They are merely carrying over the minds of earlier years.

I can't help but conclude that we are steadily declining in influence, certainly in membership and income, and the future looks dark. New labor movements do not spring up over night...

You may wonder why I hold on to my job. Well, a job is a job in these hard times, and then, too, I know the need for the labor move-

ment. I know what has been done in the past and why a labor movement will be needed in the future. I am trying as best I can, from
within the present movement, to add my little energy to whatever
progress may seem possible in the future. I know that the average
worker today who still has a job is getting an awful pounding by
high-speed pressure, wage-cuts, etc.; and without some organization—even such as ours—he will be out of luck altogether. It's a
desperate and complicated situation...

I'm telling you the truth as I see it, in the hope that you can
strain something to our credit.

One *can* "strain something" to the credit of individual local unions,
here and there, and even of some of the national unions; but there is
almost nothing one can strain to the credit of "trade unionism pure and
simple" or of the A.F. of L. as a whole and of its leadership.

The decline of the federation and some of its most important affiliates became apparent early in the last decade, soon after the death of
Samuel Gompers. By this I do not mean to imply that, if Gompers had
lived, the A.F. of L., which was in large part a creation of his energy,
would have been on the upgrade and a source of strength and hope to
at least a substantial body of the American working people in the darkest years of the great depression. I mean only to suggest that, if he were
still its president, the organization would not have sunk to quite the low
level, morally and otherwise, that it did just before the New Deal came
along and, to all seeming, gave it a new lease on life.

For one thing, with all his faults as a labor leader, and he had many,
Gompers had more innate strength and independence of character than
any of the men now in charge of the federation. And, while Gompers
was anything but a Marxist, early in his career he had studied Marx and
associated with Socialists who spoke of the Class Struggle, and thus he
had been influenced in his formative years to think in terms of conflict,
at least in periods of crisis. This the genial, polite, and charming Mr.
William Green, the present head of the A.F. of L., is quite incapable
of doing at any time and under any circumstances. Then, too, Gompers
was an immigrant and a Jew, and as such naturally distrustful and wary
of the world in which he found himself functioning... I feel certain that,
in the fall of 1929, Gompers would not have trusted, as, to all appearances, did Mr. Green, to the "honor" of Herbert Hoover, the bankers,
and the industrialists who met with labor leaders in the already referred
to White House conferences and "promised" not to cut wages during
the slump—a slump which all these leading men of the nation, along

with Mr. Green, expected to last only a couple of months!... Gompers was nearly always on his guard, a close student of forces and conditions, and at times proved himself a shrewd and forceful man, a schemer and politician of great acumen. Aggressiveness, as I have said before, perhaps was, up to the McNamara case, one of his main personal assets, and it is not one of Mr. Green's, who, as Benjamin Stolberg puts it, "rose in world by standing still." Gompers was never guilty of naïveté, which has been Mr. Green's characteristic, not only during the depression but ever since his ascension to the important office he holds.

But Gompers's supreme virtue as a labor leader was that "boodle"— wealth, graft—had no lure for him. The federation, as I have said in a previous chapter, was his very life; and his ruling ambition for forty years was to serve it the best he knew how, irrespective of personal gain. This cannot be said of more than two dozen men among the several hundred who attend the annual A.F. of L. conventions, and their influence counts for little in the organization.

Yet the sad state of the A.F. of L. just before the depression and from 1929 to 1932 was due in great part to Gompers—to the ideology which he developed, personified, and through the long years of his leadership made an integral element of the federation's basic psychology and policy.

Gompers (at the risk of repeating some of the things I say earlier in this book) grew up as a piece-work cigar maker at a time when cigars, in common with many other articles, were still made by hand. For years prior to the formation of the A.F. of L. he served as an officer of the large cigar makers' union in New York, whose members were a proud lot, a branch of the "aristocracy of labor," as unionized skilled craftsmen were then beginning to characterize themselves in contradistinction to the ordinary unskilled proletariat. The union was affiliated with the Knights of Labor; but the cigar makers, like most other skilled crafts, were uncomfortable in that amalgamation, which was open to common laborers as well as to skilled workmen. It was one of the best-organized and most successful trade unions in the seventies and as such was not a class-conscious group in the Marxian sense. With a mingling of contempt and pity, the cigar makers and the rest of the "aristocracy" looked down from their middle-class vantage-point upon the slaves who were doing the hard and dirty work of the country, and upon men and women who were mere appendages to the machines. They thought they had no interest in common with them. So to the devil with them!

And, logically enough, Gompers evolved his A.F. of L. policy out of the policy which had made his own union of piece-work handicraftsmen a success in his youth. It was the hard-boiled policy of "trade unionism, pure and simple," subscribing to the philosophy of opportunistic practicality, which was then—in the "gilded age"—becoming prevalent in America, and which urged all to seek only the obvious and reach for the immediate; for life in these free, democratic States consisted merely of problems at hand, the future promising to take care of itself. The thing to do was to raise the wages and shorten the hours of those who had the sense and the initiation fee to join the unions. To increase the wages and reduce the hours, the unions had to raise "war funds" for strikes and lockouts by adopting the high dues and initiation fees system, which made it impossible for most workers to join the unions; and the latter became closed corporations—"labor trusts"—Mr. Stolberg's "Indian tribes."

Late in the nineteenth and early in the twentieth century this was the most sensible policy for a realistic labor movement to adopt. Indeed, as I have suggested before, it was the only policy with which a labor movement could have become effective to any great extent in that extremely chaotic, dog-eat-dog, narrowly pragmatic, unidealistic, semi-frontier, and blindly dynamic period. Besides, in those years labor still could be classified into trades. The "aristocracy of labor" was yet a well-defined class of workers.

Ten or a dozen years ago, however, this policy ceased to be sound; but Gompers and his successor have been unwilling and unable to adapt it to meet the new facts and circumstances in industry.

The trouble with Gompers was that, psychologically, he was a piece-work cigar maker and handicraftsman all his life. Machines which could be operated by almost anybody after a few hours' instruction pushed tens of thousands of piece-work cigar makers on to the scrap-heap outside the labor market, and the membership of Gompers's old union went down; for the ill-paid machine operators were not really cigar makers in the old sense and, therefore, could not be admitted into the union. But that made no fundamental difference to Gompers. He remained a "trade-unionist, pure and simple," although the fate of his own union, of course, was representative of that of many once strongly organized and successful trades.

Then, too, quite apart from the influence of his cigar-making youth upon his later career, Gompers was caught in his own game, in the politics of the organization. During his declining years there were still several unions in the A.F. of L. which were not immediately threatened by modern mechanization or "rationalization," and for this reason were the strongest members of the federation and stood for the old idea *in toto*. If Gompers (assuming that he could have ceased being a piece-work cigar maker) had tried to overhaul the "pure and simple" policy and reorganize the federation, the still successful and powerful trades—the remaining "aristocracy"—would have turned against him and possibly dethroned him as the big boss of American labor; and this he could not have endured, for, as I have said, the A.F. of L. was his life. So he played the game and grew older refusing to recognize the fact that handicrafts-manship was doomed by the machine, and that the future of organized labor, if any, lay in unions formed along industrial, not craft lines.

What was true of Gompers early in the 1920s is true today of Mr. Green and of his "colleagues," as he calls them, by whose sufferance he stays in office. They blindly stick to "pure-and-simpletonism"— "carrying over the minds of earlier years"—and, naturally, by 1929, the federation became even weaker than it had been when Gompers died. "Rationalization" achieved its height after the old man's death, and more and more, just before and during the depression, "aristocracy" was being swept into the common proletarian class, either to work at low non-union wages "on the belt" or to lengthen the breadlines.

In fact, Mr. Green and the other officials were (and are) even less in position to adapt themselves and the federation to new problems than was Gompers. They were all caught in the almost inflexible system of A.F. of L. tradition. They were committed to carry on the policy of "Gompers the Immortal."

VIII

For over a decade now the federation has lacked not only the ability to adapt itself to new conditions, but also—equally important—the chief virtue of labor unionism from the members' immediate point of view: namely, successful aggressiveness in the industrial field. During this pe-riod the organization was not instrumental in the raising of wages and the shortening of the work-day. Many unions, in fact, have failed even to maintain the wages won before the war. This cannot be blamed solely or even mainly on the depression and the recent wholesale wage-cuts. Union wage scales were being reduced long before October 1929, and the A.F. of L. unions were unable to do anything effective about it.

The efforts of the federation and its branches during the last ten years for the betterment of working conditions were marked by faintheartedness, insincerity, corruption, confusion, and futility; and "labor racketeering," such as I describe in Chapter 30, increased in all sections of the country. Most of the official energy was spent within the organizations in intense factional squabbles and so-called jurisdictional disputes. (Should carpenters or sheet-metal workers put sheet metal on woodwork?) Ever since he became president, Mr. Green has spent most of his time in office work, trying—with scant success—to keep peace among factions and within unions.

During all these years, the A.F. of L. unions have conducted no successful strikes and, until the New Deal came, no effective organizing campaigns, although eighty-five per cent of American workers were unorganized even when the federation's membership was highest. Almost no effort was made to unionize workers in such basic industries as steel and iron, automobile, aircraft, rubber, oil, electrical manufacturing, meat packing and food in general, lumber and chemicals, in which labor is not definitely and simply "aristocratic" enough in the old sense. One difficulty was (and still is) that the separate unions are unable to decide among themselves under whose jurisdiction these various machine workers should be put. Another reason why the unions conducted no organizing campaigns was that the officials did not want to risk whatever "boodle" was still left in the treasuries. Organizing work is dangerous and expensive; and should their unions spend too much money on such things, where would their huge salaries come from in the future? The unions had "organizers" on their staffs, but, as members of inner-office cliques, their only duty was to cash their pay checks. In the last ten years they have drawn out of various treasuries nearly two million dollars of workers' hard-earned money in salaries and expenses, and early in 1933 there was literally less than nothing to show for it. The A.F. of L. membership dwindled from more than four million in 1920 to, perhaps, less than half that number in 1932; and during the early years of the depression I spoke with numerous union men in various crafts who wished they could get jobs in their lines without belonging to unions, not a few of which had degenerated into mere labor contracting agencies operated, by means of violence, corrupt political connections, and other racketeering tricks, in part for the benefit of the members and in part for the deep pockets of the men who ran them.

No wonder that workers were "indifferent and sour, or selfish," as my correspondent described them in the letter I have quoted. One union man who had to "belong" in order to work, said to me in 1931: "No kiddin', but I'd feel better as a man if I wasn't part of the racket"—

the latter word being a common term among trade unionists when they spoke of their organizations. Moreover, I was distantly conscious of tens of thousands of men within the A.F. of L. unions who were in a state of frustration and bewilderment. Their old trade-union morale was gone. They were leaderless and ignorantly cynical. They knew of widespread and still spreading corruption in their unions and attended as few meetings as possible. "What's the use!" They saw no future for themselves or their local unions under the old trade-union policy and the present A.F. of L. bureaucracy, but for the time being at least, as one of them put it to me, they were "stuck." The intelligent workers were frank in stating to one who asked them that in their opinion the chief function of the A.F. of L. was to prevent the emergence of a new labor movement. This was also true of the more conscientious local union officials, but their number was not large.

The A.F. of L. executive council and the "big skates" in charge of State federations, national and international unions, and other central bodies—in short, the men who attend the annual conventions—failed to manifest any real understanding of the modern industrial and economic forces either during the prosperity era or since the beginning of the depression. Through the last decade they exhibited intellectual, intestinal, and moral inadequacy, if not total bankruptcy, as leaders of labor and social-minded men. They lost sight, if they ever had it, of the larger aims of the organized labor movement. They were incapable of thinking in terms of conflict. Many of them, as already suggested, were downright racketeers, referred to as such by the sour, frustrated, and futile rank-and-file element in the unions. Some of the A.F. of L. leaders were, perhaps, the worst enemies that organized labor had and were recognized as such by large groups in the unions; but in numerous cases, where democracy gave way to racketeering, the membership could not remove them from their commanding, high-salaried positions.

IX

But let us take a close look at these "big shots" in the A.F. of L. who run the central office and the big unions and attend the conventions, at which they decide on the course their organization is to take; so that we can have some idea what we—American labor and the country as a whole—are to expect from them.

Most of them are prosperous-looking, Babbitt-like, middle-aged or elderly men, well-dressed, carefully barbered, fat-cheeked, double- and triple-chinned, vast-bellied, with gold watch-chains across their paunches and stickpins in their ties. They drive good cars or travel in taxis between their hotels, which are the best in town, and the convention hall. Their hands are soft and pudgy, eager for the shake. They are breezy, genial men, professional good fellows. The bulk of them have "grown up" together in the "movement," which now is *their* "movement." They practically own it. They have been coming to conventions for ten or fifteen years, and a few of them for as long as forty years. The A.F. of L. has a provision in its time-honored constitution which is inimical to "undesirables"—i.e., radicals, upstarts, anti-traditionalists—becoming delegates, and strongly favorable to "the right sort."

They all know one another, these panjandrums of American labor. They are, for the most part, presidents and vice-presidents and chief organizers of the various national and international unions with salaries ranging from $7,500 to $20,000 a year "and expenses." Prosperity or depression, their salaries never stop. Under their brilliant leadership some of the unions have so amended their constitutions that now the presidents—"Tsars"—can raise their own salaries almost at will. But these salaries "and expenses" are only a part of the income. When they get together in their hotel rooms during conventions they talk of stocks and bear and bull markets and short-selling, and compare notes on Buicks and Chryslers and on private schools for boys and girls. Some are powerful in local and State politics. The New York "bunch," for instance, used to be "pretty thick" with Tammany Hall. A few of them are on the payrolls of closed-shop firms. Heads of painters' and paperhangers' unions are silent partners in paint and wallpaper stores. Heads of carpenters', plasterers', lathers', and plumbers' unions have interests in building contracting concerns.

They are solid citizens, go-getters, full of upper-middle-class respectable pretensions and ambitions. They belong to Elks, Moose, and Odd Fellows. They play golf, belong to country clubs. They have no interest in

Tom Mooney and Warren Billings. What impresses them are such facts as that "Bill" Green's boy Harry is a junior at Princeton, where one of the Rockefeller boys is a student, too, and, according to report, on good terms with him. They are against the Soviet Union and hate the Communists on general principles.

In the convention hall they all look as impressive as they can and listen to speeches in favor of beer and against strikes. They vote on the resolutions as the central bureaucratic group wants them to vote. They applaud the suggestion of the executive council (as they did in 1931)

that the best way to reduce the number of the unemployed from eight to a mere two million is to induce each of the 3,000,000 employers in the United States to take on two more employees!

Mr. Green makes a charming, kindly, fair, and efficient convention chairman. He is a soft, round, graying, bright-faced man in his early sixties. His voice is mild and sonorous; only now and then, in speaking of his lowly working-class origin, he punches his chest and raises his pitch by way of emphasis. His income from his job runs into five figures a year. He sends out his official correspondence on elegant engraved stationery. He might easily be taken for a bank or railroad president or a United States senator. He deplores strikes and walkouts and considers friction between employer and worker an unfortunate result of misunderstanding of economic conditions. He believes in "moral suasion" and "collective bargaining." He goes even so far as to say that "capital is the worker's best friend."

He is a careful man. He has to be. There are potent politicians in the federation who keep their eyes on him. They are stronger men than he, and as such have enemies, which prevents them from being elected to the presidency; while Mr. Green has no real enemies and, by keeping as neutral as possible, does his best not to make any. Benjamin Stolberg compares him to the late Warren Harding: "a kindly and easy man, essentially a small-town man, a joiner and good fellow; a deacon in the Baptist Church of his native Coshocton, Ohio, where he used to teach Sunday school and lecture for the Anti-Saloon League."

Mr. Green is a respectable, high-toned man. He is indeed ultra-respectable. He has to be. As I have said, nearly all the rest of the A.F. of L. bureaucracy are men of upper-middle-class respectability, and secretly they contemplate their president with critical and jealous eyes. To make them more or less look up to him in official life he must strive for correctness with all his might, and of late the desire for respectability has become almost a neurosis with him.

The central A.F. of L. bureaucracy is held together chiefly by individual self-interest. There is not much harmony. Each of them, including Mr. Green, probably sees that "pure-and-simpletonism" is obsolete, but none of them would think of starting a movement for the overhauling of the federation. If one should do so, his political rivals would immediately pounce on him. So they all play the game.

X   313

Another close-up of the A.F. of L. bureaucracy's mentality may be had through the files of the *American Federationist*, official organ of the executive committee, edited by Mr. Green. Let us, particularly, read the editorials written or inspired and signed by Mr. Green, and fully realize his and his "colleagues'" terrible inadequacy to deal with the problem of labor today.

In March 1927 he wrote, in the face of the crisis in many unions brought about by "rationalization," that "the function of unions remains unchanged when machine tools replace hand tools," and congratulated the working people of America on "having a hand in the adventure of creation." Now and then he became inspirational. In August he warned "our union movement" against "falling into the mistakes of selfishness and materialism"!

In October 1927: "Unions have done much for industry and they would do more. We again offer employers our proposal of cooperation... We hope and confidently expect our proposals will gain in favor and practical application." This was at the time that the A.F. of L. "organizers" were approaching the Ford Motor Company and Dodge Brothers in Detroit with the polite request that they be allowed to organize the workers in their plants!

And so on through 1928 and 1929. Throughout this period Editor Green betrayed no suspicion of the coming of the depression.

In December 1929, as already mentioned, he attended the White House conference in which the depression was "prevented," and for four months thereafter he gushed editorial optimism. He did not discover unemployment till May 1930, and then it occurred to him that "the only cure for unemployment is jobs for those who must work to live." He also expressed his eagerness to collaborate with the government and industry and finance on a plan which would prevent "the next depression." The depression had not yet begun, so far as Mr. Green was aware!

Finally, in July 1930, the depression started, and Mr. Green found consolation in the fact that, apparently, it was "world-wide." In August, in an editorial entitled "Unemployment, a Most Urgent Problem," he seemed really disturbed, but in September he was once more optimistic: "We look forward to the opportunities of business revival with fresh confidence and courage." In September he wrote an indignant editorial against a textile company in North Carolina which refused to employ union workers. This, he said, was "tyranny...tyranny which kills the

314 hope for progress in life and work." He did not mention how he, as head of labor, proposed to combat this tyranny. In October he was against unemployment and in favor of "employment security," admitting, however, that the A.F. of L. had no idea what the real situation was. "We need to know the extent of the [unemployment] problem before we undertake a general plan of relief... In the meanwhile we should study all plans and proposals so that we may know what plans offer real help." In the same month the executive council of the A.F. of L. reported to the convention in Boston that there was "serious unemployment" and that they were emphatically opposed to it. In November Mr. Green discovered that unemployment was a "national calamity," and stated again that he was in favor of work and wages. In the December number he urged that the Christmas spirit should pervade the world, and remarked again that he was in favor of finding work for the jobless, and once more sought consolation in the fact that unemployment was "world-wide."

In January 1931, the official A.F. of L. was for "a life of fellowship between men" and for making that fellowship a practical guide in the world of industry, "so that we should not lose our souls" and "our national wealth." In February Mr. Green still found consolation in the fact that the depression was world-wide, was against unemployment because it was an "evil" and against wage reductions for the same reason, and in favor of "security for workers"; and emphatically declared that "lower standards of living do not create prosperity." In March unemployment was "no small problem," and Mr. Green was against poverty because it was bad for health, and in favor of leisure as a change from unemployment. In April he continued to be against wage reductions as advocated by certain short-sighted bankers because "their [the bankers'] dividends and profits need a permanent foundation in prosperity for all groups."

In September:

Working people must earn money in order to live. Money is necessary for food, shelter and clothing. Wage-earners depend upon wage-earning opportunities for earning their incomes. That is why a job is so important... The high-wage principle has planted itself firmly in our business system. Business at last realizes that high wages are an investment in the stabilization of prosperity...

And in the very week that the magazine with this editorial was distributed the largest employers in the country declared the most sweeping wage reductions in the history of their industries!

In brief—only blah-blah and confusionism. Mr. Green and his "colleagues" carried their talents to the 1931 convention in Vancouver. There Mr. Green spoke in his mild Odd-Fellows-Baptist-conservative voice: "I warn the people who are exploiting the workers that they can drive them only so far before they will turn on them and destroy them... Revolutions grow out of the depths of hunger." Which caused the newspaper reporters to grin. Such great capitalists as Owen D. Young and Thomas L. Chadbourne had spoken similarly a year and a half before!

And so on till the spring of 1933, when unemployment reached the peak figure of probably nearer twenty than fifteen millions.

XI

Then, in June 1933, began the New Deal with its National Industrial Recovery Act or NIRA, its NRA, in charge of the cavalry general, Hugh Johnson, and its Blue Eagle. Section 7A of the NIRA provided that "employees shall have the right to organize and bargain collectively through representatives of their own choosing...[and] that no employee...shall be required to join any company union."

Here, of a sudden, seemed to be the greatest opportunity American labor ever had, delivered on a platter. The President of the United States, with full power of the federal government behind him, wanted all labor to have the right to organize! But it only *seemed* so. Actually, as it became quite obvious before the NIRA was a year old, it was just a trick, only a gesture on the part of the original New Dealers, including Mr. Roosevelt and Senator Robert Wagner; a trick and a gesture invented by them in cahoots with the A.F. of L. oligarchy. The authors of Section 7A had been careful not to say that labor should organize along *industrial* lines, into so-called vertical unions, and be done with obsolete "pure and simple" horizontal unionism. Such a provision, in all likelihood, would have kicked the A.F. of L. jobholders out of their positions and probably made labor far too powerful to suit the vague and "liberal" calculations of Mr. Roosevelt and his yacht-owning friends.

As the New Dealers must have known, the A.F. of L. as a whole was totally unfitted, *by its very nature*, to take advantage of the provisions of Section 7A. Only two big unions in the federation were so constituted that the NIRA benefited them in a big way. These were the semi-industrial needle trades and the industrial United Mine Workers. Most of the "pure and simple" craft unions are no better off in consequence of the New Deal than they were before; a good many of them continue to hang on the brink of collapse.

As I write this, the A.F. of L. membership is less than 4,000,000. The approximate gains of 2,000,000 include about 700,000 needle trades and mine workers and about a million workers newly organized into the so-called "federal labor unions," which is a device of granting A.F. of L. charters to separate factories—a device (put into practice to keep a big rival organization from springing up) which in nine cases out of ten tends toward ruinous jurisdictional friction among the crafts represented in a given factory, and therefore is worse than nothing. The rest is the total of small gains in the regular craft unions. About a million workers are organized outside the A.F. of L. There still remain about 35,000,000 working people unorganized in the United States! And the A.F. of L., as it is today and always has been, can't take them in. The A.F. of L. bureaucracy is afraid of them, doesn't want them, doesn't want a new organization to come into existence, and does its best to sabotage every new movement that tries to get started.

It is not my purpose here to tell the full story of the New Deal as it touched labor. That is a vast and complicated tale, which, if told in all its details, would fill a volume as thick as this one; and much of it is irrelevant to the subject of this book. Then, too, most of the main facts of the story, as, for instance, the superb measure abolishing child labor, are generally known. The following, however, is apropos and needs to be stressed:

Whether originally intended by the New Dealers or not, Section 7A in the NIRA and the tremendous hullabaloo that accompanied the launching of the NRA powerfully stirred vast masses of the American working people from the lethargy and hopelessness into which they had sunk as a relief from bewilderment during the previous three years, and suddenly gave them a fresh aggressiveness in their socio-economic problem, a tremendous impulse toward organization.

Bewilderment and confusion still—or rather, again—are general among the working classes; there still is no real, effective leadership, and the A.F. of L. bureaucrats and other misleaders are busy confounding labor still more; but during the first half of 1934—as it became quite evident that Section 7A was largely a trick, an empty, insincere gesture, or at best a half-hearted measure, on the part of the Roosevelt regime, and that the NRA under General Johnson and its labor boards were deliberately and consistently playing into the hands of big industrialists who wanted to trap labor into company unions—the workers' unrest and feverish, militant efforts to form their own unions became marked by a profound sullenness, a great anger, a fighting mood—the sort of

mood that used to characterize large sections of American labor preceding the big struggles in the past decades that I have tried to chronicle
in this book.

As I write this, in mid-June 1934, several hundred strikes are in
progress all over the United States, most of them to force recognition of
the new unions or shop committees. In connection with a few very recent walkouts there were sudden, sharp outbursts of violence—as for instance, in Minneapolis—in San Francisco, San Pedro, and the Imperial
Valley, in California—in the Alabama coal fields—in New York City
during the taxi-men's strike—in Toledo, Ohio, and so on. In most cases
it was violence against the newly aggressive striking workers on the part
of the police, special deputies, employers' gunmen, and the militia after
the labor elements had begun to show signs of desperation or revolutionary spirit in their cause.

Let us look, briefly, at the Toledo case, which occurred in May 1934
and probably is the most interesting and significant one.

XII

Late in February the workers of the Electric Auto-Lite Company, one
of the largest manufacturers of automobile parts and one of the biggest concerns in Toledo, associated with the anti-union Automobile
Chamber of Commerce, walked out. In common with workers in hundreds of other factories all over the country, they had started a union
and wanted the company to recognize it. They also demanded an increase in wages. A day or two later the workers in two of Auto-Lite's
affiliated plants, the Logan Gear Company and the Bingham Stamping
Company, struck. They, too, had started new unions. And all together,
with the fervor of people in a new cause, they displayed great militancy.
They ran picket lines day and night. They put up tents as strikers' relief
stations.

Production of auto parts was then at its height, so the companies,
eager to fill their orders, soon yielded. The "settlement" which the workers accepted was a compromise. They took a five per cent wage boost
and the employers recognized the shop committees. The question of
union recognition was put off till April 1, the employers promising that
they would then enter with the workers' leaders into negotiations for a
union contract.

On April 1, however, Auto-Lite, Logan Gear, and Bingham
Stamping flatly refused to have anything to do with the union officials,
duly elected by the workers to represent them as Section 7A provided.

So, in mid-April, the workers in all three factories struck anew. Mass picketing was on again, and the strikers' committees requested the local Unemployed Council and Unemployed League to join them on the picket lines. These organizations, the former fostered by the regular Communist Party and the latter by the American Workers Party (under the leadership of A. J. Muste and Louis Budenz, one of the best strike tacticians in the country) were formed on a national scale in recent years to help unions on strike by keeping the desperate jobless from scabbing.

The employers succeeded—doubtless with no great difficulty—in getting a local judge to issue an injunction against the union and the Unemployed League, under which only twenty-five pickets were allowed at each factory gate. The strike committee decided to observe the court order and try to annul it by legal action. Mass picketing stopped, hundreds of strike-breakers were brought into the factories through the inadequately picketed gates, and the strike spirit began to wane.

The union leaders tried desperately to overcome the injunction legally. They appealed to the NRA's regional labor board. No result. They appealed to the NRA's national labor board in Washington. This body referred them to the regional labor board. There again no result. Back to Washington—back to the regional labor board. In brief, the NRA, that great friend of labor, was giving the Toledo strikers a run-around.

On May 7, seeing the hopelessness of the legal-action idea, the leaders of the Unemployed League decided deliberately and with full knowledge to defy the injunction. They were arrested, tried, and released on suspended sentences; released, obviously, because the judge did not want to make them into even more dramatic heroes in the strikers' eyes than they already were.

In the forenoon of May 21, Louis Budenz, who I imagine had been directing the injunction defiance from the start, appeared at the Auto-Lite plant gates. Soon about one thousand workers gathered. Budenz made a short speech, announcing he would defy the injunction and called upon the workers to join him in peaceful mass picketing and "smashing the injunction, once and for all." The vast crowd cheered. Budenz, carrying a banner which read "*1776—1865—1934*," headed the picket line. By evening the number of workers at the factory gates increased to two thousand. Budenz, who is a rather slight, harmless-looking fellow but full of courage and sincerity, spoke again. The next day he addressed before the plant over four thousand workers, and the third day nearly six thousand.

The Central Labor Union of Toledo suggested to Sheriff Krieger that he deputize union workers (non-strikers) as guards around the plant. He refused and, instead, deputized men chosen by Auto-Lite, paid by the company and not by the county.

On May 24, as the picket line began, these deputies appeared on the roof of the plant with boxes of tear-bombs. Almost immediately thereafter, the scabs inside commenced to throw iron bolts and nuts from the windows. One of these hit a girl picket behind the ear, and she had to be taken to the hospital.

Budenz and other leaders shouted to the strikers: "Don't be provoked! Continue peaceful mass picketing no matter what the scabs may do!"

The crowd in front of the plant had increased to ten thousand.

Suddenly the sheriff ordered the arrest of Budenz and four other pickets carrying banners. They were immediately taken to jail and kept there till noon of the next day. A few minutes after Budenz and the other banner-carriers were hustled off, a deputy sheriff (actually a company guard) seized an old man and in full sight of most of the ten thousand people hit him a terrific wallop.

This was a little too much for the crowd, which began swiftly to surge around the deputies and police, while the deputies on the plant roofs commenced to bombard the great space before the plant with tear gas.

In no time scores of persons lay in the street, overcome by gas or injured by bolts and other iron articles which the scabs within the plant continued to hurl from the windows.

Incensed by this terrorism (which had obviously been prearranged by company representatives and the officers of "law and order"), some of the people in the crowd started to throw bricks and stones into the plant windows, others cut off the light supply (for night was coming), and rammed the factory doors with great timbers. Groups fought with the police and deputies through most of the night, while the scabs were prisoners in the lightless plant.

On May 23 the company officials had asked for the National Guard, evidently because they had known what would happen on the twenty-fourth. On the latter date, National Guard officers were on the scene as observers, and immediately after the strikers began to throw stones and bricks and to fight the police, they, jointly with the sheriff, called for state troops. All this, without an iota of doubt, as the strikers subsequently charged, was "framed up" the previous day, or probably even two or three days before.

Early on the twenty-fifth the troops arrived in a heavy rain, which tended to disperse the immense crowd before the plant. Nonetheless, fights between the soldiers and the strikers began almost at once and continued for two days, at the end of which two workers were dead and over sixty workers and a few soldiers and bystanders wounded or injured.

The public reaction to the incident all over the country was generally favorable to the workers' side. I received a letter from an acquaintance, a school teacher in Cleveland, in which she says: "I guess we're in for great changes in this country, and when they come we shall probably realize that Toledo was not in vain—that no head was cracked in vain by a policeman's club during this depression, nor a drop of blood foolishly shed."

The story of Toledo is not yet concluded. Louis Budenz is charged with contempt of court. However, we can say that the first chapter of it is finished. The troops were withdrawn and a "settlement" was effected which was a victory for the workers. The company recognized the union, signed a contract with it, giving the employees an additional five per cent raise, and all the strikers were promised re-employment. But Auto-Lite is part of the anti-union Automobile Chamber of Commerce, and as such it will break the contract with the union as soon as it can.

Toledo gave millions of workers all over the country, who are sick of the A.F. of L.'s inaction and in danger of being trapped in thousands of company unions, an important lesson, a clear suggestion—namely that they physically and openly defy injunctions, and face danger to their lives. Thousands of new labor leaders realize that the Toledo strike would not have ended in a victory for workers, as the *Nation* for June 13 said editorially, "had it not been for the audacious violation of the injunction. The Auto-Lite workers, aided by the Unemployed League, did force a showdown and the employers yielded. In that sense a fighting union policy [in contradistinction to the typical A.F. of L. flabbiness, respectability and racketeering] has scored a great victory in Toledo, just as in Minneapolis the militant spirit and excellent organization of the striking truckmen forced a favorable settlement."

XIII

American labor, as I say, is still bewildered, deeply distraught by the suffering and humiliation of the past several years, unconsciously ashamed of its own ineffectiveness, frightfully unclear as to what it thinks it wants or ought to want; but lately large sections of it—the rank and file, the unorganized, and those in the new, loosely formed unions, all over the land—are beginning to see that they cannot trust their old "leaders," nor the NRA, nor the charming social worker who sits in the White House; that they cannot trust anyone but their own power and ability to turn that power into action, into force—FORCE.

In April 1934, the automobile workers of the country, their affairs in charge of A.F. of L. "leaders," were on the verge of a great strike, to force from the auto industry the recognition of their right to organize; but their leaders "settled" the threatened walkout with President Roosevelt, who appears to think that the country is just one grand settlement-house in which peace and order and a fantastic thing called Recovery are of more immediate importance than the rights of labor which he pretended to be championing in Section 7A of his NIRA. The labor situation in the automobile industry was anything but "settled" and will never be settled by A.F. of L. fakers and the nice gentleman in the White House. Toledo indicated that.

In mid-June 1934, the steel workers of the country, their affairs also in charge of A.F. of L. "leaders," were on the verge of a great strike, to force from the steel industry the recognition of their right to organize; but their leaders got together with President Roosevelt and the other New Dealers, and the strike was suppressed.*

There will *doubtless* be other strikes, hundreds of them, during 1934 and 1935—except, of course, if the "liberal" Roosevelt Administration goes full Fascist so far as labor is concerned and creates machinery to keep down industrial upheavals, which is not impossible; but even in case of such a development in our national situation all strikes will not be suppressed—for, as I say, the mood that I describe on the preceding several pages is widespread and intense among workers in all important industries.

The story I tell in this book is still developing, and developing rapidly. The climax is still in the future. Perhaps in a not so distant future.

American labor is faced with the *immediate* necessity of breaking up the oligarchy of the A.F. of L. and overhauling that organization to be able to meet the new problems, and of ridding itself of the NRA-supported company unions, which lately have been formed by the industrialists for the purpose of preventing regular unionization. Both of these aims can be achieved *only* by an avalanche of rank-and-file strikes

---

* See Postscript II, "Tragedy in Steel," page 329.

with full union recognition as their chief objective. Should any considerable number of strikes be successful, recognition of unions would have to be followed by campaigns, under new leadership, for the organization of unions along industrial lines; which eventually, I hope, will lead to the formation of a new movement, a *real* American labor movement, fresh, radical, and revolutionary, along industrial and political lines—a realistic *American* movement of the producing masses, born of the economic and social problems here in America, in tune with the future psychology and philosophy of American life, which will be along collectivist lines, just as the A.F. of L. was in tune with the American philosophy and psychology in the past.

But many, perhaps most, of the strikes are almost bound to be accompanied by violence as was the strike in Toledo.

THE END

POSTSCRIPTS

I. A Note on Violence as Publicity

When the fateful crash came in October 1929, the United States had, perhaps, close to two millions unemployed, and, as suggested elsewhere, in the ensuing winter months that number probably doubled. But no newspaper and no person of any importance manifested the least awareness of the national unemployment situation till March 1930.

Then, of a sudden, unemployment hit the front page everywhere and became the talk of the country, because on March 6, 1930, the Communists staged large "hunger demonstrations" in various cities. Some of the demonstrations—the one in New York, for instance, which I witnessed—were extremely impressive and culminated in riots, during which the police rode down people and clubbed them, causing bloodshed.

These demonstrations became sensational front-page news all over the country—not because they were demonstrations or because the Communists organized them, but because they produced bleeding heads. Newspapers printed full pages of riot and mob pictures and close-ups of injured persons. The publicity which resulted from these riots, of course, was not of the most favorable sort, but, unfavorable as were some of the write-ups, picture captions, and editorials, they began to force the unemployment situation, which was growing rapidly worse, on the national consciousness.

Late in March and early in April 1930, there were more demonstrations and riots in various cities and towns, and unemployment stayed on the front pages of even the most conservative anti-labor papers till the middle of April, when it was relegated for about two weeks to inside pages. On May first more "hunger parades" and riots, and, as if by magic, labor and unemployment once again reached the front page, and editorial writers began to take notice of the situation, some of them going so far as to question President Hoover's unceasing optimism. But by mid-May the labor problem was off page one once more, to stay off it till early fall.

In September more demonstrations, in which the police clubbed the workers, and, presto! front page again for labor and unemployment. I think that largely as a result of this publicity President Hoover admitted in October that there was a national unemployment emergency and abruptly created a federal relief organization to help the jobless during the winter, and in December the official Washington estimate of the number of unemployed in the United States was six million.

From November 1930 to March 1931, unemployment was front-page "stuff" in the large cities on an average of twice weekly. The various relief organizations got no end of valuable newspaper space for the asking. But one who takes the trouble of going through the files of New York, Chicago, Detroit, Cleveland, and Philadelphia papers for those months notices this striking fact—that unemployment and jobless relief were played up in a specially big way on the front pages for three or four days immediately after every Communist demonstration, "food raid," or riot.

Millions of jobless and work-eager people were not newsworthy in the eyes of the press in any big way—or at least the press did not become acutely cognizant of their existence and their plight—until the situation was dramatized or intensified with demonstrations which the police, following their natural tendency, turned into bloody riots. Quietly suffering millions are not news; they are not dramatic enough. When one of them commits suicide in some alley, he gets possibly three lines on page ten, or not even that. But when a crowd comes in the street and a few persons get their heads banged up, that is front-page news; that is dramatic.

Which, I think, is rather interesting, especially since the newspapers, to say nothing of the self-righteous general public, are inclined to get morally indignant when riots occur, usually (and in most cases unjustly) blaming them on labor. Publishers and editors do not realize that by playing up largely news of violence and ignoring most of the non-violent labor news, they indirectly—and unwittingly, of course—urge leaders of labor, who as a rule are naturally peaceable, to desire violence. Yet this obviously is so, not only in the great matter of nationwide unemployment, but, as I shall show, also in local strikes and other disputes between capital and labor.

This has been so for decades; but let us look—from this angle—at some of the recent labor history.

In the early spring of 1929, after suffering for years conditions which were worse than slavery, about 20,000 in the Southern textile region left their looms in a series of strikes, which, in many respects, were extremely impressive and nationally important. But these upheavals did not become big national news and the sermon subject of preachers who think they are socially minded until violence broke out in Gastonia and Marion, North Carolina, and Elizabethton, Tennessee, and seven men and one woman were killed and over two dozen wounded. Then all the big Eastern and Mid-Western papers sent special reporters to the scene of the strife, which had been going on for years. And the strikes were not a complete failure, which they had threatened to be before the outbursts of violence brought the whole abominable situation to the attention of the American people, who, much to the annoyance of the mill owners, commenced to interest themselves, here and there, in the plight of Southern textile labor.

All through 1928, 1929, and 1930, the labor conditions in the bituminous regions of West Virginia, Pennsylvania, Ohio, and Kentucky were worse than the slavery conditions eighty years ago which produced the Civil War. But they were not important news to the American press until the summer of 1931, when the miners heaved up violently and bombs began to explode and some eight or ten pickets were butchered by the "Cossacks."

Evil labor conditions or even strikes in the United States are big news, as a rule, only after either the workers or the police or both employ violence. In the spring of 1931 I happened to witness an intensely dramatic and complicated dispute in the anthracite towns of Pennsylvania. Thirty thousand men were on strike, not only against the employers but also against their union, which sided with the bosses. But they and their cause were not important or interesting news—not even in Pennsylvania—till they began to march on the highways in mass formation and engage in battles with scabs and "Cossacks," and a few of them died, and some mine shafts were dynamited. After that they became big news, not alone in Pennsylvania, but elsewhere; even *The Bronx Home News*, a purely neighborhood paper, featured a story about them on page one.

In May 1931 there was a small laborers' strike in Greenwich, Connecticut, because contractors engaged on public works were reducing wages. No one outside of Greenwich, perhaps not many people even in Greenwich, heard of the dispute for weeks after it started. Then in a few hours it became national news because a mob of strikers and their wives stormed the Town Hall, smashed doors and windows, and for three hours resisted the efforts of policemen, several of whom were injured, to disperse them. The largest press associations handled the story. The New York *Herald Tribune* printed a long "special" on the front page. And mainly in consequence of this publicity the workers won the strike.

I could cite not a few similar cases in recent years. In the winter of 1928 there began a great lockout-strike of hosiery workers in Wisconsin, on which I happen to have authentic data. It was a dramatic and important strike, and the leaders tried to present the strikers' side of the question to the public through the newspapers, but for five months, while remaining peaceful and non-violent, their efforts were in vain. Then, when the strike seemed almost "dead," bombs began to explode and guns to pop, and suddenly the strike became lively news throughout the country. Within a few days twenty-eight houses in and around Kenosha, which was the center of the strike, were dynamited, including the home of the vice-president and manager of one of the hosiery companies, which burned to the ground. Of the other houses bombed, two were inhabited by strikers and twenty-five by strike-breakers. In the same period twenty-four scabs and six strikers were shot and three thousand windows in the homes of non-union employees of the mills were "bricked," while for a whole week one floor of a large hosiery factory was peppered with fire from rifles equipped with Maxim silencers. Efforts of the police to locate "the brains" of this reign of terror were unsuccessful, and a special grand jury, meeting for six weeks, failed to return any indictments. The publicity which resulted from this violence was for the most part, of course, unfriendly to the strikers, but the leaders were clever enough to organize at the same time patriotic demonstrations and "stunts," such as conducting a pilgrimage of strikers to the grave of Robert La Follette, which tended to offset the violence and win for the strikers a public sympathy, aiding them to score a partial victory in the end. According to the labor leader who took a part in the strike and who gave me these facts, "violence was the only thing." Without it the strike was not news, not even in Wisconsin; it was "dead," not sufficiently dramatic to be worthy of the editors' and reporters' efforts to bring it to the attention of the wide public.

Just one more recent incident. On May 15, 1931, a group of Communists staged a demonstration at the Ellis Island ferry in New

York, protesting against the deportation by the Federal Government of a young Chinese student at Columbia University because he was a Red. There was a riot and bloodshed, and the next day most of the New York papers featured the occurrence on page one. The tabloid *Daily News* gave almost its entire front page to one of the best riot pictures I have ever seen. The incident was big news in other cities. *The New York Times* ran a "story" occupying four-fifths of a column on page three, and immediately beneath it printed a *one-inch* item about the non-violent "fight" of a great international garment workers' union against wage-cuts!... That is to say, *The Times* saw fit to feature an incident which had to do with the fate of one obscure Chinese student, palpably because it was a violent incident, and treated in five lines the non-violent efforts of the officials of a big union on which depended the future earnings and welfare of over one hundred thousand workers and their families.

Now, if I were the only person aware of the newspapers' great preference for violent labor news, it probably would not be wise for me to point it out as I do here, for I might be accused of slyly urging labor to violence. But it so happens that scarcely anything I say will be new to most experience leaders and many members of the rank and file in either the right or the left wing of the labor movement. Late in 1931, a labor-union official in New York said to me:

Circumstances keep me in the _____ Union [an A.F. of L. organization], but I know that the A.F. of L., with its polite attitude toward unemployment, has done no service to the American working class during this depression that compares with that rendered by the Communists, with their demonstrations and cracked heads. They got the publicity which scared the government and capitalists, made many people think, and benefited labor as a whole.

A well-known radical laborite, active in the tri-state coal region of western Pennsylvania, Ohio, and West Virginia in the summer of 1931, remarked to me, with the understanding that I would not quote him by name:

Often there is nothing that throws as bright a spotlight on the sufferings and unrest of the working stiff as a flare-up of violence. The capitalist sheets don't pay any attention to him except when he gets rough or his head gets bloody.

Labor leaders recognize the importance of getting their causes before the public. Often the only way they can get it is to resort to, or provoke the police to, violence. To accomplish the latter is the easiest thing in the world, but, in fact, as we have seen throughout this book, in nine cases out of ten, the police or deputy sheriffs are the ones who fire the first shot, release the first tear or stench bomb, heave the first brick, or swing the first club; whereupon, in most cases, it is next to impossible, as well as tactically wholly inadvisable, for leaders to control the strikers.

That happened in Toledo in May 1934; and, since we mention Toledo again, let us have another glimpse at that incident, which is more fully described toward the end of the last chapter. The Auto-Lite labor dispute, as we have seen, had started in February. The strike was nationally important news throughout the month of April and through part of May, but few people, no matter how carefully they read their newspapers, knew anything about it till the end of May, after the riots occurred.

Even Norman Thomas, who, on the whole, is by nature strongly anti-violence, disagrees with those who say that "violence never works." In his book *As I See It*, he says that violence

...may be terribly costly, but it has gotten results. In moderate doses, as Louis Adamic has said, it has seen publicity for the underdog. [This material was originally published in *Scribner's Magazine* for February 1932. L.A.] It also serves as warning that he may have power. Slaves content to be slaves, workers content to starve quietly, never get deliverance from heaven or from sheer human kindness. And the natural vehicle of their protest, especially given our Western traditions (quite unlike the Indian tradition to which Gandhi has appealed), is some degree of violence. No honest and intelligent person can say that in our imperfect democracy we have a polite and easy substitute for violence in the right to organize unions and to vote. The most we can say is that there is a power in them not adequately asserted by the workers of America. Ballots are better than bullets and an organized strike than a riot. The history of such considerable labor violence as was used by the Molly Maguires, the Pittsburgh and Baltimore rioters of the seventies, and the dynamiters in Los Angeles, is a history of a great setback for labor. It was not altogether useful publicity for the underdog! Yet he lacks imagination who does not see why the harassed worker or striker, seeing his job taken and his struggle defeated by a scab under police protection, finding himself evicted, perhaps at night, from his home, takes to himself a stone, a club, or a gun rather than a ballot. *No exploited class can afford to let the masters think it will not use violence unless it can discover a more effective instrument of struggle than violence... For*

workers merely to renounce violence with no substitute in sight would be
to play into the hands of the oppressor. [My italics. L.A.]

II. Tragedy in Steel

During the revising of this book, in mid-June 1934, the *Nation* asked me to go to Pittsburgh and cover it for the threatened steel strike. In its July 4, 1934 issue, I published the following "story" of a significant incident in contemporary developments in the American labor movement:

Pittsburgh, June 20.

For two weeks or longer, large sections of the American people of all classes stood on their toes, tense with hope or apprehension or both, watching—through the poorly focused telescope of the daily press reports—the onrush of developments in the threatened strike of the Amalgamated Association of Iron, Steel, and Tin Workers, with its 230 lodges or unions in the various steel-producing centers of the United States. For days, toward the middle of June, it looked—through the aforesaid telescope—as though a strike in the country's basic industry was inevitable at midnight June 15, or soon thereafter; and numerous persons everywhere believed that it probably would be one of the bitterest, bloodiest, most consequential class-war battles ever fought in America.

The special "strike" convention of the A.A., called for Thursday, June 14, was considered so important that on Wednesday the thirteenth, some of the country's foremost newspapermen rushed into Pittsburgh to cover the situation, and simultaneously there arrived also a flock of excited mediators, conciliators, observers, spies, and other such factotums sent out by federal offices in Washington and by the governments of the various steel states, notably Pennsylvania. Many of these persons believed that a strike was almost certain within two days, and, once called, was likely to become the spark for a bloody social revolution. With Toledo still fresh in their minds, they expected labor, employed and jobless, all over the United States to rise against capitalism, unemployment, company unionism, the New Deal, and what not.

Yet less than twenty-four hours later the strike idea completely fizzled out, and Mr. Green, it immediately appeared, was not the only, nor even the chief, factor in this fizzling out; while less than a week subsequently, as I write this, it is obvious that the idea for a nationwide steel strike in mid-June had been doomed to a tragic end from its inception, six weeks before.

And thereby, it seems to me, hangs an immensely interesting and significant tale worth telling, I think, in some detail because it so clearly mirrors the whole contemporary labor situation in this country, and also because it is likely soon to have a sequel which will be difficult to understand without a knowledge of what really happened in the steel-labor situation during the past few months.

To begin at the beginning, the Amalgamated Association of Iron, Steel, and Tin Workers is one of the oldest bodies affiliated with the A.F. of L. It came into existence fifty-seven years ago, when a group of highly skilled metal workers seceded from the Sons of Vulcan. Until very recently it never was anything more than a collection of fraternal benefit lodges of the "aristocracy of labor" in the steel, iron, and tin (mostly tin) industries, and a convenient stepping-stone for its so-called executive officers who had ambitions (and most of them had) for political and economic self-advancement. One president of the A.A. left his office to become secretary of the American Tin Plate Company, then United States Consul at Birmingham, England, and finally a business man in Pittsburgh; another became inspector of immigration in New York; a third, a Republican Congressman; a fourth, a Republican city councilman in Pittsburgh; a fifth, secretary of the steel manufacturers' association on the Pacific Coast.

During the last forty years no one could possibly have accused the outfit of being a labor movement. Its central office was nearly always on good terms with the managers of most of the mills. It never made any effort to organize the industry. Several of the local lodges, composed exclusively or mainly of highly skilled wrought-iron and sheet-metal men, have been recognized by otherwise anti-union bosses and have wage-and-hour contracts with them. The organization played a semi-strike-breaking role in the great steel strike of 1919.

Its present president is a fattish, drooling, loose-lipped, watery-eyed old codger in his late seventies, one M. J. Tighe, familiarly known as "Old Mike" or "Grandmother" Tighe. He has been with the organization from its birth. A typical old-time trade-union bureaucrat, he is profoundly ignorant of the forces now operating in the world or in the country; he is narrow, fussy, old-womanish, but, as he lately demonstrated, deeply experienced in the parliamentary tactics and "practical trade-union politics" long since perfected by leaders in A.F. of L. affiliates. In his official duties Tighe is ably assisted by the secretary-treasur-

er, Louis (Shorty) Leonard, a round, compact little fellow, somewhat
younger than the president but also an old-timer in the outfit, with a
loud Fourth-of-July voice and an inexhaustible supply of labor blah-
blah; of much the same stamp, both as a person and a labor-union official as Tighe. Ed Miller and Tom Gillis, the two vice-presidents, are
essentially of the same type. All these men draw a salary (and expenses)
they could not conceivably hope to receive in any other "racket" except
by some fluke, and they naturally think a great deal of their positions
and want to keep them.

For fourteen years the A.A. was on the toboggan. By the middle
of 1933 its membership had fallen to 4700, of whom fewer than 3000
were paying their dues. Then the New Deal came with its Section 7A
in the NIRA, which gave the nearly 500,000 steal, iron, and tin workers
in New York, Pennsylvania, Ohio, West Virginia, Indiana, Michigan,
Maryland, Alabama, Kentucky, California, and elsewhere a sudden and
powerful impulse to unionization. Tens of thousands of workers, full of
old Hoover-era jitters and new Roosevelt-inspired hope, were asking:
"Which union can I join?" Communist organizers were in the field with
their Steel and Metal Workers Industrial Union. A good many men
joined that organization. At the same time the Iron and Steel Institute,
under the direction of Arthur Young (now getting $40,000 a year for his
work), started its big push for company unions. Sincere, if none too intelligent, would-be leaders of non-Communist but radical independent
unionization movements appeared among the steel people. And there
were lively stirrings in several lodges of the A.A. The leaders of these
locals appealed for advice and help to the central office of the A.A. in
Pittsburgh. They wrote letters and went to the office in person. They
telephoned "Old Mike" and wired "Shorty" Leonard. But the "executive
officers" did nothing for three months, until some of the lodge presidents threatened to start organizing what possibly might turn out to be
a new union movement in the steel industry.

Then, in September 1933, largely to stop the growing Communist
and other independent-radical movements, "Grandmother" and
"Shorty" decided—possibly as the Communists maintain, on the urging
of Iron and Steel Institute agents—to send out three dozen "organizers," most of whom were unemployed old-time trade unionists, friends
of the central office, with no experience as organizers. These men receive
considerable salaries (and expenses), although in most cases their sole
qualification was that they wrote a legible hand; but that was enough,

for all that was necessary was to fill out union cards for the thousands of men who eagerly stood in line to be signed up.

The only aggressive organizer for the A.A. was Mrs. Cornelia Bryce Pinchot, the Governor's wife, who had no connection with the union. She is a rich woman with red hair and an overabundance of nervous energy, who gets more thrill out of labor agitation and strike picketing than out of bridge and society and has, besides strong political ambitions for her husband and herself, a few vague notions that something is wrong with our social system. She attracted vast crowds of steel workers and their wives and spoke at scores of meetings in Pennsylvania, Ohio, and West Virginia, urging the men to sign up and get behind the NIRA and the President. But the A.A. "executives," apparently, were anything but enthusiastic about the help the lady was trying to give the organization. They sent no one to her mass-meetings to sign up the men. The old fogies in the central office were beside themselves with fear of what was happening to their hitherto nice, quiet old outfit, and soon after starting the organizing "campaign" they began to do everything in their power to restrict its success.

But, despite all this, in less than two months the A.A. had more than 125 new lodges, many of them called by such names as the Blue Eagle Lodge, Recovery Lodge, and Nira (or Arin) Lodge, and its membership was raised from 4700 to anywhere from 60,000 to 100,000. Nobody knows yet what the new total is. The central office so far has made no real effort to find out. The officials in that office know that, whatever it is, the number is too high for the good of the organization as they want it to continue.

In short, the old, dying A.A. suddenly bulged out into a vast organization, a great, virile new body full of raw, undisciplined, undirected strength and spirit, with but a few sick old cells here and there, and, alas, with the same old head, the same senile "executive" officers, utterly lacking in real brains, in knowledge of what is going on in the country, in honesty and social vision. Suddenly the big, healthy body and the small, hollow head were at violent cross-purposes. But for some time the body didn't realize that. It merely felt very strong and very comfortable, and anxious to be doing something.

Toward the end of 1933 the situation began to clarify itself a bit. Several men of the new element and a few older but more or less progressive fellows who had helped to bring in the new ones began to feel that there were two factions in the organization, sharply opposed one to the other. They started to refer to themselves as the Young Boys, and to the old-timers in power and the old craft lodges, which supported the central office, as the Old Boys. The Young Boys were, for the most part, the presidents of the newly formed industrial lodges and the newly elected district chairmen, who—to the great annoyance of the central office—gradually began to act as spokesmen for the new element in its differences with the Old Boys—differences which rapidly increased both in frequency and bitterness. Unlike the leaders of the Old Boys, they were actual steel workers employed in mills, unless lately discharged for rank-and-file union activities; none of them received any salary from their lodge treasuries, and some of them covered even their expenses on union business out of their own pockets; some of them were still in their early and middle twenties, small-town boys, "little men," with scant education and less natural ability or experience as labor-union leaders and politicians.

For months these new leaders and would-be leaders talked among themselves, and plotted against the Old Boys and against one another, for there was a good deal of suspicion and jealousy among them. They hardly knew one another, and several wanted to be the big leader. But as time passed they became united on one point—action. The entire rank-and-file element, growing conscious of its overwhelming numerical strength in the A.A. wanted action.

Thousands of workers on signing up with the A.A. lodges paid no initiation fees or dues, promising to pay when the union started to do something for them. Having been fooled before, they did not trust the A.A. or the rank-and-file leaders. Lodge members would ask their presidents: "Well, when are we going to start doing something? How can I raise a family on $15 a week? When are we going to make the bosses recognize our union? Is this NRA stuff straight or just a lot of so-and-so? Is Roosevelt going to help us get recognition? We got a union, ain't we? Let's have an election in the mill; we'll win against the company union. Then they'll have to recognize us, deal with us. How about it? How about a strike?"

This matter of union recognition was on everybody's mind. Lodge presidents asked the A.A.'s central office what they could do. "Old Mike" and "Shorty" stalled; they didn't know. So some of the lodge leaders took the matter into their own hands. They visited the Pittsburgh NRA office. No result. They wrote letters to Washington. No answer, or they received printed material on what a wonderful thing the NRA was for labor. A few went to Washington and called on the A.F. of L. and National Labor Board, not once, but four and five times. They talked with Senator Wagner and other New Dealers and demanded elections in the mills. The National Labor Board stalled, promised them action, but for a month, two months, nothing happened. The board was afraid to tackle the Iron and Steel Institute. The gentlemen in the A.F. of L. urged patience. The boys tried to see the Secretary of Labor, "Ma" Perkins, as they called her, who some months before had been in the steel region and had seemed interested in the steel people; but most of them got only as far as her assistant, Mr. McGrady. No result anywhere, no satisfaction. Washington was full of fuss and fury which had no relation to the steel workers of America. Bill Spang of Duquesne, one of the lodge leaders who journeyed several times to Washington, finally came to the conclusion that Roosevelt, evidently, had not meant what he signed in the NIRA and, in all probability, was afraid of the iron-and-steel gang. Bill made a report to that effect to his lodge and the leaders of other rank-and-file lodges. NRA, he said, meant "National Run Around" for the workers, and Washington was "a labor college where a working stiff like me can get an education like he can get nowhere else."

The rank-and-file boys, like workers in many other industries throughout the land, rapidly developed a strike mood. In this mood, in mid-April, the rank-and-file delegates, still lacking a real leader, assembled with the Old Boys in the annual convention of the A.A. in the Elks' Hall in Pittsburgh. They had a clear two-thirds' majority over the Old Boys, and Tighe and Leonard were at their wits' end. The Young Boys shouted: "Action! Action!" The Old Boys, trying to wear them down, stretched the convention by various parliamentary tricks, with which the new men had no acquaintance, to more than two weeks. To no avail. "Action!" There is a bar in the Elks' Hall and there was some drinking, which made the Young Boys even stronger for action. The end of it all was that they passed a resolution with the so-called seven-point program which included the call for a national steel strike in the middle of June if the bosses refused to grant the union's demand for recognition and collective bargaining before then. No strike plan was outlined for the eventuality that the bosses did no recognize the union. The Young Boys invented no way to make the Old Boys in the central office prepare the organization for the big walk-out. They merely appointed a committee of ten to get busy about the matter as soon as possible.

Tired from the long sessions both in the hall and at the bar, the committee did not meet till May 20. After much squabbling among themselves, on the twenty-second, they formed a "strike committee of five" and demanded of the executive officers that one of its members be allowed to take a desk in the central office and work on strike preparation. Tighe, Leonard, and their colleagues, having, in the face of the Young Boys' now patent ineptitude, regained their composure, said: "nothing doing!" Then the whole committee of ten, duly appointed in the convention, asked the executive officers for a conference on the morning of May 26. When, on that day, the committee arrived at the A.A.'s central office, only the janitor was there to receive them. This made the Young Boys "pretty sore" and they began to call the old-timers Yellow Dogs, while the latter, in turn, started to refer to the rank-and-filers as Greenhorn Goats.

On the suggestion of a journalist friend of theirs, a group of Greenhorn Goats then journeyed to Washington to ask for an interview with the President. They meant to tell him that they were about to call a strike to help him fetch the steel trust to book, and ask him to accept their aid—the aid of the workers in the steel industry—and meet the issue squarely. "We will shut down the mills," they wished to say to Mr. Roosevelt, "until the steel magnates sign before you their acceptance of the law and actually begin collective bargaining with our unions." They did not expect to get any results. The real idea was to get publicity for the strike. But though they did not get to the President, they were received by everyone else of any importance in the NRA, scared a lot of people, caused much discomfort in the White House and the A.F. of L. Building, engaged in a hot exchange of insults with General Johnson, and before departure signed a sizzling open letter to the President which landed them on the front pages of all important papers in the country. They said, in effect, that they were going back home to call the strike. In all this they were coached by friendly journalists.

The Iron and Steel Institute announced it never would recognize the A.A. or any other outside union, and proposed a plan similar to that in effect in the automobile industry, which the boys scorned. Meanwhile, William Green called Tighe to Washington, and the Old Boy, by now quite sure of his ground again, smiled as broadly as his old face permitted, talked with General Johnson and other big people there, and let the Greenhorn Goats do what they liked. Then—very probably with the full approval of the A.F. of L. panjandrums, who were in touch with the National Labor Board, Miss Perkins, and the White House—he announced that he would reconvene the delegates of the last annual convention and let them decide what the organization would do in the matter of the threatened strike.

And on June 14, when the A.A. convention met again two floors above the luminous Elks' barroom in Pittsburgh, large sections of the American people raised themselves as high on their toes as possible, and glued their eyes closer to the poorly focused telescope of daily press reports. They expected hell to break loose within a couple of days. They didn't know (neither did I) that the whole thing was practically cut and dried, and that, save for an unlikely slip-up, the boys would not call the strike.

When the delegates reconvened, most of the Greenhorn Goats were for calling the walkout, if for no other reason than that they could see no other way out. But many of them had begun to develop, already when on the way to the convention, serious misgivings about such an action. Some of the mills were armed. Because of this fact their wives had begged them not to call the strike. And with times so hard, how many workers would really walk out at their call? It probably was true, as it was generally said, that the bosses would welcome a strike at this time; it would give them an opportunity to beat down the workers' militancy during a slack in production. All these and similar considerations were heavy on the Young Boys' minds. On the other hand, they figured, if they didn't strike, they wouldn't get anything. After all, perhaps, the only thing to do was to have the strike and some bloodshed; then Roosevelt probably would act and force the bosses (but could he?) to recognize him and the unions. They discussed Toledo. Well, maybe——

At the opening of the convention the most aggressive of the strike-minded Greenhorns had in their hands copies of two resolutions—one calling the strike and setting up the strike machinery, the other calling upon the A.F. of L. for financial and moral support. But the "Yellow Dogs" running the convention from the platform gave them no chance to present them. Parliamentary trickery was utilized to the utmost. They killed time on the rules of procedure. Who was to be admitted besides the delegates? Resolutions. Amendments. Amendments to amendments. Which confused the inexperienced boys, made them feel like "a bunch of damn fools." Then serious difficulties with roll call. More resolutions. Amendments. Amendments to amendments.

Finally, at 11:30 they adjourned till 3:30 to "fix up the roll call," but actually, of course, to stretch the convention, to give William Green time to see President Roosevelt between one and two and to come to Pittsburgh. At 3:30 a squabble over credentials. Pointless, time-wasting resolutions. Delegations were asked to report whether or not the bosses had recognized their respective unions. A Slovak priest, one of the few "guests" in the hall, made a long speech urging the boys, with several of whom he had some influence, to postpone the strike. Then it was announced that word had been received from Washington that William Green, the great leader of organized labor in America...was coming to Pittsburgh to address the convention tomorrow, and meantime his brotherly appeal to the boys was to keep their shirts on. Convention adjourned.

Confused, their spirit down, uncertain what would be the best or most sensible thing to do, some of the Young boys proceeded to get drunk, much to the glee of "Grandmother" Tighe, a teetotaler who generally frowns on hard liquor. I do not mean to say that any considerable number of the delegates got drunk, but enough of those who did were leaders, and the fact that they incapacitated themselves for leadership the next day tended further to demoralize those who stayed sober. Only a few newspapermen know of this, and they were kind enough not to tell about it. I mention it because it is so important. It is a lesson to rank-and-file labor leaders in steel as in other industries.

By the time Mr. Green arrived, the strike idea was practically dead. Then he dug up the grave for it; the boys themselves, half-consciously, half-unconsciously, buried it. From the Old Boys' and Bill Green's viewpoint it all worked to perfection, just as they had hoped it would when plotting the whole show, perhaps as long as a week before. Bill Green stepped before the boys as a "fellow-worker," a "miner," and begged them to be calm and not allow their judgement to give way to their feelings. But many had no judgement or feelings, except bewilderment, in the matter. Several of them had katzenjammers; a few were in their cups during Mr. Green's speech and throughout the rest of the day. He proposed a peace plan which he was sure President Roosevelt would accept and support. As a matter of fact, it was essentially the President's own plan, which as Mr. Green spoke was on the way to Congress to be (and was) made a law. When Mr. Green finished, Shorty Leonard and the other Old Boys leaped to their feet and led the applause. The convention promptly accepted Mr. Green's proposition and "postponed" the strike call till the end of June. Telegrams were sent to the lodges for the workers, tens of thousands of whom were ready to strike at midnight, to stay put.

The farce was carried still farther. The final important question was: Who will present President Green's plan to President Roosevelt? There was a little squabbling over that. Then someone rose and said: "Boys, let's show we have confidence in our executive officers, who all these years, blah, blah... Let's authorize them to take our proposition to Washington." This was quickly seconded, and Old Mike put up the motion for a vote so quickly that the majority, when they lifted their hands, had no idea what they were voting for. The hands were not counted. Passed! Shorty Leonard whispered a joyous remark to Old Mike, who grinned cynically, and a few hours later one of the other Old boys remarked: "Now we got 'em where we want 'em. Now we'll teach 'em discipline."

Immediately after the conclusion of the convention I spoke to one of the more intelligent of the young militants. He said: "I feel like Carnera must of felt last night." Others, even among the sober ones, told me they didn't know exactly what had happened. "Things were done so fast." I overheard a conversation of two Young Boys. One said: "The strike is only postponed, ain't it?" "Yeah, I guess." "Have we, I mean the Young Boys, any authority left to call the strike in case we don't get what Green said we want." "Damn' if I know. Don't think we have." "Well, I guess we sold ourselves out." A third young fellow, a little drunk, who stood by, listening, said: "Nuts!" and walked off.

Bewilderment, bewilderment. I had a feeling, in that dismal hall, that I was witnessing the whole essential tragedy of American labor. On the platform, surrounded by reporters, Old Mike drooled away: "We're not Communists...no, not Communists. We're trade unionists. I'm a highest type of trade unionist... Strike? Haw-haw! There ain't gonna be no strike. All over! We ain't a strike organization... I'm tired, boys, nothin' else to say, nothin' to say, boys. Haven't had a bite all day, now it's midnight. Good night, boys."

The sense of tragedy deepened in me during the ensuing few days as I motored through the steel towns in Pennsylvania, Ohio, and West Virginia, and talked with "leaders" and ordinary members of A.A. lodges. Bewilderment. None knew what really happened in Pittsburgh or what would happen in Washington.

One thing is sure, as sure as anything nowadays: there will be no national steel strike this summer. There may be one or two "wildcat" strikes, à la Toledo, but even that is a remote possibility. Whether or not there will ever be a steel strike or a respect-commanding steel-labor organization depends on many things, but mostly, perhaps, on the ability of the rank-and-file leaders to realize what happened to them at the convention, what happened immediately after the convention, and what may, will, or should happen this summer and next fall; and on their ability, too, to regain their lost morale by honestly admitting their

shortcomings so far, and trying to improve themselves for future work
and to communicate that morale to their membership. They should try
to realize as soon as possible the following things:

1. That, no matter whom the President will appoint to the board to
determine who shall represent steel labor in collective bargaining, the
dice will be loaded against any real workers' union; and that should a
real union win the election in a given mill, the bosses will not recognize
it but will turn the matter over to the courts, where it will be hung up
for months and possibly for years.

2. That William Green and the whole A.F. of L. oligarchy, in their actual function, are closer to the interests of the Roosevelt Administration
and, *ipso facto*, of the employers than to the interests of labor; that the
plan Mr. Green brought with him to Pittsburgh was not his plan but the
President's and General Johnson's.

3. That even if Mr. Green and the A.F. of L. send thirty organizers and a $200,000 organizing fund to the steel region, as Mr. Green
promised they would, steel will never really be organized; that fully
to organize steel, if they could, would be against their interests, their
nature; that if the A.F. of L. makes any attempt to organize steel, it
will be largely frustrated in jurisdictional disputes. (Important jurisdictional disputes are already pending in the A.A., and the A.A. has all but
stopped organizing unorganized workers. And why hasn't the A.F. of L.
tried to organize steel long before this?)

4. That the future of American labor lies only in clear struggle,
not in playing along with social workers like President Roosevelt and
Secretary Perkins, who appear to consider the United States one vast
settlement house in which everything should be nice and peaceful; and
that in that struggle, as things stand today, there is not time to lose.

In September of this year the A.A. has general elections. Here will
be the rank-and-filers' first big opportunity. Will they be able to oust
the Old Boys? Will they, meantime, continue organizing their local
lodges, apart from any A.F. of L. "organizing," and thus prepare themselves, at least in part, for a national strike in October, when production
will be at its height? Will they, in the event of such a strike, be able to
join hands with other labor movements in the industry, including the
Steel and Metal Workers Industrial Union? And will they, eventually,
be able to overhaul the A.A. and make it a straight industrial union, and
develop social vision, which any American labor movement, to be worth
anything, will have to have in the future?

The answers to these questions, when they come and whatever they may be, will be of supreme importance not only to American labor but to the whole country.

III. Leon Samson on Violence

In his interesting book *Toward a United Front* (chapter on "Substitutive Revolution") Leon Samson writes on violence in general as follows:

> Violence is the defeat of force. And the weakness for violence everywhere in evidence on the American scene is the impotence of revolutionary energy in America, its inability to organize itself and become force. The American atmosphere is surcharged with violence because American society is ripe for revolution while the American mind is not.

In fine, the American working class will be violent until the workers become revolutionary in their minds and motives and organize their revolutionary spirit into force—into unions with revolutionary aims to power. Then they will be able to afford to dispense with such violence as has been described in this book.

BIBLIOGRAPHY*

T. S. Adams and Helen L. Sumner: LABOR PROBLEMS. 1905.

John P. Altgeld: REASONS FOR PARDONING FIELDEN, NEEBE, AND SCHWABE. 1893. (*A pamphlet.*)

American Civil Liberties Union: THE ISSUES IN THE CENTRALIA MURDER CASE. 1920. (*A pamphlet.*)

Edward B. Aveling: THE CHICAGO ANARCHISTS. 1887.

Mary Beard: A SHORT HISTORY OF THE AMERICAN LABOR MOVEMENT. 1920.

Genevieve LeC. Bergstresser: THE HISTORY OF THE HAYMARKET RIOT. 1917.

Alexander Berkman: PRISON MEMOIRS OF AN ANARCHIST. 1912.

Anthony Bimba: HISTORY OF THE AMERICAN WORKING CLASS. 1912.

E. L. Bogart: THE ECONOMIC HISTORY OF THE UNITED STATES. 1918.

J. G. Brissenden: THE LAUNCHING OF THE INDUSTRIAL WORKERS OF THE WORLD. 1913.

Katherine Brody: NOBODY STARVES. 1932. (*A novel.*)

John Graham Brooks: AMERICAN SYNDICALISM: THE I.W.W. 1913.

Fielding Burke: CALL HOME THE HEART. 1932. (*A novel.*)

William J. Burns: THE MASKED WAR. 1913. (*Dealing with his part in the McNamara and "Dynamite Conspiracy" cases.*)

Robert Cantwell: THE LAND OF PLENTY. 1934. (*A novel.*)

F. T. Cantwell: The History and Problem of Organized Labor. 1911.

John Chaberlain: FAREWELL TO REFORM. 1933.

Ralph Caphlin: THE CENTRALIA CONSPIRACY. 1920. (A pamphlet.)

THE FAMOUS SPEECHES OF THE EIGHT CHICAGO ANARCHISTS IN JUDGE GRAY'S COURT. 1886. (A pamphlet.)

John R. Commons, Ulrich B. Phillips, and Others (editors): A DOCUMENTARY HISTORY OF AMERICAN INDUSTRIAL SOCIETY. 1910–1911. 10 vols.

Jack Conroy: THE DISINHERITED. 1933. (*A novel.*)

Jacob S. Coxey: THE COXEY PLAN. 1914

J. A. Dacus: ANNALS OF THE GREAT STRIKES. 1877.

F. P. Dewees: THE MOLLY MAGUIRES. 1877

---

* As it appeared in the 1934 edition.

342   John Dos Passos: FACING THE CHAIR. 1927. (*A pamphlet, dealing with the Sacco-Vanzetti case.*)

Robert W. Dunn: THE AMERICANIZATION OF LABOR—THE EMPLOYERS' OFFENSIVE AGAINST THE TRADE UNIONS. 1927

———.LABOR AND AUTOMOBILES. 1929

Justus Ebert: THE TRIAL OF A NEW SOCIETY. 1913. (*Dealing with the I.W.W.'s part in the Lawrence Strike in 1912.*)

R. T. Ely: THE LABOR MOVEMENT IN AMERICA. 1886.

Elizabeth G. Evans: OUTSTANDING FEATURES OF THE SACCO-VANZETTI CASE. 1924. (*A pamphlet.*)

Arthur Feiler: AMERICA SEEN THROUGH GERMAN EYES. 1928.

William Z. Foster: THE GREAT STEEL STRIKE AND ITS LESSONS. 1920

Felix Frankfurter: THE CASE OF SACCO AND VANZETTI. 1927.

———.THE LABOR INJUNCTION. 1930.

W. J. Ghent: THE NEXT STEP: A BENEVOLENT FEUDALISM. 1902. (*A pamphlet.*)

Samuel Gompers: LABOR AND THE EMPLOYER. 1920.

Ethelbert V. Grabill: SACCO AND VANZETTI IN THE SCALES OF JUSTICE. 1927. (*A pamphlet.*)

G. G. Groat: AN INTRODUCTION TO THE STUDY OF ORGANIZED LABOR IN AMERICA. 1916.

Albert Halper: UNION SQUARE. 1933. (*A novel.*)

———. THE FOUNDRY. 1934. (*A novel.*)

———. SCAB! (*A short story in American Mercury, June, 1934.*)

Henry Harrison (editor): THE SACCO-VANZETTI ANTHOLOGY OF VERSE. 1927.

Bill Haywood's Book. 1929.

J. A. Hobson: RATIONALISATION AND UNEMPLOYMENT. 1930.

J. H. Hollander and G. E. Barnett (editors): STUDIES IN AMERICAN TRADE UNIONISM. 1905. 2 volumes.

Robert Hunter: VIOLENCE IN THE LABOR MOVEMENT. 1914.

Mother Jones: AUTOBIOGRAPHY. 1927.

Lloyd Lewis and Henry Justin Smith: CHICAGO—A HISTORY OF ITS REPUTATION. 1929.

Lewis L. Lorwin, with the assistance of Jean Atherton Flexner: THE AMERICAN FEDERATION OF LABOR. 1933.

Grace Lumpkin: TO MAKE MY BREAD. 1932. (*A novel.*)

Jeannette A. Marks: THIRTEEN DAYS. 1929. (The Sacco-Vanzetti case.)

Helen Marot: AMERICAN LABOR UNIONS. 1914.

James Dabney McCabe: THE HISTORY OF THE GREAT RIOTS. 1877.

J. Ramsay MacDonald: SYNDICALISM. 1912.

Ortie E. McManigal: THE NATIONAL DYNAMITE PLOT. 1913. (*A pamphlet.*)

Donald Le Crone McMurry: COXEY'S ARMY. 1929.

G. E. McNeill: THE LABOR MOVEMENT: THE PROBLEM OF TODAY. 1892.

John Mitchell: ORGANIZED LABOR. 1913.

Johann J. Most: THE BEAST OF PROPERTY—TOTAL ANIHILATION PROPOSED

AS THE ONLY INFALLIBLE REMEDY. 1885(?). (*A pamphlet.*)   343
Scott Nearing: VIOLENCE OR SOLIDARITY?—OR, WILL GUNS SETTLE IT?
1919. (*A pamphlet.*)
Stephen H. Olin: SUGGESTIONS UPON THE STRATEGY OF STREET FIGHTING.
1886. (*A pamphlet for private circulation.*)
Selig Perlman: A HISTORY OF TRADE UNIONISM IN THE UNITED STATES.
1923.
Allan Pinkerton: MOLLY MAGUIRES AND THE DETECTIVES. 1978.
Emile Pouget: SABOTAGE. *Translated from the French, with an Introduction,*
by Arturo M. Giovannitti. First published in the United States in 1913.
Ragnar Redbeard: MIGHT IS RIGHT. 1895(?).
William Rollins, Jr.: THE SHADOW BEFORE. 1934 (*A novel.*)
THE LETTERS OF SACCO AND VANZETTI: *Edited by Marion Denman*
Frankfurter and Gardner Jackson. 1928.
Leon Samson: THE AMERICAN MIND. 1932.
———. TOWARD A UNITED FRONT. 1933.
Michael J. Schaack: ANARCHY AND ANARCHISTS. 1887.
Theodore A. Schroeder: MARTYRS OR CRIMINALS? 1915. (*A pamphlet dealing*
with the McNamaras' guilt.)
Art Shields: THE SACCO-VANZETTI CASE AND THE GRIM FORCES BEHIND
IT. 1920. (*A pamphlet.*)
A. M. Simons: SOCIAL FORCES IN AMERICAN HISTORY. 1913
Upton Sinclair: BOSTON. 1929. (*A novel of the Sacco-Vanzetti case.*)
Georges Sorel: REFLECTIONS ON VIOLENCE. 1912.
Benjamin Stolberg: A GOVERNMENT IN SEARCH OF A LABOR MOVEMENT.
(*Article in* Scribner's Magazine, *December 1933.*) *Also an article on William*
Green in Today, *May 10, 1934.*
Vincent St. John: THE I.W.W. 1912. (*A pamphlet..*)
Courtney Terret: ONLY SAPS WORK. 1930.
Norman Thomas: AS I SEE IT. 1932.
Wm. E. TRautmann: DIRECT ACTION AND SABOTAGE. 1912. (*A pamphlet.*)
———. ONE BIG UNION. 1912. (*A pamphlet about the I.W.W.*)
Bartolomeo Vanzetti: BACKGROUND OF THE PLYMOUTH TRIAL. 1926.
H. Vincent: THE STORY OF THE COMMONWEAL. 1894. (*Dealing with the*
Coxey Movement.)
Mary Heaton Vorse: MEN AND STEEL. 1920. (*Dealing with the Steel Strike*
in 1919.)
———. STRIKE. (*A novel about textile workers in the South.*)
James P. Warbasse: THE ETHICS OF SABOTAGE. 1913. (*A Pamphlet.*)
The following magazines and newspapers: THE AMERICAN MERCURY,
THE OUTLOOK, the Chicago TRIBUNE, TIMES, and DAILY NEWS, the
Los Angeles TIMES, RECORD, HERALD, and EXPRESS, the San Francisco
ARGONAUT, the APPEAL TO REASON, and the New York TIMES, WORLD,
SUN, and EVENING POST.

INDEX

Printed in the USA
CPSIA information can be obtained
at www.ICGtesting.com
JSHW011417160824
R13664500003B/R136645PG68134JSX00034B/11

9 781904 859741